LIST OF ILLUSTRATIONS

	PAGE
George Washington,	*Frontispiece*
A Ship of the Norsemen,	2
Christopher Columbus,	3
The *Nina*,	4
The *Pinta*,	4
The *Santa Maria*,	5
Sebastian Cabot,	8
Columbus at the Court of Ferdinand and Isabella after his Return from the New World, *facing page*	8
Americus Vespucius,	9
Cortez,	13
Old Spanish Mission, New Mexico, Built 1604,	14
Spanish Gateway, St. Augustine, Florida,	14
Balboa,	15
Fernando de Soto,	16
Queen Elizabeth,	20
Sir Walter Raleigh and Autograph,	21
The Destruction of the Spanish Armada,	22
Philippe II., King of Spain, 1527–1598,	23
An Indian Village at Roanoke,	24
English Explorers Bartering with Indians for Land,	25
Queen Elizabeth's Signature,	27
Signature of James I.,	28
Ruins of Old Church at Jamestown,	30
Captain John Smith,	31
Tobacco-plant,	34
A Wild Dash for Life,	35
George Calvert (Lord Baltimore),	38
A Maryland Shilling,	39
A Puritan,	42
Oliver Cromwell,	43
The *Mayflower*,	46
A Chest which came over in the *Mayflower*,	47
Myles Standish,	48
Pilgrim Types,	49
Myles Standish's Bill of Expenses after his Visit to the Indians,	50

PAGE

Hooker's Emigration to Connecticut, ... *facing page* 50
Gov. John Winthrop, ... 51
First Church at Salem, ... 54
Facsimile of Opening Lines of the Massachusetts Charter, . . . 56–57
Sir Edmund Andros, ... 58
The Charter Oak, ... 60
A Dutch Officer of the Seventeenth Century, ... 64
A Group of Seventeenth Century Dutchmen, ... 65
The Earliest Picture of New Amsterdam, ... 66
Henry Hudson's *Half Moon* on the Hudson, ... 67
An Early Dutch Man of War, ... 69
William Penn, ... 70
Penn's Treaty with the Indians, ... *facing page* 70
An Indian Camp, ... 76
Wampum received by Penn from the Indians, ... 77
Indian Whip (Quirt), War-Club, and Hunting-Arrow, ... 78
Indian Snow-shoes and Pappoose-case, ... 79
Totem of the Five Nations, ... 80
Totem of the Illinois, ... 80
Totem of the Sioux, ... 81
Totem of the Hurons, ... 81
Carved Pipes from an Indian Mound, ... 82
Big Elephant Mound, ... 83
Indians Carrying Canoes over a Portage, ... 85
French Soldiers of the Time of the French Exploration, . . . 88
Samuel Champlain, ... 89
La Salle Claiming for France all the Territory through which the Missis-
        sippi and its Tributaries Flowed, ... *facing page* 90
Robert Cavalier De La Salle, ... 91
French Soldiers and Officers of the Time of the French War, . . . 95
Quebec in 1730, ... 97
General Braddock's Troops in an Indian Ambuscade, . . *facing page* 98
Maj.-Gen. James Wolfe, ... 101
Marquis de Montcalm, ... 102
Puritans Going to Church, ... 108
A Wanton Gospeller, ... 110
The Pillory, ... 112
Colonial Relics, ... 113
Early New Amsterdam, Showing Costumes, Amusements, and Architec-
        ture, ... 114–115
Old Spinning-wheel, ... 117
Title-page of "Poor Richard's Almanac," 120
John Hancock House, Boston, Mass., ... 126
James Otis, ... 127

PAGE

A Royal Stamp, ... 128
Faneuil Hall, Boston, Mass., ... 129
Old State House, Boston, Mass., ... 130
Patrick Henry, ... 131
The "Boston Massacre," 133
Old South Church, Boston, ... 135
St. John's Church, Richmond, Va., ... 137
The Fight on Lexington Common, April 19, 1775, . . *facing page* 138
Old North Church, Boston, Mass., ... 140
The Retreat from Concord, ... *facing page* 140
The Battle of Bunker Hill, ... *facing page* 142
The Washington Elm at Cambridge, ... 144
The Craigie House, Washington's Headquarters at Cambridge (afterward the
    residence of Longfellow), ... 146
Samuel Adams, ... 149
Independence Hall, Philadelphia, Pa.   Chestnut Street Front, . . . 150
Signing the Declaration of Independence, ... *facing page* 150
The Jumel Mansion, New York City, Washington's Headquarters, . . 153
John Burgoyne, ... 159
Lafayette, ... 160
Benjamin Franklin, ... 162
The Attack on the Chew House, Germantown, . . . *facing page* 164
A Revolutionary Gun, ... 168
A Revolutionary Flint-lock Pistol, ... 168
Clark on the way to Kaskaskia, ... 170
John Paul Jones, ... 172
The *Bonhomme Richard* and the *Serapis*, ... 173
The Escape of Benedict Arnold, ... 178
Nathaniel Greene, ... 180
Washington Firing the First Gun at the Siege of Yorktown, *facing page* 180
Nelson House, Yorktown, Va., ... 182
Three Shilling Massachusetts Bill of 1741, ... 186
Celebrating in New York the Adoption of the Constitution, . . . 189
Washington's Mansion—South and West Fronts—Mt. Vernon, Va., . 196
Washington's Bedroom, Mt. Vernon, Va., ... 197
Servants' Quarters, Mt. Vernon, Va., ... 198
A Mail Carrier, ... 199
A Fast Mail—1876, ... 199
A Twentieth Century Flyer, ... 199
John Jay, ... 200
How Washington Signed his Name at Various Ages, . . . 201
Alexander Hamilton, ... 202
A Primitive Cotton-gin, ... 204
Whitney's First Cotton-gin, ... 205

PAGE

John Adams, ... 209
School-house where Thomas Jefferson Received his Early Education, . . . 214
Monticello, the Home of Jefferson, ... 215
Thomas Jefferson, ... 216
A Pack-horse, ... 217
A Hand Corn-mill, ... 217
A Sweep-mill, ... 218
Breaking Flax, ... 218
An Ohio River Flatboat, ... 219
Early Settlers Crossing the Plains, ... *facing page* 220
Lewis's First Glimpse of the Rockies, ... *facing page* 222
James Madison, ... 228
American Seamen Boarding the *Frolic*, ... *facing page* 232
Old State House, where the Hartford Convention Met, . . . 237
James Monroe, ... 241
Henry Clay, "The Great Peacemaker," 244
John Quincy Adams, the Anti-slavery Statesman, . . . 246
Andrew Jackson, ... 251
John C. Calhoun, the Defender of Slavery and State Rights, . . 253
Daniel Webster, ... 255
Robert Y. Hayne, ... 256
The Boston & Worcester Railroad in 1835, ... 258
The Baltimore & Ohio Railroad, 1830–35, ... 258
A Railway Coach of 1830, ... 261
Martin Van Buren, ... 262
William Henry Harrison, ... 268
John Tyler, ... 269
Facsimile of the Heading of Garrison's Paper, ... 272
James K. Polk, ... 275
The Storming of Chapultepec, ... 276
Sutter's Mill, where Gold was first found in California, . . . 279
Zachary Taylor, ... 280
Modes of travel in the West. An Old Stage-coach and Prairie Schooner, . 282
Millard Fillmore, ... 283
Fugitive Slave Advertisements, ... 284
Franklin Pierce, ... 286
Charles Sumner, ... 289
Old Plantation Days, ... 292
James Buchanan, ... 294
Engine House, Harper's Ferry, ... 296
Abraham Lincoln, ... 300
Lincoln's Birthplace, ... 301
Jefferson Davis, ... 303

A HISTORY OF

THE UNITED STATES

FOR SCHOOLS

BY

WILBUR F. GORDY

FORMERLY SUPERINTENDENT OF SCHOOLS, SPRINGFIELD, MASS.; AUTHOR OF "ELEMENTARY HISTORY
OF THE UNITED STATES," "AMERICAN LEADERS AND HEROES," "AMERICAN BEGINNINGS IN
EUROPE," "STORIES OF AMERICAN EXPLORERS," "COLONIAL DAYS," "STORIES
OF EARLY AMERICAN HISTORY," "STORIES OF LATER AMERICAN HISTORY"

WITH MANY ILLUSTRATIONS AND MAPS

NEW EDITION

CHARLES SCRIBNER'S SONS
NEW YORK   CHICAGO   BOSTON

M

To
I. H. G.

PREFACE

THE function of both the writer and the teacher of history is to explain the meaning of human life as revealed in the records of the past. In the case of both the historian and the teacher much depends upon a nice discrimination in choosing typical facts, for their *nature* rather than their *number* should be the guiding principle. This is especially true in the teaching of history in grammar grades, where the purpose is not so much to acquire a considerable body of knowledge as to develop in the pupil an interest in history and a taste for historical reading. In this book care has been taken not only to select typical events but so to group them that their full value may be appreciated as causes or as results.

The reader is invited to examine briefly the plan of the book. After a short chapter on early discoveries follows an account of the struggle, on the part of the Spaniards, the English, the Dutch, and the French, for control in the New World. In accordance with the general purpose of selecting significant events, many romantic and interesting adventures have been omitted from the body of the text, in order to give more space to topics of greater importance. But enough has been told to explain the nature of the explorations, their objects, and methods, and the reasons for failure or success in planting colonies.

In the treatment of the English colonies, only typical

ones are chosen and they are divided in three groups. Virginia and Maryland represent the Southern group; Massachusetts and Connecticut, the New England group; and New York and Pennsylvania, the Middle group.

A few things should be noted in connection with the treatment of the colonies. In the first place, the history of each group is brought down to 1689, a turning-point in American history. The pupil can thus study separately the three parallel streams of colonial history, without the inevitable and almost inextricable confusion which must attend a strictly chronological treatment of the thirteen colonies, whether taken up singly or all together. In the second place, emphasis is laid upon what is important; the selection of typical colonies and of typical events in the life of these colonies must, of course, give more space for intelligent and interesting treatment of illustrative facts. In the third place, certain definite characteristics of the people in any one of the groups can, by comparison and contrast, be distinctly brought out by this method of study.

Of course there is an elimination of some matter generally used in text-books. At the ends of chapters, however, may be found, in the "Notes," reference to the colonies not treated fully in the body of the text. The subject-matter of these "Notes" has been carefully selected and will, it is believed, supply nearly all that is needed in schools where the conditions require a special handling of the colony in question.

Up to 1689 there was little of the spirit of union among the colonies. To a great extent each went its own way. But after 1689, three sets of influences—Indian wars, troubles with the French, and difficulties with the royal and the proprietary governors—gradually brought the colonies into closer sympathy and prepared them for union. To make clear the working of these three sets of historic forces, the topics introducing them are given in the following order: " Life among the Indians " and " Indian Wars "; " French Explorations " and the " Last French War "; and " Life among the Colonies " and " Growth toward Union."

Special attention is called to the facts selected to explain the real meaning of the intercolonial struggle between the English and the French. Of the four Intercolonial Wars, the only one worthy of study in grammar schools is the Last French War. By omitting the other three, space is gained for a more complete discussion of the one that had altogether the most important bearing upon American history. If the pupil thoroughly studies this war he will know the meaning of the struggle between England and France for control in America.

In the Revolution, as in all other wars, causes and results are emphasized rather than campaigns and battles; military details are avoided, only a few significant battles being given to enable the pupil to understand the character of the fighting. The pertinent question here as elsewhere is: Does the fact serve to give the pupil clear ideas of the past as an interpreter of the present? In applying this test in the study of history, we soon find ourselves passing lightly over or omitting altogether much that has found a conspicuous place in class-room work.

In the Constitutional period, the traditional grouping of topics according to Presidential administrations has been abandoned in the belief that the sequence of events can be more clearly understood by a *logical* grouping. But those who prefer to use the traditional method can easily adapt it to this book. Numerous references are made, in the notes " To the Pupil," to the Presidents and their terms of office, and a carefully prepared table containing a list of the Presidents and important facts about them may be found in the

Appendix.   Moreover, portraits of all the Presidents and sketches of their lives have been given an appropriate place.

Inasmuch as the colonization of the West has played so large a part in our history, no apology need be made for the prominence given to Western settlement, Western life, the difficult problems of connecting the East and the West, the effect of Western expansion upon the slavery controversy and immigration, the influence of the prairies and the Pacific railroads, and so on.

In discussing the development of the West, the intimate relation existing between man and the physical conditions that surround him is made evident.   Indeed, throughout the book the marked influence of geography upon history has been distinctly recognized.

But, however important physical conditions may be, history concerns itself more largely with moral than with material life.   Accordingly, the personal actor has been given emphasis.   In portraits, autographs, biographical sketches, and in the conspicuous mention made of representative men, the moral element has been kept uppermost. For man dominating his physical and social surroundings is the central fact of history.

The very cordial reception given to the previous editions of this book has been most gratifying.   In this new edition the history has been brought down to date.   Although many changes in the text have not been found necessary, yet, whenever in the interests of a more useful book such changes have seemed advisable they have been unhesitatingly made.   The excellence of the maps and pictures in the editions already published has won hearty commendation for their helpfulness in illuminating and supplementing the text.

In closing, the author wishes to express his deep obligation to Dr. Thomas M. Balliet, Dean of the New York University of Pedagogy, and to Professor William E. Mead, of Wesleyan University, Middletown, Conn., for their many invaluable suggestions; also to Miss Elizabeth M. Worthington, of Hartford, Conn., for her great care in reading the proof.

WILBUR F. GORDY.

CONTENTS

DISCOVERY OF AMERICA

CHAPTER   PAGE
I. Discovery of America, ... 1

EXPLORATION AND COLONIZATION

II. Spain in the New World, ... 13
III. England in the New World, ... 20
IV. The English in Virginia and Maryland (1607–1689), 28
V. The Pilgrims and Puritans in Massachusetts and
    Connecticut (1620–1689), ... 42
VI. The Dutch in New York and the Quakers in
    Pennsylvania (1609–1689), ... 63
VII. Life Among the Indians, ... 75
VIII. Early Indian Wars, ... 84
IX. French Explorations, ... 87
X. The Last French War, ... 93
XI. Life in the Colonies at the Close of the French
    and Indian Wars, ... 105
XII. Growth toward Union in the Colonies, . . . 118

THE REVOLUTION, THE CONFEDERATION, AND THE FEDERAL UNION

XIII. The Revolution, ... 125
XIV. The Breakdown of the Confederation and the
    Formation of the Constitution (1781–1789), . 185
XV. The New Struggle for Political Independence
    and the Growth of National Feeling (1789–
    1829, ... 194

CHAPTER   PAGE
  XVI. JACKSONIAN DEMOCRACY AND THE WEST (1829–1841), . 250
 XVII. THE SLAVERY QUESTION (1841–1859), ... 267
XVIII. SECESSION AND THE CIVIL WAR (1860–1865), . . 298

RECONSTRUCTION AND THE NEW UNION

  XIX. RECONSTRUCTION DAYS (1865–1871), ... 356
   XX. THE NEW SOUTH (1877–   ), ... 365
  XXI. THE NEW WEST (1865–   ), ... 372
 XXII. THE NEW UNION (1865), ... 382
XXIII. THE SPANISH–AMERICAN WAR AND RECENT EVENTS
           (1898–   ), ... 410
XXIV. SOME INDUSTRIAL, ECONOMIC, SOCIAL, AND POLITICAL
           CONDITIONS AND PROBLEMS OF THE PRESENT, . 451

TOPICAL REVIEWS IN AMERICAN HISTORY, ... 472

APPENDICES

A. THE DECLARATION OF INDEPENDENCE, ... 481
B. A CHART ON THE CONSTITUTION, ... 485
   CONSTITUTION OF THE UNITED STATES, ... 486
C. TABLE OF STATES AND TERRITORIES, ... 501
D. PRESIDENTS OF THE UNITED STATES, ... 503

INDEX, ... 505

	PAGE
Interior of Fort Sumter after the Bombardment in 1863,	306
Long Bridge Across the Potomac at Washington, D. C.,	308
George B. McClellan,	309
Deck of the *Monitor*,	312
The Battle between the *Monitor* and the *Merrimac*, *facing page*	314
Parapet at Fortress Monroe,	316
Grant's " Unconditional Surrender" Letter,	317
A Mortar Battery in front of Yorktown,	321
A Federal Battery in the Field,	323
Robert E. Lee,	324
Fugitive Negroes Fording the Rappahannock,	326
Thomas J. (" Stonewall ") Jackson,	327
George G. Meade,	329
The First Reading of the Emancipation Proclamation,	331
A Federal Cavalry Camp—Winter Quarters	332
George H. Thomas, " the Rock of Chickamauga,"	333
General Grant and Staff on Point Lookout, 1863,	334
General U. S. Grant,	337
Building a Pontoon Bridge,	338
Philip H. Sheridan,	339
Destroying a Railroad at Atlanta, Ga.,	340
William T. Sherman,	341
David Glasgow Farragut,	343
Farragut in Mobile Bay, *facing page*	344
A Council of War at Massaponax Church,	347
The Surrender of Lee to Grant at Appomattox, *facing page*	348
A Sanitary Commission Lodge near Alexandria, Va.,	351
Andrew Johnson,	357
A Ku-klux " Warning" in Mississippi,	362
Rutherford B. Hayes,	366
Eads Bridge over the Mississippi at St. Louis,	367
A Cotton Press Yard, New Orleans,	368
A Sugar Plantation,	369
State Buildings, Atlanta, Ga.,	370
A Cripple Creek Mine,	374
A Reaper,	375
A Steam-Driven Gang-Plow,	376
A Thresher,	377
Indian Warfare in the West, *facing page*	378
Artesian Well System, Riverside, Cal. An Aerator in foreground,	379
An Irrigated Orange Grove, Riverside, Cal.,	380
A Midship View of the *Great Eastern*, showing one of the Paddle Wheels and the Launching Gear,	383
Samuel F. B. Morse's Original Model of the Telegraph Instrument,	384

PAGE

R. F. T. Allen's Original Model of the Typewriter, ... 385
Alexander Graham Bell's Original Model of the Telephone Receiver and
    Transmitter, ... 386
Elias Howe's Original Model of the Sewing Machine, ... 387
Opening Day at the Philadelphia Centennial, 1876, ... 388
Samuel J. Tilden, ... 389
James A. Garfield, ... 390
Supreme Court Room, Capitol, Washington, D. C., ... 391
Chester A. Arthur, ... 392
Grover Cleveland, ... 393
Brooklyn Bridge. One of the Largest Suspension Bridges in the World, . 394
The Statue of Liberty in New York Harbor, ... 396
Senate Chamber, Washington, D. C., ... 398
Hall of the House of Representatives, Washington, D. C., ... 399
James G. Blaine, ... 400
The New Battleship *Maine*, ... 401
Benjamin Harrison, ... 402
At the World's Fair, ... *facing page* 402
William McKinley, ... 404
The Inauguration of William McKinley, ... 406
The Wreck of Cervera's Flagship *Colon*, ... 410
W. S. Schley, ... 411
George Dewey, ... 412
Shipping and Docks, Pasig River, Manila, ... 413
United States Troops Landing at Baiquiri, Cuba, ... 415
The Palace at Santiago on which the American Flag was Raised when the
    American Troops Took Possession, ... 416
Theodore Roosevelt, ... 417
William T. Sampson, ... 418
Nelson A. Miles, ... 420
Native Tagalo Children, Malabon, ... 421
Wireless Telegraph Station at Wellfleet, Cape Cod, ... 424
The Atlantic Fleet Starting on its Voyage Around the World, Dec., 1907, . 426
Peace Palace, The Hague, ... 428
Natural Forest Regions of the United States 434
William H. Taft, ... 435
The New Department of State Building,. 437
Woodrow Wilson 438
The Round-Up, ... 451
A Textile Mill, ... 452
Anthracite Coal Mine, ... 454
Goods Awaiting Exportation, ... 457
Transportation in a Large City, showing Elevated Road, Surface Line and
    Subway, ... 459

PAGE

A Crowded Street in a Tenement District, ...   461
New Steel Tower Bridge Across the East River, New York,   .   .   .   462
Ralph Waldo Emerson, ...   464
John Greenleaf Whittier, ...   464
The Louisiana Purchase Exposition, St. Louis, 1904. One of the Bridges
        and Lagoons, with the Palace of Education, ...   465
The Capitol, Washington, D. C., ...   466

LIST OF MAPS

	PAGE
The World as Known in the Time of Columbus,	7
English and Spanish Explorers in America,	10
Routes of Narvaez, De Soto, and Ponce de Leon,	17
The United States as it was in 1650,	*between pages* 28 and 29
Plymouth and London Grants, 1606,	29
England and Holland,	45
New England,	53
Province Ruled over by Sir Edmund Andros, 1688,	59
Colonies between Potomac and Hudson Rivers,	71
Routes of Champlain, Marquette, and La Salle—also English Possessions, French and Spanish Claims,	*between pages* 88 and 89
Quebec and Vicinity,	100
Results of the French and Indian War,	107
Boston and Vicinity,	143
New York and Vicinity,	151
Washington's Retreat across New Jersey,	155
Burgoyne's Invasion and Howe's Capture of Philadelphia,	161
War in the South and the Northwest Territory,	171
Scene of Arnold's Treason,	177
North America at the Close of the Revolution,	*between pages* 182 and 183
Louisiana Purchase and Lewis and Clark Route,	221
War of 1812,	*between pages* 234 and 235
Oregon Country,	270
Area in Dispute at Time of Mexican War,	*facing page* 274
The Mexican Cession, Gadsden Purchase, etc.,	*facing page* 280
Acquisition of Territory,	*facing page* 294
The First and Second Secession Areas,	*between pages* 304 and 305
Campaigns in the West, 1862-63,	318
Virginia Campaigns and McClellan's Route,	320
The Battle of Gettysburg,	328
Vicksburg and Vicinity,	330
Chattanooga and Vicinity,	335
Sherman's March to the Sea,	342
Cuba,	414
Porto Rico,	419
The United States in 1910,	*between pages* 420 and 421
Philippine Islands	422
Trade Routes with Distances by Existing Lines and by the Panama Canal,	444, 445

HISTORY OF THE UNITED STATES

PART I

Discovery of America

CHAPTER I

DISCOVERY OF AMERICA

REFERENCES: **Scribner's** Popular History of the United States, I.; **Wright's** Children's Stories in American History; **Richardson's** History of Our Country; **Coffin's** Old Times in the Colonies; **Eggleston's** Household History; **Bancroft's** United States, I.; **Andrews's** United States, I.

OUTSIDE READINGS: **Irving's** Columbus; **Prescott's** Ferdinand and Isabella; **Winsor's** Columbus; **Fiske's** Discovery of America; **Towle's** Heroes of History (Marco Polo; also Vasco Da Gama); **Brooks's** The Story of Marco Polo.

1. European Trade with Asia in the Fifteenth Century.—For many hundred years there had been more or less trade between the people of Europe and Asia. Silks, spices, and precious stones had been brought by ships and caravans from India, China, and Japan, enriching the cities of southern Europe. Genoa and Venice, especially, had been made rich by this eastern trade, which continued to grow until 1453, when the Turks conquered Constantinople. This was thirty-nine years before Columbus discovered America. At this time European vessels on the Mediterranean Sea were no longer safe from the attack of these fierce and warlike people. Therefore Europe began to look for another and safer route to the Indies.

2. Aids to Discovery.—Three inventions which had recently come into practical use had made discovery less difficult than it had ever been before. (1) Gunpowder made easier the conquest of uncivilized peoples; (2) the

A SHIP OF THE NORSEMEN.

Remains of a viking ship and a sketch showing steering board.

mariner's compass encouraged the sailor to venture far out into the sea; (3) and the printing-press spread abroad the knowledge of new-found lands. Men were full of curiosity, and the more they learned the more they wished to know. With this burning desire for knowledge went hand in hand the spirit of adventure. There was a longing to go into distant lands, to perform great deeds, and to bring home gold and jewels. In these far-away lands men thought they should find honor, wealth, and fame.

3. **Portugal Leads in Discovering an Eastern Route.** —Portugal is to-day a very unimportant country. At the time when men were trying to find a safe water route to the Indies, she was one of the great powers of the world. She was the leader in many adventures and discoveries reaching through a period of two centuries. Early in the fifteenth century, Portuguese vessels and seamen were slowly and cautiously skirting the coast of Africa, and after seventy years of brave struggle they found the Cape of Good Hope.[1] Portugal had at this time many vessels and

[1] Diaz reached the southern point of Africa in 1487 and called it the Cape of Storms. It was afterward significantly named the Cape of Good Hope.

CHRISTOPHER COLUMBUS.

From a portrait by Antonio Van Moor painted in 1542. By permission of Charles F. Gunther.

seamen, and was the first country to find a new route to the Indies.

4. Plans of Columbus.—In the meantime Christopher Columbus, in common with some learned men of his time, had decided that the eastern coast of Asia could be reached by sailing westward across the Atlantic. Columbus thought, also, that Asia was no farther from Europe on the west than we now know America to be. He thought the East Indies were directly west from the Canary Islands. This being so, the easiest way of reaching China, India, and Japan would be to sail down to the Canaries, and from them straight across the Atlantic in a westerly direction. To us, with our knowledge, all this seems simple and natural enough, but it was not so then. Men knew little of the world outside of their own country. Sailors were afraid to venture upon the trackless ocean, or Sea of Darkness, as they called the Atlantic, where death seemed likely to meet them. Moreover, practical difficulties stood in the way. **Difficulties of Columbus.** Such an enterprise would require the equipment of vessels at much expense. Money and influence were essential. Columbus had neither, but he was eager to fit out an expedition. He went with his plans to his native city, Genoa, and then to Portugal and Spain.

THE *NINA*.

THE *PINTA*.

He sent his brother to England and to France. Then he went to Spain again. He was nowhere successful. Some thought he was an idle dreamer, and others that he was a madman. But he never despaired, because he had faith in himself and believed also that his work was under the special direction of God.

5. **First Voyage of Columbus (1492).**—Finally, after seven years of anxious waiting, the brave Columbus found success. Isabella, Queen of Spain, agreed to aid him in carrying out his plans. Still there were difficulties. Sailors were unwilling to go on the dangerous voyage, but were compelled to yield to the mandate of the king. Three small vessels, only one of which had a deck, were fitted out. The largest of these, the *Santa Maria*, was commanded by Columbus. The others were the *Nina* and the *Pinta*. Before sunrise, August 3, 1492, this little fleet, with one hundred and twenty men and provisions for a year, sailed out of the port of Palos. It was a sad hour for the poor sailors. Columbus steered for the Canaries, where he stopped over three weeks to make a rudder for one of his **Columbus sets sail.** vessels. He then set sail again. As soon as they could no longer see land, the sailors were overcome with fear and cried like children. At the end of a week the compass needle did not point to the North

Star. Failing to understand the reason for this, the sailors were struck with terror. Three days later the vessels entered wide stretches of sea-weed. It was then feared that the vessels might strike upon hidden rocks and be dashed to pieces. But they passed on in safety.

Soon afterward the sailors were gladdened by the sight of birds, which they thought indicated that land was near. It was an idle hope, for, no land appeared. Again and again the cry " Land " was shouted, but in every case the cry was called forth by the sight of distant clouds. **The sailors in despair.** The poor sailors were in despair. They were now in the belt of the trade-winds, which were steadily and certainly blowing them farther and farther from home and friends. "We can never return to Spain," they said. "What shall we do?" They begged Columbus to turn back. He refused. They became angry and talked of throwing him overboard. He knew he was in danger and tried hard to quiet their fears and to give them hope. It was then that his great influence over men was shown. His tall and manly figure gave him a commanding presence, but his greatest strength in these trying days lay in his noble soul and his lofty purpose. His courage never failed him. Sometimes he

THE *SANTA MARIA.*

heartened the sailors with promises of wealth and fame, and again, as occasion demanded, he threatened them with punishment from the Spanish king.

At last, after a voyage of ten weeks, land was discovered **October 12,**[1] **1492.** In a full suit of armor and bearing the

[1] October 21 by the present method of reckoning time.

flag of Spain, Columbus landed. With tears of joy he
knelt upon the ground and offered thanks to God. Then,
Land discovered.   planting the royal banner, he took possession
of the land in the name of the king and queen
of Spain. He had discovered one of the Bahama Islands
which he called San Salvador (Holy Saviour). He coasted
along the shores of Cuba and Hayti, touched the coast here
and there, and sent reconnoitring parties inland to examine the land. He did not find the cities of Asia as he had
expected, but he had no doubt that he was in the East Indies, and therefore called the natives Indians.

  6. Other Voyages of Columbus.—When Columbus returned to Spain with the news of his discovery, the people
were enthusiastic with delight. The idle dreamer became
suddenly great and famous, and honors were heaped upon
him from every side. It was easy enough to find sailors
and vessels for a second voyage, which was made in the
following year, 1493. Men were now eager to go where
they expected to get all kinds of wealth. Four voyages
were made in all, but when the adventurers reached the
land of their hopes, and found no silks, no spices, no precious stones, no gold, they reproached Columbus. The
Court of Spain, also, finding no return for the great expense of fitting out these expeditions, censured him. His
Last days of   enemies increased, and his last days were spent
Columbus.   in disappointment and neglect. Heart-broken,
he died ignorant of the greatness of his own discovery.

  **7. John Cabot Discovers the Mainland of North Amer-
ica (1497).**—In consequence of the discoveries by Colum-
The "Line of De- bus in the West and of those by Portuguese
marcation" di-   captains in the East, it was feared there might
vides the heathen be trouble between Spain and Portugal over
possessions of
Spain and Portu- the new-found lands. To keep the peace,
gal.   therefore, between these two great Catholic
countries, a treaty was signed in 1494, dividing between
them the heathen lands that had been, or should be, discovered. "The Line of Demarcation," extending north and
south three hundred and seventy leagues west of the Cape

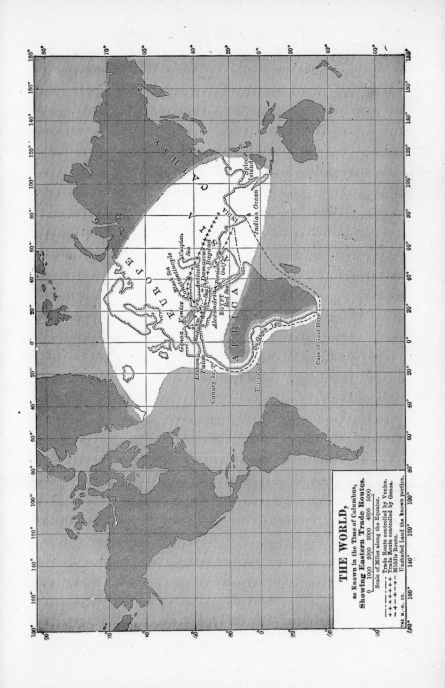

THE WORLD,
as Known in the Time of Columbus,
Showing Eastern Trade Routes.

Scale of Miles along the Equator.
0 1000 2000 3000 4000 5000

– · – · – · – Trade Route controlled by Venice.
+ + + + + + Trade Route controlled by Genoa.
– · · – · · – Middle Route.
Unshaded Land the known portion.

THE M · M · CO.

Verde Islands, ran between Spain's possessions on the
West and those of Portugal on the East.   The powerful
navies of these two countries were sufficient to make good
their claims against England or any other nation.   But England was determined to have some share in the discoveries
that were stirring the hearts of men.   Hence, in 1497, Henry
VII. sent out John Cabot, accompanied possibly by his son
Sebastian, to find a short northwest passage to Asia.   By

sailing across the northern part
of the Atlantic, England avoided
difficulties likely to arise from
coming in contact with Spanish
or Portuguese discoverers farther south.   John Cabot landed
Voyages of the
Cabots.   somewhere on the
                eastern coast of
North America, possibly on the
coast of Labrador.   He was
therefore the first to discover
the mainland of the Continent
of North America, and he
claimed it in the name of Eng-

SEBASTIAN CABOT.

land.   The next year Sebastian Cabot sailed from England
and explored the coast of North America from Nova Scotia
down as far as North Carolina or farther.   Upon these
discoveries England based her claim to North America.

8. **Americus Vespucius and the Naming of America**
(1499-1503).—Americus Vespucius, a native of Florence and
a navigator, was first employed by Spain and later by
Portugal, to make explorations.   In 1499 he skirted the
coast of Venezuela and northeastern South America.
During the next four years he made several voyages to
Brazil, and explored its coast as far south as the mouth
of the La Plata River.   On returning to Europe he wrote
a good description of what he had seen.   This was published in 1504, and constituted the first printed account of
the mainland of the New World.   Up to that time Europe,
Asia, and Africa were known as the three parts of the

COLUMBUS AT THE COURT OF FERDINAND AND ISABELLA AFTER HIS RETURN FROM THE NEW WORLD.

world, and one distinguished geographer believed there was an unknown southern continent which constituted the fourth part. It now seemed clear that Americus Vespucius had proved the existence of the fourth part. In consequence of this belief a German professor, **New World called America.** who printed a little treatise on geography a few years later, suggested that the fourth part should be called America, after Americus Vespucius. According to this suggestion the name America was at first applied to Brazil, later to South America, and later still to the whole of the New World.

9. **Magellan Proves America to be a Continent (1519–1521).** —What America and the New World meant was as yet by no means clear. By some, America was supposed to be an immense island, like Australia; by others, a peninsula extending in a southeasterly direction from Asia. In 1519 Magellan, a Portuguese captain in command of a Spanish fleet, started on a voyage whose object was to reach Asia by way

AMERICUS VESPUCIUS.

From statue by G. Grazzini in the Uffizi Gallery, Florence, Italy.

of a passage through America. After coasting down much of the eastern shore of South America, he discovered and sailed through the strait now bearing his **Wonderful voyage of Magellan.** name. Mutiny, starvation, and other hardships that would have driven back a less heroic man were bravely endured. He sailed for some distance up the western side of South America, and then steered his way across the Pacific. He was killed by the natives in the Philippine Islands, but a part of his men succeeded in finding their way back to Spain. This was the most wonderful voyage that had ever been made, because it proved that the earth was a globe, and that America was a distinct continent.

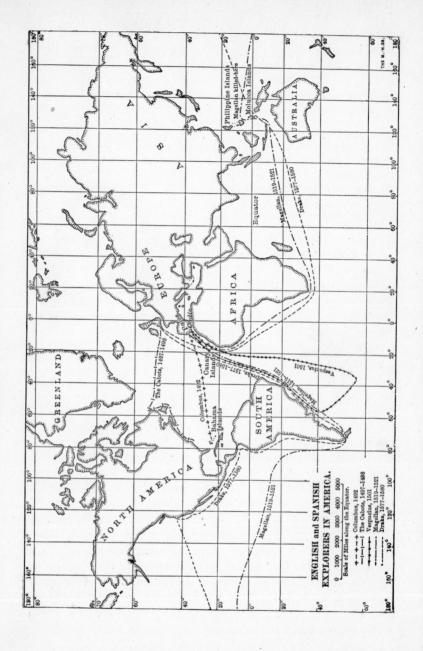

ENGLISH and SPANISH
EXPLORERS IN AMERICA.

Scale of Miles along the Equator.
0   1000   2000   3000   4000   5000

+—+—+—+ Columbus, 1492
—·—·—·— The Cabots, 1497–1498
———————— Vespucius, 1501
············ Magellan, 1519–1521
•—•—•—• Drake, 1577–1580

TO THE PUPIL.

1. Trace on the map the Eastern trade routes in the fifteenth century. In what way did printing aid discovery? What advantage did the control of the water route to India give to Portugal?
2. Imagine yourself to be Columbus and write an account, in the first person, of your plans, your difficulties, and your first voyage. Trace this voyage on the map. What do you admire in the character of Columbus?
3. How did America receive its name? Was this fair to Columbus? Give reasons for your answer.
4. What was the distinctive work of Columbus? Of Americus Vespucius? Of Magellan?
5. Read in Fiske's Discovery of America the account of Magellan's wonderful voyage.

NOTES

Lief Ericsson and the Northmen.—The old inhabitants of Norway were called Northmen or Norsemen. These people were bold and hardy sailors, and in the ninth and tenth centuries were famous sea-robbers. In order to find new fields for plunder and adventure they sought strange coasts. On one of these expeditions they reached Iceland and on another Greenland. In each of these islands they made settlements. The brave deeds of these old warriors are preserved in the so-called "Sagas," which were written in Icelandic prose. For a long time these Sagas were transmitted orally, but finally they were committed to writing. Three of the Sagas tell us of the daring adventures of Lief Ericsson in his wanderings in the year 1000 A.D. along the eastern coast of North America. As the story goes, Lief Ericsson, with a crew of thirty-five men, started out in search of a land which had been visited by another Northman. Sailing west, Lief touched upon the coast of Labrador and thence, proceeding south, he landed, built huts, and spent the winter near the coast. Finding vines hung with grapes, he called the country Vinland. Some historians have supposed that Lief Ericsson's Vinland was somewhere on the coast of Massachusetts, but the weight of authority is in favor of Cape Breton Island or Nova Scotia. Other Northmen visited Vinland but they made no permanent settlements. Nothing reliable can be found out about these early expeditions, and nothing of importance ever came of them.

CHRONOLOGY

870. ICELAND DISCOVERED BY NADDOD, THE NORTHMAN.

1000. LEIF, SON OF ERIC THE RED, DISCOVERS AMERICA.

1450. INVENTION OF PRINTING, ABOUT THIS DATE.

1453. THE TURKS CAPTURE CONSTANTINOPLE.

1492. FIRST VOYAGE OF COLUMBUS ; DISCOVERY OF WEST INDIES.

1497. JOHN CABOT DISCOVERS NORTH AMERICA.

1498. THIRD VOYAGE OF COLUMBUS ; HE DISCOVERS THE CONTINENT OF SOUTH
       AMERICA.

       VOYAGE OF SEBASTIAN CABOT.

1499. FIRST VOYAGE OF AMERICUS VESPUCIUS.

1504. AMERICUS VESPUCIUS'S NARRATIVE PUBLISHED.

1507. AMERICA NAMED.

1513. DISCOVERY OF FLORIDA BY JUAN PONCE DE LEON.

       PACIFIC OCEAN DISCOVERED BY VASCO NUNEZ DE BALBOA.

1519–21. CORTEZ CONQUERS MEXICO.

1519–21. A SHIP OF MAGELLAN'S EXPEDITION SAILS AROUND THE WORLD.

Exploration and Colonization

CHAPTER II

SPAIN IN THE NEW WORLD

REFERENCES: **Scribner's** Popular History of the United States, I.; **Wright's** Children's Stories in American History; **Richardson's** History of Our Country; **Bancroft's** United States, I.; **Higginson's** American Explorers; **Morris's** Half Hours with American History, I.; **Andrews's** United States, I.

OUTSIDE READINGS: **Prescott's** Conquest of Mexico; **Prescott's** Conquest of Peru; **Fiske's** Discovery of America; **Winsor's** Narrative and Critical History, II.; **Higginson's** American Explorers; **Parkman's** Pioneers of France in the New World (Huguenots).

FICTION: **Henty's** By Right of Conquest; **Wallace's** The Fair God; **Munroe's** Flamingo Feather; **Munroe's** The White Conqueror.

CORTEZ.
An early Spanish explorer.

10. **Precious Metals the Main Object of Spaniards.**—Spain is to-day a third-rate power, but in the early part of the sixteenth century she was the greatest power in Europe. She had a mighty navy, manned by daring and patriotic seamen, and she was ambitious to extend her sway over much of the heathen world. The marvellous stories of the treasures to be found in the New World dazzled the imagination of the Spaniards. Believing that gold and silver made the only true wealth, they were willing to undergo almost any suffering to secure them.

11. **De Leon Discovers Florida (1513).**—Among these fortune-hunters was an old

13

OLD SPANISH MISSION, NEW MEXICO, BUILT 1604.

man, Ponce de Leon, who had been governor of the island of Porto Rico. He had heard the natives tell stories of rich gold mines, and of a wonderful fountain in the land of the North, the drinking of whose waters would restore youth and vigor to old age. De Leon conducted an expedition

SPANISH GATEWAY, ST. AUGUSTINE, FLORIDA.

northward by which he hoped to secure for himself wealth and young manhood. The gold and the fountain he did not find, but he discovered something of much greater value to Spain, a beautiful land covered with flowers. This he named Florida (1513). A few years later De Leon returned to Florida with the purpose of planting a colony, but he was killed by an unfriendly Indian.

12. De Soto Explores Florida and Discovers the Mississippi (1539-1541).—The failure of De Leon and Narvaez did not prevent other Spaniards from making sim-

ílar attempts. In 1539 De Soto, with about six hundred men, two hundred horses, and bloodhounds to hunt the Indians, landed on the west coast of Florida in search of the new kingdom of gold. The Indians did not fear the bloodhounds more than they hated the Spaniards, whom they fiercely opposed. Northward and westward the Spaniards wandered in their fruitless search for gold mines. They found, instead, "fighting, fever, and famine." One great, unlooked-for discovery it was their fortune to make. That was the discovery of the Mississippi River. They journeyed many miles beyond it but soon returned, and at last, after two years of hopeless wandering, De Soto, worn out and sick at heart, died and was buried in the great river which he had discovered (1541). His surviving companions sailed down the Mississippi and found shelter in the Spanish settlement of Mexico.[1] De Soto, like De Leon,

BALBOA.
An early Spanish explorer.

failed; nor were any Spanish explorations in the country north of Mexico successful.

13. The Spaniards Drive the Huguenots out of Florida. (1562–1565).—For more than twenty years after De Soto's failure the Spaniards made no further efforts in Florida. In the meantime a bitter religious war broke out in France between the Catholics and the Huguenots.[2] Coligny, the distinguished leader of the Huguenots, desired to establish

---

[1] Cortez had conquered Mexico and established Spanish colonies there (1519–1521). Pizarro had conquered Peru (1531–1533).

[2] French Protestants.

a commonwealth of his own religious sect in America. Accordingly he sent over in 1562 a small number of settlers **Huguenot settlements.** who tried to plant a colony where Port Royal, South Carolina, now stands. The colony having failed, another expedition under good leadership was sent out in 1564. This time the French planted a fort not far from the mouth of the St. John's River, Florida. But for several reasons Spain laid claim to Florida: (1) By

FERNANDO DE SOTO.

right of discovery through Columbus; (2) by the explorations of De **Why Spain laid** Leon and De Soto; and **claim to Florida.** (3) by the Pope's decree, which assigned that part of the heathen world to Spain. The king of Spain, therefore, was indignant that the French should make any settlement there, and at once decided to send out a force to destroy the insolent intruders. This Spanish force was under the command of Menendez, who in 1565 landed in Florida and built a stronghold which later became St. Augustine. Then he marched across the country, and by surprise and treachery succeeded in destroying all but a miserable remnant of the **The Spaniards destroy the Huguenot settlement in Florida.** unfortunate Frenchmen who had established the settlement. It was a cruel work, thoroughly done.[1] The French learned a lesson from their unpleasant experience with the Spaniards at this time, and made no further attempt to plant colonies in the southern part of what is now the United States.

14. Advantages of Spain in the New World.—The advantages of Spain in the New World were many, two of which we will notice. In the tropical regions of Mexico,

---

[1] Although at this time France and Spain were at peace, the French did nothing to resent this wrong. A French captain, Dominic de Gourgues, however, determined upon revenge in the name of his country. Having a private grudge against the Spaniards, who had imprisoned him and made him work in the galleys, he fitted

South America, and the West Indies, the Indians lived in a warm climate, supported themselves by a rude tillage of the soil, and could be easily enslaved. In this respect Spain had a decided advantage over the nations colonizing in the North, where the Indians had been made hardy and brave by exposure to rougher climate and almost continuous inter-tribal warfare. These Indians were dangerous

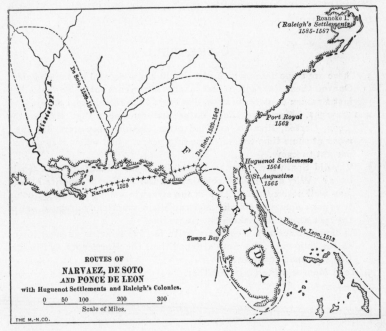

ROUTES OF
NARVAEZ, DE SOTO
AND **PONCE DE LEON**
with Huguenot Settlements and Raleigh's Colonies.

0 50 100   200   300
Scale of Miles.

THE M.-N.CO.

enemies to the white settlers. And surpassing all other advantages was the possession of the Gulf of Mexico and the mouth of the Mississippi River.

15. Reasons for Spanish Failure.—But in spite of these advantages the Spaniards failed, and they failed because

out at his own expense an expedition to Florida. Until the proper time he concealed his real purpose. Then he sailed straight to Florida, and with the aid of the Indians surprised the Spanish forts on the St. John's River and put to the sword nearly all the Spanish soldiers. As his force was too small to attack St. Augustine he returned to France, leaving Spain in control of Florida.

their conceptions and aims were wrong. Their greatest desire was for gold and silver, conquest, and adventure. They did not understand that the soil must first be conquered, and that in order to develop agriculture, trade, and commerce, a life of patient toil was necessary. As they wished to get rich without work, the gold and silver which they found made them poor because it took away habits of industry. In North America Spanish colonization was a total failure.

TO THE PUPIL

1. There are some dates which you should know as well as the alphabet. One of these is 1492. Just about fifty years later De Soto, the last Spanish explorer of note, discovered the Mississippi River.
2. 1492–1541. Memorize these dates and remember that Balboa, De Leon, Cortez, Pizarro, and the other Spanish explorers did their work at some time within these fifty years. Just when, it is not important to know.
3. Why did Spain lay claim to Florida? What advantages did Spain have? Why did Spanish colonization fail in North America? You may well notice the fact that in the struggle among European countries for colonizing North America, Spain practically dropped out of the race after establishing St. Augustine.
4. To develop accuracy, frequently write for five minutes on such topics as the following: De Soto's expedition, the Huguenots in Florida. Use your map constantly.
5. Read Munroe's Flamingo Feather.

NOTES

Balboa Discovers the Pacific (1513).—Balboa, a Spaniard in command of a company of men at Darien, made his way across the Isthmus of Panama (then known as the Isthmus of Darien) and discovered the Pacific Ocean. He took possession of the sea in the name of his king.

Cortez Conquers Mexico (1519–1521).—In 1519 Hernando Cortez began the conquest of Mexico. Although his army numbered less than five hundred Spaniards, he burned his fleet behind him at Vera Cruz and boldly set forth against the powerful Mexican ruler, Montezuma. Under an ordinary leader the Spaniards must have been destroyed, but Cortez, with rare courage and foresight, led them on to victory. Before the close of 1521 Mexico had become a Spanish province.

Narvaez Explores Florida (1528).—As the greedy Spaniards now had fresh hopes of finding gold and silver in the new country, Narvaez fitted out an expedition that landed on the western coast of Florida (1528.) After passing through the severest hardships, he and many of his men were drowned. His secretary, Cabeza de Vaca, and three companions fell into the hands of the Indians. Passing through many thrilling experiences, they wandered during eight years over two thousand miles of territory and finally joined, on the Gulf of California, a body of Spaniards from Mexico.

Pizarro Conquers Peru (1531–1533).—In 1531 Pizarro sailed from Panama, with the purpose of conquering Peru for Spain. By bravery, cruelty, and treachery, he succeeded in carrying out his plan (1533). Peru, like Mexico, yielded to Spain vast quantities of gold and silver, which greatly aided her in carrying on her European wars.

CHAPTER III

ENGLAND IN THE NEW WORLD

REFERENCES: **Scribner's** Popular History of the United States, II.; **Wright's** Children's Stories in American History; **Richardson's** History of Our Country; **Morris's** Half Hours with American History, I.; **Eggleston's** Household History; **Winsor's** Narrative and Critical History, III.; **Andrews's** United States, I.

OUTSIDE READINGS: **Towle's** Heroes of History (Drake and Raleigh); **Higginson's** United States; **Montgomery's** English History; **Camden's** History of Queen Elizabeth; **Creasy's** Fifteen Decisive Battles.

FICTION: **Scott's** Kenilworth; **Kingsley's** Westward Ho!; **Henty's** Under Drake's Flag.

16. Relations Between Spain and England.—England's claim to North America was based upon the discoveries of

QUEEN ELIZABETH.

the Cabots, who reached the mainland shortly after Columbus made his first landing on the West Indies. But Spain was the leading naval power in Europe. She controlled the Netherlands, and her mighty fleets sailed far and wide over the seas. England was not then the power she is now, and she was not strong enough to prevent Spain from carrying out her plans in America. So English explorers did not venture into that part of America to which Spain laid claim. Their efforts were directed chiefly to

20

discovering a northwest passage to Asia, since they regarded America as only a barrier between Europe and Asia.

During the latter part of the sixteenth century, however, conditions changed. In 1567 the Netherlands revolted against the rule of Spain, and for forty years carried on war with that country. In this war, which was partly religious, England was on the side of the Netherlands. Thus Spain had to contend with two countries at once, and found the great struggle a constant drain upon her strength. During these forty years of warring Spain received blows from which she never recovered. The "Invincible Armada," her mighty **Defeat of the** fleet of war vessels,[1] **Spanish Armada.** met with crushing defeat at the hands of English seamen (1588). From that date England's naval power was on the increase.

17. **English Sea-rovers and Explorers.**— After 1570 the English did not confine themselves to the northern ocean but explored in waters that Spain claimed as hers alone. English ships, manned by fearless sea-captains ready to do and dare anything for old England and their queen, began to sail in every direction. As soon as it became clear that for carrying on her wars Spain depended largely on the gold and silver[2] coming from the mines of Mexico and Peru, there was a fresh

SIR WALTER RALEIGH AND AUTOGRAPH.

---

[1] The Invincible Armada consisted of 130 warships carrying 2,500 cannon and about 30,000 men. Philip II., the Spanish king, expected to humble England with this fleet.

[2] It has been estimated that the gold and silver Spain got from America would be now valued at five thousand million dollars.

THE DESTRUCTION OF THE SPANISH ARMADA.

motive for English voyages to the New World. To cut off
the supply of these metals bold sea-captains like Drake and
Hawkins scoured the sea in search of Spanish vessels. They
cruised about the coasts, burning and plundering Spanish
fleets and settlements, and thus did very great injury to
Spain and her colonies in South America and Mexico.

18. Sir Walter Raleigh's[1] Attempt to Colonize America (1584–1587).—In 1578, ten years before the Invincible Ar-

---

[1] Sir Walter Raleigh, born in 1562, was in his own time rightly called the
"Great Englishman," for he ranked high as historian, navigator, soldier, and
statesman. In 1579, when only seventeen years old, he fought on the side of the
Huguenots in the religious wars in France. He is said to have won the admiration
of Queen Elizabeth by a simple act of gallantry. Meeting her one day as she was
walking across a muddy street, he spread his cloak in her pathway for her to walk
upon. From that time the queen took him into her court as a favorite. So entirely did he win her favor that she made him a knight.

In 1588 Raleigh commanded one of the vessels in the English fleet that defeated the "Spanish Armada." Later he was thrown into the Tower of London on
an unproved charge of treason. After remaining twelve years in the Tower he
was beheaded (1618). Just as he was about to lay his head upon the block he felt
the keen edge of the axe and said, "This is a sharp medicine, but a sound cure for
all diseases."

mada sailed for England, a scheme was laid to plant on the coast of America an English settlement, or military post, from which attacks might be made upon Spanish fleets. Sir Humphrey Gilbert, the author of the scheme, failed, but the idea of making a settlement in America had found a lodging-place in the English mind. *Sir Humphrey Gilbert's scheme.*

A little later Sir Walter Raleigh determined upon another effort. He saw that America's greatest wealth did not consist in gold and silver, but in the opportunities it offered for the growth of a great people. He earnestly desired to plant an English commonwealth in America, and he had the honor of making the first English settlement. After obtaining a patent from the queen, he sent out in 1584 two vessels to make explorations. The explorers returned with glowing accounts of the new land and its people, and Queen Elizabeth was so delighted with the reports of the new country that she called it Virginia in honor of herself, the " Virgin Queen." *Raleigh sends an exploring party to Virginia.*

PHILIPPE II., KING OF SPAIN
1527–1598.

In 1585 Raleigh sent out one hundred colonists, who landed on Roanoke Island, bright with hope. As soon as the ships sailed back to England the unfitness of the colonists for their new trials became apparent. Like all who had come before them they failed because of their thirst for gold. Instead of building homes and trying to cultivate the soil, they gave themselves up to searching for gold and silver. Moreover, they showed so little wisdom in dealing with the Indians that the latter became bitter enemies, eager to destroy the white strangers. The natural result of the experiment was failure. Fortunately for them Drake, who was returning from one of his cruising expeditions, happened along and *Raleigh's first colony fails.*

carried the colonists back to England. The expedition
was not wholly fruitless, however, for they took back to
England on their return two products which were evidence

AN INDIAN VILLAGE AT ROANOKE.
From an old print.

of the real wealth and promise of the new country. These
products were tobacco and the common potato.

Raleigh did not lose hope. Two years later he made
a second attempt. He sent out a much larger number of
settlers, among whom were women and children. The new

ENGLISH EXPLORERS BARTERING WITH INDIANS FOR LAND.

settlement was made at Roanoke under the leadership of Governor White. He was soon compelled to return to England for supplies, where he found all the people astir in preparation for the attack about to be made by the Spanish Armada. As every man was needed to fight the coming enemy, three years passed before Governor White sailed again for Roanoke. Not one of the colonists was ever found.

Raleigh's second colony fails.

Raleigh sent out several expeditions in search of the lost colony, but finally gave up hope of finding it or of planting another. He had spent what was equivalent to more than a million dollars of our present money. Although nothing remained to be seen in return for this vast expenditure of money, Raleigh's work was not a failure, for his efforts had suggested to England that the real wealth of America lay in the opportunity it afforded for planting colonies which in time would become the foundation of a new English nation.

Raleigh's lost colony.

19. England's Need of America.—There was special need at this time for such an opportunity to relieve the crowded industrial conditions at home. The great demand for wool by Flemish weavers made wool-growing very

profitable in England. Therefore, English landowners engaged largely in raising sheep instead of cultivating the
Large numbers of soil. The result was that but one man was
men thrown out of now required to watch sheep where formerly
work in England. many had been needed to raise wheat and
barley. Large numbers of men were thrown out of work,
and there was great distress among the laboring classes.
The closing of the monasteries by Henry VIII., a few
decades earlier, had had a similar effect, and the return of
soldiers from European wars increased the difficulty. What
to do with this large body of the unemployed was a trying
problem. America seemed to furnish a solution, and to
America men eagerly turned for help in the hour of England's need.

TO THE PUPIL

1. As the defeat of the "Invincible Armada" by England is a great
   landmark in history, 1588 is another date you should know with
   certainty. You will notice that this defeat, which had a large influence upon colonization in America, occurred about one hundred years
   after 1492. You will notice, also, that Raleigh's attempts to plant
   colonies took place only a short time before 1588.
2. If you will learn important dates like 1492 and 1588 and group about
   them others of less importance, you will remember your history much
   better.
3. Why can you say that Raleigh's work in America was not a failure?
   Make a chart outline of the most important events for the first hundred years after the discovery of America by Columbus.
4. You can easily make a review outline from the topics in the three
   chapters now studied. Do it. It would be well for you to read the
   life of Sir Walter Raleigh and also Scott's Kenilworth.

NOTES

Sir Francis Drake (1577).—Sir Francis Drake was one of England's
famous navigators and admirals. In 1577 he set sail from England with
five vessels ; in 1580 he returned with but one. In the meantime he had
doubled the Cape of Good Hope, as Magellan's men had done sixty years
before, and sailed entirely around the world. He was the first English sea-
captain to accomplish this great undertaking.

Bartholomew Gosnold (1602).—In 1602, the same year in which Raleigh sent out his final expedition in search of the lost colony at Roanoke,

Bartholomew Gosnold set sail from England. He had with him twenty-three men, eleven of whom were to remain in America to make a settlement. Reaching the coast of Massachusetts, he sailed around Cape Cod, which he so named on account of the abundance of cod fish near its coast. Then steering his course southward, he entered Buzzard's Bay and landed on an island which he called Elizabeth, in honor of the Queen of England. On his return homeward the eleven men, who were expected to remain and make a settlement, insisted upon returning with him. But Gosnold's interest in America bore fruit, for it kept alive the interests of other Englishmen in colonizing the New World.

QUEEN ELIZABETH'S SIGNATURE.

CHAPTER IV

THE ENGLISH IN VIRGINIA AND MARYLAND (1607–1689)

REFERENCES: **Scribner's** Popular History of the United States, III.; **Wright's** Children's Stories in American History; **Drake's** Making of Virginia and the Middle Colonies; **Richardson's** History of Our Country; **Coffin's** Old Times in the Colonies; **Cooke's** Stories of the Old Dominion; **Andrews's** United States, I.

OUTSIDE READINGS: **Fiske's** Old Virginia and Her Neighbors; **Fisher's** Colonial Era; **Eggleston's** Pocahontas and Powhatan; **Bancroft's** United States, I.; **Eggleston's** The Beginners of a Nation; **Doyle's** English Colonies; **Lodge's** Short History of the English Colonies in America; **Thwaites's** The Colonies; **Cooke's** Virginia; **Browne's** Maryland; **Wilson's** A History of the American People, I.

FICTION: **Johnston's** Prisoners of Hope; **Johnston's** To Have and to Hold.

20. **London and Plymouth Companies.** — Raleigh assigned his interests to a number of merchants and capitalists, who received a charter from King James in 1606 and formed two companies for the purpose of colonizing America. One of these companies was located in London, and was called the London Company. The other was located in Plymouth, and was called the Plymouth Company.[1] The former was to occupy the land between 34 degrees and 38 degrees north latitude, extending from Cape Fear to the mouth of the Potomac River; the latter, between 41 degrees and 45 degrees, extending from the mouth of the Hudson River to New Brunswick. By a

SIGNATURE OF JAMES I.

[1] The Plymouth Company sent out to the Kennebec the following year a settlement which proved a failure. No further attempt was made by this company.

charter granted in 1609, the Pacific Ocean was made the western boundary of Virginia. The area lying between these two belts, 38 degrees to 41 degrees, might be occupied by either company provided it came no nearer than one hundred miles to a settlement made by the other.

The most notable provision of the charter was that the colonists, as citizens in America, should have the same rights and privileges as belonged to citizens of England. It will be well to bear this great principle of the charter in mind when we study later the causes of the American Revolution. In addition to the charter, **The charter and the common store-house.**

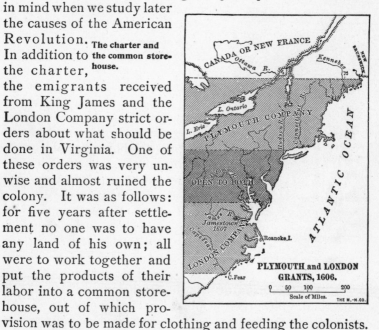

PLYMOUTH and LONDON GRANTS, 1606.

0   50   100   200
Scale of Miles.
THE M.-N.CO.

the emigrants received from King James and the London Company strict orders about what should be done in Virginia. One of these orders was very unwise and almost ruined the colony. It was as follows: for five years after settlement no one was to have any land of his own; all were to work together and put the products of their labor into a common storehouse, out of which provision was to be made for clothing and feeding the colonists.

21. Settlement of Jamestown (1607.)—On New Year's day, 1607, the first colony, consisting of one hundred and five men, set sail from London. About half of these men were gentlemen, whose aim, like that of previous settlers, was to make their fortunes in the New World and then return home. The other half consisted mostly of mechanics and tradesmen. There were no farmers and no women in the new colony, for the colonists did not come to make homes and settle down to earning their living by patient labor. Their aim was to find gold as the Spaniards had done in Peru and Mexico. Such men were not the right material to make a successful colony, as soon appeared after they had reached Virginia. In May they sailed up the James River and made a settlement. This they called Jamestown, in honor of King James, from whom they received their charter. Being for the most part a lazy, shiftless set, they did very little to prepare for the future. They were so

slow that by the time they were settled it was too late for the **The settlers and their sufferings.** spring planting. Soon their provisions began to fail, and famine, along with the fever which seized them in the warm climate, rapidly thinned their ranks. Sometimes there were hardly enough well persons to bury the dead. In about four months half their number had died, and the rest were discouraged. During these weary months of suffering some of the settlers lived in miserable dwellings made of boughs of trees or old sails, and some dug holes in the ground for shelter.

RUINS OF OLD CHURCH AT JAMESTOWN.

22. The Services of Smith.—But for one courageous man, John Smith, they would probably have perished. He so managed the Indians as to secure food enough to preserve the lives of the wretched colonists. Two years later more colonists joined them, but the new-comers were as unfit as those who came first. During this time John Smith not only kept the colony from ruin but found opportunity to do some valuable exploring. While on one of these expeditions he sailed, in search of the Pacific, up the Chickahominy River,[1] where he was captured by the Indians and

[1] North America at this time was supposed to be a narrow strip of land.

taken before their chief, Powhatan. Smith tells a thrilling story [1] of the saving of his life by Powhatan's young daughter, Pocahontas. However much truth there may be in the romantic incident, Pocahontas herself is an attractive character, and her relation to the colonists is full of interest. [2]

23. Smith Returns to England; the Suffering Colonists (1609-1610).—After two more years of famine and hardships, five hundred additional colonists came over. It was the old story over again. Paupers, criminals, and otherwise worthless men made up the greater part of this wretched company. About this time the colonists suffered a severe loss, also, for Smith, having been wounded by the accidental discharge of a gun, was obliged to return to England. The colony was thus left without a leader. At once the Indians, whom Smith had managed with great skill, began to rob

CAPTAIN JOHN SMITH.

[1] As Smith in his efforts to prevent capture had killed two Indian warriors, Powhatan decided that he must be put to death. In the meantime Smith had won the warm friendship of Pocahontas, a kind-hearted girl about ten years old. This little friend saved his life. For the Indians, having bound Smith hand and foot and laid his head upon some stones, were gathered about their captive to see him put to death. Then a warrior raised his club, but before it could fall upon Smith's head, Pocahontas threw her arms about the prisoner's neck and begged her father not to kill him. Powhatan's heart being touched, Smith was released and allowed to return to Jamestown. Although this story has been discredited by some historians, there is pretty good evidence for its truth. Later, Pocahontas carried food to the starving settlers at Jamestown, and gave Smith warning of an Indian plot to kill him.

A young Englishman, John Rolfe, fell in love with Pocahontas and married her. He took her to England, where she was treated with great kindness. Just as she was on the point of returning to America she died, leaving a son who became a man of influence in Virginia. John Randolph, of Roanoke (Va.), was one of her descendants.

[2] According to his own romantic account, John Smith had many thrilling adventures before he went to Virginia. Running away from his home in England, while

and plunder the settlers, and famine and disease aided the work of destruction. The famine became so severe that

" The starving time." the colonists ate the bodies of their own dead. Every day the numbers were thinned by death, and at the close of that dreadful winter (1609–1610), long known as " the starving time," barely sixty of the five hundred were left alive. Lord Delaware, the newly appointed governor, came in June, 1610, just in time to prevent the miserable remnant from sailing away to England. On account of ill-health he could not remain long in the colony, and left Sir Thomas Dale in charge of affairs.

24. Dale's Great Reform: He Establishes Individual Ownership of Land and Goods (1611-1616). — Dale was, like Smith, a vigorous and able ruler. He quickly saw that he must be extremely severe in governing the lawless men in the colony. He not only flogged the unruly but inflicted the severest kind of punishment upon those who

Dale's severe measures. said anything against his mode of governing. He even went so far as to burn some of the most rebellious, and in one case he sentenced to death by starvation a man who had stolen food. Of course these oppressive measures made Dale unpopular, but a stern ruler was just what was needed to put the colony on a firm footing. Its future soon began to look hopeful.

Perhaps Dale's wisest act was the abolition of the system of a common storehouse. This had been one of the

Dale abolishes the system of the common storehouse. greatest evils of the colony. The settler had no land of his own and had to put the products of his labor into a common stock which all shared alike. It was a foolish system. The idlers,

---

yet a boy, he went to Holland and became a soldier. From Holland he wandered to other parts of Europe, and in course of time fought against the Turks, three of whom he slew in single combat. After being captured and enslaved by the Turks he made his escape, and in 1604 returned to England, at the age of twenty-five, in time to join the movement for planting a settlement in Virginia. On his return to England in 1609 he sailed to New England and made a map of much of its coast. In addition to an account of his own life, he wrote several books on America. He was a man of immense courage and energy, and doubtless saved the Jamestown colony from ruin.

knowing they would be fed and clothed whether they worked or not, willingly let the industrious ones support them. As a result, thirty or forty energetic men had been supporting four or five times as many lazy, good-for-nothing men. Dale's great reform consisted in giving every man his own plot of ground. After the owner had turned into the common stock two and one-half barrels of corn, the remainder of his crop was his own. Under the new law the idle were compelled to work, and the thrifty were encouraged to produce all they could by their labor.

25. Tobacco the Main Source of Wealth.—About the time that this working spirit began to direct the colonists, they found that raising tobacco was immensely profitable. The soil and climate of Virginia specially fitting it for growing tobacco, after 1616 this product was the principal source of wealth. Now that the colonists could have their own land and could make money by raising tobacco, they were ready to work with a will. Farmers in England were glad to come to Virginia, and the success of the colony was no longer doubtful.

26. The Second Great Reform: Self-government (1619).—Up to 1619 the people had little or no voice in their government. This state of things they did not like, for they had been accustomed in England to sending representatives to their governing body, Parliament. In 1619, therefore, they were granted a new charter, which provided for a representative assembly consisting of two delegates from each of the eleven settlements. As these settlements were called boroughs, the assembly was known as the House of Burgesses. The new government   The new government. consisted of a governor, council, and assembly. This threefold government was modelled after the English form [1] and furnished later a basis for our own State and national governments. The private ownership of land and the culture of tobacco were two great inducements to

[1] The English Government consists of the King, House of Lords, and House of Commons. The Cabinet, and not the King, is the real executive in England. The two Houses constitute what is known as Parliament.

emigration. Now that the people had a voice in making their own laws and levying their own taxes, Englishmen flocked to Virginia. Within a year after the people began to govern themselves, the population increased from 600 to

TOBACCO-PLANT.

4,000. With the coming of women about that time family life found a place in Virginia, and the people became prosperous and contented.

27. Great Need of Labor; Labor Supply.— A very different class of men now came to Virginia. Men with families and capital were ready to plant homes where returns for labor were so promising. The great need was for laborers, and to supply this need indented servants in large numbers were brought over. At first these were poor boys and girls who were bound to service until they became of age. Then adult servants, required to serve a term of years to pay for their passage, were sent. **White servants sent to Virginia.** There were also kidnappers in England whose special duty it was to procure men for service in Virginia.

But all these sources of labor did not supply Virginia's demand; for it frequently happened that the indented servant, when free, himself became a landowner **The first cargo of negro slaves.** and required laborers. Naturally, then, the slave-trader sought this inviting market, and in 1619 landed the first cargo of negro slaves in Virginia. At that time able-bodied negroes could be bought on the coast of Guinea for a few shillings apiece. These negroes were packed so closely for sailing that a vessel would bring hundreds of them over in a single voyage. Reaching Virginia they could be sold for about the price of a good horse. The profits were immense both to the slave-trader and the slave-owner. What the tobacco grower needed was an abundance of cheap labor, a need which negro slavery supplied. Tobacco, therefore, was largely responsible for the introduction of negro slavery into Virginia.

28. Tobacco Establishes Rural Life.—It was found that tobacco quickly exhausted the soil. This led to taking up much new land as soon as the old was worn out. Large plantations were the result. Each planter tried to secure a plantation on one of the many rivers. He could then have his own wharf, where he could ship his tobacco and receive in exchange manu-

A WILD DASH FOR LIFE.
An incident of the early slave trade.

factured goods from England. Under such a system, where each planter held thousands of acres of land, no large town could grow up, and life was wholly rural.

29. Berkeley and the People.—In 1660 after the over-throw of the commonwealth (see par. 35), Charles II. ascended the throne of England, and Sir William Berkeley for a second time[1] became governor in Virginia. Governor Berkeley cared very little for the rights and wishes of the people. He was trying to rule in America as his despotic king was ruling in England. Hence in 1660 there began, between the people on the one side and the king's party headed by Berkeley on the other, a struggle that grew more and more bitter until it ended in Bacon's Rebellion in 1676. As this rebellion is an event of some importance, we may well notice how it came about. We shall see in the chain of events some of the causes of the American Revolution which occurred one hundred years later.

30. Bacon Leads an Uprising of the People (1676).— Charles II., early in his reign, decided to enforce the Naviga-
The Navigation Laws. tion Laws as a means of increasing his revenue. These laws wer. very severe upon the tobacco trade of Virginia. They required that the planters should send their tobacco in English vessels and to none but English ports. They required also that the planters should buy in England all the European goods they might need, and that these goods should be brought over in English vessels. In other words, the planter had to sell his tobacco and buy his manufactured goods at prices set by English merchants. This nearly ruined the leading industry of the planters, and they became discouraged and exasperated. In 1670 they received almost nothing for their tobacco, and paid high prices for goods manufactured in England.

At the same time the Virginia Assembly no longer represented the wishes of the people, but the tyrannical ideas
Tyranny of Berkeley. of Berkeley. Having found in 1660 a set of men[2] that suited his views, Berkeley for sixteen years kept these men in office, without an election by

---

[1] Berkeley was governor from 1642–1651.

[2] Between 1650 and 1660, when the Puritans were in control in England, hundreds of the Stuart followers, called cavaliers, came to Virginia (see par. 103). Many of these cavaliers became planters of large influence and naturally supported Berkeley.

the people, by adjourning the assembly from year to year.
Popular rights were thus despised.   Moreover, suffrage
was taken from all except land-owners and " housekeepers."

All these things were bad enough, but in 1673 the king
did something far worse.   He actually gave away Virginia
to two of his favorites for thirty-one years.   This action
made the colonists uncertain about the titles to their land
and aroused them to a high pitch of indignation.   When a
little later the lives of the settlers were threatened by
attacks from the Indians and Berkeley refused to send
troops against them, the people were ready
for open rebellion.   Nathaniel Bacon, a young   **Bacon's Rebellion.**
man of wealth and influence and a leader among the peo-
ple, sought a commission from the governor to march
against the Indians, but the governor, fearing a revolt,
refused to give it.   Without the commission, therefore,
Bacon led his troops against the Indians and routed
them.   The governor declared him a rebel and traitor.
Civil war followed.   Governor Berkeley was driven out of
Jamestown, and the town was burned by owners of property
in order to prevent his coming back.   But Bacon suddenly
died of fever, and Berkeley returned to take revenge by
putting to death more than twenty of Bacon's leading
followers.   Not pleased with Berkeley's management of
affairs, the king summoned him to England where, disappointed and heart-broken at the king's rebuke, he soon
afterward died.   Bacon's Rebellion showed that the 40,000
people in Virginia loved liberty well enough to shed their
blood in its defence.

We have shortly to study settlers of a very different
type,—the New England Pilgrims and Puritans,—but before
doing so we must glance at the fortunes of the Catholics in
Maryland.

31. Lord Baltimore and the Catholics Settle Maryland
(1634).—At the time the Puritans[1] were coming over to
America on account of religious persecution in England,
the Catholics also were being badly treated because they

[1] See par. 40.

were unwilling to conform to the English church. Lord Baltimore, a prominent Catholic, wishing to secure freedom of worship for English Catholics, obtained from Charles I., who was his personal friend, a charter granting him the land lying north and east of the Potomac River and on both sides of the Chesapeake Bay. Lord Baltimore died before the charter was issued, and it was transferred to his son. The latter made a settlement in 1634 near the mouth

of the Potomac River, at St. Mary's, and named his colony Maryland in honor of the queen, Henrietta Maria. Before proceeding to build houses for themselves the colonists bought the land of the Indians, and paid for it with axes, hoes, and cloth. Their relations with the Indians were, with rare exceptions, most friendly.

32. **Lord Baltimore's Proprietary Rights.**[1]—The charter granted **The liberal charter.** to Lord Baltimore was extremely liberal. The king made him proprietor, requiring, as a token of his

GEORGE CALVERT (LORD BALTIMORE).

allegiance to the crown, two Indian arrows yearly and one-fifth of all the gold and silver. Lord Baltimore had almost the powers of a king in the new colony. He could call together an assembly of the people's representatives, whose laws were in force as soon as he signed them, the king's assent not being required. The proprietor could coin money, establish at his will courts of law and pardon criminals ; and these proprietary rights were to remain with Lord Baltimore's descendants. Thus we see that he had almost as much power in Maryland as King Charles had in England.

Besides, the Maryland charter contained a remarkable

[1] Maryland, Pennsylvania, and Delaware were the only Proprietary colonies at the time of the Revolution. See par. 111.

provision denying the right of the English government to tax the colonists within the province. The colonists were to enjoy all the rights of freeborn Englishmen in the mother country, and no taxes could be levied without being voted by the people's representatives in their colonial legislature.

33. Disputes About Boundaries and Religion.—The Virginia colonists were greatly dissatisfied on account of the king's grant of land to Lord Baltimore, because the same land, they claimed, had already been granted to them. This dispute led to fighting and bloodshed, but the king finally decided the question in favor of Lord Baltimore. Much later, after the settlement of Pennsylvania, there was a dispute also about the boundary between that colony and Maryland. After a long time two surveyors, Mason and Dixon, established the boundary since known as Mason and Dixon's line (1763–1767).

A MARYLAND SHILLING.

Mason and Dixon's line.

In the early days of the colony every settler was allowed to worship as he pleased—provided he worshipped in a Christian church; all were equally protected under the laws. But later, during Cromwell's rule in England, the Protestants,[1] getting control of the government, began to persecute the Catholics, and serious trouble followed.

34. Prosperity of the People.—But in spite of many disputes about boundaries and religion the colony prospered. The land was fertile, the climate delightful, and the colonists could make their own laws. As in Virginia, life was almost wholly rural during the seventeenth century. The numerous rivers, creeks, and inlets made communication so easy that towns, or centres for collecting and distributing articles of trade, were unnecessary. Ships could bring whatever the planter needed

Rural life of the people.

[1] Protestants were always more numerous in the colony than Catholics.

to his door, and carry away in exchange the products of the
plantation,—tobacco and Indian corn.   Like Virginia, Maryland derived much wealth from growing tobacco, which
was for a long time the staple product of the two colonies.

TO THE PUPIL

1. What was the most notable provision of the charter granted by James
   I. to the London Company ?   What bad results followed the establishment of the common storehouse ?   What did John Smith do for
   the Virginia colony ?   Tell all you can about his character.
2. Imagine yourself in Virginia during these early years, and give an
   account of your life there.   Impersonating Pocahontas, speak in the
   first person of your relations to the whites.   Compare the work of
   Smith and Dale.
3. Do not be satisfied until you understand clearly the two great reforms.
4. Study the relation of soil and climate to tobacco, and of tobacco to
   plantation life and to negro slavery.
5. What was Berkeley's attitude toward the plain people ?   How did the
   Navigation Laws bear heavily upon the Virginia planters?   In
   what way was Berkeley tyrannical ?   Write a simple outline of the
   events which led to an uprising of the people under Bacon in 1676.
   What were the results of this uprising ?   Contrast Bacon and Berkeley, and show why you like or dislike either of them.
6. Subject for debate : Resolved that Virginia owed a greater debt to
   John Smith than to Governor Dale.
7. Why did Lord Baltimore wish to plant a colony in the New World ?
   What singular powers did the king confer upon Lord Baltimore as
   proprietor of Maryland ?   Be sure that you know what a proprietor
   was.
8. What remarkable provision did the Maryland charter contain ?   Note
   the important clause in the Maryland charter about "no taxation
   without representation."   What was Mason and Dixon's Line ?   In
   what respect was the life of the Maryland colonists like that of the
   settlers of Virginia ?   If you can see the relation of cause and effect
   between events, history at once becomes full of meaning and life.
   In looking for such relation, you will find it a great help to bring to
   your recitation at least one written question on every lesson.
9. The account of Bacon's Rebellion, as told in Cooke's Virginia, is well
   worth reading.

NOTES

North and South Carolina (1663-1729).—In 1663-65 Charles II., desiring to reward eight of his favorite noblemen, gave them a grant of all the land between the Atlantic and the Pacific and extending from Virginia to a point some distance below St. Augustine. Thus we see that this land, called Carolina, had eight proprietors, just as Maryland and Pennsylvania each had one.

The form of government for Carolina was aristocratic. It was called the Grand Model, and is said to have been outlined by a great English philosopher, John Locke. A few noblemen were to own all the land, make the laws, and have all the powers of government in their hands. The people were, like the old Russian serfs, to be bought and sold with the land. Of course this absurd scheme was a failure. The people made so much trouble for the proprietors that the latter were glad to sell in 1729 all their rights to the king of England. The king then divided Carolina into North and South Carolina, appointing a governor for each colony and allowing the people in each to choose their own assembly.

The population of the two colonies was composed of Englishmen, Huguenots, Germans, Scotch-Irish, and Scotch Highlanders. When the Revolution began, North Carolina was the fourth colony in population. The staple products of South Carolina were rice and indigo, and of North Carolina were tar, pitch, turpentine, and lumber.

Georgia (1733).—James Oglethorpe, a brave soldier and wealthy member of Parliament, knowing how eager the Spaniards were to destroy the weak English settlements in South Carolina, wished to plant a colony that should serve as a military outpost to ward off the Spanish attacks. But this was not his only motive. Being a man of warm sympathies, he desired to find relief for imprisoned debtors suffering in English prisons. He therefore secured from the king a grant of the land lying between the Savannah and the Altamaha Rivers and extending westward to the Pacific. In 1733 he planted at Savannah a colony in which freedom of worship was allowed to all but Catholics. For many years neither rum nor slaves could be imported. But, believing that these restrictions interfered with the prosperity of the colony, the people finally secured their removal. At the end of twenty years the trustees, to whom the king had granted the original charter, gave it up. Georgia then became a royal colony and remained so until the Revolution.

CHAPTER V

THE PILGRIMS AND PURITANS IN MASSACHUSETTS AND CONNECTICUT (1620–1689)

REFERENCES: **Scribner's** Popular History of the United States, I. and II.; **Drake's** Making of New England; **Coffin's** Old Times in the Colonies; **Wright's** Children's Stories in American History; **Winsor's** Narrative and Critical History, III.; **Eggleston's** Household History; **Andrews's** United States.

OUTSIDE READINGS: **Fisher's** Colonial Era; **Doyle's** English Colonies; **Dodge's** Short History of the English Colonies in America; **Thwaites's** The Colonies; **Hawthorne's** Grandfather's Chair; **Hale's** Story of Massachusetts; **Fiske's** Beginnings of New England; **Abbott's** Captain Myles Standish; **Earle's** Child Life in Colonial Days; **Earle's** Home Life in Colonial Days; **Drake's** On Plymouth Rock; **Drake's** Making of New England.

FICTION: **Stowe's** Mayflower; **Austin's** Standish of Standish, Betty Alden, A Nameless Nobleman, Dr. Le Baron and His Daughters; **Cogswell's** Regicides.

POETRY: **Longfellow's** Courtship of Myles Standish.

A PURITAN.

35. England Under the Stuarts (1603–1649 and 1660–1688).—We cannot understand who the Pilgrims and Puritans were, why they left their homes in England, and what they did after they came to America, unless we know something of English history from 1603 to 1689. With the exception of eleven years (1649–1660) the Stuart kings[1] reigned in England during

[1] James I. (1603–1625), Charles I. (1625–1649), Charles II. (1660–1685), James II. (1685–1688).

this period. These men were oppressive rulers and aroused the opposition of many of the best people in England. When James I. ascended the throne he seemed to think that all England and its people were his personal property. He claimed that he ruled by divine

The tyrannical Stuarts.

right, which was another way of saying that his will was law and that the people had no rights which he was bound to respect.

OLIVER CROMWELL.

Accordingly, there at once began a struggle between the throne and the people, who were represented by Parliament. The great majority of the people claimed that they could not lawfully be taxed without their consent; in other words, that no taxes could be levied unless voted by the people's representatives in Parliament. The Stuarts tried to plan various ways of raising

No taxation without representation.

money without asking Parliament to vote it. But this was very difficult.

For eleven years (1629–1640) Charles I. ruled England without Parliament, and he was so arbitrary that he brought on the war which ended in the loss not only of his crown but of his life (1649). The Commonwealth followed (1649–1660), England being ruled by Oliver Cromwell and later by his son Richard. Oliver Cromwell became even more autocratic than Charles I. had been.

After the Restoration Charles II., son of Charles I., reigned till 1685, when he was succeeded by his brother, James II. The latter was so despotic that the people rose

against him in the revolution of 1688 and drove him out
of England. It will greatly help us to understand Berkeley
James II. driven   in Virginia and Andros in New England, if
from England.   we remember that these men were trying to
rule in America as their royal masters were ruling in
England.

James I. was determined to make every one conform to
the Established Church in England. But there were many
The Church of   people who did not like its forms and cere-
England and the   monies and wished to modify them. They
Puritans.   were called Puritans because, it was said, they
wished to purify the Church. The Puritans wished to remain in the Church and reform it. Another party wished to
leave the Established Church, or separate themselves from
The Separatists.   it, and were therefore known as Separatists or
Independents. They not only disliked the
forms and ceremonies of the English Church, but they also
disapproved of church-government by bishops. They
wished to have a church in which the people only should
rule. Such a self-governing church, where each congregation could elect its minister and manage its own affairs without interference from king or bishop, afterward became
known as Congregational.

36. Pilgrims Migrate to America (1620).—In the early
part of the reign of James I. a number of people in the
village of Scrooby, a small village in Nottinghamshire, under-
took to form such a church. But they were regarded as
The Pilgrims es=   rebels and were hunted down, and some of
cape to Holland.   them were thrown into prison. At last, in
1608, they escaped to Holland, where they were allowed to
remain in peace and to worship as they pleased.

But they were not satisfied to settle permanently in Holland, because they did not wish their children when grown
up to intermarry with the Dutch. They wished to make
homes in a new land and there establish a free government
and their own religion. After remaining in Holland twelve
years, therefore, they decided to go to America, in order to
establish a self-governing community and bring up their

children to be liberty-loving and God-fearing men and women. By reason of their wanderings these people were called Pilgrims. The Pilgrims were poor, but they were men of strong will and noble purpose. They tried to get a charter from the king, but he refused to give it. He led them to believe, however,

Their aims and character.

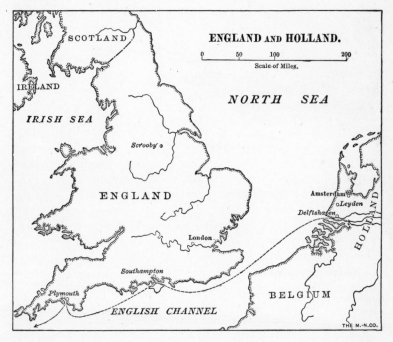

ENGLAND AND HOLLAND.

that he would not interfere with their project if they did not make themselves troublesome to him.

37. Voyage and First Winter.—After getting money on hard terms they started[1] over from Plymouth, England, in the *Mayflower* and the *Speedwell*. On account of a leak the *Speedwell* was obliged to return, and the *Mayflower*, with about one hundred people on board, sailed for America.

[1] The Pilgrims sailed in July, 1620, from Delftshaven, the Port of Leyden, Holland, in the *Speedwell* for Southampton, England, where the *Mayflower* awaited them.

After a stormy voyage they anchored about the end of November, 1620, on the northern shore of Cape Cod. As this place was not suitable for a settlement, they sailed

across the bay to a good harbor and made their final landing at Plymouth December 21, 1620. The suffering during the first winter was severe, and before spring half their number were dead. But when spring came they had no disposition to return to England. Weak as they were in numbers and possessions, they

THE *MAYFLOWER*,
From a model in the Smithsonian Institution.

were strong in manly purpose and brave enough to face any danger that threatened their little settlement.

38. The Covenant, Democracy, and the Church.—Before landing they signed, in the cabin of the *Mayflower*, a covenant in which they agreed to make and support such laws as should seem for the best interests of all. John Carver was chosen governor. The laws were made in town-meetings, in which every man could vote. The Pilgrims at Plymouth believed that the people should rule; they planted democracy in their church and state. Some years later,[1] after

Pilgrim leaders. population had increased, this pure democracy was obliged to give place to representative government. Governor Carver died during the first winter, and William Bradford was chosen to succeed him. Elder Brewster was the minister, and Captain Myles Standish was chosen military leader. These stout-hearted leaders well represented the character of the Plymouth settlers.

39. Relations with the Indians.—For a better defence against the Indians the Pilgrims organized their able-bodied

[1] In 1630 there were only 300 settlers. By 1639 representative government became necessary, and in 1642 the population numbered 3,000. This increase was due to surrounding settlements which began to spring up about 1630.

men into small companies who took turns in guarding the settlement against surprises by the Indians. Fortunately for the Plymouth settlers, so many of the Indians of that region had recently died from a pestilence that the remaining natives were not troublesome. Massasoit, chief of the Wampanoag Indians, visited Plymouth in the spring of 1621, and Governor Bradford made a treaty of peace with him that lasted fifty years.[1]

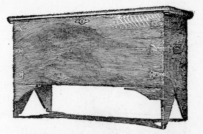

A CHEST WHICH CAME OVER IN THE *MAYFLOWER.*

40. The Puritans and the Massachusetts Bay Colony (1628–1630).—Encouraged by the successes of the Pilgrims, many Puritans began to follow their example. In 1628 some of the leaders of the Puritan party in England, men of wealth and influence, formed a trading company. They bought of the Plymouth Company a tract of land along the Massachusetts coast, extending between the Charles and Merrimac Rivers and to within three miles beyond each, and sent out men to occupy it. Endicott was their leader, and they settled at Salem.

The following year the same trading company, with increased numbers, obtained a charter from the king, incorporating it as the Governor and Company of Massachusetts Bay. Very likely Charles I. was quite willing to be rid of these liberty-loving, unruly subjects. At any rate he granted them a charter which was very liberal in its terms. It allowed the freemen of the company to choose their own governor, his deputy, and a council of eighteen assistants, and to manage in every way their own affairs. It did not restrict its holders in the place of meeting. Of course this was a distinct advantage to the promoters of the new enterprise. Accordingly,

The Puritans secure a liberal charter.

[1] Later the Narragansett chief, Canonicus, sent to Plymouth a rattlesnake skin containing a bundle of arrows; Governor Bradford removed the arrows and, filling the skin with powder and shot, returned it to the Indians. This hint was sufficient.

in 1629, when the king was ruling with a high hand and setting at naught the will of Parliament by levying taxes himself and by throwing into prison those who refused to pay such illegal taxes, these Puritans decided upon the bold step of removing with their chartered rights to New England, where they might find a refuge from the tyranny of the king and build up a government according to their own ideas.

In 1630, under the leadership of John Winthrop, about 1,000 persons, with horses, cattle, and stores of various kinds, sailed for **The Puritan settlements in 1630.** Massachusetts. This new colony, called the Massachusetts Bay Colony, made settlements at Charlestown, Boston, Roxbury, and Watertown. John Winthrop was made the first governor. Like the Plymouth colony they established a government democratic in form, but unlike the Plymouth colony they were men of wealth and culture. Some of them were relatives of the greatest men of the day. They were men of wisdom and energy also, and might have made great names [1] for themselves in England. It must have been a strong motive that led them to sacrifice so much. We shall see how tenaciously they held to the rights which those sacrifices had bought.

MYLES STANDISH.

41. The New England Township.—Unlike ordinary colonists, the Puritans came in large communities with their plans of government fully matured. They were not Separatists in England as the Pilgrims had been, but the church they established in Massachusetts was independent and Congregational. Each congregation formed a settlement, and

---

[1] Stoughton, lieutenant-governor of Massachusetts (1692–1701), said, "God sifted a whole nation that He might send choice grain over into this wilderness."

each settlement consti-
tuted a township and
parish whose boundaries
were one and the same,
and usually included an
area of from forty to
sixty square miles. Each
parish had one church
or meeting-house, where
all business, *The meeting-house*
church or *and the village.*
civil, was transacted.[1]
Later the people erected
a separate building for
their town meetings and
called it a town-house
or town-hall. The meet-
ing house and the town-
house were the centres

PILGRIM TYPES.

about which clustered the villages. In order to meet the
more easily for worship the settlers built their houses close
together. Perhaps another reason was to secure a better
defence against the Indians.

42. Church and State.—The charter permitted all freemen to vote, but the Puritans came to New England to
establish and preserve what was most dear to them, their
own religious and political freedom—in no sense religious
toleration. When the first elections were held, *Puritans allow*
therefore, it was enacted that no one should *none but church*
be admitted a freeman and so have a right to *members to vote.*
vote who was not a member of one of the churches of the
colony. The union of church and state was thus complete.

At first the freemen met with the governor, his deputy,
and council of assistants to make such laws as pertained to
the general welfare of the several towns. But after a time,
when the towns and freemen had so multiplied that it be-

[1] As early as 1631 it was decided that none but church members should be
admitted as freemen.

came inconvenient for them all to meet, each town began to send representatives, or deputies, to the legislature, or General Court (1634), just as each settlement or borough in Virginia sent representatives to the House of Burgesses.

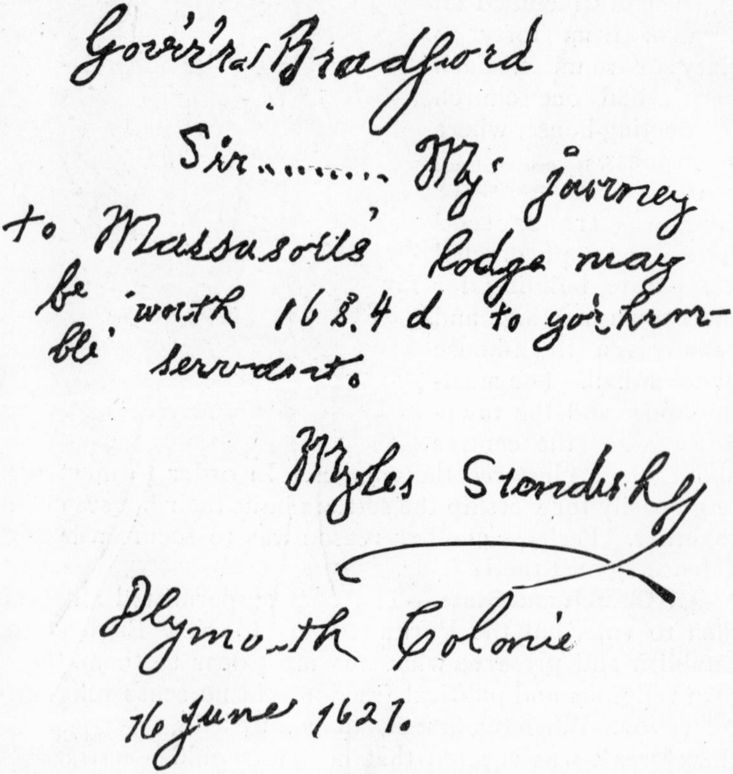

Govr'ras Bradford

Sir.......... W[y] journey to Massasoits lodge may be worth 16 s. 4 d to yor hum-ble servant.

Myles Standish

Plymouth Colonie
16 June 1621.

MYLES STANDISH'S BILL OF EXPENSES AFTER HIS VISIT TO THE INDIANS.

43. Massachusetts Gets Control of the Connecticut Valley (1633–1636).—Some time before the Massachusetts Bay Company had made settlements on the New England coast the Dutch had become established in New York (then New Amsterdam) on the Hudson, where they were engaged in the fur trade with the Indians. Claiming the land as far east as the Connecticut River, they built a small fort at

HOOKER'S EMIGRATION TO CONNECTICUT.

Hartford in the interest of the fur trade. In 1633 Massachusetts sent up the Connecticut a vessel, which in spite of Dutch protests sailed to Windsor, six miles **The Dutch at** above Hartford. There the Massachusetts **Hartford.** men built a house for trading with the Indians. Two years later John Winthrop, by building a fort called Saybrook at the mouth of the river, cut off the Dutch fort at Hartford from the support of New Amsterdam. The way was now open for Massachusetts to send settlers into the valley of the Connecticut.

44. Massachusetts Settles the Connecticut Valley (1635-1636).— In 1635 3,000 more settlers came from England to Massachusetts, where, some of them maintained, there was not enough good land for the many people now in that colony. The complaint of the lack of land came mainly from three of the eight Massachusetts towns. On hearing of the fertile soil of the Connecticut valley a great part of the people of these three towns decided to make settlements there. When they migrated

GOV. JOHN WINTHROP.

to Connecticut they settled the three towns of Hartford, Wethersfield, and Windsor. The principal **Settlement at** settlement was made at Hartford in June, **Hartford.** 1636. Under the leadership of their minister, Thomas Hooker, one hundred men, women, and children came overland from Cambridge (then Newtown), driving their cattle before them. It took them two weeks to make the toilsome journey through the woods to their new home.

45. Thomas Hooker and Democracy.—There is not much doubt that the principal reason why these three towns

wished to move to Connecticut was political. Many people did not approve of the Puritan idea held in Massachusetts
of allowing only church members to vote. Nor did they
like to have the clergy take a controlling part in political
life. Thomas Hooker, the minister at Cambridge, was the
leader of this movement in favor of a more democratic system. John Winthrop and other Puritan leaders believed
in government by only a part of the people. They did not
believe that all the people were wise enough to govern
well. But Thomas Hooker, like Abraham Lincoln, believed
in government " of the people, by the people, and for the
people."

46. The Connecticut Constitution (1639).—In 1639 the
three towns of Hartford, Wethersfield, and Windsor united
under one government. The constitution which they
adopted was the first written constitution in all history
upon which a government was built up. Another interesting fact about this constitution is that in it no mention was
made either of the king or of the English company[1] hold-
Government by   ing a patent of the land. This constitution
the people.   was made by the people, in the interests of the
people, and showed that Thomas Hooker and his followers
had faith in the ability of the people to manage their own
affairs.[2] In the Connecticut colony all freemen, whether
church members or not, could vote.

The New Haven colony was founded in 1638 by a
small body of men under the leadership of John Daven-
New Haven col- port and Theophilus Eaton. They based
ony.   their laws strictly upon the Bible, and like the
Massachusetts Bay colonists allowed none but church
members to vote.

After the Restoration Connecticut, in order to confirm

---

[1] In 1630 the Council for New England granted the patent to the Earl of War-
wick. In 1631 he assigned it to Lord Say-and-Sele and others.

[2] Alexander Johnston says: " It is on the banks of the Connecticut, under the
mighty preaching of Thomas Hooker, and in the constitution to which he gave life
if not form, that we draw the first breath of that atmosphere which is now so familiar to us. The birthplace of American democracy is Hartford."

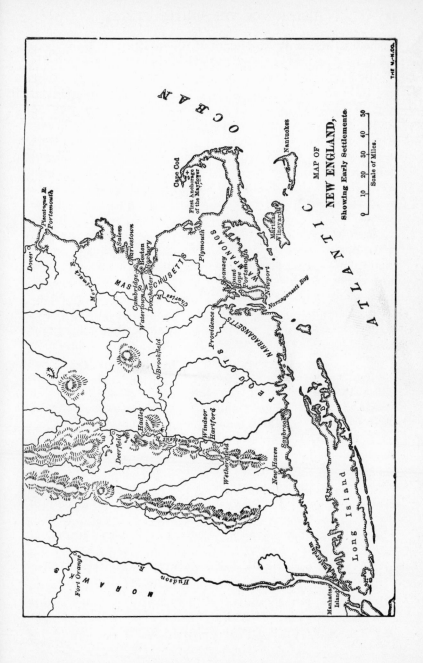

MAP OF
NEW ENGLAND,
Showing Early Settlements.

Scale of Miles.

0   10   20   30   40   50

THE W.M.CO.

her rights, thought it best to secure, if possible, a charter from the king. Governor Winthrop was sent to England, and by his tact and pleasing address succeeded in obtain-

The Connecticut charter. ing a charter (1662) for the territory which included Hartford, New Haven, and all the other settlements[1] that had been made in what is now Connecticut. This charter was so liberal and satisfied the people so well that it afterward became the State Constitution and remained in force till 1818.

FIRST CHURCH AT SALEM.

47. Religious Intolerance in Massachusetts Leads to the Settlement of Rhode Island (1636).— We must remember that the Puritans did not come to New England to establish religious freedom, but to form a state where they should have freedom for their own religion. They thought their own safety, certainly their own welfare, depended upon having none but members of the church take any part in government. But while none but church members could vote, all were obliged to pay taxes for the support of the church and were com-

Roger Williams and his views. pelled to attend its services. Roger Williams, a young man of pure spirit and strong conviction, who had become pastor of a church at Salem (1633), declared this system to be wrong. He asserted that no man should be obliged to pay taxes to support any church, nor should he be punished by the magistrates for not attending church services. His belief was that

[1] Saybrook was purchased by the Connecticut colony in 1644.

every man should settle all such matters with his conscience and his God. Williams stirred up the Puritans by declaring, also, that they had no just claim to the land they lived on. The land was theirs because the king had granted it to the Massachusetts Bay Company. But the land, Williams said, had never become the king's property; it belonged to the Indians; and the king, therefore, could not grant to anybody what was not his own.

This strange way of looking at the authority of the magistrates and at property rights alarmed the Puritans, especially as the English government was already none too friendly. They very much feared that the English king, hearing of the disturbance which these new teachings had caused in the colony, would hasten to take away the charter. Hence they looked upon Roger Williams as a dangerous person and drove him out of the colony.[1] He went to Rhode Island and made a settlement at Providence (1636). Rhode Island became a refuge for all who were seeking for a place to worship freely in accordance with their chosen faith.

Roger Williams driven out of Massachusetts.

Another disturber of the public peace was Mrs. Anne Hutchinson, an able woman who had recently come from England. She gave religious lectures which were opposed in their doctrines to those of the regular clergy, and caused great excitement. Although some of the leading men were included among her followers she was banished from the colony.

48. The New England Confederacy (1643). — The Dutch, angry at the loss of their fur trade in the Connecticut valley, had twice tried to drive the English away. The French in Canada were trying to push their claims to the

[1] As soon as Roger Williams learned that the Puritan magistrates had decided to send him back to England, he made his escape in midwinter to the wilderness. Here he wandered about for fourteen weeks, through deep snows, sometimes sleeping in hollow trees at night and sometimes getting food from the Indians. Early in the following summer, with five friends from Salem, he crossed the Narragansett Bay in search of a new home. Canonicus, chief of the Narragansetts, gave him a tract of land where he made a settlement, calling it Providence, in token of God's care for him during his time of trouble.

kinge of England Scotland ffraunce and ireland defender of the faith, of
Loyall ffamier kinge, famed of blessed memory by his highnes letters
paigne **Oath** given and graunted unto the Comitt established at
England in America and to their Successors and assignes for ever.
from the Equinoctiall lyne to forty eight degrees of the saide North
landes from Sea to Sea, together also with all the firme landes,
Mynes of Gould and Silver as other Mynes and Myneralls, precious
ffranchesies and preheminences both within the said Draft of Lande
What the saide, Islandes or any the premisses by the said letters Pai
Christian Prince or State, nor within the boundes Lymitt or Berri

south, and the Indians, either as allies of the French or the
Dutch or on their own account, threatened on all sides.

Enemies of the New England colonies. Connecticut, therefore, proposed to Massachusetts a union of the New England colonies for mutual defence. In 1643 articles were agreed upon at Boston by representatives from Massachusetts, Plymouth, Connecticut, and New Haven, uniting the colonies in a confederation for " mutual safety and welfare."

This confederacy was important because it taught the colonies how to unite and made stronger their feeling of independence. It prepared the way for the Albany Congress, the Continental Congress, and the union of the States in 1789.

49. The Quakers in New England.—In 1656 the Massachusetts colonists were greatly alarmed to learn of the arrival of two Quakers. These persons were at once thrown into prison until the ship in which they had come should sail, and boards were nailed on their prison windows **Punishment of the Quakers.** to prevent them from communicating with people outside. But in spite of this harsh treatment the Quakers continued to come. Fined, imprisoned, whipped without mercy, mutilated, and driven from the colony on penalty of death, they still persevered.

OF THE MASSACHUSETTS CHARTER.

Not until four of them were hanged did a reaction in their favor set in.

We are led to ask why the Quakers persisted in coming to Massachusetts in the face of such deadly opposition, and why the Puritans were so horrified to have them in the colony. The first question is quickly answered. The Quakers were zealous to make converts and were more than willing to suffer for their teachings. In answering the second it may be said that the Quakers held **Peculiar ideas of** in small esteem both the political and religious **the Quakers.** system of the Puritans. The ideal of the Quakers was a separation of church and state. They were guided by what they called the "inner light," or conscience. This was to them a supreme authority to be obeyed in spite of law or punishment. As they did not approve the Puritan system they refused to take the oath of allegiance, to pay taxes, or do military service.

To the Puritans the success of Quakerism meant the overthrow of Puritanism. The Puritans said, **Why the Puritans** "We have come over to New England to es- **persecuted the** tablish a church and state after our own ideal. **Quakers.** If the Quakers and others do not like our system let them go elsewhere, as we did when we left England."

50. Trouble with England and Loss of the Massachusetts Charter (1684).—During the first thirty years of its existence, Massachusetts, left pretty much alone by

Independent attitude of Massachusetts. England, had improved her opportunities to build up a strong and independent government. The stormy reign of Charles I. had

not permitted any oversight on the part of England. The commonwealth which succeeded (see par. 35), being Puritan

SIR EDMUND ANDROS.

in its sympathies, allowed the colony to follow its own course. But the conditions which had favored her growth thus far were giving way. After the Restoration (1660), it was not to be expected that Charles II. would overlook the growing importance and independent attitude of the Massachusetts colony. That would be too much to expect of any king, especially of a Stuart king. Moreover, Massachusetts had used her power in such a way as to make many enemies. Her custom of excluding from

the colony people like Roger Williams and Anne Hutchinson, whose religious views differed from her own, had

Enemies of Massachusetts. driven some men of influence back to England. Others who were not members of the Congre-

gational Church had of their accord returned to England, because in Massachusetts they could get no voice in the government. As a result, these men cherished only ill-will toward the colony which had caused them so much trouble.

All these aggrieved persons found means of carrying into the king's court mischievous reports of the doings of the colony. For instance, it was rumored that Massachusetts had raised money without the king's sanction, and had given a hearty welcome to two of the judges who had sentenced Charles I. to death, and who afterward had escaped to Massachusetts. Furthermore, it was said that Massachusetts had broken the Navigation Laws, which forbade the colonies to receive foreign vessels into their ports or to trade with any except English ports or ports belonging to England. This political sin was especially grievous to English merchants, and robbed the king of his revenue.

Complaints against Massachusetts.

The time had therefore arrived for England to find means of humbling her ambitious colonists. But it was not until after a long struggle that the charter was finally annulled in 1684. The Government and Company of Massachusetts then passed out of existence.

51. Andros, the Stuart Governor in New England (1686–1689).—Charles II. died and James II. succeeded him. In 1686 he appointed Sir Edmund Andros governor of all New England and, later, of New York and New Jersey also. Andros truly represented the despotic will of his royal master. He was especially tyrannical in Massachusetts, because this colony had taken such an independent attitude toward England. He at once declared that inasmuch as the colonists had lost their charter they could no longer lay any legal claim to their lands. They could hold them only by paying money as a quit-rent to the king. The privilege of making their own laws and levying their own taxes in town meetings and General Court[1] was also taken

Tyranny of Andros in Massachusetts.

---

[1] General Court was the name for the colonial legislature. The term is still applied to the Massachusetts legislature.

away. Andros and a council of his own choosing now made the laws and levied the taxes. The colonists rebelled, but the king stood back of the governor, and resistance was useless. Freedom of the press was no longer allowed, and men were illegally thrown into prison. Indeed, the condition of the people was little short of slavery.

THE CHARTER OAK.

In 1687 Andros went to Hartford to secure the Connecticut charter. The conference was so long and heated that it continued till dark, when suddenly the candles were blown

Andros fails to secure the Connecticut charter. out and, as the traditional story goes, the charter was snatched from the table and hidden in an oak-tree[1] afterward historic as the "Charter Oak." But the colonists were obliged to give up their charter government and to acknowledge Andros as Governor.

[1] In 1856 the noble old tree, which stood in what is now Charter Oak Place, Hartford, was blown down. A marble tablet marks the spot.

Andros, however, pressed his tyranny too far. As soon as the people heard that King James II. was driven from the throne of England, they seized Andros, threw him into prison, and later sent him back to England. Andros in Massachusetts and Berkeley in Virginia were both intensely hated and bitterly remembered.[1]

52. Industries and Trade in New England.—As we have seen, soil and climate favored the growth of tobacco on large plantations in Virginia, where life was rural. This was not true in New England. There the soil was rocky, and the climate was too cold for the growth of tobacco. The people lived mostly in towns, usually not far from the coast. Near the towns were the farms of those who tilled the soil.

In Virginia the many sluggish rivers made it easy for vessels to reach the wharves of the plantations. In hilly New England the swift-running streams were not so navigable, but were useful for turning the wheels of mills and factories. Naturally, manufacturing on a small scale began early in New England. In addition to saw-mills and weaving-mills the New Englanders had factories for making salt, gunpowder, and glass-ware. Good fishing off the coast led to a considerable export trade in dried fish. The extensive forests furnished lumber for ship-building and commerce. At an early day New England started the ship-building industry, for which, in later New England history, the people became famous.

TO THE PUPIL

1. In what ways were the Stuart kings tyrannical? Name two or three results of their struggles with the people of England.
2. Who were the Puritans? the Pilgrims? Why did the Pilgrims wish to emigrate to America?
3. Explain how the settlers at Plymouth first made their laws. What were their relations with the Indians?

---

[1] It is only fair to say that Andros was personally a far more honorable man than Berkeley.

4. State the leading provisions of the charter which the Puritans obtained from the king. What was the township? Why would the
Puritans allow none but church members to vote? What form of
government did they have?

5. Name points of difference between the Pilgrims and the Puritans.
Which do you like the better, the Pilgrims or the Puritans? Give
your reasons.

6. How did the Massachusetts people get control of the Connecticut
valley? How did Thomas Hooker and John Winthrop differ in their
ideas of government? Tell all you can about the Connecticut Constitution.

7. Why did the Puritans send Roger Williams out of their colony?
Subject for debate : Resolved, that the Puritans were right in their
treatment of Roger Williams.

8. What were the causes and results of the New England Confederacy? Do you think that if you had been a Puritan you would have
joined in persecuting the Quakers? Give your reasons.

9. What enemies did Massachusetts make? What complaints did they
raise against the colony? Compare the rule of Andros in Massachusetts with that of Berkeley in Virginia. In what respects were
these governors like the Stuart kings?

10. How did the life and occupations of the people in Virginia differ from
those of the people in Massachusetts?

11. Read Austin's Standish of Standish and Longfellow's Courtship of
Miles Standish.

NOTES

New Hampshire (1623).—Two years after the Pilgrims landed, the
Council of Plymouth granted to Sir Ferdinando Gorges and Captain John
Mason the territory between the Merrimac and the Kennebec Rivers. In
1623 fishing stations were begun at Dover and Portsmouth. Later,
Mason and Gorges divided the territory between them. Mason took the
part west of the Piscataqua, which he named New Hampshire after his
own county of Hampshire in England; Gorges took the part east of the
same river, naming it Maine. The proprietors left the early settlers to do
pretty much as they liked. Massachusetts claimed all the territory, but to
make certain her claim bought out the heirs of Gorges (1677) for $6,000.
Maine continued as a part of Massachusetts till 1820. New Hampshire remained for a long time under the protection of Massachusetts. After sever-
ing connection with Massachusetts three times, New Hampshire became a
separate royal colony in 1741, and so continued until the Revolution.

CHAPTER VI

THE DUTCH IN NEW YORK AND THE QUAKERS IN PENN-SYLVANIA (1609–1689)

REFERENCES: **Scribner's** Popular History of the United States, II. and III.; **Wright's** Children's Stories in American History; **Drake's** Making of Virginia and the Middle Colonies; **Richardson's** History of Our Country; **Morris's** Half Hours with American History; **Andrews's** United States, I.

OUTSIDE READINGS: **Fisher's** Colonial Era; **Doyle's** English Colonies; **Lodge's** Short History of the English Colonies in America; **Thwaites's** The Colonies; **Bancroft's** United States, I.; **Winsor's** Narrative and Critical History, III.; **Fiske's** The Dutch and Quaker Colonies in America; **Buell's** William Penn.

FICTION: **Irving's** Knickerbocker's History of New York.

53. Henry Hudson Seeks the Northwest Passage (1609).—In 1609 Henry Hudson, an English navigator, was employed by the Dutch East India Company to sail in search of a short northwest passage to India. Holland was then one of the greatest commercial countries in the world, and, like the other great European powers, desired to find a shorter route for the trade that was making her people rich. Hudson crossed the Atlantic, and with a crew of twenty men, in the *Half-moon*, sailed up the river which now bears his name. He held the familiar belief of his time, that the East Indies could be reached by a short water-route through North America, which was supposed to be a narrow continent. But after sailing as far as the present site of Albany he could go no farther, and gave up his plan of finding the East Indies by that route. Although he did not find a short passage to the Pacific, he discovered the Hudson River, which was a great water-way for the Dutch fur traders coming later. He also won the good-will of the Indians.

It was worth much to the Dutch that Hudson came to the Indians as a friend. The same year Champlain, a French

Hudson wins the good-will of the Indians for the Dutch.

explorer and trader, made deadly enemies of these same Indians, the Iroquois, who gave him great trouble and hindered the French in their work of exploration and colonization.

54. Dutch Claims to New Netherland.—During the next few years Dutch traders continued to visit the region

A DUTCH OFFICER OF THE SEVENTEENTH CENTURY.

of the Hudson, and in 1615 the Dutch States-General gave a charter to a company of merchants. In this charter the new country was named New Netherland. A small trading-house was erected on the present site of Albany, and a similar one was built on Manhattan Island at the mouth of the river.

Real colonizing did not begin until 1623, when the West India Company, which had been chartered two years before for purposes of settlement and trade, began to send out colonists. Some of these settled on the Delaware, or South River, some on the Hudson, or North River, some on Long Island, and a few remained on Manhattan Island. The Dutch built Fort Orange, where Albany now stands. In 1626 Peter Minuit, governor of New Netherland, founded

Dutch settlements and forts.

New Amsterdam (now New York City) on Manhattan Island, which he bought from the Indians for trinkets worth twenty-four dollars. These early colonies opened a successful trade with the Indians, with whom they kept on good terms, but they did not cultivate the soil and, therefore, their settlements did not thrive.

55. The Patroons.—To encourage emigration the States-General of Holland granted to the company a new charter by which the patroon system was established. This system permitted any member of the Dutch West India

A GROUP OF SEVENTEENTH CENTURY DUTCHMEN.

Company who would, within four years, bring into the colony fifty settlers, to own a landed estate with a water front of sixteen miles if on but one side of the Hudson, or of eight miles if on both sides. This great land-owner or patroon might extend his estate inland as far **Power and duties** as he thought desirable. In all cases the land **of the patroons.** was to be fairly bought of the Indians. These patroons exercised almost absolute power over their tenants. In fact the patroons resembled feudal lords, and the tenants resembled the vassals of feudal times. It should be noted that the patroons were each required to support a minister and a school teacher, in order that religious education should not suffer. This wise provision indicated the sturdy, wholesome character of the Dutch people.

56. The Dutch Win the Friendship of the Iroquois Indians and thus Secure an Extensive Fur Trade.—By treating the Iroquois justly the Dutch won the warm friendship of these powerful Indians, who engaged in an extensive fur trade with them. By honest dealing the Dutch fur-traders avoided costly Indian wars, and easily secured all the furs coming through the hands of the Iroquois from numerous tribes around the Great Lakes and between the Ohio and the Mississippi. The results of this

friendship were important : (1) Dutch commerce was en-
riched ; (2) the Iroquois received for their furs the fire-
Results of the friendship of the Iroquois for the Dutch. arms which enabled them all the more suc-
cessfully to prevent the French from getting
possession of New York ; (3) unwittingly the
Dutch were doing the English a great favor, for after
New Netherland passed into the hands of England, the
Dutch remained along the Hudson as before, and helped

THE EARLIEST PICTURE OF NEW AMSTERDAM.

to maintain the fur trade with the Iroquois, much to the
advantage of England.

**57. New Netherland Under Dutch Governors[1] (1623-
1664).**—There was less political freedom in New Netherland
The government. than in New England. The people could not
make their own laws nor levy their own taxes.
The town meeting, which was such a characteristic feature
of New England life, had no existence here. Religious freedom was all that the most liberal could desire. As Holland
welcomed the Pilgrims when driven by persecution from

---

[1] New Netherland had four Dutch governors: Peter Minuit, Walter von Twil-
ler, William Kieft, and Peter Stuyvesant. Stuyvesant was the only governor
worthy of the name. With great reluctance did he yield to the English.

England, the Dutch in New Netherland welcomed the victims of Puritan intolerance in New England. People from all parts of Europe were attracted to New Netherland, and a very mixed population was **The mixed population.** the result. It was said that in 1643 eighteen languages were spoken in New Amsterdam. In such a mixed community there could not be the same intense loyalty to the ruling power as if all the people had been of one nation.

58. New Netherland Becomes New York (1664).—The Dutch were now, as the Spaniards had been the century before, the great naval and commercial rivals of England. It was natural that England should be jealous of Dutch trade. The Dutch held the best

HENRY HUDSON'S *HALF MOON* ON THE HUDSON.

Why England wished to get control of New Netherland.

harbor on the Atlantic coast and the best highway to the Indian fur trade in the interior. No other river equalled the Hudson in this respect; its advantages were superb. Moreover, the Dutch colonies separated the English colonies north and south, and England, not foreseeing that the union of the English colonies could prove disastrous to the mother country, conceived the idea that the intrusion of the Dutch was a great obstacle to their growth.

Therefore, after allowing the Dutch to remain fifty years in the territory they had settled, England suddenly brought forward her claim to the land by the discovery of the Cabots. Accordingly, in 1664, while Holland and England were at peace, Charles II. sent over a fleet to attack the Dutch colony at New Amsterdam.[1] Governor Stuyvesant made frantic appeals to the people to assist in warding off the at-

The Dutch yield to the English. tack, but the Dutch were outnumbered,[2] and resistance was useless. Without a blow New Amsterdam fell into the hands of the English, and with it the whole of New Netherland. Charles II. gave the newly conquered territory to his brother, the Duke of York, and changed the name of both the colony and its capital to New York.

Dutch colonization, like Spanish, failed, and for a similar reason. The Spaniards were allured by gold, the Dutch by

Why the Dutch failed. trade. They both lacked the colonizing instinct which puts home-making before wealth-getting. Though the Dutch failed as a nation in colonizing America, their influence was indelibly impressed for good on the part of the country which they settled.

59. New York Under English Governors.—New York prospered under English rule, but the people there were disappointed because they were not given as much political freedom as the English colonists enjoyed in New England. The feeling became so strong that in 1683 they were allowed an assembly elected by the freeholders, which could meet with the governor and council to make laws and levy taxes.

In 1686, however, the Duke of York, having become king, took away this representative government, and two years later annexed New York to New England, under the rule of Andros.[3] The later English governors were so exasperating and tyrannical, that a people's party arose in the colony. When in 1689 news came that James II. had been driven from the throne, the people of New York, like

---

[1] Connecticut readily came forward to assist in defeating her old enemy in the Connecticut valley and on Long Island, where English settlers had come into collision with the Dutch.

[2] At this time the population of New Amsterdam was about fifteen hundred, and of New Netherland about seven thousand.

[3] Andros, while governor of New England, New York, and New Jersey (1686–1689), remained in New England. Nicholson represented him in New York as lieutenant-governor.

AN EARLY DUTCH MAN OF WAR.

From a model in the Musée de Louvre, Paris.

their New England neighbors, put aside the king's government and established one of their own. Their party was headed by Jacob Leisler, an energetic tradesman without education or political experience. He made many mistakes and aroused the opposition of his own party, but he managed to hold office for three years. The people finally appealed to the king (William III.), who sent over in 1691 a new governor. Leisler was tried for treason and hanged. With the new governor, the assembly was restored, and from this time the colony was governed in a constitutional way.

> Leisler leads an uprising of the people against Andros.

60. The Quakers in England.—The direct cause of the settlement of Pennsylvania was the bitter persecution

of the Quakers in England.[1] They had no respect for
forms and ceremonies; they were extreme dissenters from
the Established Church, and did not believe in paying
taxes for its support; they would use no titles of honor to
any man, not even the king; they counted it a sin to take
oath even in a court of justice, or to pay taxes for war.

61. **William Penn and the Quakers Settle Pennsylvania (1681).**—William Penn was the most illustrious con-

WILLIAM PENN.

vert of the Quakers in the seventeenth century. He was a young
man of wealth, education, culture,
and political promise. His father,
Admiral Penn, had been active in
bringing about the restoration of
the Stuarts, and was therefore held
in high esteem by King Charles II.
and his court. Penn early cherished an idea of founding a settlement for the Quakers in America.
He had taken a leading interest in
a colony in West Jersey, where
many Quakers had found a refuge.[2]
The colony was not altogether sat-
isfactory, and he was led to obtain a grant of land from the
king, in payment of a claim of $80,000 which he had inher-
ited from his father.

The king, always short of money, was glad to discharge
his debt in this way. He granted Penn a large tract of
land west of the Delaware River (1681), and named it Pennsylvania in honor of his friend, the admiral. Penn was
made proprietor of the new colony, and by the terms of

**Penn becomes pro-
prietor of Penn-
sylvania.** the charter, which was drawn by his own
hand, the proprietor, with the consent of the
freemen, was to make all necessary laws.
Having obtained the charter, Penn offered land on liberal
terms, and promised the settlers a popular government,

[1] At one time there were 4,000 Quakers in English prisons.
[2] Some of the New England Quakers came here, and many came from England.

PENN'S TREATY WITH THE INDIANS.

with justice to all regardless of religious belief. The people of his faith throughout England responded with such enthusiasm that he sent out a large colony.

62. The Quakers Live in Peace with the Indians.— William Penn came to America in 1682, and in the follow-

ing year he laid out the city of Philadelphia on a tract of land lying between the Delaware and Schuylkill Rivers. Under the spreading branches of an elm-tree[1] he made a treaty[2] of peace with the Indians. By this treaty he paid them fairly for the land and made them presents. So honest were the Quaker colonists of Pennsylvania in all their dealings with the natives that for a long time the highest compliment an Indian could pay

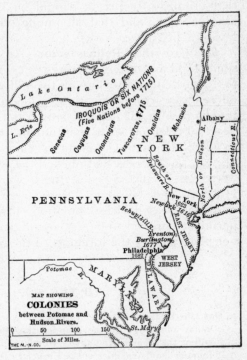

a white man was to liken him to Penn. They kept their treaty with them for sixty years.

63. Penn's Liberal Government.—The government was very liberal. The proprietor named the governor, but the

[1] This tree was blown down in 1810. A monument marks the spot where it stood.

[2] Penn said to the Indians: "The friendship between you and me I will not compare to a chain, for that might rust, or the falling tree might break. We are the same as if one man's body were to be divided into two parts. We are all one flesh and blood." When the Indians handed to Penn the wampum belt of peace, they said: "We will live in love and peace with William Penn as long as the sun and the moon shall endure."

people chose the members of the council and the assembly. Every tax-payer and freeholder was to have the right to vote. The first laws reflect the benevolence of Penn and his people. These laws provided that the Indians should be treated kindly ; that each child should be taught a trade ; that criminals in prison should be kept busy with some kind of work ; and that all public officers should be professing Christians.

64. Growth of Pennsylvania.—In spite of internal feuds, some slight and others serious, the colony continued to prosper. The climate was good, the soil was fertile, and rivers offered easy communication. These natural advantages, together with the liberal spirit, the good laws, and the peaceful relations with the Indians, caused the settlement to grow rapidly.[1] Colonists were not afraid to come where Mixed character of others had opened the way. Besides English the population. and Swedes, there were many from Wales, Holland, and Germany. Industries were built up, and wealth increased with population. Thus Penn's "Holy Experiment" proved to be successful, and Pennsylvania took her place among the foremost of the original colonies.[2]

TO THE PUPIL

1. Describe Hudson's attempt to find the Northwest passage to India. What advantage did he gain for the Dutch by winning the goodwill of the Iroquois Indians ? How did Champlain make these same Indians deadly enemies of the French ? In what way did the friendship of these Indians to the Dutch aid the English later ? Note the importance of the fur trade.

2. Bear in mind the mixed population in New York and in Pennsylvania, for you can use this knowledge to a good purpose when you study the Revolution.

[1] In three years Philadelphia had gained more in population than New York had in a half century. Toward the close of the century Philadelphia was a "noble and beautiful" city, as a history of that time describes it, containing two thousand houses, most of them "stately," built of brick.

[2] Although Penn's colony prospered, it caused him much anxiety and the loss of a large fortune.

3. Why did England wish to secure New Netherland? What does the series of years, 1609-1664, cover in the history of New Netherland? Why did Dutch colonization fail?

4. What was the condition of New York under the English governors? What led to a popular uprising under the leadership of Leisler?

5. Find interesting facts about the following: The Quakers, William Penn, his charter, his liberal ideas of government in the new colony, and his relations with the Indians. Write five minutes on one of these.

6. You began with 1492: you have now reached 1689, about two centuries later. Learn these dates thoroughly: 1492, 1588, 1689. 1492-1898: observe that 1689 is almost half-way between the two. How many of the thirteen original colonies had been settled before 1689? Make out a chart with the following facts in separate columns: Name of colony, when settled, where settled, by whom settled.

7. You have seen how the Spanish, the English, and the Dutch tried to establish colonies. In the "Notes" you will find an account of similar attempts made by the Swedes.

8. It would be a good plan for you to make out a chronological chart, beginning with 1492 and ending with 1689, including dates of principal events in three parallel lines, one for the Spanish, one for the English, and one for the Dutch.

NOTES

New Jersey (1618).—As New Jersey was at first included in New Netherland, the Dutch erected, as early as 1618, a small fort at Bergen, on the west bank of the Hudson River. When in 1664 New Netherland passed into the hands of the English, the Duke of York sold the land between the Hudson River and the Delaware to his friends, Lord Berkeley and Sir George Carteret. He named the province New Jersey, after the island of Jersey, which Carteret had bravely defended for the king's father, Charles I., during the Civil War in England. The first permanent English settlement was made at Elizabethtown in 1665. As the people were allowed freedom of worship and a part in making the laws, a good class of settlers was attracted to New Jersey. The Indians were so kindly treated that they gave no trouble.

In 1674 the province was divided into East and West Jersey, for many years known as "The Jerseys." By 1682 both the Jerseys had been sold to a number of Quakers, among whom was William Penn. There were now so many proprietors that much confusion over land titles resulted. The proprietors therefore sold in 1702 all their claims to the English Crown. From that time the Jerseys were known as New Jersey and were united to New York. New Jersey and New York now had the same governor, but each province had its own assembly. In 1738 New Jersey was made a royal province, which it continued to be until the Revolution. Benjamin Franklin's son was the last royal governor.

Delaware (1638).—In 1638 a number of Swedes and Finlanders landed near the present site of Wilmington, Delaware, and built a fort which they called Christina, in honor of their queen. Later, the Swedes made settlements along the Delaware River as far as the site of Philadelphia. Their colony they called New Sweden. But the Dutch claimed all this region as a part of New Netherland, and in 1655 they sailed up the Delaware, captured all the Swedish forts, and made New Sweden a part of New Netherland.

When in 1664 the English took New Netherland from the Dutch, Delaware became an English possession. In 1682 William Penn, wishing to secure a free outlet to the ocean, bought from the Duke of York this territory, then known as the "three lower counties on the Delaware." Delaware then became a part of Pennsylvania. In 1703 the people of Delaware were allowed a separate assembly; but they had the same governor as Pennsylvania until the Revolution.

CHAPTER VII

LIFE AMONG THE INDIANS

REFERENCES: **Scribner's** Popular History of the United States, I., II., III.; **Drake's** Making of New England; **Drake's** Making of the Great West; **Wright's** Children's Stories in American History; **Morris's** Half Hours with American History, I.; **Richardson's** History of Our Country.

OUTSIDE READINGS: **Catlin's** North American Indians; **Chapin's** Land of the Cliff Dwellers; **Fiske's** Discovery of America; **Ellis's** Red Man and White Man; **Drake's** Indian History for Young Folks; **Parkman's** Conspiracy of Pontiac; **Hart's** Colonial Children.

POETRY: **Longfellow's** Hiawatha.

65. The People Columbus Found in America.—When Columbus came to America he found a people very different from the Spaniards or other Europeans. As he believed he had reached the Indies he called these people Indians. They were alike in having high cheek-bones, black eyes, coarse black hair, and beardless faces. But with respect to their size, dress, houses, and manner of life there was as much difference as there was among people living in various countries of Europe.

66. Division into Families of the Indians East of the Mississippi.—The Indians whom the French and English found living East of the Mississippi were divided into three great families. First, there were the Southern, or Maskoki, Indians, who were spread over the country extending from the Tennessee River to the Gulf of Mexico and from the Mississippi to the Atlantic. The most important tribes were the Chickasaws, Choctaws, Cherokees, Creeks, and Seminoles. Secondly, there were the Iroquois Indians,

AN INDIAN CAMP.

who included the Five Nations[1] in Central New York, the
Tuscaroras in North Carolina, the Hurons north of Lake
Erie, and the Eries south of it.   Thirdly, all the other tribes
spreading northward from the Tennessee and eastward
from the Mississippi were Algonquins.

67. Character.—The Indian was a true child of the forest.
He had a wild love of liberty, which refused control by any

[1] The Five Nations included the Mohawks, Oneidas, Onondagas, Cayugas, and
Senecas, who formed a loose confederacy.   The Five Nations were very powerful
Indians till their defeat by Frontenac in 1697.   They firmly controlled the Mohawk
River valley and prevented the French from using the best natural highways from
Lake Erie to the Ohio.   Their population at the time of their greatest strength was
under 20,000.   After the Tuscaroras from North Carolina joined them in 1715
they were known as the Six Nations.

will except his own. He was cruel to his enemy and often tortured him or burned him alive. But the Indian was generous and kind. In the midst of famine he would cheerfully share the last morsel with a fellow-sufferer, and in the hour of danger would lay down his life for a friend.

68. Occupations.—The squaw did nearly all the work. She dug the soil with shells and pointed sticks, gathered the crops, dressed skins, dried meat, and made moccasins and various articles of clothing out of *What the squaw* the skins of animals. The Indian was first *did.* of all a warrior. His weapons were the war-club, the bow and arrow, and the tomahawk. A sharpened *Indian weapons.* stone served for the blade of his tomahawk, and bone or flint pointed his arrows. He was also fond of

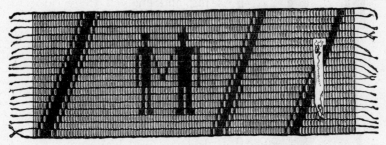

WAMPUM RECEIVED BY PENN FROM THE INDIANS.

hunting and fishing, and to assist him in these occupations he made the canoe and the snow-shoe.

69. The Canoe and the Snow-shoe.—In the fishing season he sought the side of lake or stream, and he was always eager to go where game was thickest and where the scalps of his enemies could be taken in greatest numbers. The canoe was therefore a necessity. Before the whites came it was to him horse, steamboat, and railroad, all in one. In travelling on land he followed the trail of *The canoes and* the deer or the buffalo. But water-ways were *the water-ways.* so much easier that he travelled ten miles on water to one on land. Between the water-ways there were " carrying places," or portages, over which he had to carry the canoe and all its load of fur and other goods. In other words, sometimes the canoe carried its owner and sometimes the owner carried his canoe. It was therefore necessary that it should be both light and strong. Such was the birch-bark canoe, which was made by stripping off the bark of the birch in one piece and carefully fitting it over a light wooden frame. Another Indian invention of great use was the snow-shoe, which was three or four feet in length, curved and tapering, and enabled the wearer to go along easily on the surface of the snow at the rate of forty miles a day.

70. **Wampum.**—Wampum consisted of small shells, or beads made from shells, perforated and strung together, and often wrought into belts. The Indians used wampum for personal adornment and also for more serious purposes, such as summoning the tribes to war, and recording treaties, laws, and speeches. Ten thousand beads have been known to be worked into a single war-belt four inches wide. The colors and the patterns of the belt varied with its purpose, peculiar signs and figures enabling the Indian to remember certain parts of a speech or a treaty. This was necessary because the Indian

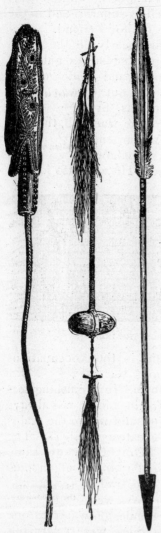

INDIAN WHIP (QUIRT), WAR-CLUB, AND HUNTING-ARROW.

could not write. Apart from other uses it was valued also as money.

71. Religion.—The Indian believed that all Indians, good and bad, would after this life go to the Happy Hunting Grounds. This was his name for Heaven. The Happy Hunting Grounds. Life there would be the same as life in this world, but without pain or trouble of any kind. It is

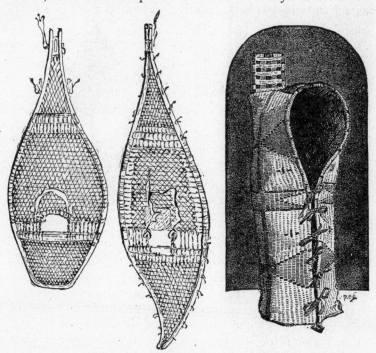

INDIAN SNOW-SHOES AND PAPPOOSE-CASE.

thought that the practice of scalping enemies killed in battle was associated with the belief that the loss of the scalp prevented the spirit from entering the Happy Hunting Grounds. The Indian would therefore risk almost anything to save the dead body of his chief or his friend from being scalped by the enemy. As in the Happy Hunting Grounds he would need arms to defend himself, these and other things of use in this life were buried with him for use in the other life.

72. The Clan and the Tribe.—According to language and locality the Indians were separated into families, such as the Maskoki, Algonquin, and Iroquois. According to government the family was separated into distinct tribes, and again, by relationship more or less remote, the tribe was separated into clans. Each clan had its name, usually

TOTEM OF THE FIVE NATIONS.   TOTEM OF THE ILLINOIS.

that of some bird, beast, or reptile, and the picture of this animal became the peculiar emblem or "totem" of the clan. The animal represented in the totem of each clan was supposed to favor and protect that clan and was sometimes tattooed on the breast.

The totem.

Every clan selected a sachem, or civil ruler, and at least one war-chief. The sachems exercised but little authority. They acted as advisers and, when assembled together in tribal councils, freely discussed important questions. The Indian government was therefore democratic, each warrior being to a large degree his own master.

Indian government democratic.

73. Communal Living.—The Indians knew but little of real estate. The tribes occupied the land but did not own it in the sense in which white men own land now. They had very little personal property except such objects as weapons, trinkets, and clothing, and held all other property in common. Their architecture was adapted to their communal life. Interesting illustrations of this are to be found in the " Long Houses "of the Iroquois. These The " Long Houses " of the Iroquois. houses, made of wood and bark, were in some cases one hundred feet long, and would accommodate as many as twenty families. As a rule, each house was occupied by families of which the mothers were members of the same clan. Whatever these families obtained

TOTEM OF THE SIOUX.

TOTEM OF THE HURONS.

by hunting or by the rude culture of the soil they owned in common, and all their food they kept in a common storehouse.

74. The Mound Builders.—Many thousands of mounds have been found in Ohio and in other parts of the United States. Some have the shape of birds, fishes, and reptiles; some of the square, circle, and other mathematical figures. The Big Elephant Mound, a few miles below the mouth of the Wisconsin River, is 135 feet long; the Serpent Mound, in Ohio, is 1,000 feet long, with a gracefully curving body. These mounds have gateways, outlooks, and parallel lines, showing that they were probably used as fortifications. Of late years very careful explorers The mounds. have been at work among these mounds, opening many of them and taking out relics. These relics include kettles, pipes, axes, arrowheads, tools for weaving and spinning, and other things. They have been examined with the great-

Relics found in the mounds. est care, because they help us to understand what kind of people made and used them. At one time it was thought that the Mound Builders were a people of a very superior civilization, because of the artistic

skill they showed in their sculptured relics. Accordingly, the Mound Builders were spoken of as a "lost race" that numbered many millions and constituted a mighty empire.

The character of the mounds and of the relics found in them leaves no

Mound Builders probably American Indians. doubt that they were the work of

various tribes, differing from each other quite as much as Indian tribes differ now. The Cherokees, who are known to have built mounds some time after the whites came to America, probably built those found

CARVED PIPES FROM AN INDIAN MOUND.

in the western part of North Carolina and the eastern part of Tennessee. It seems altogether probable that the Mound Builders were nothing more than American Indians, like those found by the English and the French colonists.

75. Number of Indians.—There are at present about 250,000 Indians in the United States. Very likely the number is quite as large now as it was when the English and the French began to plant settlements. It has been thought that the coming of the whites prevented the destruction of large numbers of Indians by war and famine.

76. Influence of the Indians Upon the Whites.—The influence of the Indians upon the whites, especially from the time of the early settlements to the Revolution, was considerable. They often saved struggling settlers from starvation by furnishing them food, and they taught the whites how to cultivate Indian corn. But, as we shall see in later chapters of this book, the principal influence of the Indians upon the whites was through the numerous Indian wars, which

Indian wars taught the colonists the advantage of union.

helped the colonists to know one another better, and taught them what they most needed to learn—the advantage of union. In fighting against a common danger the colonies were brought into closer sympathy with one another. Let us briefly refer to two of those wars, the Pequot War and King Philip's War, both of which were fought before the beginning of the Intercolonial Wars.

BIG ELEPHANT MOUND.

CHAPTER VIII

EARLY INDIAN WARS

77. The Pequot War (1637).—The leading cause of each of the Indian wars in New England was the same— the feeling on the part of the Indians that the whites were **Leading cause of** getting possession of the lands, and would **early Indian wars.** in time drive the Red Men away from their hunting grounds. The Indians did not at first understand that sales of land meant their giving it up entirely. But even when they understood the nature of land sales, they thought the whites had taken advantage of them.

When the people from Massachusetts settled in Connecticut in 1636 they found themselves neighbors to a strong, ferocious tribe of Indians, called Pequots, living in the eastern part of the State. These Indians attacked the little settlement of Wethersfield, where they killed a number of persons. Captain John Mason, with ninety men from the **Captain Mason's** towns of Hartford, Wethersfield, and Wind- **expedition against** sor, started in pursuit. The party came to **the Pequots.** anchor in Narragansett Bay about three weeks after leaving Hartford. Mason marched westward across Rhode Island, and at the end of two days halted the expedition just north of the present town of Stonington. Before daybreak next morning he and his men surprised the Indian fort, and destroyed nearly all the Indians in it, consisting of from 400 to 600 men, women, and children. The war resulted in the destruction of the Pequot tribe, and so awed the Indians in that part of the country that there was no more trouble with them for about forty years. Then came King Philip's War, which lasted two years and was much more extensive than the Pequot War.

78. King Philip's War (1675–1676).—King Philip, chief of the Wampanoags, a Rhode Island tribe, was a leader of much ability. He united the New England   King Philip's Indians from Maine to the Hudson River in   purpose. a league whose aim was to destroy all the whites in New England. The war broke out in Swansea, Massachusetts.

INDIANS CARRYING CANOES OVER A PORTAGE.

and spread through the towns in the southern and western parts of the State. Deerfield and Hadley were among the places pillaged and burned. The war was stubbornly fought, and finally ended with the death of King Philip, who was shot while trying to escape capture at Mount Hope (Bristol), Rhode Island, which was his home.   Results of King The remnant of his tribe were either killed or   Philip's War. sold into slavery, and the power of the New England Indians was completely broken. The war was a severe strain upon the New England colonists. Six hundred of them were killed, and thirteen of their towns were destroyed. It cost the colonists a large sum of money and imposed heavy burdens upon them in the way of taxation.

But the Indians having the greatest influence upon colonial development were the Iroquois. These we have already mentioned in their relation to the Dutch, and we shall now speak of their immediate influence upon the French and the English colonies.

TO THE PUPIL

1. Why were the canoe and the snow-shoe of great value to the Indian? What was his religious belief? Tell what you can about communal living; about the Mound Builders.
2. Why did the absence of such animals as horses and oxen retard the progress of the Indians? Discuss the influence of the Indians upon the whites.
3. What were the causes and results of the Pequot War? of King Philip's War? Impersonating King Philip, write an account of the wrongs you suffered at the hands of the whites.
4. Subject for debate: Resolved, that the Indians have been unjustly treated by the white people.
5. If you rightly study the facts about the Indians, you will be prepared to understand the Indian problem which the American people are now trying to solve. As in the case of all other problems of to-day, we study the past that we may learn how to interpret the present. Even the Indian question has two sides. Read the first chapter of Parkman's Conspiracy of Pontiac; also Longfellow's Hiawatha.

CHAPTER IX

FRENCH EXPLORATIONS

REFERENCES: **Scribner's** Popular History of the United States, I. and II.; **Wright's** Children's Stories in American History; **Drake's** Making of the Great West; **Drake's** Making of New England; **Morris's** Half Hours with American History; **Richardson's** History of Our Country.

OUTSIDE READINGS: **Parkman's** La Salle and the Discovery of the Great West; **Parkman's** Pioneers of France in the New World; **Winsor's** Narrative and Critical History, IV.; **Winsor's** The Westward Movement; **Bancroft's** United States, II.; **Hinsdale's** Old Northwest; **Hildreth's** United States, II.; **Thwaites's** Father Marquette; **Wilson's** A History of the American People, II.; **Dix's** Champlain.

FICTION: **Catherwood's** Romance of Dollard; **Catherwood's** Story of Tonty.

79. The French Discover and Explore the St. Lawrence.—By reason of the discoveries of Verrazano (1524) France laid claim to the Atlantic coast between Cape Fear, North Carolina, and Newfoundland. Ten years later Jacques Cartier discovered the St. Lawrence and sailed up the river as far as an Indian village on the present site of Montreal. He returned *Cartier discovers the St. Lawrence (1534).* in 1540 and in the name of King Francis I. took possession of Canada, as the Indians called the country. Immediately attempts were made to colonize, but they were unsuccessful. In 1603 the French again attempted settlement in the region extending from New York harbor to Cape Breton, called Acadia,[1] and again they failed.

But these failures only shed the greater lustre about the name of Samuel de Champlain, the "Father of New France." When he first penetrated the St. Lawrence val-

---

[1] Acadia was afterward restricted in meaning to its present boundaries.

FRENCH SOLDIERS OF THE TIME OF THE FRENCH EXPLORATION.

ley he was impressed with its great beauty and its valuable resources, for it was rich in forests and furs.   Next
Champlain makes to the gold and silver, the fur trade furnished
the first perma= the best means of securing the coveted wealth
nent French set=
tlement in Canada. which the New World offered.   Champlain
was a man of culture and refinement, earnest, patriotic, and
religious.   He wished to extend the glory of France and
the Catholic Church.   Moreover, he saw that the St. Lawrence valley, and not Acadia, was the promising field for
France in the New World.   In 1608 he made the first permanent French settlement in Canada, at Quebec.   The following year he discovered the lake which bears his name.

80. Champlain and the Iroquois.—It was a curious coin-
cidence that two years after the settlement of Jamestown
Hudson should have sailed up the Hudson River and
Champlain and   Champlain should have explored Lake Cham-
Henry Hudson.   plain (1609).   These two events had a large
influence on American history.   The Dutch on the Hudson
and the Iroquois in the Mohawk River valley stood in the
way of French success in America.   The story containing
the reasons for French failure is full of interest, and we will
now begin to read it.

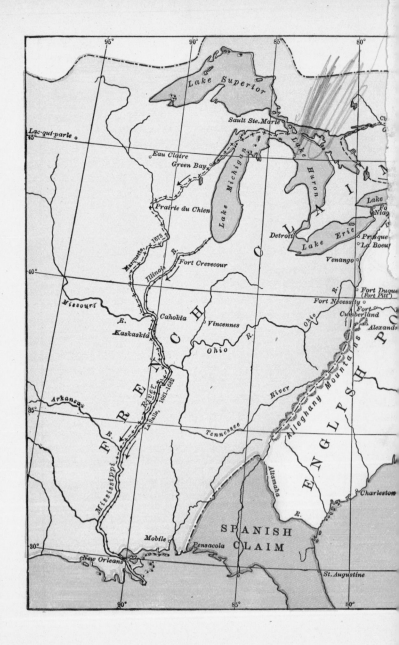

Lake Superior

Sault Ste. Marie

Lac-qui-parle
45°

Eau Claire
Green Bay

Lake Michigan

Lake Huron

C   L   A   I   N

Lake
Fo
Niag

Prairie du Chien

Detroit

Lake Erie

Presqu
La Boeuf

Marquette, 1673

Fort Crevecour

Venango

40°

Illinois

R.

F   R   E   N   C   H

Missouri

R.

Cahokia

Vincennes

R.

Ohio

Fort Duque
(Fort Pitt)

Fort Necessity

Fort
Cumberland

Alexandr

Kaskaskia

Ohio

R.

35°

Arkansas

R.

R. 1681-1682

La Salle,

River

Tennessee

Alleghany Mountains

E   N   G   L   I   S   H

R.

Altamaha

R.

Charleston

30°

Mississippi

Mobile

Pensacola

SPANISH   CLAIM

New Orleans

St. Augustine

90°   85°   80°

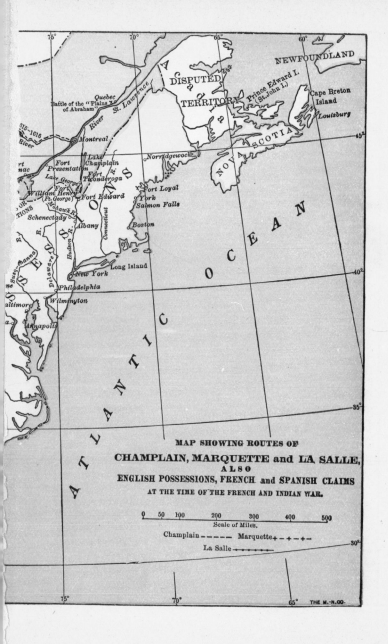

MAP SHOWING ROUTES OF
CHAMPLAIN, MARQUETTE and LA SALLE,
ALSO
ENGLISH POSSESSIONS, FRENCH and SPANISH CLAIMS
AT THE TIME OF THE FRENCH AND INDIAN WAR.

Scale of Miles.

Champlain − − − − − Marquette + − + − + −
La Salle • • • • • • •

When Champlain settled at Quebec in 1608, he found that the neighboring tribes of Algonquin Indians were bitter enemies of the Mohawks, one of the Five Nations, or Iroquois, in New York. It was hard for him to keep out of their deadly feud, and he decided to take the side of the Algonquins because their lands were nearer to him. Accordingly he joined them in a battle with the Mohawks near Ticonderoga, on Lake Champlain, and shot some of the latter with his gun. As the Mohawks had never before heard the report of a gun **Champlain makes** they were overcome **the Iroquois enemies of the French.** with superstitious terror and defeated. The Frenchman enabled the Algonquins to triumph over the Mohawks, but that shot was fatal to the future success of the French in America. The Iroquois were from that day

SAMUEL CHAMPLAIN.

the unrelenting enemies of the French colonists, and did all they could to prevent them from carrying out their plans of exploration and trade.

81. The French Reach the Mississippi Valley.—It is important to remember that this battle of Ticonderoga took place in 1609, when only a handful of Englishmen were at Jamestown. The French had control of the St. Lawrence, one of the three great water-ways to the interior of North America. If they could get control of **The three great** the Mississippi valley and the Hudson-Mo- **water-ways.** hawk River route they would hold the other two, and North America would be in their grasp. The distance from the St. Lawrence to the Mississippi was not great. One route lay through Lake Ontario and Lake Erie, by portage into French Creek, through the Alleghany and Ohio Rivers into the Mississippi. Another lay through the same lakes into the Maumee, by portage into the Wabash, and through the Ohio into the Mississippi. But the ever-watchful Iroquois, whose territory stretched along the shore of Lake Erie, blocked the way and baffled the French here. The latter were obliged to seek a route farther north, which was much longer and more difficult. Slowly and patiently they worked their way up the Ottawa River into Georgian Bay, through Lake Huron, Lake Michigan, across into the Illinois River, and from there into the Mississippi.

The Iroquois force the French to seek a long and difficult route.

The Jesuit missionaries bore a large part in this toil-some work of exploration. These brave men were eager to Christianize the Indians. They built mission stations and in their zeal braved many dangers. Not only did they gain converts to their faith, but with rare intelligence they made important explorations and discoveries. It was one of their number, Marquette, who succeeded in reaching the Mississippi. Attended by Joliet, he sailed, in 1673, as far down the Mississippi as the mouth of the Arkansas. This was two years before King Philip's War and three years before Bacon's Rebellion.

Important work of the Jesuit missionaries.

82. La Salle Plants the Arms of France at the Mouth of the Mississippi.—But the most valuable explorations were made by the daring and tireless La Salle. He was an earnest Catholic, and was full of plans for his own success and ambitious for the success of France. In 1666, at the age of twenty-three, he came out to Canada, filled with the passion of his age, the desire to discover a water route to India. Not much is known of his early explorations, but it is supposed that he discovered the Ohio River and partially explored it. In 1679 he set out on an expedition to explore the Mississippi. By this time he had given up the idea of a water route to India. His great ambition was to reach the mouth of the Mississippi and secure the valley for France. Having built the *Griffin*, a small boat, on the Niagara River, he sailed in it through Lakes Erie and Huron and landed on the shore of Lake Michigan. He then sent back his boat for

La Salle sets out to explore the Mississippi.

LA SALLE CLAIMING FOR FRANCE ALL THE TERRITORY THROUGH WHICH THE
MISSISSIPPI AND ITS TRIBUTARIES FLOWED.

supplies, but he never heard from it again. This was only one of the many trials and disappointments in his troubled life. A little later he reached the Illinois *La Salle reaches the mouth of the Mississippi.* River, and sailing about half way down, built a fort afterward fitly named Crevecœur (Heart-break). In 1682 he found the Mississippi and explored it to its mouth. There, according to French custom, he planted the French arms and claimed all the country through which the river and its tributaries flowed. He called the country Louisiana in honor of the French King, Louis XIV. This was the year in which Penn was laying the foundations of Philadelphia.

ROBERT CAVALIER DE LA SALLE.

83. Attempt to Plant a Colony at the Mouth of the Mississippi. —La Salle's aims were two-fold: (1) To establish military and trade centres at various *La Salle's two aims.* points and (2) to plant a colony at the mouth of the Mississippi River. In this way he hoped to get control of the fur trade for France. He had built many forts. He now returned to France to get people for his colony. He succeeded in getting men for this new scheme, but in sailing for the mouth of the Mississippi he missed it and landed several hundred miles to the west at Matagorda Bay. Trials and difficulties grew thick about him until, at the end of two years, he started overland to get assistance from Canada. While he and his wretched followers were wandering through the dense forests, he was waylaid and shot dead by some of the men of his own company (1687). He had not accom- *What La Salle did.* plished his full purpose, but in exploring the Ohio and the Mississippi and in building forts in the unoccupied territory he had done a great work for his country.

84. On Account of La Salle's Exploration the Mississippi Valley Becomes a Part of New France.—The planting of French arms at the mouth of the Mississippi was a very significant event in American history. It was the declaration to the world that France laid claim to the whole Mississippi valley from the Rocky to the Alleghany Mountains. Spain had failed to follow up her discovery of the Mississippi by making the country known to the world or by colonizing it. It had been the dream of La Salle to

La Salle's dream. unite this immense and valuable territory with the St. Lawrence valley, making a vast empire which would crowd out the English. The English had planted their colonies on the Atlantic sea-coast, and he wished to keep them shut in behind the Alleghanies forever. The Mississippi and St. Lawrence valleys would form the New France of America, with the seat of government removed to the Mississippi.

TO THE PUPIL

1. You have been studying colonial history from the earliest settlements to 1689. Before that date, each colony largely went its own way, with but little interest in any other. After that date, the colonies were gradually drawn nearer together by the necessity of uniting for a better defence against common enemies. One of these common enemies was the French and the Indians, and another the royal and proprietary governors.

2. What was done for France by Verrazano? by Cartier? by Champlain? You cannot too carefully note the results of Champlain's mistake (1609) in making enemies of the Iroquois.

3. Trace carefully on the map the various water-ways by which the French could reach the Mississippi valley. What part did the Jesuit missionaries bear in the toilsome work of exploration?

4. Describe the work of La Salle. What were his aims? Notice what he did in 1682, only seven years before the great landmark 1689. What were the results of his work? Write an essay on his explorations.

5. Learn all you can about the Iroquois Indians, as their influence upon colonial history was remarkable. You will find a good account of them in the first chapter of Parkman's Conspiracy of Pontiac.

CHAPTER X

THE LAST FRENCH WAR

REFERENCES: **Scribner's** Popular History of the United States, III.; **Wright's** Children's Stories in American History; **Sloane's** French War and the Revolution; **Cook's** Stories in the Old Dominion; **Coffin's** Old Times in the Colonies; **Fiske's** War of Independence; **Richardson's** History of Our Country; **Hart's** Formation of the Union.

OUTSIDE READINGS: **Winsor's** Narrative and Critical History, V. and VI.; **Parkman's** Montcalm and Wolfe; **Parkman's** Conspiracy of Pontiac; **Parkman's** Old Régime in Canada; **Bancroft's** United States, V.; **Morris's** Half Hours with American History, I.; **Hinsdale's** Old Northwest; **Wilson's** A History of the American People, II.; **Frothingham's** Rise of the Republic; **Rossiter Johnson's** Old French War; **Scudder's** George Washington; **Franklin's** Autobiography; **Wilson's** George Washington; **Ford's** The True George Washington.

FICTION: **Cooper's** Last of the Mohicans; **Thackeray's** Virginians; **Henty's** With Wolfe in Canada; **Munroe's** At War with Pontiac.

POETRY: **Longfellow's** Evangeline (the Acadians).

85. England and France Struggle for Control in America (1689-1763).—These events in the Mississippi valley occurred just before 1689. In 1688 James II., one of the Stuart kings, was driven out of England and found refuge in the court of France. There France took up his cause, and England and France began a series of wars which did not end until 1763. While these wars were going on in Europe there was fighting between the French and English colonies in America.

The Iroquois stood in the way of French success, for the French sought the fur trade, and the Iroquois largely controlled it in the region of the Great Lakes. But since the day that Champlain had joined the Algonquins and helped them defeat the Iroquois, the French had been persistently hindered and harassed by these powerful tribes in the Mohawk valley. It will be remembered that the English, when they conquered New Netherland, inherited from the Dutch the good-will and friendly alliance of these Indians.

Both the French and the English encouraged their Indian allies to make attacks upon frontier settlements during the years that France and England were at war. The vari-

The Intercolonial Wars.

ous wars in the colonies were called Intercolonial Wars.[1] The last one is the most interesting one to us. It is known as the Last French War[2] in America and the Seven Years' War in Europe (1756–1763).

86. Causes of the Last French War.—Both England and France claimed the territory between the Alleghanies

Reasons why France and England claimed the Mississippi valley.

and the Mississippi. England claimed it by the discovery of the Cabots and by Indian treaty, and France by reason of exploration. France had done much more than England to make this region known, but had not occupied the country. When, therefore, the English colonies, which had been taking root on the Atlantic coast, had spread as far west as the eastern base of the Alleghanies, a struggle for possession was inevitable.

By 1750 the French had built a line of sixty forts by

[1] The first three of the Intercolonial Wars, named after the English sovereign reigning at the time, were as follows: King William's War (1689–1697), Queen Anne's War (1702–1713), and King George's War (1744–1748). During the last one the New England colonists, led by Colonel Pepperrell, captured Louisburg, a great fortress on Cape Breton Island. The French had thought that this stronghold could withstand any attack, and were therefore amazed at the success of the New England farmers and fishermen. At the end of the war, however, England gave up Louisburg to France.

[2] To develop union among the English colonies, there were needed such common interests as the Intercolonial Wars furnished. Massachusetts, Connecticut, and New York united in King William's War; South Carolina, New England, New York, and New Jersey organized separate expeditions against the French and Indians in Queen Anne's War; the northern colonies engaged in King George's War; and in the Last French War all the colonies stood side by side in a solid array against the French and Indians. This war was national, and led the provincial to begin to think of himself as an American.

FRENCH SOLDIERS AND OFFICERS OF THE TIME OF THE FRENCH WAR.

way of the Great Lakes, from the St. Lawrence to the mouth of the Mississippi. Great skill was shown in locating them at points of military importance. In many cases they afterward became great business French forts and and trade centres. Detroit, Chicago, Nat- colonies. chez, and St. Louis mark the sites of some of these forts. The French had planted colonies also at Mobile and New Orleans early in the eighteenth century. Thus far they had outgeneraled the English in establishing a claim to such a vast extent of territory, for the English colonists had been so busy with their own affairs that they had thought very little of the land lying west of the mountains. But at last they had waked up and were ready to make a stubborn fight if necessary.

French and English traders had come into collision in the disputed territory, and both the French and the English appreciated the need of immediate action. About the same time that the French governor was once more trying to make friends with the Iroquois[1] Indians, and urging the

---

[1] The Iroquois were the great barrier between the French and the disputed territory. During this war the Iroquois were neutral.

home government to send colonists to the Ohio valley, the Ohio Company was formed by some gentlemen in Virginia. This company received from the king, on condition of set-

The Ohio Company. tlement, a grant of 600,000 acres of land between the Great Kanawha and Monongahela Rivers. Lawrence Washington had a large interest in the Ohio Company, and his younger brother George was employed as surveyor. The Ohio Company at once began to send explorers into the disputed region, and at the same time the French were taking formal possession by sinking lead plates with inscriptions at the mouths of the streams.

To get ahead of the English the French built a line of forts on the direct route to the Ohio.[1] Governor Dinwid-

Washington's journey to the French forts. die sent George Washington, then adjutant-general of the Virginia militia, to inform the French commander[2] that he was building on English territory and would do well to depart peaceably. Washington at this time was twenty-one years old and over six feet tall. Cool-headed and fearless, with seven companions, all on pack-horses, he started from Williamsburg, Va., on his perilous journey late in October, 1753. About the middle of January, 1754, he returned with the refusal of the French commander to withdraw.

As the juncture of the Alleghany and Monongahela Rivers was the "Gateway of the West," a fort here would control the entrance to the Ohio valley. Both nations had their eyes upon this important site. The English reached

[1] These forts included Presque Isle, Le Bœuf, and Venango on the Alleghany.

[2] To reach Fort Le Bœuf, situated only fifteen miles from Lake Erie, Washington had to travel five hundred miles through the wilderness. By the time he was ready to start back from Fort Venango, it was Christmas. The pack-horses were so weak that Washington and a single companion pressed forward on foot. They had many narrow escapes from death. A treacherous Indian guide, who was not three rods in advance, turned suddenly and shot at Washington, but missed him. Washington took the Indian's gun away and let him go. On reaching the Alleghany River Washington and his companion found it full of floating ice. With nothing but a hatchet, they made a raft and began crossing the river. Shortly afterward Washington was struck by a piece of floating ice and knocked into the water. Darkness falling upon them before they could reach the opposite side of the river, they spent the night on an island, where they nearly froze to death.

it first, but were driven off by a larger force of French, who put up a fort and called it Fort Du Quesne. Washington, who was on his way from Virginia to occupy the new fort, was met by the unsuccessful party of English. He pushed on to Great Meadows (Pennsylvania), and there learned that the French were marching toward him. Advancing with the aid of an Indian guide and forty men, he met a French party in a dark glen near by, and exchanged shots with them. The French leader and most of his men were killed. This encounter began the war. Washington returned to Great Meadows

The fighting begins at Great Meadows.

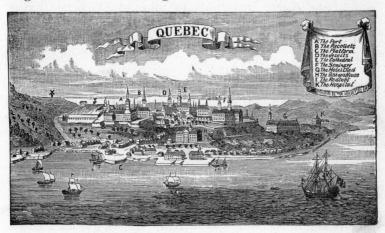

QUEBEC IN 1730.

and threw up intrenchments which he called Fort Necessity. Here he was defeated by the French and obliged to retire (July, 1754). This handful of men with their youthful leader had fired the shot which set in motion European armies. The war which followed was but little less important in its issues than the Revolution. Let us now follow it in some of its most important engagements.

87. Plan of the War.—The plan of the English in 1755 and their general plan for the war was four-fold. An expedition was to be sent against Acadia; a second against Crown Point, a French fort on Lake Champlain, which

controlled the route to Canada from the south ; a third was
to move through the Mohawk valley and capture Fort
Niagara, the key to the Great Lakes ; and a fourth, the most
important, under the leadership of General Braddock, had
for its object the capture of Fort Du Quesne, the " Gateway of the West."

88. Braddock's Defeat (1755.)—In 1755 General Braddock was sent over to take command of the English forces
in America.   He was a brave soldier with much experience, but he knew nothing of fighting the Indians in
woodland warfare.   Self-confident and headstrong, he was
quite unwilling to take advice from Wash-
General Braddock. ington or Franklin,[1] who both warned him
against Indian ambuscades.   He trusted all things to his
English regulars.   The colonial troops were to his mind
very inferior, the colonial officers inexperienced, and he
regarded them with contempt.   With 2,000 men Braddock
started from Alexandria, Virginia, toward Fort Du Quesne.[2]
His purpose was to capture this fort and then to march
north along the Alleghany River, capture the line of forts
upon its banks, and join the other forces at Niagara.   In
marching his troops he insisted upon the same order and
precision as in the open fields of Europe, and would listen
to no suggestions of avoiding risks from ambush.   Finally,
when within eight miles of the fort, the fears of the despised American militia were realized.   Braddock's army
The ambush and marched into an ambush.   The attack came
the battle.   from an unseen foe, who shot down by scores
the surprised English soldiers.   The regulars tried to fight
in ranks, but in doing so were the more easily struck down

---

[1] Benjamin Franklin was at this time forty-nine years old.   He had been for
many years a member of the Pennsylvania Assembly and was now Postmaster-general for America.

[2] Braddock was in great need of horses and wagons, which for a long time he
was not able to secure.   At Frederick, Maryland, he was met by Benjamin Franklin, who used his powerful influence to procure from Pennsylvania farmers one hundred and fifty wagons, six hundred draft-horses, and fifteen hundred pack-horses.
Franklin promised to see that the farmers were paid for their horses and wagons,
and he kept his word.

GENERAL BRADDOCK'S TROOPS IN AN INDIAN AMBUSCADE.

by the indians firing from behind trees. Braddock made a brave effort to bear up against the foe. Four horses were killed under him, and he was on the fifth when he received a mortal wound. Washington, one of Braddock's staff, had three horses shot under him, and four bullets passed through his clothes.

Finally, after suffering severely, the regulars fled in shameful rout. The brave Virginians, led by Washington, fought behind trees in true Indian fashion, and saved the army from utter ruin. Out of Braddock's army of 2,000, 700 men and three-fourths of the officers were killed. Such was the dismal **Dismal failure of Braddock's expedition.** failure of Braddock's expedition. The miserable remnant of his army retreated, and the Indians laid waste the settlements in western Virginia, Maryland, and Pennsylvania.

89. Removal of the Acadians (1755).—During the same summer that Braddock was defeated the people of Acadia were removed from their homes. Acadia was included in what is now Nova Scotia and New Brunswick. It was settled by the French early in the seventeenth century, and about one hundred years later (1710) was captured by the English. For forty-five years it had been un- **The Acadians take sides with the French.** der English rule. But the simple-minded, ignorant peasantry continued to speak the French language and to take sides with the French in every struggle with the English. In this way they did much injury to the English cause. Accordingly, in 1755, some troops from New England landed in Acadia and told the inhabitants they must promise to support the English king or they would be sent out of the country. More than 5,000 of them refused, and they were torn from their **Their removal necessary.** homes and scattered among the colonies from Massachusetts to Georgia. A large number of them found their way to Louisiana, where many of their descendants may be found to-day. This removal caused much hardship, but it seemed to be a military necessity.

90. Montcalm and French Successes.—There had been fighting in the colonies for about two years before war was declared between England and France in 1756. The first two years of fighting in the colonies found the French successful almost everywhere. The English government sent **Weak English generals.** to America very weak and inefficient generals. These men, like Braddock, were unwilling to take any advice from colonial officers and looked down upon colonial troops. Moreover, they so managed the

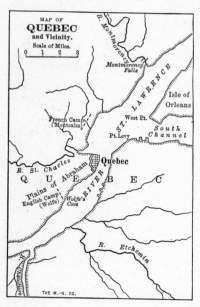

MAP OF
QUEBEC
and Vicinity.
Scale of Miles.
0   1   2   3

various armies that there was not united and harmonious action. The French, on the contrary, were ably handled by Montcalm, who so massed his forces at important points that, during these two years, he kept the English out of the disputed territory, and hemmed them in behind the Alleghanies. At the close of 1757 the outlook for England was gloomy.

91. William Pitt and English Successes.—At this critical time William Pitt became the head of affairs in England. Clear-headed and great-hearted, he was a true hero. He loved England as fondly as his own life and was willing to rise or fall with her. He said, "I can save England," and he did save England. His faith in himself and his country filled the people with hope and confidence. He appointed strong and able officers for the troops in America. He put the colonial officers and troops on an equal footing with the English and pushed forward the various armies in energetic, united action. The spirit of Pitt was everywhere. In quick succession Louisburg, Fort Frontenac, Fort Du Quesne, Fort Niagara, and other French strongholds fell into the hands of the English.

92. **Wolfe and the Capture of Quebec (September 18, 1759).**—Pitt showed great wisdom in appointing General Wolfe to take command of an expedition against Quebec, the most important place now remaining in possession of the French.[1] General Wolfe, then in his thirty-third year, had a feeble body but a fearless soul. As brigadier-general at Louisburg he had gained high praise for energy and boldness. Pitt believed in this brave young general, and therefore placed him at the head of an army of 10,000 men for the capture of Quebec. The men so idolized Wolfe that they would gladly follow him to victory or death.

General Wolfe.

MAJ.-GEN. JAMES WOLFE.

Quebec was situated on steep and lofty cliffs overlooking the St. Lawrence, and was protected by a strong fortress. This fortress was the strongest in America, and the key to Canada. Wolfe and his army tried in vain for three months to find a weak spot where they might make a successful attack, but failure met them on every hand. The English troops were discouraged, and even the brave Wolfe began to lose hope, but in spite of sickness and intense bodily suffering he resolved to make one more attempt to take Quebec.

Quebec.

At last his searching eyes caught sight of a pathway up the rugged sides of the cliffs along the river bank, some distance above the city. Here was an opportunity not to be neglected. One dark night Wolfe's army floated quietly down the river in boats and landed at the foot of the rocky heights. The brave soldiers, with immense difficulty, pulled themselves and their cannon up the steep ascent. Reaching the top, they quickly over-

The English climb the rocky heights.

[1] Crown Point and Ticonderoga were captured by the English under Amherst in the summer of 1759 (the last of July).

powered the guard, which was too much astonished to make resistance. In the morning, Wolfe's men were drawn up in line of battle on the Plains of Abraham, less than a mile from the walls of Quebec. Montcalm, astonished at what the English had done, would not wait for an attack, but at once led his army out on the open plain. The fighting was terrible, and the French could not stand up against the withering fire of the English. Wolfe led in a furious charge

MARQUIS DE MONTCALM.

and, although twice pierced with bullets, refused to give up until he received a mortal wound. It was **Wolfe's victory and death.** hard for him to die as long as the issue was in doubt, but when, in his last moments, he heard the shout of victory, he said, "Now, God be praised, I will die in peace." Montcalm was also mortally wounded, and in the hour of death was equally heroic. When told that he could not live more than ten or twelve hours, he exclaimed, "Thank God, I shall not live to see Quebec surrendered." A few days later Quebec passed from French into English hands (September 18, 1759).

93. The Treaty of Peace (1763).—With the fall of Quebec the last stronghold of the French in America passed into the hands of the English. The following year Montreal surrendered, and the colony of New France ceased to exist. Although the war was over in America, it still continued for three years in Europe, and Spain joined France against England. It was finally closed by the treaty of Paris, signed in 1763. By this treaty France ceded to Spain all the territory lying between the Mississippi and the Rocky Mountains; also the town of New Orleans, which controlled the navigation of the Mississippi. To England she gave Canada and all her territory east of the Mississippi.[1] Spain gave Florida to England in ex-

[1] France retained for fishing stations two small islands, St. Pierre and Miquelon, in the Gulf of St. Lawrence.

change for Havana, which the English had captured during the war. The English had driven out of North America successively the Dutch (1664) and the French (1763). England and Spain alone remained. Thenceforward these two had control in North America.

94. Other Results of the War.—But there were other far-reaching results of the Last French War which largely affected the future of the English colonies: (1) Up to this time there had been little of common interest among them. But all were engaged in this struggle, and they fought side by side. Thus the war taught them to know and respect each other, gave them a mutual interest, and prepared them for union. (2) They were made to realize their own strength and to see that their military ability was quite equal to that of the English soldiers. (3) The war was a preparatory school for the Revolution. Such officers as Marion, Stark, Putnam, and Washington received a military training of great value. (4) Although in fighting the French in America, England felt that she had been protecting the colonies, the colonies felt that they had been helping England in establishing English against French authority. This attitude explains their growing sense of power and independence which led, after the removal of the French, to their resistance against British interference and their final separation from the British crown.

NOTE

The Conspiracy of Pontiac.—When, at the close of the Last French War, England tried to take possession of the territory west of the Alleghanies and north of the Ohio, trouble with the Indians in that region at once arose. The French, embittered by their loss of this territory, stirred up the Indians against the English, and the conspiracy of Pontiac was the outcome. This able and daring chief of the Ottawas organized a widespread movement for the purpose of destroying all the English settlers west of the Alleghanies. Having won over to his scheme many tribes, he succeeded in capturing eight out of twelve forts, whose garrisons he put to death. This fierce and bloody war lasted two years and ended in the complete failure of Pontiac.

TO THE PUPIL

1. What was the leading cause of the Last French War? What did the Ohio Company set out to do? What journey did Washington make and with what results? Write an account of this journey.
2. How did the war begin? In outlining the plan of the war use the map freely.
3. What do you think of Braddock and of the causes of his defeat? Was the removal of the Acadians just? Give reasons for your answer.
4. Account for French successes in the early years of the war. What had William Pitt to do with English successes later?
5. What do you admire in the character of General Wolfe? For many interesting facts about the personality of this heroic man, see Parkman's Montcalm and Wolfe.
6. Imagine yourself to have been one of Wolfe's soldiers and write an account in the first person of scaling the Heights of Abraham and of the battle on the following day.
7. What were the results of the war? Make two brief outlines, one containing the advantages the French had in America and the other containing the advantages the English had.
8. Subject for debate: Resolved, that the French had a just claim to the Ohio valley.
9. Subject for essay: Cooper's Last of the Mohicans.
10. To aid you in an intelligent review from the beginning of the book, you can supplement the chronological chart suggested at the end of Chapter VI. by adding a fourth parallel line for the principal events connected with French exploration and colonization. Such a review will help you to understand clearly the nature of the struggle, mainly on the part of four European countries, to get control of North America. By 1763 England had come out ahead in this struggle.
11. As you may know, Francis Parkman is the standard historian on the relations between the English and the French colonies in America. Read his Montcalm and Wolfe and Longfellow's Evangeline.

CHAPTER XI

LIFE IN THE COLONIES AT THE CLOSE OF THE FRENCH AND INDIAN WARS

REFERENCES: **Drake's** Making of New England; **Richardson's** History of Our Country; **Barnes's** Popular History of the United States; **Sanford's** History of Connecticut; **Thwaites's** Colonies; **Scudder's** Men and Manners in America One Hundred Years Ago; **Eggleston's** Household History.

OUTSIDE READINGS: **Earle's** Customs and Fashions in Old New England; **Earle's** Sabbath in Puritan New England; **Earle's** Costume of Colonial Times; **Weeden's** Economic and Social History of New England; **Earle's** Margaret Winthrop; **Irving's** Knickerbocker's History of New York; **Irving's** Sketch Book; **Hart's** Colonial Children.

95. The Colonies in General.—At the close of the French and Indian Wars in 1763, the colonies mainly occupied a strip of land lying along the Atlantic coast and stretching all the way from Maine to Florida. There were thirteen of these original colonies, which, by reason of difference in soil, climate, and other natural as well as social and economic conditions, may be divided into three groups: the New England group, or New Hampshire, The three groups of colonies. Massachusetts, Rhode Island, and Connecticut; the Middle group, or New York, New Jersey, Pennsylvania, and Delaware; and the Southern group, or Maryland, Virginia, North Carolina, South Carolina, and Georgia. The population was about two million souls,[1] one-fourth of whom were slaves. The people lived mainly along the seacoast and large rivers, although a few settle- Population and large towns. ments stretched back into the forests. As many of the people were engaged in farming there were few large towns. Philadelphia, with a population of about

[1] The population of New York City in 1900 was 3,437,202.

25,000, was the largest town; Boston was not far behind; and New York contained 10,000 or 12,000 people.

Money being scarce, trade was mainly by barter. There were much comfort and prosperity and some wealth, but there was great need of labor to develop the resources of the West, which was now under the control of the English and open to settlement.

THE NEW ENGLAND GROUP OF COLONIES

96. Occupations of the People.—By reason of the poor, rocky soil of New England, agriculture yielded a meagre return for a great deal of hard labor. Farming on a small scale was extensive, but much more important sources of wealth were the cod and whale fisheries. By 1763 New England had built up a flourishing trade with the West India Islands. Cargoes of dried fish from New England were exchanged in these islands for sugar, molasses, and slaves. Large forests furnished excellent material for shipbuilding. Boston alone had six hundred vessels engaged in foreign commerce and a thousand in the fisheries and trade along the coast. All this fishing and trading developed a hardy and expert class of sailors that later furnished excellent material for our navy.

The fisheries and the trade with the West India Islands.

97. Religion and Church Worship.—Religion came first with the Puritan. The minister was usually the leading man in the community, and he did much to form public opinion in political as well as religious matters.

The churches were plain within and without. They were not heated, even in the coldest weather. But for all this, everybody was expected to attend, absence without good excuse being punishable by a fine. The minister sometimes preached in overcoat and mittens. Women carried heated stones in their muffs, and later handstoves took the place of the stones. When going to church the men sometimes carried their muskets and left sentinels outside to watch against sudden attack from the Indians. People were carefully seated according to their

Church attendance.

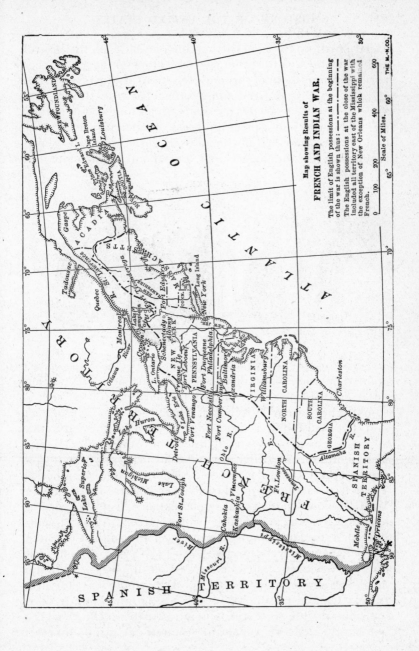

Map showing Results of
FRENCH AND INDIAN WAR.

The limit of English possessions at the beginning
of the war is shown thus : ....—..—..—..

The English possessions at the close of the war
included all territory east of the Mississippi with
the exception of New Orleans which remained
French.

Scale of Miles.
0   100   200   300   400   500   600

THE M. M. CO.

social position, the men sitting on one side of the church
and the women on the other.   As the minister often preached
two or three hours, the congregation at times naturally
The tithing grew tired and sleepy.   But the tithing man
man. was always present with his long rod of authority.   This rod had a piece of brass on one end and a hare's
foot on the other.   If a woman went to sleep she was gently
touched with the hare's foot, but if an unfortunate boy

PURITANS GOING TO CHURCH.

nodded or otherwise failed in reverent attention, he was less
gently rapped on the head with the hard end of the rod.

98. **The Salem Witchcraft (1692).**—It has often been
said that the gloomy religious life of the Puritans led to that
strange delusion known as the Salem Witchcraft.   As a
matter of fact, the belief in witchcraft in 1692 was not confined to the Puritans, for such a belief was almost universal.
The witchcraft craze in Massachusetts started from Salem
Village (now Danvers) a short distance from Salem.   A
half dozen girls and young women, from ten to twenty
years old, became almost insane over the subject of witchcraft.   They mewed like cats, barked like dogs, and went
into fits, declaring that certain persons, in league with the
devil, bit them, pinched them, or in some way tortured
them.   On the testimony of these silly girls hundreds of
innocent people were thrown into prison on the charge of
witchcraft.   Before the frenzy had spent itself, nineteen

people were hanged, including a clergyman, and one old man eighty years of age was pressed to death with heavy weights. But when, after six months, some of the magistrates and even the governor's wife were accused, the people realized their folly and stopped punishing for witchcraft.

99. Education.—Education stood next to religion and, from the Puritan standpoint, was almost a part of religion. The Puritans therefore established a system of public education soon after reaching New England. Every town was required to have a school, and before 1650 each New England colony, except Rhode Island, had passed laws enforcing some degree of education. Everywhere there was training in reading and writing. As a consequence, public education was so general that there were few people who could not read and write. As early as 1636 Harvard College was established at Cambridge, Mass., and in 1701 Yale College at New Haven, Conn.

100. Crimes and Punishments.—Laws were severe, and few crimes were committed. Many offences were punishable by death, and all kinds of punishments were inflicted in the most public way. Stocks, pillories, ducking-stools, and whipping-posts could usually be found in every village of any size. The pillory was a wooden frame, so constructed as to hold fast the head and hands of the offender. The stocks held fast the offender's feet only. In some cases he was confined in a cage and ex- *The stocks and the pillory.* posed to the public gaze; in others, he was branded with the initial letter of his crimes or compelled to wear, in a conspicuous place, a big initial letter indicating his crime.

101. Life and Manners.—The New England diet was simple. Cider and rum were favorite drinks, used often as we use tea and coffee now.

The best room and the kitchen were the principal rooms in the house. The most noticeable thing in the kitchen was the fireplace. It would accommodate a *The old-time fireplace.* backlog five or six feet long and two or three feet in diameter, and was large enough for roasting an entire sheep.   As there were no stoves all cooking was done here.   By such firesides the mothers and daughters would sit during the long winter evenings with their knitting, spinning, or quilting, while the father read his Bible or smoked his pipe.   Sometimes as the fire blazed, cider-drinking, nut-cracking, and story-telling helped to while away the evening hours.

In general, however, life was neither bright nor cheerful, as the Puritans were shy of most kinds of enjoyment. But the young people were not without simple amusements,

Amusements.

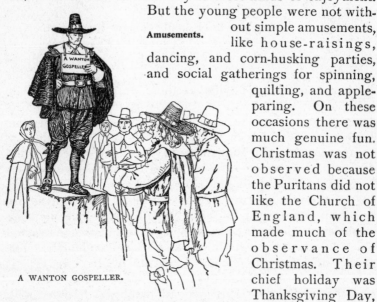

A WANTON GOSPELLER.

like house-raisings, dancing, and corn-husking parties, and social gatherings for spinning, quilting, and apple-paring.   On these occasions there was much genuine fun. Christmas was not observed because the Puritans did not like the Church of England, which made much of the observance of Christmas.   Their chief holiday was Thanksgiving Day, which they celebrated, as now, in the autumn.   This was made the occasion for family reunions.   At the Thanks-

The Thanksgiving reunion.

giving dinner the table was loaded with chicken, turkey, nuts, plum-puddings, mince-pies, pumpkin-pies, and many other toothsome varieties of food.   Weddings were festive occasions.   The friends and

Weddings and funerals.

neighbors were generally entertained at the bride's home, the wedding feast often lasting several days.   Funerals were very expensive.   Gifts such as scarfs, gloves, and rings were generously distributed to the guests, and an elaborate feast of meats and drinks was regarded as an essential feature of the occasion.

TO THE PUPIL

1. Prepare yourself to write five minutes on any one of the following topics : Occupations of the people, church worship, education, crimes and punishments, the old-time fireplace, and amusements.
2. Imagine yourself to be a New England boy or girl in colonial days and write a story of your experiences. Such work will greatly aid you in reviving the past.
3. What do you like in the manners and customs of Early New England ? Read Earle's Customs and Fashions in Old New England.

THE SOUTHERN GROUP OF COLONIES

102. Occupations of the People.—In the Southern colonies, a rich soil was general, rivers made excellent highways, and the climate was well suited to agriculture. The plantations were scattered along the rivers, *The plantation and* sometimes many miles apart, with thickly *the planter.* wooded stretches of land between. Each planter in Virginia had his own wharf, from which his produce was carried to England, and to which manufactured goods of every sort were brought in exchange. The planter needed but little that he did not obtain on his plantation or at his wharf. His slaves were not only cultivators of the soil, but they included skilled workmen, such as millers, tailors, carpenters, and shoemakers. Under such an independent system of life, towns were not needed, and before the Revolution there were only a few towns of any size in Virginia.

103. Education.—The facilities for common school education were poor. Governor Berkeley said (1670), " I thank God there are no free schools, nor printing, *Berkeley opposes* and I hope we shall not have them these hun- *free schools.* dred years." The scattered condition of the population did not favor the establishment of good common schools. The rich planters had tutors at home for their children and often sent their sons to Europe to be educated, but the schools for the masses were so few that the poorer people generally grew up in ignorance. The wealthy planters could live without work and formed a leisure class. Many of them owned fine libraries.

Although Virginia had been settled as early as 1607, the most important additions were made to her population in the time of the Commonwealth (1649–1660.) During this time hundreds of the king's followers, or cavaliers, came to Virginia. These men were usually from the higher ranks of English society, and had been prominent in public life in England. Their descendants in Virginia naturally inherited their political tendencies and included the ancestors of George Washington, Thomas Jefferson, James Madison, James Monroe, Patrick Henry, the Lees, and the Randolphs. We need not be surprised, then, that Virginia furnished more leaders in the Revolution than any other colony and afterward became the "Mother of Presidents."

The cavaliers and political leaders in Virginia.

104. Life and Manners.—The mansion of the planter, built of wood or brick, was two stories high, with a spacious veranda and a wide hallway. Close by the mansion were the slave quarters, consisting of wooden cabins surrounded by gardens and poultry yards. These negro quarters, on a large plantation, made a small village, and all about them could be seen swarms of negro children. Planters on the large plantations lived in wasteful extravagance, with choice dogs, fine horses, and a coach-and-six for great occasions. They were fond of such sports as horse-racing and fox-hunting, and were so generous and hospi-

The mansion and the slave quarters.

Manner of life of the planters.

THE PILLORY.

COLONIAL RELICS.

table that the doors of their mansions were always open to respectable travellers. Though, as we have seen, Thanksgiving was the feast-day of the year in New England, Christmas was celebrated in a festive manner in the South, when everything was gay and bright in the planter's house. A great dinner was followed in the evening by dancing to the music of the harpsichord and the violin.

Christmas a festive occasion.

TO THE PUPIL

1. Find points of difference between the people in New England and in the South in respect to occupations, education, and life and manners.
2. Write an essay on life in Virginia just before the Revolution. Read Scudder's George Washington.

THE MIDDLE GROUP OF COLONIES

105. The People and Their Occupation.—The people in the New England and Southern groups of colonies were largely English, but this was by no means true of New York, Pennsylvania, and the other Middle colonies. Here the population represented many of the countries of Europe. Trade and agriculture were of about equal importance in New York. The fur trade claimed most attention in New York and

A mixed population in New York and Pennsylvania.

EARLY NEW AMSTERDAM, SHOWING

Pennsylvania. Besides furs, the principal exports were grain and flour. The principal port for foreign trade was then, as now, New York, whose merchants were busy and prosperous, employing many ships in their extensive com-

**Trade, agricult-
ure, and manu-
facturing.**
merce with England, the West Indies, and other parts of the world. Most manufactured goods came from England and the continent of Europe. As in New England, the spinning-wheel and loom took their place in the domestic economy. The ship-building industry and the saw-mill were of necessity early developed, and the Dutch wind-mill became a striking feature of the landscape. Outside of New York agriculture was the most extensive industry.

106. Education.—While the Dutch were in control, common schools were well supported in New York, but under the English they were not in a flourishing condition. The Episcopalians founded King's College, now Columbia University, New York, in 1754. Although in New Jersey and Pennsylvania but little was done to provide for general education, outside of a few larger towns, the Presbyte-

COSTUMES AMUSEMENTS, AND ARCHITECTURE.

rians founded Princeton College, New Jersey, in 1746; and Benjamin Franklin founded the University of Pennsylvania at Philadelphia in 1749.

107. Crimes and Punishments.—Crime was not widely prevalent in the Middle colonies, although piracy had a most demoralizing influence. Hanging, whipping, and the pillory were forms of punishment frequently practised under the public gaze, as was the case in New England.

108. Life and Manners Among the Dutch.—The Dutch house had a pointed gable roof with a weather-vane on top and a porch in front of the house, where the family sat during summer evenings to enjoy the air. There were great wide fireplaces with seats *The Dutch house.* for reading or sewing. The walls were without paper, but many pictures in small frames hung upon them. The Dutch women were noted for their neatness and for their excellent housekeeping. They scrubbed the *Neat housekeeping.* floors and sprinkled them with sand every day. The men were slow and easy-going, but they were honest, thrifty, and industrious. They were fond of smoking and liked story-telling and good eating, the Dutch housekeepers being noted for their skill in making dough-nuts, crullers, and various kinds of cakes. The Dutch intro-duced "Santa Claus" and "St. Nicholas" at Christmas time, and New Year's visiting. Among them a funeral was a most expensive affair. Not only did

Funeral customs.

they distribute to the guests gloves, scarfs, and rings, as was the custom in New England, but to each friend a bottle of wine. In Albany the funeral expenses in one instance were $20,000.

The towns were situated mostly about the mouth of the Hudson, and from there the settlements extended through the Hudson valley to Albany and then followed the Mo-hawk valley. The patroons lived on their vast estates in

Life among the patroons.

grand and richly furnished houses facing the Hudson. They had about them many ser-vants and rented to numerous tenants the farms into which their estates were divided. These great estates, lying on the rivers, where goods could be easily landed and cargoes sent off, did away with the necessity of trade centres or towns.

The people were more social and fond of merry-making than the New Englanders. Their most noted holidays were Christmas, New Year's, St. Valentine's Day, Easter, and May Day. In the country, spinning-bees, house-rais-

Social life of the people.

ings, corn-huskings, and dancing parties were favorite amusements; in towns, horse-racing, cock-fighting, balls, and picnics. There was little luxury, but much quiet contentment with the simple ways of living.

TO THE PUPIL

1. What points of difference do you find between the people of the Middle colonies and those of New England? Those of the South?

2. Write a short account of life and manners among the Dutch, adding as many facts as you can to those given in the text.

3. The Legend of Sleepy Hollow, in Irving's Sketch Book, is delightful reading.

MODES OF TRAVEL AND COMMUNICATION

109. Modes of Travel.—It was difficult for the colonies to know and understand each other because their means of communication were so restricted.   The usual mode of travel on land was on foot or horseback ; and not only were the roads poor, but very few of the rivers had bridges. People living near the rivers journeyed much by row-boats, and those along the coast made great use of sloops. The trip by water from New York to Philadelphia, with a fair wind, required three days.

A wagon ran twice a week from New York to Philadelphia, and, in 1766, a stage-coach was put on which made the trip in two days. This stage, greatly

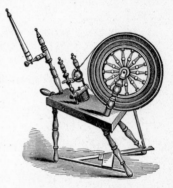

OLD SPINNING-WHEEL.

shortening the time, was called a "flying machine." It could make the journey from Boston to New York in four days. When the coach was ready the driver gave notice by sounding a horn, and then, with **The old stage-coach.** a crack of the whip, away it went on its slow and toilsome journey, during which it was no uncommon thing for the travellers to be compelled to alight and help pry the coach-wheels out of the mire.

Mails were carried mostly on horseback, and people depended mainly on letters for news. Newspapers did not at this time tell much about local or colonial news. They were full of advertisements and **Newspapers.** news from Europe. The first newspaper was the *Boston News Letter* (1704). At the close of the Last French War there were from thirty to forty newspapers in the whole country.

CHAPTER XII

GROWTH TOWARD UNION IN THE COLONIES

REFERENCES: **Scribner's** Popular History of the United States; **Fisher's** Civil Government in the United States; **Thwaites's** Colonies; **Fiske's** Colonial Era; **Bancroft's** United States, II.

OUTSIDE READINGS: **Frothingham's** Rise of the Republic; **Eggleston's** Household History; **Macy's** Our Government; **Franklin's** Plan of Union (Old South Leaflets); **Fiske's** Civil Government in the United States; **Woodburn's** The American Republic.

110. Colonial Government.—The various colonial governments were modelled after the English and were there-
<small>The governor, the council, and the assembly.</small> fore much alike in form. Each colony had its governor and a law-making body consisting of the Council,[1] and the Assembly. The Council was the governor's body of advisers. They aided the governor in executing his duties, and generally took part in making laws. The Assembly was elected by the people and was therefore the stronghold of their rights. It alone could levy taxes, and in this way it controlled the public money.

But the manner of choosing the governor made all the difference in the amount of freedom which each colony
<small>The three kinds of colonies.</small> enjoyed. In 1763 there were three political groups[2] of colonies. The first, containing Rhode Island and Connecticut, may rightly be called the *republican*, or self-governing, group, because the people elected the governor; the second, containing Pennsylvania,

---

[1] The members of the council were chosen in various ways: by the king, as in Virginia; by the proprietary governor, as in Pennsylvania; by the legislature, as in Massachusetts; or by the people, as in Connecticut.

[2] These political groups should not be confused with the groups named in par. 94.

Delaware, and Maryland, may be called the *proprietary* group, because the proprietors appointed the governor; and the third, containing the remaining eight colonies, may be called the *royal* group, because the king of England appointed the governor.

111. Republican, Proprietary, and Royal Colonies.— Connecticut and Rhode Island had very liberal charters and governed themselves without any interference from the mother-country. They were, even at this early period, little republics. In the royal and proprietary colonies there was an almost continual struggle going on between the governors and the colonial assemblies. The points at issue were sometimes petty, sometimes serious, and the discussions were often bitter. In New York, for instance, the burning question was whether the governor should receive a fixed salary (1745–1755). The members of the assembly objected, for they feared that the governor might thus become independent of the people. They believed a fixed salary would be in the nature of a tax by the crown, and, true to the instincts of their forefathers, they declared that no taxes should be levied without the consent of the people. In all the proprietary and royal colonies, long and bitter conflicts were waged over raising money for public defence, especially during the Intercolonial Wars (1689–1763). As the real source of power in any government is the authority that lays the taxes, the assemblies usually came out ahead.

Struggle between the royal and proprietary governors and the assemblies.

No taxation without representation.

The results were twofold: (1) The people received valuable political training, and (2) they learned that they had a common interest in contending against the personal rule of the king of England. The attempt to enforce personal rule, or royal prerogative, as it was called, is most familiar in the case of Berkeley in Virginia and Andros in Massachusetts, who did much to arouse the spirit of opposition in the two leading colonies. These colonies were afterward the first to break out in open rebellion against English authority.

Two results of the struggle.

112. Need of Union Among the Colonies.—The great need of the thirteen colonies was union. We have seen how the feeling of common danger from Indian Wars, and later from the various wars with the French. drew the colonists together. The common grievances of the assemblies against their royal and proprietary governors united the people still more closely, when the latter realized that their liberties were endangered by the British crown.

The royal governors appreciated the need of union, and they naturally sought the advantage of the crown. They urged union as a means of checking the people's power. As representatives of the king they wished (1) to get control of colonial trade, and (2) to take the right of taxation out of the hands of the colonial assemblies. For the people, under the various colonial governments, had acquired much more power

Why the royal governors wished union.

than the king wished them to have. For instance, the different assemblies, in their narrow, provincial spirit, would not act together, and were slow to enlist soldiers, build forts, or send armies into the field, where their own territory was in no danger of attack. As a result, there was little united effort to ward off a great danger such as threatened the colonies in the Last French War and in Pontiac's conspiracy. This lack of union ex-

Weakness from lack of union.

Poor Richard, 1733.

A N

Almanack

For the Year of Christ

1 7 3 3,

Being the First after I EAP YEAR:

And makes since the Creation   Years
By the Account of the E stern Greeks   7241
By the Latin Church, when ☉ ent ♈   6932
By the Computation of W W·   5742
By the Roman Chronology   5682
By the Jewish Rabbies   5494

Wherein is contained

The Lunations, Eclipses, Judgment of the Weather, Spring Tides, Planets Motions & mutual Aspects, Sun and Moon's Rising and Setting, Length of Days, Time of High Water, Fairs, Courts, and observable Days

Fitted to the Latitude of Forty Degrees, and a Meridian of Five Hours West from London, but may without sensible Error serve all the adjacent Places, even from Newfoundland to South-Carolina.

By RICHARD SAUNDERS, Philom.

PHILADELPHIA:
Printed and sold by B FRANKLIN. at the New Printing Office near the Market

TITLE PAGE OF " POOR RICHARD'S ALMANAC."

plains the purpose of James II. in appointing Andros governor of New England, New York, and New Jersey. He supposed he would strengthen the Northern colonies by uniting them under one government that could act with energy and promptness, but, as we have seen, he failed.

The colonies sought union, in so far as they sought it at all, for an entirely different purpose—to ward off the offensive restrictions and impositions of England and to extend and increase the rights of the people.   **Why the colonies sought union.**

From the beginning of the English settlements in America, a democratic spirit was developed by the situation and life of the colonists. But Benjamin Franklin[1] saw that something more than a spirit of democracy or self-government was needed to make a strong people. He saw that they needed a central authority to lay taxes for their mutual defence. Clearly understanding this need, Franklin proposed his famous Plan of Union at the Albany Convention[2] (1754). According to this plan each colony was to elect representatives to a Grand Council, similar to our present National Congress. This Grand Council was to have the power of levying taxes upon the people for raising and maintaining armies and otherwise providing for the defence of the colonies. Moreover, like our present Congress, this Council was to exercise supreme   **Franklin's Plan of Union.**

[1] Benjamin Franklin was born in Boston in 1706 and died in 1790. His father, a soap-boiler and tallow-chandler, had seventeen children, of whom Benjamin was the youngest son. At ten years of age the lad was set to work in his father's shop, but was dissatisfied with the business. Then he tried printing with his brother, but suffered from harsh treatment. Finally, at the age of seventeen he ran away from home to seek his fortune. One Sunday morning he landed in Philadelphia, cold and friendless, and with only a single dollar in his pocket.

In 1732 he began to publish Poor Richard's Almanac, which he continued to publish for twenty years. Full of witty maxims which people could apply with profit to every-day living, it became extremely popular and had an immense sale. Franklin became rich and devoted himself to science. By simple experimenting with a kite, he discovered that lightning is nothing more than discharges of electricity. He invented a kind of open stove which is in use at the present time. At the close of the Revolution he was associated with John Adams and John Jay in securing a treaty of peace with England.

[2] Only seven colonies were represented. This Convention was called to form a closer alliance with the Six Nations.

authority in questions affecting all the colonies alike. This was known as the Albany Plan of Union.

The king of England did not like it, because he feared it might encourage the colonies to form a union in which the people would exercise too much power. The colonists did not like it[1] because they were unwilling to give up **Reasons for its failure.** the right of taxation by their colonial assemblies. Franklin's Plan of Union failed, but it was of great value because it led the people to think seriously about the advantages of union.

TO THE PUPIL

1. How did the Council differ from the Assembly?
2. What were the three political groups of colonies? What was the distinguishing feature of each group?
3. Discuss the nature of the struggle between the various assemblies on the one side and the loyal and proprietary governors on the other. What were the results? In this connection, review the struggle between Governor Berkeley and the people of Virginia and that between Governor Andros and the people of New England. If you get clear ideas about these struggles, you will better understand the causes of the Revolution.
4. Why was there need of union among the colonies? What attempts at union had been made? Why did the royal governors wish union among the colonies? On what grounds did the colonies seek union? What was Franklin's Plan of Union? Why did it fail and what were its results?

CHRONOLOGY

1524. FRENCH EXPEDITION TO AMERICA UNDER VERRAZANO.
1528. PAMPHILO DE NARVAEZ LANDS IN FLORIDA.
1531-33. PIZARRO CONQUERS PERU.
1534. CARTIER SAILS TO THE GULF OF ST. LAWRENCE.
1539. DE SOTO LANDS IN FLORIDA.
1540. CORONADO'S EXPEDITION IN SEARCH OF CIBOLA.
1541. DE SOTO DISCOVERS THE MISSISSIPPI RIVER.
1562. COLIGNY'S FIRST COLONY SENT TO FLORIDA UNDER RIBAULT.
1565. FOUNDING OF ST. AUGUSTINE.
1576. MARTIN FROBISHER DISCOVERS THE STRAIT SINCE CALLED BY HIS NAME.
1579. DRAKE ON THE CALIFORNIA COAST.

[1] The plan was presented to the several legislatures, and they all rejected it because they did not strongly feel the need of union.

1584. SIR WALTER RALEIGH'S FIRST EXPEDITION.

1585. RALEIGH'S FIRST COLONY.

1587. RALEIGH'S SECOND COLONY.

1603. FIRST VOYAGE OF SAMUEL DE CHAMPLAIN TO AMERICA.

1606. PATENT GRANTED TO THE VIRGINIA COMPANIES.

1607. FIRST PERMANENT SETTLEMENT OF VIRGINIA AT JAMESTOWN.

1608. FOUNDING OF QUEBEC BY SAMUEL DE CHAMPLAIN.

1609. THE DISCOVERY OF LAKE CHAMPLAIN.

HENRY HUDSON DISCOVERS THE HUDSON RIVER.

1611. SIR THOMAS DALE, GOVERNOR OF VIRGINIA.

1619. FIRST CARGO OF SLAVES BROUGHT TO JAMESTOWN.

FIRST LEGISLATIVE ASSEMBLY OF VIRGINIA MEETS IN JAMESTOWN.

1620. THE PILGRIMS LAND AT PLYMOUTH.

1623. SETTLEMENT OF NEW HAMPSHIRE AT PORTSMOUTH AND DOVER.

1630. SETTLEMENT OF BOSTON AND NEIGHBORING TOWNS.

1634. SETTLEMENT OF MARYLAND.

1635. PERMANENT SETTLEMENT OF CONNECTICUT BY EMIGRANTS FROM MASSACHU-
SETTS BAY.

1636. PROVIDENCE FOUNDED BY ROGER WILLIAMS.

1637. THE PEQUOT WAR.

1643. THE CONFEDERATION OF NEW ENGLAND COLONIES FORMED.

1663. CHARTER OF RHODE ISLAND AND PROVIDENCE PLANTATIONS GRANTED BY
CHARLES II.

FIRST GRANT OF CAROLINA.

1664. GRANT OF NEW NETHERLAND TO THE DUKE OF YORK, AND ITS SURRENDER
TO THE ENGLISH.—NAMED NEW YORK.

GOVERNMENT OF NORTH CAROLINA ESTABLISHED.

GRANT OF NEW JERSEY TO BERKELEY AND CARTERET.

1665. SECOND GRANT OF CAROLINA.

ARRIVAL OF PHILIP CARTERET AS GOVERNOR OF NEW JERSEY.—ELIZABETH
FOUNDED.

1673. MARQUETTE EXPLORES THE MISSISSIPPI.

1675. OUTBREAK OF KING PHILIP'S WAR IN NEW ENGLAND.

1676. BACON'S REBELLION IN VIRGINIA.

1679. NEW HAMPSHIRE MADE AN INDEPENDENT ROYAL PROVINCE.

1680. HENNEPIN'S VOYAGE ON THE MISSISSIPPI.

1681. THE GRANT OF PENNSYLVANIA SIGNED.—EMIGRATION BEGUN.

1682. THE FRIENDS BUY EAST JERSEY.

PENN SAILS FOR AMERICA.

PHILADELPHIA FOUNDED.

PENN'S INDIAN TREATY.

LA SALLE'S VOYAGE ON THE MISSISSIPPI.

1685. LA SALLE'S COLONY FOUNDED IN TEXAS.

1686. ANDROS GOVERNOR-GENERAL OF NEW ENGLAND.

1687. ANDROS ATTEMPTS TO SEIZE THE CONNECTICUT CHARTER.

1689. ARREST OF ANDROS AT BOSTON.

1692. OUTBREAK OF THE WITCHCRAFT PANIC AT SALEM, MASS.

1700. IBERVILLE ESTABLISHES A SETTLEMENT AT POVERTY POINT, LA.

1702. BEGINNING OF QUEEN ANNE'S WAR.

1715. FIVE NATIONS BECOME SIX BY ADDITION OF THE TUSCARORAS.

1733. OGELTHORPE'S COLONY SETTLES IN GEORGIA.

SUGAR AND MOLASSES ACT.

1744. BEGINNING OF KING GEORGE'S WAR.

1745. CAPTURE OF LOUISBURG.
1748. OHIO COMPANY FORMED.
      LOUISBURG RESTORED TO FRANCE.
1754. COLONIAL CONGRESS AT ALBANY, AND FRANKLIN'S PLAN OF UNION.
1755. BRADDOCK'S DEFEAT.
      BANISHMENT OF THE ACADIANS.
1756. FORT OSWEGO SURRENDERED TO THE FRENCH.
      BEGINNING OF THE LAST FRENCH WAR.
1757. MASSACRE OF FORT WILLIAM HENRY.
1758. DEFEAT OF ABERCROMBIE AT FORT TICONDEROGA.
      RECAPTURE OF LOUISBURG.
1759. FORT TICONDEROGA TAKEN BY AMHERST.
      CAPTURE OF FORT NIAGARA BY THE ENGLISH.
      WOLFE CAPTURES QUEBEC.
1761. ATTEMPT TO ENFORCE WRITS OF ASSISTANCE IN MASSACHUSETTS.
1763. PONTIAC'S WAR.
      TREATY OF PARIS.

The Revolution, the Confederation, and the Federal Union

CHAPTER XIII

THE REVOLUTION

REFERENCES: **Scribner's** Popular History of the United States, III. and IV.; **Andrews's** United States, I.; **Fiske's** War of Independence; **Sloane's** French War and the Revolution; **Hart's** Formation of the Union; **Channing's** United States; **Richardson's** History of Our Country; **Coffin's** Boys of '76; **Barnes's** Popular History of the United States; **Cooke's** Stories of the Old Dominion; **Hale's** Stories of Massachusetts.

OUTSIDE READINGS: **Trevelyan's** The American Revolution; **Winsor's** Narrative and Critical History, VI. and VII.; **Bancroft's** United States, III.; **Fiske's** American Revolution; **Hildreth's** United States, II. and III.; **Lossing's** Field Book of the Revolution; **Lecky's** England in the Eighteenth Century, III.; **Wilson's** History of the American People, II.; **Frothingham's** Rise of the Republic; **Goldwin Smith's** United States; **Morris's** Half Hours with American History, II.; **Hale's** Franklin in France; **Hart's** Camps and Firesides of the Revolution; **Roosevelt's** Winning the West, I. and II.; **Greene's** Historical View of the American Revolution; **Hinsdale's** Old Northwest; **Green's** History of the English People, IV.; **Drake's** Burgoyne's Invasion; **Abbot's** Blue Jackets of '76; **Brown's** Mercy Warren; **Wharton's** Martha Washington; **Hosmer's** Samuel Adams; **Henry's** Patrick Henry; **Morse's** John Adams; **Scudder's** George Washington; **Hale's** George Washington; **Abbot's** Paul Jones; **Spark's** Life of Arnold; **Arnold's** Life of Arnold; **Lossing's** Two Spies; **Spear's** The History of Our Navy; **Ford's** The True Benjamin Franklin; **Thwaites's** Daniel Boone; **Greene's** General Greene; **Brady's** Commodore Paul Jones; **Wilson's** George Washington; **Ford's** The True George Washington.

FICTION: **Cooper's** Lionel Lincoln; **Henty's** True to the Old Flag; **Cooper's** Spy; **Harte's** Thankful Blossom; **Cooper's** Pilot; **Simms's** Partisan; **Mitchell's** Hugh Wynne; **Brady's** For Love of Country; **Churchill's** Richard Carvel; **Thompson's** Alice of Old Vincennes; **Comfort's** Arnold's Tempter.

POETRY: **Holmes's** Grandmother's Story of Bunker Hill Battle; Independence Bell; **Bryant's** Seventy-six; **Bryant's** Song of Marion's Men.

The Causes of the Revolution

113. England Tries to Control American Commerce.— In the seventeenth and eighteenth centuries European countries planted colonies as a means of increasing their own trade. In accordance with this theory, England valued her American colonies according to the wealth she gained from them. To secure control of colonial trade, therefore, Parliament began in 1651, thirty-one years after the landing of the Pilgrims, to pass the famous Navigation **The Navigation Laws and Acts of Trade.** Laws and Acts of Trade. These laws required (1) that all trade between the colonies should be carried on in ships built in England or in the colonies; (2) that the colonies should not export such colonial products as sugar, tobacco, iron, furs and lumber to any part of the world except England, or

JOHN HANCOCK HOUSE, BOSTON, MASS.

some English colony; (3) that all European goods should be bought in England and brought over to the colonies on English vessels; (4) that the colonies should not manufacture any article that could be manufactured in England.

The carrying out of these laws would injure the colonists in the following ways: **These laws injure the colonies in four ways.** (1) A profitable trade with the Dutch would be cut off at a single stroke; (2) whatever colonial products the English manufacturer needed he could buy of the colonies at his own price; (3) as the colonists were compelled to buy European goods in England, they had to pay whatever English merchants charged, or not buy at all ; (4) while the law providing that all European goods should be imported in English ships would put money into the pockets of the English ship-owner, it would almost ruin the ship-building industry in the colonies and throw thousands of sailors out of employment.

114. The Sugar Act and Smuggling.—In 1733 the famous Sugar Act was passed to protect the English West India sugar islands. By this act a prohibitory duty was laid upon the sugar and molasses imported into the colonies from the French islands in the West Indies. The principal exports of New England were lumber and fish. The inferior qualities of fish were carried to the French islands and exchanged with profit for sugar and molasses. There was thus a double advantage to New England

JAMES OTIS.

in this trade : (1) The French would buy fish which were not salable elsewhere ; (2) they were willing to sell at a low price their sugar and molasses. On the other hand, the New Englanders made the sugar and molasses into rum, part of which they consumed *Advantages of trading with the French West Indies.* at home, and the remainder they took to Africa, where they exchanged it for slaves to be sold to the Southern colonies. All this trade was extremely profitable for New England, and was one of the principal sources of wealth. New England merchants saw that if the Sugar Act should be enforced the profits of their West India trade must be greatly diminished. Financial ruin *Smuggling or financial ruin.* threatened them. They had to choose between that and smuggling. They chose smuggling, because they believed the law was an unjust interference with the natural rights of free-born Englishmen.

115. James Otis Defends New England Merchants against Writs of Assistance.—As long as England allowed this smuggling to go on, all went well with the colonies. But after the Last French War the English Government decided to put a stop to this contraband trade. England was greatly in debt. Money had to be raised, and it was thought that by enforcing the Navigation and Trade Laws the profits of colonial trade would be turned over to English merchants.

A ROYAL STAMP.

Legal papers called Writs of Assistance were issued (1761). They were general search-warrants, which empowered officers to go into any warehouse or private dwelling in search of contraband goods. With these odious papers in hand, custom-house officers could at any time enter a warehouse or a private dwelling, and ransack it from garret to cellar. In this way many thousand dollars' worth of goods were seized and confiscated.

England issues Writs of Assistance.

The people were furious. James Otis, of Massachusetts, defended the colonial merchants in a test case. He made a great speech, in which he earnestly contended that the colonists were not bound to obey any law not made by their own representatives. The keynote of his speech was "Taxation without representation is tyranny," and it sounded from Massachusetts to Georgia.

Otis declares that "Taxation without representation is tyranny."

116. Parliament Passes the Stamp Act.—We have just seen how England, in protecting her merchants, shipowners, and manufacturers, had indirectly [1] taxed the colonies. In thus taxing them England regarded the colonies as trading companies whose main purpose, from her standpoint,

[1] A tax levied directly on a person or property is a direct tax. One levied on trade is an indirect tax. When a man pays a tax on his house, his horse and carriage, or any other form of property, he pays a direct tax. When a merchant imports goods upon which a duty has been laid by the government, he pays this duty to the government through the custom-house. Such a duty is called an indirect tax. The taxes for the support of our national government are usually indirect.

was to enrich the mother-country. The colonies had submitted to such indirect taxation of their trade The colonies sub-
and industries because (1) it was usual, the mit to indirect
world over, for colonies to have their trade taxation for three reasons.
thus taxed by their mother-country; (2) the English navy
protected the commerce of the colo-
nies; and (3) the Trade Laws were
not strictly enforced.

But in 1764 the English Government decided to levy a *direct* tax upon
them. As we have seen, England, by
reason of the expensive Intercolonial
Wars (1689–1763), was greatly in debt.
The king's representative in the min-
istry, Lord Grenville, maintained that this debt was
incurred in the defence of
the colonies. He said that
it was now time that the
colonies should pay their
share of their defence.
Grenville seemed to forget
that the colonies *had* paid
their share and were themselves heavily in debt. He
seemed to forget, also, that
all these wars were fought
quite as much to protect

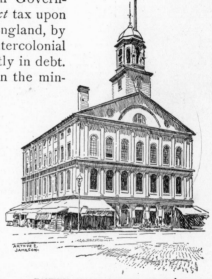

FANEUIL HALL, BOSTON, MASS.[1]

the English trade as to defend the colonies. Now that the
French were driven out, a standing army of from 10,000 to
20,000 men was to be kept up in America for the The colonies to be
purpose, among other things, of protecting the required to help
colonies from the Indians. A standing army, to maintain a standing army
it was argued, would prevent a repetition of an in America.
Indian uprising such as Pontiac's conspiracy. Moreover, if
such a permanent standing army was to be maintained in

[1] Faneuil Hall was built in 1742 by a Boston merchant named Peter Faneuil
and presented by him to the town of Boston. The first floor was to be used as a

the colonies for their defence, it seemed fair to Grenville
and to the king that the colonies should share in the
expense.

During the Intercolonial Wars the various colonies paid
Colonies slow in paying taxes during the Intercolonial Wars. their share of expense by raising money in
response to requisition made by the king's
agents. But they were very slow about it.
It was difficult to get any legislature to vote money for

soldiers and supplies
unless the danger
threatened its own
colony. Such a sys-
tem was weak and
lame, and it prevented
prompt and united
action. Some more
effective plan of taxa-
tion seemed not only
desirable but impera-
tive. The Stamp Act
offered such a scheme,
and it became a law in
March,[1] 1765.

**117. How the
Stamp Act Was Re-
ceived in America.—**
This act required the

OLD STATE HOUSE, BOSTON, MASS.

colonies to use stamped paper for newspapers, almanacs,
The Stamp Act. pamphlets, advertisements, and all kinds of
legal documents. These stamps cost all the
way from six cents to thirty dollars each. Grenville

market house ; the second as a town hall. Just before the Revolution, so many
public meetings were held in Faneuil Hall that it was called "The Cradle of
Liberty." In "The Cradle of Liberty" the people met, day after day, in 1773
(see par. 127) to decide upon some plan of action about the tea in Boston Harbor.
The last of these meetings was so large that it had to be held in the Old South Church.

[1] It is certain that up to this time, as later during the Revolution (1775–1783),
and the critical period (1783–1789), the American people suffered greatly for lack of
some central taxing power. England's purpose was to supply this lack by a system
of direct taxation furnished in the Stamp Act.

thought this tax would be fair because it would fall upon all alike.

But he found that the Stamp Act aroused a storm of angry opposition throughout the colonies.[1] Organizations called "Sons of Liberty" were formed. Merchants banded together to import no more goods from England until the Stamp Act should be repealed. *Its effects upon the colonists.* They urged the necessity of manufacturing in the colonies. They decided to stop eating mutton, that they might have more wool for making cloth. The day the Stamp Act went into effect was made a day of mourning.[2] Bells tolled, flags were lowered, and business houses were closed to indicate that liberty was dead.

PATRICK HENRY.

118. Patrick Henry Introduces the Virginia Resolutions. —In May the Virginia Legislature met at Williamsburg. It included the most eminent men of Virginia, and they were anxious to act wisely. In the midst of the general doubt and perplexity, Patrick Henry[3] arose and introduced his famous resolutions. In these he declared that the "General Assembly

---

[1] At Portsmouth, New Hampshire, the people bore to an open grave a coffin with this inscription: "Liberty, aged CXLV years." The solemn procession marched to the beating of muffled drums. On reaching the grave the people listened to a funeral oration over Liberty, which was supposed to be lying dead, but just as they were lowering the coffin some one cried, "There are signs of life!" The coffin was eagerly raised, and "Liberty Revived" was inscribed upon it. At once the people shouted themselves hoarse because Liberty was once more alive.

[2] The brave women did their share, also. They formed organizations called "Daughters of Liberty," and agreed to buy no more goods imported from England. They formed "Spinning Societies," and wove cloth for the men to wear.

[3] He was at this time just twenty-nine, tall in figure, but stooping, with a grim expression, small, blue eyes which had a peculiar twinkle, and wore a brown wig without powder, a "peach-blossom coat," leather knee-breeches, and yarn stockings. He had ridden to Williamsburg on "a lean horse," and carried his papers in

of the colony had the sole right and power of laying taxes
in the colony." An exciting debate followed. George

Patrick Henry's famous resolutions

Washington was present, and Thomas Jefferson stood at the door earnestly listening.
He tells us later that the discussion was
"most bloody." The opposition only fired the passion of
Henry, and in a burst of wrathful eloquence he ended

and speech.

his speech in words never to be forgotten:
"Cæsar had his Brutus, Charles the First
his Cromwell, and George the Third" — "Treason!
Treason!" wildly shouted some of the members. The
orator paused a moment and then calmly added, " may
profit by their example. If this be treason, make the most
of it." The excitement caused by this speech travelled like
wildfire through the colonies. Massachusetts and Virginia
had declared themselves and were ready to join hands in
open resistance.

119. The Stamp Act Congress (1765).—The English
Government made a great mistake in passing the Stamp

England's mistake in passing the Stamp Act.

Act. The enforcement of the Sugar Act
affected the Middle and Southern colonies so
little that they doubtless would not have joined
New England in resistance to Parliament on this issue alone.
But in the Stamp Act a grievance was presented which
affected all the colonies alike. It furnished them a common
ground for resistance and a common purpose for united
action. Accordingly, the passing of the Stamp Act had a
most important and significant result in strengthening the
union of the colonies. In June Massachusetts sent out a
call for a general congress to discuss the situation and agree
upon some plan of action. Representatives from nine of
the colonies met at New York in October and passed resolutions similar to those of Virginia. They sent a memorial
to the king acknowledging his sovereignty, and a remon-
strance to Parliament declaring it had no right to tax

a pair of saddle-bags. . . . As Henry came out of the Capitol a man of the
crowd slapped him on the shoulder and cried:
"Stick to us, old fellow, or we are gone."—COOKE'S VIRGINIA.

them. This congress should have been a warning to George III.

120. Repeal of the Stamp Act (1766).—But the most effective action of the colonists was their non-importation agreements. One-third of England's trade was with the colonies. In 1772 it amounted to $30,000,000. Non-importation, therefore, *Effect of non-importation upon English merchants.* caused a serious loss to English merchants, and they eagerly begged Parliament to repeal the Stamp Act. The debate

THE " BOSTON MASSACRE."

After an engraving by Paul Revere.

in Parliament over the repeal showed that many English statesmen stoutly defended the colonies in their opposition to the direct taxation without representation. Said William Pitt in a stirring speech in the House of Commons: "Sir, I rejoice that America has resisted! Three millions of people so dead to all the *William Pitt opposes the Stamp Act.* feelings of liberty as voluntarily to submit to be slaves would have been fit instruments to make slaves of all the rest." Parliament voted to repeal the act, but declared its *right* to *bind* the colonies in all cases. It was this very *right* to tax an unrepresented people that the colonies called in question.

121. Taxation Without Representation in America.— The colonists claimed that as freeborn Englishmen in America they had, granted to them in their charters, the same rights and privileges as freeborn Englishmen in the mother-country. The only difference between the man of Kent (England) and the man of Massachusetts was in the authority that taxed him. The government in Kent consisted of the king and Parliament; the government in Massachusetts of the king and the colonial assembly. The king could exercise no more power in Massachusetts than in Kent, while the taxing power in Kent was Parliament and in Massachusetts was the colonial assembly. This was the position taken by the Whig[1] party in America, not by all the colonists.

122. Taxation Without Representation in England.— We cannot understand the real meaning of the Revolution in America without looking into a similar struggle that was at the same time going on in England. Some Americans did not oppose England and some Englishmen did not join hands against America. It was in each country the same kind of struggle—a struggle between hostile principles. There was taxation without representation in England as well as in America, and many Englishmen, like William Pitt, were as much opposed to it there as men like Samuel Adams and Patrick Henry were opposed to it in America. William Pitt and his followers represented the true feeling of the English people toward America.

At this time Parliament did not fairly represent the people of England. Great towns like Manchester, Liverpool, Birmingham, and Leeds were not represented at all, and members were returned for boroughs that had no existence except in name. Such boroughs were called rotten boroughs, or pocket boroughs,

The English people not fairly represented in Parliament.

---

[1] The Whigs were those who opposed the king's schemes of taxing the Americans without their consent. The supporters of the king, who at this time included a large part of the American people, were called Loyalists, or Tories.

which were owned by the great families. Long after Old Sarum, a noted rotten borough, had no population, a member, representing its owner, was returned to the House of Commons. In a population of 8,000,000 only about 160,-000, or one-tenth of the men of voting age in England, could vote.[1] A few great families controlled the House of Commons. Certainly the mass of Englishmen could justly complain of taxation without representation. Among them was the great William Pitt, who urged upon the people the justice of parliamentary reform, with a fair and full representation of the English people in the House of Commons.

OLD SOUTH CHURCH, BOSTON.

123. George III. and Personal Government.— "George, be King," said George the Third's mother when he was crowned. That advice pleased the young ruler, who was then only twenty-two years old. His controlling purpose was to establish personal government in England. His desire for arbitrary power, together with his narrowness and bigotry, had much influence in bringing on the Rev- **The views of** olution. He cared little for the rights of **George III.** the people. The more power they had the less he would enjoy. By the corrupt use of money he succeeded in con-

---

[1] In our own country the people are fairly and equally represented in the national House of Representatives. The unit of representation, or the number of people entitled to one representative since the last census of 1900, has been 194,182. This means that the number of representatives in Congress from any State may be found by dividing its population by 194,182. For example, Pennsylvania has 32

trolling the elections. His desire was to make Parliament
represent him and a few great families that were in the
political ring with him. He maintained his influence largely through boss-like methods, keeping his followers under
control by the use of an immense corruption fund. As long
as a large number of small boroughs remained under the
control of his friends, the king could maintain his tyrannical
hold upon the government.

But if the Americans should succeed in their struggle
for "No taxation without representation," there was little
doubt that in time Englishmen would succeed in a similar

**Why the king
wished to tax the
Americans.**
struggle for parliamentary reform, or "No
taxation without representation" in England.
If the Americans were not repressed, their
success would make certain the failure of the king's pet
scheme of personal government. King George, therefore,
was deeply chagrined when the Stamp Act was repealed.
He could not let the matter rest here, however, but the
next year (1767) he again tried to force new taxes upon
America. We shall see how well he succeeded.

124. The New Taxes of 1767.—In 1767 Townshend,
acting as the king's tool, induced Parliament to levy new
port duties on a few articles, including glass, lead, paper,
and tea. The colonies had objected to a stamp tax because
it was a direct tax. As these new taxes were indirect,
Townshend and King George thought the Americans might
not refuse to pay them. But in this they wholly misunder-
stood the temper and feeling of the American people. The
new taxes were opposed quite as violently as the Stamp Act
had been.

We can easily understand the feelings of the colonists
when we see the purpose of the taxes. The Sugar Act

**Purpose of the
new taxes.**
(see par. 114) was to be strictly enforced by
commissioners who were to use the hated
Writs of Assistance in searching for smuggled goods. The
money raised by these taxes was to be used not only to pay

representatives and Delaware but one. But every State, large or small, has two
members in the Senate.

ST. JOHN'S CHURCH, RICHMOND, VA.

Where the famous orator Patrick Henry made his great speech.

the colonial governors, judges, and crown attorneys, and thus make all these officials independent of the people, but also to maintain a small English army in the colonies. The remainder, if there should be any, was to be used in pensioning men of influence. This last was in reality a corruption fund to bribe men to become the king's tools. Thus we see that the colonists themselves were to pay the taxes which should keep their governors and judges independent of them.

When we recall the bitter struggle between the people and the royal governors over this question of allowing a fixed salary, we can easily realize why this **Bitter opposition** measure was so unpopular. Then, too, in pay-**to the new taxes.** ing this tax the people were supporting a standing army whose presence was plainly intended to enforce the personal rule of the king. In a word, the people were to pay taxes whose real purpose was to deprive them of the rights of freeborn citizens.

Massachusetts led in the opposition. She sent a circular letter to the other colonies for the purpose of securing some united plan of action against the Townshend Acts.

Results. The result was that the colonies again agreed to import no more goods from England, and they thus greatly injured English ship-owners and merchants. In the next two years English imports to New England fell off one-half, and to New York five-sixths.

125. **The Redcoats[1] and the "Boston Massacre"** (1770).—King George at length decided to send troops to America to enforce the revenue laws. In the autumn of 1768 they arrived in Boston. Their presence was regarded as a menace and was a constant source of annoyance. Quarrels between them and the people were of frequent occurrence ; and finally one evening in March, 1770, the crisis came in a disturbance which took place in State Street in front of what was then the Custom House but is now the old State House. The soldiers fired upon the people, killing three and wounding many others. This was called the "Boston Massacre." The next day an immense town meeting was held, and the people, through Samuel Adams as spokesman, demanded that the troops should be removed. They were withdrawn to an island in the harbor.

126. **Committees of Correspondence (1772-1773).**—The need of united action among the towns of Massachusetts was now pressing. It was hard to tell what new danger might at any hour fall upon the people. So Samuel Adams proposed, in town meeting, that committees of correspondence should be appointed in the towns. His plan was carried out (1772). In the following year Dabney Carr of Virginia suggested committees of correspondence for the various colonies. When these committees were organized the colonies rapidly drew closer and closer together in their sympathies. This was a bold step, which led later, as we shall see, to the Continental Congress and open war.

[1] The English soldiers wore red uniforms. They were therefore called Redcoats.

THE FIGHT ON LEXINGTON COMMON, APRIL 19, 1775.

127. Samuel Adams[1] and the "Boston Tea Party" (1773).—The new duties were no more successful than the Stamp Act had been, for again colonial merchants refused to import English goods. Again English merchants begged for a repeal. But the stupid king could not understand the Americans. Thus far he had failed. He now resorted to a trick by which he hoped to induce the colonists to pay a small tax levied by Parliament. He took off all the new taxes except the one on tea. "There must be one tax to keep the right to tax," he said. The tax on tea was to be only threepence a pound in America, instead of sixpence, as in England. This not only enabled the colonists to buy tea cheaper than it could be bought by the people in England, but also cheaper than it could be bought when the colonists smuggled it from Holland. But still they refused to import the taxed tea.

George Third's trick in levying the tax on tea.

The East India Company decided to ship cargoes to such important ports as Boston, New York, Philadelphia, and Charleston. When the tea arrived the people in New York and Philadelphia refused to let it land, and the people in Charleston stored it in damp cellars where it spoiled. In Boston the people were determined to send it back, but Governor Hutchinson refused to let this be done. For nineteen days the struggle continued. On the nineteenth day the excitement in Boston was intense. If the cargo of tea should remain in the harbor till the twentieth day the law permitted it to be landed. All day long the town meeting continued in Boston. Seven thousand men crowded the Old South Church[2] and the streets outside.

Taxed tea sent to America.

[1] Samuel Adams has been called the "Father of the Revolution." He was distinguished for his courage and perseverance and for his ability as a leader of men. Like Jefferson, he was full of sympathy for the toiling masses and easily won their confidence. In 1774 General Gage offered him money and official advancement if he would give his influence and services to the king. Although Samuel Adams was poor, yet true to himself and to his countrymen, he scorned the offer. He was the first American to advocate independence of England, and was one of the foremost leaders that prepared the people to adopt the Declaration of Independence.

[2] The Old South Church is still standing on Washington Street, at the corner of Milk Street.

At nightfall a messenger brought word from the governor that he would not permit the tea to be returned to **The "Boston Tea Party."** England. At once Samuel Adams, moderator of the meeting, arose and said: "This meeting can do nothing more to save the country." As if this were the signal, a warwhoop was heard, and forty or fifty men,

OLD NORTH CHURCH,
BOSTON, MASS.

disguised as Indians, proceeded down the street toward Griffin's Wharf.[1] Boarding the tea-ships they ripped open every chest and spilled the tea into the harbor. A large party of people stood by while the "Indians" were emptying the chests, but everyone was quiet and orderly. This was the famous "Boston Tea Party," at which some of the best people of Boston were present (1773).

128. Boston Punished for its Tea Party.—King George was very angry at these high-handed proceedings. In order to punish the Boston people for what they had done, Parliament passed the Boston Port Bill, which closed the port of Boston to all trade until the town should pay for the tea that had been destroyed. Another law, known as the Massachusetts Act, annulled the charter and took away free government from the people. A military governor, General Gage, like the Stuart governor, Andros, was appointed to stand for the tyranny of an arbitrary king. Surely George III. and his followers little realized the love of self-government in these stubborn, unruly colonists!

129. The Colonies Unite in Support of Massachusetts.—The English Government determined to make an example of Boston, and hoped in this way to frighten the

[1] A tablet on Atlantic Avenue now marks the spot where the Tea Party reached the wharf.

THE RETREAT FROM CONCORD.

other colonies into submission. Contrary to the expectation of the Government, the effect of the oppressive measures was to unite the colonies in sympathetic support of the Massachusetts people. Through the committees of correspondence the colonies could now act together more promptly than ever before. Provisions were sent from every direction to the suffering people in Boston. Help came from even the far-away Carolinas. Patrick Henry[1] angrily cried : " We must fight. I repeat it, sir; we must fight. I know not what course **"We must fight."** others may take, but as for me, give me liberty or give me death."

The excitement was everywhere intense. United action was a necessity. The Continental Congress, meeting in Carpenters' Hall, Philadelphia, was the out- **The Continental Congress.** come (September 5, 1774). All the colonies except Georgia[2] were represented. This Congress declared the colonies had a right to govern themselves and levy their own taxes. It further declared that, should England attempt to force Massachusetts to submission, the other colonies would join Massachusetts in forcible resistance.

TO THE PUPIL

1. Name four requirements of the Navigation Laws and the Acts of Trade. In what four ways did these laws injure the colonists?
2. What advantages did New England merchants have in trading with the French islands in the West Indies? Do you think these merchants were right in smuggling? Give reasons for your answer. How were the Writs of Assistance connected with smuggling?
3. What is the difference between a direct and an indirect tax? Why had the colonies submitted to indirect taxation?
4. What was the object of the English Government in levying the stamp tax? From the English stand-point, give reasons why it was just that such a tax should be imposed upon the Americans.

[1] This great speech by the famous orator of the Revolution was made in "Old St. John's Church," Richmond, Va. This church is still standing.

[2] Georgia people were in sympathy with the Congress, but her royal governor prevented the appointment of delegates.

5. Subject for debate: Resolved that England had the right to levy the stamp tax upon the colonies.

6. What colonies did the Sugar Act of 1733 affect most seriously? What colonies did the Stamp Act affect? How, then, did the English Government make a great mistake in passing the Stamp Act?

7. Why did England repeal the Stamp Act?

8. What did James Otis mean by saying that "taxation without representation is tyranny"? In what way did Otis and those agreeing with him think that direct taxes should be levied in America? Was Otis right in his views of taxation? Give reasons for your answer.

9. Why were William Pitt and his followers in England opposed to the Stamp Act? Do you see clearly what was meant by taxation without representation in England?

10. What were King George's ideas of government for both England and America? If a man like William Pitt had been king of England, do you think there would have been any American Revolution? Give reasons for your answer.

11. What was the purpose of the new taxes of 1767? Why were committees of correspondence organized and with what result? Find out all you can about the influence of Samuel Adams in these trying times.

12. What events led to the Boston Tea Party? You can easily trace the connection between the destruction of the tea and the Continental Congress.

13. Make an outline of the topics discussed under the "Causes of the Revolution" and try to discover a causal connection between the events.

14. 1763 and 1775, between which most of these events took place, are well worth remembering.

15. In studying the Revolution, do not fail to read Fiske's War of Independence.

THE WAR BEGINS

130. Battles of Lexington and Concord (April 19, 1775). —General Gage, as military governor of Massachusetts, remained at Boston with 3,000 British troops. But the people outside of Boston refused to recognize his authority, and through their Provincial Congress governed themselves as well as they could. This Congress was a provisional government, organized by the people to take the place of the Colonial Assembly which General Gage had

THE BATTLE OF BUNKER HILL.

dissolved. John Hancock was its president, and Samuel Adams was its leading spirit. It prepared for war. Twenty thousand men were ordered to be ready, at a minute's notice, to march to any point of danger. They were called "minute-men." **The Provincial Congress and the "minute-men."**

In April General Gage received orders from England to arrest John Hancock and Samuel Adams and send them to England to be tried for treason. About the same time the governor heard that the minute-men had collected some military stores at Concord, twenty miles from Boston. As Hancock and Adams were staying with a friend in Lexington, Gage decided to send out troops for the purpose of arresting them and at the same time destroying the military stores at Concord. **English troops sent to Lexington and Concord.**

BOSTON and Vicinity.
Scale of Miles.
THE M.-N. CO.

About midnight eight hundred English soldiers started from Boston. But the minute-men were on the watch. Dr. Joseph Warren[1] sent Paul Revere and William Dawes[2] to warn his two friends and to spread the alarm, "The regulars are coming!"

[1] Dr. Joseph Warren was a prominent patriot leader and a warm friend of Samuel Adams. Referring to the British soldiers he said: "Those fellows say we won't fight. By heavens, I hope I shall die up to my knees in blood." He was killed at Bunker Hill.

[2] William Dawes rode on horseback by way of Roxbury. Paul Revere went over from Boston to Charlestown in a boat and there awaited a signal which was given by a lantern hung in the belfry of the Old North Church. At eleven o'clock on that beautiful moonlight night he mounted his horse. Speeding his way through Medford he barely escaped capture by some British officers. From Lexington, where his warning saved Hancock and Adams from capture, he pressed on toward Concord, in company with Dr. Samuel Prescott and William Dawes. Between

Early next morning (April 19, 1775), when the English troops reached Lexington, Hancock and Adams had made their escape, and a party of minute-men were drawn up on Lexington Common. Soon the English fired upon them, killing seven of their number, and then passed on to Concord. Here they destroyed the small part of the military

THE WASHINGTON ELM AT CAMBRIDGE.

stores which the Americans had not had time to conceal. Again they found minute-men, in ever-increasing numbers, **The fight at Concord Bridge.** angrily facing them. At the old Concord Bridge the fight began in earnest, and men fell on each side. From every direction the minute-men came flocking in, and the English were forced to retreat, loading and firing as they marched.

Lexington and Concord some British officers captured Dawes and Revere, took them back to Lexington, and there released them. Paul Revere's ride is graphically described in Longfellow's famous poem, but some of the details are not historically accurate.

From behind rocks and trees, fences and barns, the minute-men shot the tired soldiers. On the English soldiers pushed, but they had to leave the dead and dying scattered along the road. At Lexington they met reinforcements sent from Boston. But for these fresh troops all of the eight hundred men sent out to Concord would **Retreat of the** have been captured. As it was, the whole **English to Boston.** force of about 2,000 men fled in confusion from Lexington to Boston, barely saving themselves from capture. The British lost about three hundred men; the Americans about one hundred. The British were glad to find shelter in Boston, around which in a few days were gathered 16,000 Americans. It was a good beginning for the patriot army.

131. The Colonies Unite for Resistance.—On May 10 (1775) there was a second meeting of the Continental Congress at Philadelphia. John Hancock, of Massachusetts, was chosen president. The colonies voted to **The second meet-** unite in resisting England, and for that pur- **ing of the Conti-** pose to raise an army of 20,000 men, whose **nental Congress.** expenses were to be paid by the united colonies. George Washington was appointed commander-in-chief of the Continental army.

While Congress was passing these war measures New England was actually engaged in pushing the war. Sixteen thousand yeoman troops were already besieging Boston, and, on the day that Congress met, Ethan Allen from Vermont and Benedict Arnold from Connecticut led a force which surprised and captured Ticonderoga, **Americans capture** thus securing an important fort. Two days **Ticonderoga and** later Crown Point was taken. With these **Crown Point.** forts they secured two hundred and twenty cannon and other military supplies. The Americans now had control of the line of communication between New York and Canada. They vainly hoped Canada would join them in their struggle. In November, 1775, they captured St. John's and Montreal. On December 30th Montgomery and Arnold made a gallant attack upon Quebec but were driven back. Montgomery was killed and Arnold wounded. It was plain that the colonies meant to fight and that the war had already begun.

132. Battle of Bunker Hill (June 17, 1775).—In the meantime the English troops had been increased to 10,000, and Howe had been sent over to take the place of Gage as their commander. The English general saw the importance of occupying the heights in Charlestown known as

THE CRAIGIE HOUSE, WASHINGTON'S HEADQUARTERS AT CAMBRIDGE (AFTERWARD THE RESIDENCE OF LONGFELLOW).

Bunker Hill and Breed's Hill. If the Americans should secure them it would be very difficult for the British troops

The Americans fortify Breed's Hill.

to remain in Boston. But the English were not quick enough. About the middle of the night preceding June 17th, 1,500 Americans, led by Colonel Prescott and aided later by General Putnam and General Warren, began throwing up breastworks on Breed's Hill. All night they toiled, and in the morning the British were surprised to find that the Americans had got ahead of them in occupying this important position.

Later in the day Howe, at the head of about 2,500 men, tried to drive the Americans out of their intrenchments. The British supposed the Americans would not stand an attack, but in this they were mistaken. As the English troops marched up the hill the Americans bravely waited until the regulars were within fifty yards. Prescott's orders were "Aim low! wait till you see the whites of their eyes." They did wait, and then they poured forth such a deadly fire that the English retreated down the hill, leaving the ground covered with their dead and wounded. Before making a second attack the English set fire to Charlestown, and then a second time were driven by American bullets down the hill. By this time the ammunition of the Americans had given out, and slowly and stubbornly they retired, fighting with clubbed muskets as they went. Among their dead was the brave General Warren.

General Howe attacks the Americans.

The British lost over one thousand, or more than one-third of their attacking force, while the Americans lost about four hundred and fifty. Although the Americans had to give up their position they gained a moral victory because their brave fighting inspired the people with courage and hope. When Washington heard that the raw American troops stood fire he said: "The liberties of the country are safe." It was a glad day for the American colonies.

Results of the battle of Bunker Hill.

133. Washington Drives the British out of Boston.— About two weeks after the battle of Bunker Hill Washington arrived at Cambridge and formally took command of the American army (July 3), under the famous elm still standing near Harvard University. His army was in no condition for fighting. The men were in every way without proper equipment. Only a limited number had muskets, and very few had bayonets. Besides, there was a great scarcity of cannon and powder. Of course, under such conditions, Washington could not attack the enemy. But with patience and faith he awaited the hour when he could strike a telling blow.

Washington's army.

Early in March, 1776, having received cannon[1] and ammunition, he seized Dorchester Heights, on the south of Boston, and threw up intrenchments there as the Americans had done on Bunker Hill in the previous June. Howe saw that he must drive Washington off the heights or leave Boston. He proposed to storm the works, but bad weather delayed him until the position had been made too strong to be successfully attacked. The British therefore evacuated Boston and went to Halifax.

The Americans seize Dorchester Heights.

TO THE PUPIL

1. Why were English troops sent to Lexington and Concord? What results followed this expedition?
2. Impersonating Paul Revere, write an account of his famous ride. What did the Continental Congress do at its second meeting?
3. As an aid to the intelligent study of the Battle of Bunker Hill, draw a map of Boston and its surroundings. Why was this battle fought? What effect did it have upon the Americans?
4. Describe the difficulties Washington had to face after taking command of the American army.
5. Do not fail to read, over and over again, Holmes's Grandmother's Story of Bunker Hill Battle.

THE STRUGGLE FOR THE HUDSON RIVER AND THE MIDDLE STATES IN 1776

134. The Declaration of Independence (July 4, 1776).— When the first gun of the Revolution was fired, Samuel Adams stood almost alone in his wish for the political separation of America from England. One year later, however, the desire for independence grew rapidly. The king had refused to hear the petition sent to him by the Continental Congress; he had called the colonists rebels; he had sent his ships of war to burn their towns; and, worst of all, had

Desire for independence grows rapidly.

---

[1] These cannon, numbering fifty, came from Ticonderoga, which had been captured the previous year. Along with other supplies, they were brought down on sledges drawn by oxen.

hired Hessian[1] soldiers to make war upon them. About this time Thomas Paine published *Common Sense*—a pamphlet which urged many reasons why America should separate from England. The fact that war already existed had weakened the bond of union, and Paine's arguments led many to look with favor upon the idea of independence.

Virginia took a leading part by instructing her delegates in Congress to vote for independence. This action on the part of Virginia had its due influence upon the other colonies. The Stamp Act, the Boston Port Bill, and the other unpopular measures of the King and Parliament had drawn the colonies much closer together. They were beginning not only to realize the value of united action but to have a feeling of self-confidence leading to a desire for independence. On June 7 Richard Henry Lee, of Virginia, introduced a resolution "that these united colonies are, and of right ought to be, free and independent states."[2] This resolution was seconded by John Adams of Massachusetts. Thus did the leading colonies, Massachusetts and Virginia, join hands in this most important step toward establishing the nation.

SAMUEL ADAMS.

Before July all the colonies except New York had de-

[1] The Hessians were so called because they came from Hesse-Cassel in Germany. Thirty thousand Hessians were hired during the war, 18,000 of whom were engaged the first year. Twelve thousand lost their lives during the war. The cost to the king was $22,000,000. The English government was driven to hire Hessian troops because (at this time) the war was so unpopular in England that it was not easy to secure English volunteers to fight in America.

[2] The colonies, with the approval of Congress, began to form State governments in 1775. The change from a colonial to a State form of government was slight. In Connecticut and Rhode Island, where the people had been governing themselves by electing their own representatives, the only change necessary was to withdraw allegiance from the king.

clared themselves in favor of independence. In the meantime, the committee[1] which had been appointed to prepare

Adoption of the Declaration of Independence, July 4, 1776. the Declaration of Independence, made its report. This famous paper, written by Thomas
Jefferson, was formally adopted in Indepen-
dence Hall,[2] Philadelphia, July 4, 1776. Realizing how serious the occasion was, John Hancock said: "We must be

INDEPENDENCE HALL, PHILADELPHIA, PA.   CHESTNUT STREET FRONT.

unanimous; we must hang together." "Yes," said Franklin,
with his ready wit, "we must all hang together, or else we
shall all hang separately."

**135. The British Direct their Attention to the Middle
States and the Hudson River.**—The British[3] had failed in

[1] The committee consisted of Thomas Jefferson, John Adams, Benjamin
Franklin, Roger Sherman, and Robert R. Livingston.

[2] This building is still standing on Chestnut Street.

[3] On June 28th the British fleet attacked Fort Moultrie, in Charleston Harbor,
South Carolina. Colonel Moultrie commanded the fort. His men returned the
British fire with a precision which was surprising in untried gunners. The fleet
retired, and South Carolina and Georgia were safe for three years.

SIGNING THE DECLARATION OF INDEPENDENCE.

their attempts to crush the Revolution in New England. They had found the opposition there so stubborn that they had been driven out of Boston. Their next move was to try to get control of the Hudson River and the Middle States. There were several reasons why this movement attracted the British. In this region, on account of the mixed char-

Reasons why the English wished to secure the Hudson River and the Middle States.

acter of the population, the people were not so united and earnest in their desire for independence as in New England. A large part of the inhabitants were Tories,[1] whose influence, it was thought, would be of much service to the British. The Hudson River was of great military importance, because, along with Lakes George and Champlain, it made a natural highway[2] be-tween New York and Can-ada. If the British could

secure this river, they could cut off New England from the other States. British forces concentrated in New England would soon conquer it, and they would then make short work of the rest of America. In a word, British control of the Hudson meant certain defeat for the Americans.

136. Washington's Plan of Defending New York: Bat-tle of Long Island (August 27).—When the British evacu-ated Boston, Washington supposed that their next point of attack would be New York. He therefore proceeded to

---

[1] Everywhere in America Tory sentiment was strongest among the non-English elements of the people.

[2] Water routes were especially valuable then, because there were no railroads for the transportation of armies and military supplies.

make ready its defences. Not knowing at what point the attack would be made, he found it necessary to prepare for the defence of a line of twenty miles. Just above New York he built Forts Lee and Washington, on opposite sides of the Hudson. He also fortified Brooklyn Heights and sent Putnam with half the army to occupy them.

In the summer General Howe arrived at Staten Island with a powerful fleet and an army of about 30,000 men. Washington had only about 18,000. On August 27 Howe landed on Long Island and attacked a detachment of the Americans under Sullivan, whose forces were outnumbered four or five to one. The battle was brief and one-sided. The Americans were defeated and driven back behind their **Washington** intrenchments on Brooklyn Heights. If Howe **escapes from** had followed up his victory he might have **Long Island.** captured the American army and brought the war to a speedy end, but as usual he was too slow. Two days later Washington, perceiving that the British fleet was moving to cut him off from New York, secured all the boats he could find, and with the aid of a heavy fog escaped during the night with all his force.[1]

137. Washington's Retreat from New York and Across New Jersey.—Brooklyn Heights overlooked New York just as Bunker Hill or Dorchester Heights overlooked Boston. As soon, therefore, as the British got possession of Brooklyn Heights, Washington saw that his army could not long remain in New York.[2] A little later

[1] It is surprising that Washington could, in a single night, succeed in getting an army of 10,000 men across a river, at this point nearly a mile wide, without being discovered. It was a brilliant piece of work, which none but an able general could have achieved. Here, as at Dorchester Heights, the slow-witted Howe was outgeneralled.

[2] During the interval of about two weeks between the retreat from Long Island and the evacuation of New York, the sad episode of Nathan Hale's capture and execution occurred. Captain Nathan Hale, who was only twenty-one years of age, was quite willing to risk his life by going as a spy into Howe's camp on Long Island. Hale succeeded in getting much valuable information about the enemy's fortifications, and was on his way back to the American army when he was captured and taken before General Howe. The latter promptly ordered him to be hanged on the next (Sunday) morning. During the night Hale asked for a clergyman and

THE JUMEL MANSION, NEW YORK CITY, WASHINGTON'S HEADQUARTERS.

Howe, with the aid of his fleet, tried to prevent Washington's escape by cutting off his retreat, but Washington was too alert for him. After more or less fighting near the Hudson River, north of New York, Washington left General Charles Lee with one-half the army at North Castle while he crossed over to New Jersey. **The British capture Forts Lee and Washington.** The British captured Forts Lee and Washington and 3,000 men. This was a terrible loss at a time when everything seemed to be going against the American cause.

But even worse things were to follow. In order to prevent the British from carrying out their plan of taking Philadelphia, Washington put his troops between that city and the British army. Needing every available soldier, he sent Lee orders to join him. **Lee's disobedience and jealousy.** Lee did not move. Again and again Washington urged upon Lee the importance of joining their forces, but he re-

a Bible. Both were denied him. He wrote to his mother and to his betrothed, but the letters were torn in pieces before his eyes by the hard-hearted jailer. The last words of the martyr-spy bore witness to his brave spirit: "I only regret that I have but one life to lose for my country."

mained at North Castle. He was jealous of Washington, and, being second in command, he wished Washington to fail in order that he himself, by promotion, might become commander-in-chief. This disobedience and jealousy put Washington in a critical position.

To save his army from capture he was again forced to retreat—this time across New Jersey. On his line of march he broke down bridges and destroyed supplies which the British hoped to secure for their army. Often the rear-guard was just leaving a burning bridge when the advance of the British could be seen approaching. Washington's retreat was so skilful that the British spent nineteen days (November 19 to December 8) in marching a little
Washington's army melting away. over sixty miles. But his losses by desertion were great and his army seemed to be melting away. When he reached the Delaware River he had only about 3,000 soldiers. Having previously sent on men to secure the boats for nearly one hundred miles along the river, he got his little army across just in time to escape the British, who arrived on the evening of the same day.

138. Battle of Trenton.—These were indeed " dark and dismal" days. In the retreat across New Jersey the Amer-
Dark outlook of the American cause. icans suffered greatly. Many were without shoes and they could be tracked by crimson foot-prints upon the snow. The friends of the patriot cause, both in England and in America, thought the Americans hopelessly beaten. There was doubt and gloom everywhere. The British generals thought the war was near its close, and Cornwallis was packing up to return to England; for as soon as the Delaware should become frozen over the British intended to march across and seize Philadelphia, the "rebel" capital. It would then be useless for him to remain longer in America.

But Washington was not without hope. He noted with satisfaction the mistake the British were making in care-
Washington's plans. lessly separating their army into several divisions and scattering them at various points in New Jersey. In the meantime Charles Lee had been

captured. His troops, now under Sullivan, had joined Washington, so that the entire army numbered 6,000. Washington at once planned to attack the body of Hessians stationed at Trenton.

The attack was made on Christmas night with 2,400 picked men. They began crossing the river early in the evening. Great blocks of ice, float-ing down the swift current, made the crossing slow and difficult. Massa-chusetts fishermen skilfully directed the boats, but it was four o'clock in the morning before the soldiers were ready to take up their line of march. A furious storm of snow and sleet beat in their faces as they plodded on toward Trenton, nine miles away. By daybreak

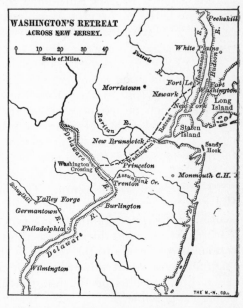

WASHINGTON'S RETREAT ACROSS NEW JERSEY.

Scale of Miles.

they had completely surprised the Hessians and, after a brief struggle, had captured the whole force **A glorious victory** of more than 1,000 men. By one bold stroke **at Trenton.** Washington had changed defeat into victory and had in-spired the patriot Americans with new hope.

Cornwallis, filled with amazement, decided to remain a little longer in America. Leaving a rear-guard at Prince-ton to protect his supplies, he speedily advanced with a superior force against Washington. At nightfall January 2, 1777, only a small creek separated the two armies, just south of Trenton. "At last," said Cornwallis, "we have run down the old fox and we will bag him in the morning." But

Washington outgeneralled him. During the night he not only escaped, but marched around Cornwallis, defeated his **Battle of Princeton.** rear-guard at Princeton, captured five hundred prisoners, and then withdrew in safety to the heights about Morristown, where he went into winter quarters.

139. Robert Morris Furnishes Money for the Army.— After the battle of Trenton Washington was in sore straits **Great need of money for the soldiers.** with his army. Many of the soldiers' terms of service were about to expire, and these men were eager to get to their homes. Washington knew that good money would hold them over for a few weeks. He wrote in haste therefore to his friend Robert Morris, a rich merchant and banker of Philadelphia, for $50,000 in hard cash. Morris promptly responded. Before light on New Year's morning he went knocking from door to door to secure the money from among his friends. **The noble task of Robert Morris.** By noon the sum was made up and on its way to Washington. The army was saved, and Washington was able to bring to an end a brilliantly executed campaign. Again during Greene's campaign in the Carolinas (1780) and during Washington's about Yorktown (1781), Morris came to the rescue of the army. His ample fortune was a silent power which none the less truly than the military genius of Washington made American independence possible.

TO THE PUPIL

1. Review the New England Confederacy, Franklin's Plan of Union, the Stamp Act Congress, and the Continental Congress. How do you account for the rapid growth of a desire on the part of the colonists for Independence? In this connection, find out all you can about the Hessians.

2. Explain the leading part taken by Virginia and Massachusetts in securing the adoption of the Declaration of Independence. Review Berkeley in Virginia and Andros in Massachusetts.

3. What were the Americans fighting for before the adoption of the Declaration of Independence? What, after it?

4. Why did the British wish to secure control of the Hudson River and the Middle States? Can you give any reason why the Tories were more numerous in this part of the country than in New England?
5. What plans did Washington make for the defence of New York?
6. Are you constantly using a map to aid you in forming vivid pictures?
7. What had Charles Lee to do with Washington's retreat across New Jersey? After chasing Washington across New Jersey, what mistake did the British make? How did Washington take advantage of this? You may well closely follow Washington at this time. What service did Robert Morris render the American cause?
8. Read the account of the battle of Trenton in Coffin's Boys of '76.

THE STRUGGLE FOR THE HUDSON RIVER AND THE MIDDLE STATES IN 1777

140. The British Plan to get Control of the Hudson in 1777.—By the capture of New York the British held the lower part of the Hudson. Their plan for 1777, like that for 1776, was to get entire control of this river. The plan was three-fold: (1) Burgoyne was to come down from Canada by way of Lake Champlain;[1] (2) St. Leger was to sail up the St. Lawrence into Lake Ontario and, landing at Oswego, was to come down the Mohawk Valley; (3) and Howe, with the main army, was to go up the Hudson from New York. All three of these divisions were to meet at Albany. The plan looks simple. It will be interesting to see how the blundering of the British led to failure.

141. Burgoyne's Brilliant Beginning.—Burgoyne, with an army of 10,000 men, including Canadians and Indians, captured Crown Point (June 26). Ten days later he forced the Americans to evacuate Fort Ticonderoga and hastily to retreat southward. Burgoyne was now confident of easy victory. King George clapped his hands and shouted, "I have beat them! I have beat all the Americans!" The English people thought the war would soon be over.

[1] In 1776 Carleton had led a similar expedition. With 12,000 troops he started from Canada to secure control of the water route to the mouth of the Hudson. Although stubbornly opposed by Arnold on Lake Champlain, he captured Crown Point, but finding Ticonderoga strongly fortified he withdrew without attacking that fort.

The Americans were everywhere disheartened. **Four days** more (July 10) found Burgoyne's army at Skenesboro (now Whitehall), about twenty miles distant in a direct line from Fort Edward.

142. Some of Burgoyne's Difficulties.—But in crossing the carrying-place between Lake Champlain and the Hudson serious difficulties stood in his way. The country was swampy and heavily wooded. General Schuyler, who was in command of the Americans, felled trees across the roads and destroyed over forty bridges. These obstructions greatly delayed Burgoyne. The British advanced only about a mile a day until they reached Fort Edward (July 30). As Burgoyne's supplies had to be sent to him from Canada, the farther he advanced the more difficult it was to feed his army. To keep his line of communication guarded it was necessary to leave troops in his rear. Every mile of advance thus compelled him to weaken his attacking force.

143. Burgoyne's Indian Allies.—Burgoyne's Indian allies were a source of more weakness than strength to his army. They murdered and scalped peaceful inhabitants every day.[1] These barbarous cruelties aroused the hottest indignation among the people, hundreds of whom eagerly offered their services to the American commander.

144. Bennington and Supplies.—While encamped at Fort Edward in August, Burgoyne's army stood greatly in need of horses and supplies. News came that at Benning-

---

[1] Near Fort Edward they killed Jane McCrea, a fascinating young woman who was engaged to be married to David Jones, an American loyalist serving as lieutenant in Burgoyne's army. Jones, having prevailed upon Miss McCrea to come within the British lines and marry him, sent a party of Indians under the half-breed Duluth to act as her guard. She was staying at the house of Mrs. McNeil, only a few hundred yards from Fort Edward. Before Duluth's party could reach Mrs. McNeil's house, however, another party of Indians under the Wyandotte Panther arrived and carried off Miss McCrea. Both parties of Indians met at a spring between Fort Edward and Glens Falls, and Duluth declared his right to take charge of the young lady. In the heated dispute which followed the Panther shot dead the unfortunate Miss McCrea. This is the version of the McCrea story as told by W. L. Stone in the "Cyclopædia of American Biography."

ton, a little village in Vermont at the foot of the Green Mountains, the Americans had collected several hundred horses, as well as food supplies and ammunition. Burgoyne was as much in need of horses to draw his can- **Burgoyne's need** non as of food to feed his troops. Besides, he **of supplies.** was told that there were many Tories in the Green Mountains who would, with a little encouragement, flock to the British army. To win over the people to the British cause was no small part of the purpose of the expedition to Bennington.

JOHN BURGOYNE.

Accordingly, about 1,000 Hessians were sent to Bennington, where nearly all of them were killed or captured by a body of militia under Colonel John Stark. Burgoyne's army was badly crippled by this disaster. Instead of bringing recruits to **Results of the** the British the expe- **British defeat at** dition to Bennington **Bennington.** only served to make the feeling of the Green Mountain farmers more bitter against the English Government. Great numbers of them speedily hastened to join the American army.

145. Failure of St. Leger.—Fortune seemed to be against Burgoyne. St. Leger, it was hoped, would gather about his standard many of the Iroquois, or Six Nations, and large numbers of Tories in western and central New York. In due time he made his way to Oswego, and from there to Fort Stanwix. St. Leger laid siege to the fort. Arnold, with a body of troops, pressed forward to its **St. Leger's** relief. He sent a messenger ahead to report **hurried retreat.** that a large force would soon attack the British. Panic-stricken, the Indians at once hurried away and were soon followed by St. Leger himself (August 22). Burgoyne could no longer look for aid in this direction. His only remaining hope was in receiving reinforcements from Howe.

Where Howe was and what his army was doing we will now consider.

146. Why Howe Failed to Unite with Burgoyne.— If Howe had gone up the Hudson and joined Burgoyne at the time planned, the latter's invasion would no doubt have been successful. Why Howe did not do the part assigned him was a question that until eighty years afterward had no satisfactory answer. An explanation was then found in a

LAFAYETTE.

document in Charles Lee's handwriting that proved him beyond a doubt to be a traitor. Lee had been captured in the autumn of 1776. While yet uncertain of his fate, he told Howe that he had given up the American cause and offered his advice for the summer campaign. Lee believed it was more important to capture Philadelphia than to get control of the Hudson. Hence he advised sending a force to take that city, which the British general called the "rebel capital." Howe might thus speedily bring Pennsylvania under subjection to England, while Burgoyne and St. Leger would easily subdue New York. To his own confusion and to the confusion of the British cause Howe followed Lee's advice.

The traitor Lee.

Lee's advice to Howe.

147. Howe's Advance Toward Philadelphia.— Howe opened the campaign (June 12) by an effort to draw Washington from his strong position among the hills around Morristown into a general engagement. But Washington was too wary to allow himself to be caught napping. After spending two or three weeks in vain attempts to provoke Washington to come out from his strongholds and fight in the open field Howe withdrew, tired out with his fruitless manœuvres.

Howe's vain attempt to bring on a battle.

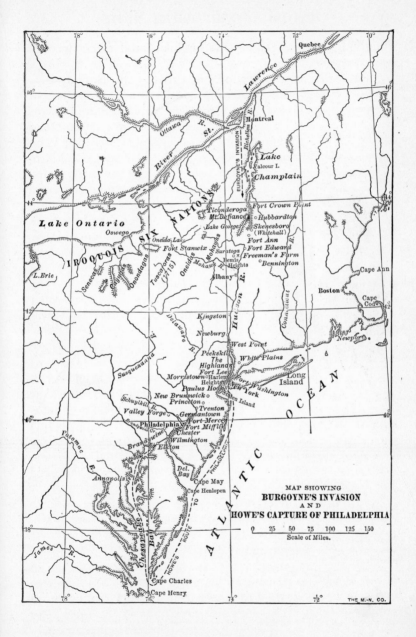

MAP SHOWING
BURGOYNE'S INVASION
AND
HOWE'S CAPTURE OF PHILADELPHIA

0   25   50   75   100   125   150
Scale of Miles.

THE M. N. CO.

Even though Howe's army numbered 18,000 men he dared not risk a march across New Jersey with Washington and an army of 8,000 in his rear. So on the last day of June he gave up his plan of marching across New Jersey to Philadelphia and withdrew his army to Staten Island.

He sails to Elkton. He then sailed southward in order to reach Philadelphia by way of the Chesapeake. When he reached Elkton, the head of the Chesapeake (August 25), he had been two months on the way. It was a precious two months to the American cause, as we shall now see.

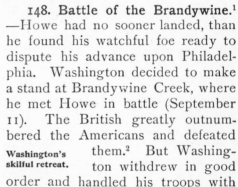

148. Battle of the Brandywine.[1] —Howe had no sooner landed, than he found his watchful foe ready to dispute his advance upon Philadelphia. Washington decided to make a stand at Brandywine Creek, where he met Howe in battle (September 11). The British greatly outnumbered the Americans and defeated them.[2] But Washington withdrew in good order and handled his troops with such skill as to keep Howe two weeks in marching to Philadelphia, only twenty-six miles from the battle-field.

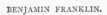

BENJAMIN FRANKLIN.

Washington's skilful retreat.

[1] When La Fayette heard that the Americans had declared their independence of England he was eager to cross the Atlantic and aid them. He was not yet twenty years of age and had just married a beautiful young woman of rank and fortune. But he was willing to leave behind him wife, family, and friends to fight in a noble cause. Accordingly, he sailed in his own vessel for this country and reached the coast of South Carolina in April, 1777.

Congress made him major-general in the Continental army, where he rendered excellent service. He fought his first battle at Brandywine, and here was wounded in the leg. He freely spent his own money for clothing and equipping the soldiers under his command. From their first meeting a warm friendship sprang up between La Fayette and Washington. After the war was over La Fayette twice visited the United States. The first visit he made in 1784 on Washington's invitation; the second, in 1824, when he laid the corner stone of Bunker Hill monument on the spot where the brave Warren had fallen in 1775.

[2] Washington had weakened his army by sending picked troops to aid the Army of the North.

It was on September 26 when the British general marched into this city, a week after the first battle of Saratoga, and altogether too late to send troops to co-operate with the unfortunate Burgoyne three hundred miles away. In delaying Howe Washington had made Burgoyne's capture certain. People did not understand the meaning of Washington's masterful strategy, but his policy of delaying Howe had been fatal to the success of the British plan to secure control of the Hudson.

149. Burgoyne's Surrender.—While Howe was on his way to Philadelphia Burgoyne was passing through a trying experience in the North. On sailing away from New York Howe left Clinton in command there. In vain Burgoyne sent messenger after messenger to Clinton, asking for reinforcements. Without Clinton's aid success was very doubtful, for the Americans were increasing daily and were threatening to cut off Burgoyne's line of communication with Canada. The American army, now commanded by Gates,[1] occupied a strong position at Bemis Heights. The situation was desperate. Bur- *Burgoyne's situation desperate.* goyne must force an advance. With great courage he fought a battle (September 19), in which his advance was stubbornly contested. Still there was no news from Clinton. In the meantime, Lincoln had succeeded in cutting off the British supplies from Canada. Three weeks later Burgoyne, whose army was suffering from want of food, again attacked the Americans (October 7) with the hope of cutting his way through their lines, and again suffered defeat. He tried in vain to find a way of escape but could not, for he was surrounded and cut off from supplies. After ten days, therefore, he

[1] Schuyler was a noble man and a good general, but he had political enemies who succeeded in having him removed. Gates was vain and weak, and his subsequent history proved him to be lacking even in personal bravery. The success of his army at Saratoga was due to the gallant leadership of Arnold and Morgan. Gates deserved no credit. His easy manner and fluent tongue enabled him for a time to influence people who did not understand his real character. In time, however, his selfishness, trickery, and cowardice brought down upon him the contempt of honest men.

surrendered his entire army of 6,000 regular troops[1] (October 17).

150. Burgoyne's Surrender Leads to Aid from France. —The surrender of Burgoyne was the turning-point in the war. Its immediate result was a treaty of alliance between France and our country. Shortly after the Declaration of Independence was signed Congress sent over three commissioners[2] to secure aid from France. The principal one of these was Benjamin Franklin, then seventy years old. His simplicity and directness charmed the French people and won him a warm place in their hearts. Before Burgoyne's invasion France had secretly sent to the Americans much aid in the form of money and ship-loads of ammunition and clothing.

Franklin's influence secures secret aid from France.

But after Burgoyne's surrender it was evident that the Americans were fighting England with success. France, England's traditional enemy, was then ready to aid them openly. She therefore entered into a treaty of alliance with the United States, agreeing to send over a fleet and an army of 4,000 men. England promptly declared war against France. She also changed her policy toward the Americans. She repealed the tea duty, the Boston Port Bill, and all the other hated measures that had driven the colonies to take up arms against the king. She promised that there should be no more taxation without representation. But it was too late. The Americans would now agree to nothing short of independence.

Results of the American treaty with France.

151. The Suffering at Valley Forge.—Even after losing Philadelphia, Washington had the courage to attack the British at Germantown. Although he made a well-planned attack, on account of a fog he suffered defeat. He then

---

[1] The Americans when marching the English soldiers off the field of surrender proudly unfurled their new flag. In January, 1776, Washington began to use an American flag. This was like the British flag, except that the thirteen stripes in the American flag took the place of the solid red of the British. Congress adopted the "Stars and Stripes" on June 14, 1777. John Paul Jones is believed to have been the first to hoist the flag at sea.

[2] These commissioners were Benjamin Franklin, Arthur Lee, and Silas Deane.

THE ATTACK ON THE CHEW HOUSE, GERMANTOWN.

withdrew his army and went into winter quarters at Valley Forge. This was a strong position among the hills, about twenty miles northwest of Philadelphia, on the Schuylkill River. But the winter was a terrible one for the army.[1] Most of the soldiers were in rags, few had any bedding, and many had not even straw to lie upon at night. Nearly 3,000 were barefoot, and could be tracked by their bloody foot-prints upon the frozen ground. Owing to mismanage. ment by Congress and the commissary department, there was often, for days at a time, no bread.

The army, though weakened by suffering and loss of food, was greatly strengthened by the systematic military drill which they received from Steuben,[2] a Prussian veteran who had joined the American cause. He was made inspector-general, and he transformed the ragged regiments into a well-disciplined army.

152. The Conway Cabal.—Petty politics and personal jealousy in Congress did much at this time and at other times to prevent the successful handling of the troops by Washington. Weak and vain men, such as Gates and Charles Lee, did all they could to destroy Washington's influence and drive him from his position as commander-in-chief. As Gates had succeeded, by his political scheming, in getting Congress to appoint him, in place of Schuyler, as head of the Northern army in 1777, so now he was busily scheming for the downfall of Washington that he might himself become the head of all the American armies. As one of the leaders in this

Washington's enemies and their petty scheming.

[1] A beautiful story is told of Washington at Valley Forge. When "Friend Potts" was near the camp one day he heard an earnest voice. On approaching he saw Washington on his knees, his cheeks wet with tears, praying to God for help and guidance. When the farmer returned to his home he said to his wife: "George Washington will succeed! George Washington will succeed! The Americans will secure their independence!" "What makes thee think so, Isaac?" inquired his wife. "I have heard him pray, Hannah, out in the woods to-day, and the Lord will surely hear his prayer. He will, Hannah; thee may rest assured He will."

[2] There were five eminent foreign gentlemen who fought in the American army. Two of these, La Fayette and John Kalb, were Frenchmen; two others, Kosciusko and Pulaski, were Poles; and the fifth was Baron Steuben, a German. These brave officers won the lasting gratitude of patriot Americans.

shameful plot was Conway, it was called the Conway Cabal. The taunt was openly made that while Gates had captured Burgoyne at Saratoga, Washington had been defeated by Howe on the Brandywine. But when people understood the meanness of all this plotting they were indignant. Washington appeared all the more noble in contrast with these selfish men, and his popularity was even greater than before.

153. The British Evacuate Philadelphia (June 18, 1778). When the British learned that a French fleet was coming over to aid the Americans, they feared it might go up the Delaware and, co-operating with Washington, capture their troops in Philadelphia. So Clinton, who had succeeded Howe in the chief command, was at once ordered to hasten away from Philadelphia and reinforce the army in New York. With 17,000 men, the British general began his march across New Jersey. Washington started in pursuit of Clinton, overtook him at Monmouth, and attacked him there (June 28). But, owing to the treachery of Charles Lee,[1] Washington failed to win a decisive victory. During the night the British hurried from the battle-field on toward New York.

Battle of Monmouth.

TO THE PUPIL

1. First review the reasons why the British wished to get control of the Hudson River and the Middle States. What was the British plan for 1777?

2. Describe Burgoyne's brilliant beginning and his later difficulties. In what way did his Indian allies affect the invasion?

3. What were the purposes and the results of the expedition against Bennington? Explain the failure of St. Leger.

4. Why did not Howe sail up the Hudson to join Burgoyne? In what way did Charles Lee show himself to be a traitor to the American cause? What was his advice to Howe?

5. Why did not Howe march across New Jersey in his attempt to capture Philadelphia? Trace his route by water to Elkton. In what way did Howe waste valuable time?

[1] For his shameful retreat and disobedience of orders Lee was tried by court-martial. He was suspended from his command for one year. Later he was expelled from the army.

6. How did Washington aid the Northern army to capture Burgoyne?
7. Give reasons for Burgoyne's failure.
8. What were the most important results of his surrender? How had France aided us before this surrender? After France entered into a treaty of alliance with the Americans what change did England make in her policy toward them?
9. Be prepared to write five minutes on any of the following topics: The suffering at Valley Forge, the Conway cabal, the British evacuate Philadelphia. Contrast Washington with such men as Lee and Gates.
10. Imagine yourself to have been with Washington's army at Valley Forge in that trying winter and write an account of your personal experiences.
11. Read Scudder's George Washington.

WARFARE ON THE BORDER AND ON THE SEA

154. England's Numerous Wars.—England's war with France made it necessary for her to protect her colonies in various parts of the world. This prevented her from concentrating her forces in America. Within the next two years she also became implicated in war with Spain and Holland; hence we need not be surprised that the English did but little fighting in America during 1778 and 1779.

155. Weakness and Difficulties of the Americans.—The United States was equally unable to engage in extensive military operations. The country was very weak in point of wealth and population. The principal industries were farming, fishing, ship-building, and commerce, and these, especially the last three, had naturally been much interfered with by the war. The Continental Congress had but little authority, and steadily lost influence until it commanded but little respect. It could not enlist a soldier or build a fort, because it had no power to levy taxes. In course of time the States paid little heed to the requisitions for money which Congress made upon them. Under such circumstances Congress had great difficulty in raising money enough to carry on the war.

The Continental Congress has little power.

Although Congress had no money and no means of get-

A REVOLUTIONARY GUN.

ting any, it could issue paper promises, and this it did in immense quantities.   These paper promises were called Con-
Continental currency.   tinental currency, and, like all such promises, they were valuable only in so far as people had confidence in the ability of the government to redeem them.   As people lost respect for Congress, this paper currency fell in value.   Before the close of 1779 the coin value of this Continental currency was only two cents on the dollar, and in the early part of the following year its coin value was nothing at all.   " Not worth a Continental " recalls the money trials of the Revolution.

156. Use of Indians by the English.—The difficulties of the situation were enhanced by the hostility of the original owners of the soil.   We have seen how Burgoyne employed Indians to help him.   It was a part of the plan of the English to get all the aid they could from the Iroquois in New York and from the Indians west of the Alleghanies. These powerful tribes, furnished with arms, ammunition, provisions, and sometimes with British leaders, were a serious annoyance to the people on the frontier.

A REVOLUTIONARY FLINT-LOCK PISTOL.

The struggle between the backwoodsmen and the red men was **Importance of the struggle between backwoodsmen and the Indians.** of great importance. The English Government wished to coop up the Americans between the Alleghanies and the Atlantic.   For, as long as the western country remained unsettled, English merchants could continue to grow rich on the immensely profitable fur trade with the Indians.   The

Americans were eager to make settlements west of the Alleghanies, but before they could occupy the land they had to conquer the Indians. Daniel Boone, George Rogers Clark, John Sevier, and James Robertson were prominent leaders in this western movement for conquest. The struggle east of the Alleghanies was for independence in territory already acquired; the struggle west of the Alleghanies was for the conquest of new territory.

157. George Rogers Clark Marches Against the British Posts North of the Ohio.—When the war began the British had possession of all the territory north of the Ohio between the Mississippi and the Alleghanies. Colonel Hamilton, the English governor of that region, wished to drive out all the American settlers. He encouraged the Indians to roam over the country, burning, murdering, and scalping without mercy.

Colonel George Rogers Clark, a backwoodsman of Kentucky, which was then a part of Virginia, decided to put a check upon Hamilton's plans. Clark got together a small body of volunteers, who numbered less than two hundred, and with these he boldly set out to capture the British posts north of the Ohio. In May, 1778, Clark's men made rude flat boats and rafts and floated down the Ohio to a point south of the Tennessee River. Here they met a party of hunters who consented to act as guides overland to Kaskaskia in the southwestern part of Illinois. Having surprised and captured this post, Clark sent a small force to seize Cahokia (Illinois), from thirty to forty miles northwest of Kaskaskia. This expedition was successful, and a message was received about the same time that Vincennes had taken the oath of allegiance to America and that the American flag floated over the fort there.

158. Clark Secures Control of the Northwest.—Hearing of Clark's success, Hamilton, who was at Detroit, at once prepared to march against him. As soon as possible the expedition started from Detroit toward Vincennes. In four or five weeks Hamilton captured Vincennes and threatened to advance upon Clark.

When the news reached the Illinois towns there was great alarm. Clark's situation was now critical. With scarcely more than one hundred men he was too far away to secure reinforcements from Virginia. Hamilton had five hundred men, including Indians, and could easily get reinforcements from his red friends.

In the midst of the excitement Clark got news that Hamilton had postponed further operations for the winter,

CLARK ON THE WAY TO KASKASKIA.

and was holding Vincennes with only eighty men in the **Clark's expedition to Vincennes.** garrison. Although it was midwinter, Clark promptly decided to march across the country and attack Hamilton at Vincennes, two hundred and forty miles away. He started from Kaskaskia (February 7, 1779). It was a fearful march of sixteen days, five of them spent in wading over the drowned lands of the Wabash.

The water was often three or four feet deep and sometimes reached the men's chins. The weather was bitterly cold. During the last six days of the march the men, drenched and half-frozen, had no regular meals, **Clark's heroic work.** and were wholly without food for two days. But Clark pressed steadily forward. On reaching Vincennes he attacked the fort with such vigor that he forced Hamilton to surrender (February 24, 1779). He had done a heroic piece of work. In capturing Vincennes Clark and his brave backwoodsmen finished the conquest of the territory in the Northwest and opened all this vast region to American settlers. The importance of this conquest will be appreciated when we see its ef-

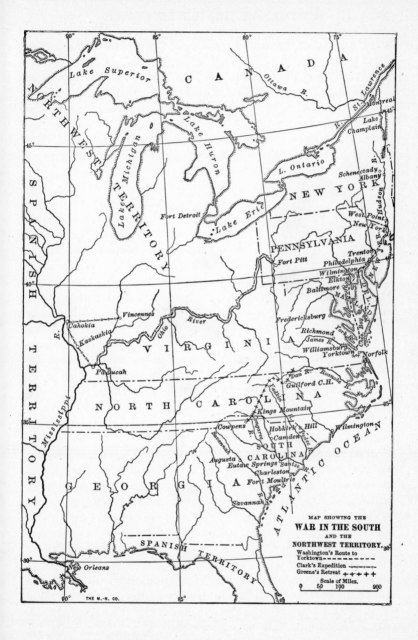

MAP SHOWING THE
WAR IN THE SOUTH
AND THE
NORTHWEST TERRITORY.

Washington's Route to
Yorktown – – – – – – – –
Clark's Expedition •—•—•—•—•
Greene's Retreat + + + + +

Scale of Miles.
0   50   100   200

THE M.-N. CO.

fects upon the treaty of peace at the close of the Revolution.

159. The American Navy.—Up to this time all the fighting, so far as we have seen, had been on land, but there was serious trouble on the sea also. When the war began the Americans were without war vessels, because up to this time they had been under the protection of England. Before the close of 1775, however, Congress had ordered a

small navy of thirteen vessels to be built, nearly all of which were captured during the war or burned to avoid capture. As a consequence we were much crippled for means of transporting troops by water. After recognizing our independence (1778), France made several attempts to aid us with her strong fleets, but owing to the supremacy of the English navy these efforts were of little service before the siege of Yorktown. Indirectly, however, they were of great assistance, because they kept England busy on various parts of the sea and in this way withdrew her strength from America.

France aids us with her fleets.

JOHN PAUL JONES.

160. American Privateering.—While England had little to fear from our navy, she suffered much from American privateers. Even as early as 1776 they captured three hundred and fifty English vessels, a few of which were loaded with powder and supplies for the British army. So much damage did they inflict upon England's commerce that her ship-owners and merchants became bitter in their opposition to the war. Governor Hutchinson of Massachusetts said there were 70,000[1] New England sailors at one time on privateers. The estimate was too high, but with-

---

[1] There were two reasons why it was easier to get men to engage in privateering than to enlist in the army: (1) Most of the men on these privateers were fishermen

out doubt many more than this number of Americans engaged in privateering during the war.

161. Paul Jones and the American Navy.—John Paul Jones, the naval hero of the Revolution, was a Scotchman by birth. At an early age he emigrated to America, and had been engaged in commerce many years before the outbreak of the war. Being placed by Congress in command of a small ship, he captured many vessels in the English Channel and thoroughly frightened the people as he sailed along the coasts of England and Scotland threatening the towns. At length, through the help of Franklin and the French king, he was placed in command

THE *BONHOMME RICHARD* AND THE *SERAPIS*.

of a small squadron. His flag-ship was called ɩhe *Bonhomme Richard*. Sailing along the eastern coast of England he saw several English merchantmen convoyed by two men-of-war. At seven o'clock in the evening (September 23, 1779), his ship attacked the larger of the two, the *Serapis*. A desperate fight followed. During the action the firing on the *Richard* slacked. The English commander shouted to Jones, "Have you struck?" Jones promptly answered, "I have not begun to fight." The two vessels coming in touch, he lashed them together with his own hands and for two hours longer continued the deadly struggle. At last some of Jones's men, from the main-yard of the *Richard*, dropped hand-grenades among the English sailors. One of

Desperate fight between the "Bonhomme Richard" and the "Serapis."

and sailors who, as we have already found, were thrown out of employment by English cruisers; (2) privateering was far more profitable than service in an ill-paid army.

these caused an explosion of a powder chest. This demoralized the English crew, and their commander struck his colors. Jones had lost in killed and wounded one hundred and sixteen men, and the *Richard* was sinking. It was a tremendous struggle and a great victory, and it caused the name of John Paul Jones to be spoken of with gratitude throughout America.

TO THE PUPIL

1. In what part of the country was most of the fighting in 1775? In 1776 and 1777? Review the leading events of these three years.

2. Why was there little fighting in 1778 and 1779? Notice with care the weakness of the Continental Congress and the disastrous effects of the Continental currency.

3. How did the English make use of the Indians? Give reasons for the importance of the struggle between the backwoodsmen and the Indians in the region west of the Alleghanies.

4. What was the purpose of George Rogers Clark's expedition? Trace it on the map. What did Clark accomplish in the Northwest?

5. Imagine as vividly as you can his heroic expedition against Vincennes and write an account of it.

6. Why were the Americans without war vessels at the beginning of the war? How were they crippled for lack of a suitable navy during the Revolution? In what way did France aid them with her fleets?

7. Who was Paul Jones? What service did he render the Americans?

8. Read Roosevelt's Winning of the West for a good account of what the Westerners did during the Revolution.

WAR IN THE SOUTH AND THE SURRENDER OF CORNWALLIS (1780–1781)

162. Reasons Why the British Tried to Conquer the South.—After failing in New England and the Middle States, the British directed their energies to the South. Their plan was to conquer Georgia and then get control of the Carolinas and Virginia. They knew that Georgia, being weak, could not offer much resistance, and that the Tories, who were numerous in the Carolinas, would join them. Moreover, should England fail in overthrowing American independence, the control of the South would help her, at the close of the war, in confining the Americans within a smaller territory than would be otherwise possible.

163. First Successes of the British.—As we have seen, there was little fighting anywhere in America in 1778 and 1779. The British had captured Savannah in 1778, but it was not until the spring of 1780 that they began the serious work of conquering the South. General Lincoln was in command of the American army in the South and was stationed at Charleston. Clinton, coming down from New York with a large force, succeeded in penning him in this place and forcing his surrender (May 12), with about 3,000 Continental troops. *Lincoln surrenders to Clinton at Charleston.* Well satisfied with this beginning, Clinton returned to New York and left Cornwallis in command of the British forces in the South.

After Lincoln's surrender at Charleston, Congress sent General Gates down to take command of the American troops. Gates, whose head had been turned by his capture of Burgoyne at Saratoga, went South confident of success. He reached the army on July 19 and at once planned to make an advance upon Camden. This was the most important place in South Carolina, *Defeat of Gates at Camden.* because all the principal roads, leading from the North and from the coast, centred here. He was met by Cornwallis (August 16) and badly defeated. This was the second American army destroyed in the South within three months.

Gates rode off the battle-field in such confusion of mind that he did not stop until he was more than sixty miles from Camden. In utter disgrace he retired from the army, to be heard of no more during *Gates in disgrace.* the war. As Gates was leaving his Virginia plantation to take command of the army in South Carolina, his friend Charles Lee had said to him, "Take care that your Northern laurels do not change to Southern willows." But Gates was bound to fail. He was too self-satisfied to listen to any advice, even that of his officers.

164. Battle of King's Mountain.—Cornwallis now advanced into North Carolina. At the same time he sent 1,200 men, mostly American Tories under the dashing Ferguson, to enlist Tories in the mountainous regions of South Carolina. Hearing of this movement, a body of American backwoodsmen hastily gathered and attacked Ferguson at King's Mountain (October 7) before he could receive reinforcements. His position was a strong one, but the backwoodsmen assailed him with great fury on three sides at once and killed or captured his entire force. Ferguson himself was killed.

This brilliant victory so severely crippled Cornwallis that it has sometimes been called the Bennington of the South. Cornwallis was compelled to return to South Carolina in order to maintain control of the territory in that State.

165. Partisan Warfare in the South.—Before returning to New York after the capture of Charleston, Clinton sent Clinton's unwise small forces into the interior of South Caro- proclamation. lina, and in a proclamation offered pardon to all who would return to allegiance to England. Those who would not actively aid in restoring the royal government were to be treated as rebels and traitors. This unwise proclamation compelled all citizens to range themselves on one side or the other.

A bitter, bloody, and cruel partisan warfare resulted. Neighbor fought against neighbor, sometimes brother against brother, in this semi-civil war. The most noted partisan leaders on the American side were Marion, Sumter, Pickens, and Lee. Marion's men were without uniforms, The Swamp Fox. without tents, and without pay. They lived in the swamps, and were so swift and cunning in their attacks that their leader was known as the Swamp Fox. With a very small force, often less than fifty men, he annoyed beyond measure the British by rescuing prisoners and capturing supply-trains, foraging parties, and outposts. When the American cause looked most gloomy in the South, these brave men, aided by noble women, kept hope alive in patriot hearts.

166. Arnold in Philadelphia.—Before we follow Greene and Cornwallis in their final struggle for control in the South, let us turn to an alarming event on the banks of the Hudson. This was Arnold's treason, which offered the British an opportunity to make a third attempt to get control of the Hudson. After the British left Philadelphia (1778) Arnold, who had not fully recovered from his wounds received at Saratoga, was placed in command there. He was popular in social circles, which included many Tories, and became engaged to a Tory's daughter. Extravagant living followed, and Arnold was soon heavily in debt.

The State government accusing him of dishonesty, Congress ordered his trial by court-mar- **Arnold tried by** tial. By its **court-martial.** verdict he was found guilty of indiscretions and mildly sentenced to receive a reprimand from the commander-in-chief. As Arnold had served his country with distinguished bravery, Washington held him in high esteem and therefore gave the reproof as gently as possible. But Arnold was indignant. He felt that he had been unjustly treated, and he secretly planned revenge.

167. Arnold Becomes a Traitor.—Arnold pretended that on account of his wound he was not able to engage in active service, and requested that he might be placed in command of the important position of West Point. Wash-

ington, suspecting nothing, granted Arnold's request. The
latter, no doubt, thought the American cause was hopeless.
At any rate he was as eager for money as he was for revenge and soon opened a treasonable correspondence with
General Clinton, commanding the British troops in New
York. The scheme was that Arnold should so dispose of
his forces at West Point that this strong fort might easily
fall into the British hands at a time agreed upon for an
attack.

168. Arnold Fails, and André is Hanged as a Spy.—
For weeks the correspondence between Arnold and the

THE ESCAPE OF BENEDICT ARNOLD.

British commander was carried on. Arnold looked forward to a successful execution of his plot; but a few details
were yet to be agreed upon. So, in September (1780),
Major André was sent by Clinton up the Hudson to make
final arrangements with Arnold.

André sailed up the river in the ship *Vulture* and met
Arnold on shore near Stony Point. An all-night interview
followed, and morning found the transaction still unfin-
The all-night ished. Before André could return to the *Vult-*
interview.   *ure* it was fired upon and withdrew down the
river. André then attempted to make his way to the British lines by land. In disguise, therefore, and with Arnold's

plans of the fort between his stockings and the soles of his feet, the next morning he was galloping rapidly down the east side of the Hudson on his way to New York. His safe arrival would secure him honor and fame.

Little did he know what fate awaited him. As he reached Tarrytown he was stopped by three militiamen lying in wait for any suspicious persons who might appear. They searched him and, finding the tell-tale papers, retained him as a prisoner. Arnold got the news of the capture in time to escape. André was tried by a fair-minded court-martial and was condemned to be hanged as a spy. *André's capture.*

Arnold received for his treason a brigadiership and about $30,000, but he spent the remainder of his life in disgrace, justly despised by Americans and Englishmen alike. He had carefully kept in his possession the old uniform in which he made his escape from West Point. Just before his death he called for this and put it on once more. " Let me die," said he, " in this old uniform in which I fought my battles. May God forgive me for ever putting on any other." *Arnold's disgrace and death.*

169. Greene and Cornwallis.—In the meantime the struggle between Greene and Cornwallis in the South was going on. When Gates retired from the command of the armies of the South, General Greene was appointed by Congress to succeed him. On reaching the Carolinas (December 2, 1780) Greene had many difficulties to face. The British, now in control of Georgia and South Carolina, were about to overrun North Carolina also. Their army was in good condition and was led by such able officers as Cornwallis, Tarleton, and Rawdon. Greene's small forces were poorly armed, without pay and clothing, and sometimes even without food. The troops were broken in spirit and discouraged, but Greene soon inspired the confidence of officers and soldiers. *Greene's difficulties.*

He sent the brave General Morgan against Tarleton. They met at Cowpens (January 17, 1781), where Morgan, with only nine hundred men, routed the British force of

1,100 picked men. The British loss was two hundred and thirty killed and wounded and six hundred prisoners. This **Morgan's brilliant victory at Cowpens.** brilliant victory destroyed nearly one-third of Cornwallis's army and, like the victory at King's Mountain, seriously interfered with his plans. At King's Mountain Cornwallis lost his best corps of scouts; at Cowpens he lost his light infantry. Both would have been of untold benefit to him when chasing Greene into Virginia immediately after this battle.

NATHANIEL GREENE.

170. Greene's Retreat into Virginia.—After his victory at Cowpens Morgan joined Greene. Cornwallis then chased them for two hundred miles northward across the Carolinas. In this famous retreat the Americans forded three rivers whose waters, swollen by rainstorms soon after the Americans had crossed, checked the British in their pursuit. Greene crossed the last of these, the Dan, just in time to escape the British, who were pressing closely upon his rear. Knowing that Greene would be reinforced in Virginia, Cornwallis dared not follow.

On receiving reinforcements Greene returned and fought his enemy at Guilford Court House, North Carolina (March 15, 1781). Here he was defeated, but withdrew his forces **Battle of Guilford Court House.** in good order. This battle was fatal to the plans of Cornwallis, for it so severely crippled his army—which lost about one-fourth of its whole number—that he would not follow Greene in his retreat. The remainder of the British army were tired out and **Cornwallis retires to Wilmington.** almost famished. With his men in this condition Cornwallis could not return to Charleston, his base of supplies, but decided to go to Wilmington, where communication with the English fleet would

WASHINGTON FIRING THE FIRST GUN AT THE SIEGE OF YORKTOWN.

A group of American and French officers to the left behind the gun.

be easy. Greene's Fabian policy had been very successful. He had worn out the enemy and forced him to seek the coast for supplies.

Greene at once greatly disturbed Cornwallis's peace of mind by marching back to South Carolina. Again and again Greene was defeated, but he skilfully handled his troops and inflicted severe losses upon the enemy. Before the close of 1781 the British *Greene's skill as a general.* held, in the States south of Virginia, only the two seaports of Charleston and Savannah. Greene was bold, cautious, active, and persevering. He had outgeneraled Cornwallis, the ablest English commander, and shown himself second only to Washington in military genius.

171. Cornwallis Goes to Virginia.—Cornwallis, disappointed in the South, and regarding Virginia as the great storehouse of the Southern armies, now marched northward to get control of that State. Here he found a considerable force of British sent there to keep the inhabitants from aiding the more southern States. Arnold had set fire to Richmond and had destroyed much property in other parts of Virginia. La Fayette was there with a body of troops to look after the interests of the Americans. When Cornwallis reached *Cornwallis tries to entrap La Fayette.* Virginia he tried to entrap La Fayette, but the wily young Frenchman was not to be caught.

Cornwallis then withdrew to Yorktown, where he could easily communicate with the English fleet. Clinton had ordered him to be in readiness to send reinforcements to New York in case the expected French fleet should co-operate with Washington in trying to capture that place.

172. Cornwallis, Entrapped at Yorktown, Surrenders.—Up to this time the French army had not been of any real service to the American cause, nor had the French fleet given much *direct* aid. Now, however, both their land forces and their fleet were to *Direct aid from the French.* help Washington in carrying out a bold plan. The latter, whose army was lying on the Hudson, had been joined the

NELSON HOUSE, YORKTOWN, VA.

Which was occupied as headquarters by General Cornwallis.

year before Cornwallis went to Yorktown by 6,000 fresh troops from France in command of Rochambeau. Clinton, who was at the head of the English forces in New York, hearing that a powerful French fleet was on its way with more land forces to America, feared that on its arrival there would be a combined attack by land and sea.

This had been the original plan, but when Washington learned that the fleet was on its way to the Chesapeake he withdrew from New York and began the execution of a Washington's brilliant movement. Leaving a small force brilliant on the Hudson, he marched the rest of his movement. army four hundred miles to reinforce La Fayette in Virginia and co-operate with the fleet in capturing Cornwallis. So secretly and skilfully did Washington make his plans that he had almost reached Maryland before Clinton found out what was going on.

Clinton at once sent a fleet to drive the French fleet away. He also sent Arnold to burn New London, Connecticut, hoping thus to draw Washington back. But the English fleet failed in its attack on the French, and Washington was not to be turned aside from his purpose. Rapidly marching to the Chesapeake, he embarked his troops at

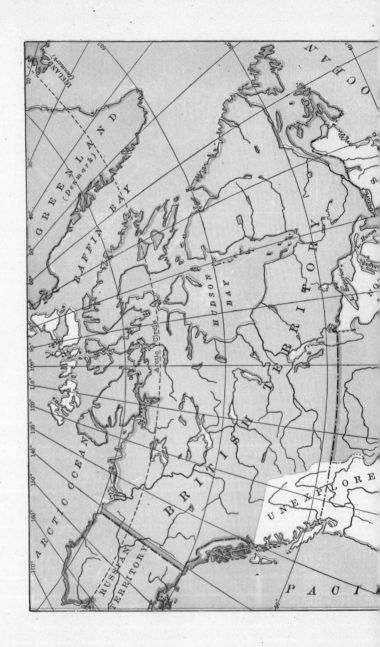

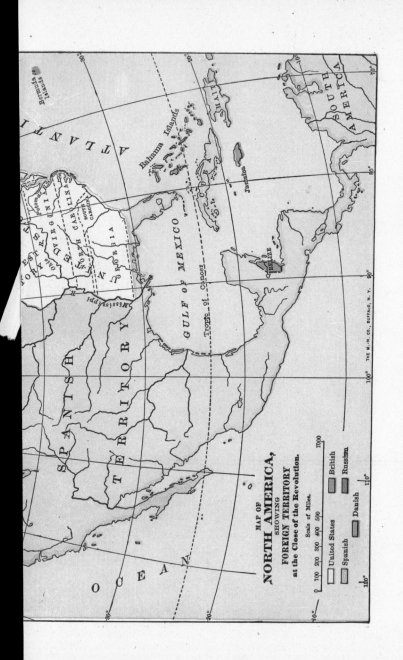

MAP OF
NORTH AMERICA,
SHOWING
FOREIGN TERRITORY
at the Close of the Revolution.

Scale of Miles.
0 100 200 300 400 500   1000

United States   British
Spanish   Russian
Danish

THE M.-N. CO., BUFFALO, N. Y.

Baltimore and Elkton, and united with La Fayette, who had already been reinforced by a French land force from the fleet. Cornwallis, entirely surrounded, saw but one chance of escape. That was by crossing the York River and making a rapid retreat northward. A violent storm upset his plans.

Cornwallis surrenders.

As his army of 8,000 was matched against an army of 16,000, to say nothing of the fleet, a successful resistance was hopeless. Therefore, after a siege of about three weeks he surrendered his army (October 19, 1781).

173. The End of the War and the Treaty of Peace (1783).—The Americans everywhere rejoiced. Congress, adjourning in a body, attended church to offer thanksgiving for the great victory. It was plain to Americans and Englishmen that Cornwallis's surrender must end the war. Peace commissioners from both countries were therefore appointed to agree upon a treaty of peace.

The French Government tried hard to confine the Americans to the region east of the Alleghanies. But the work of George Rogers Clark and other Westerners who had bravely conquered and settled the vast regions north and south of the Ohio, aided our commissioners in securing for American independence the territory lying between the Alleghanies and the Mississippi, and between the Great Lakes and Florida. Florida was ceded back to Spain.

George Rogers Clark and the West.

George the Third's plan of personal government in America had failed. The Revolution secured independence in America; it overthrew the personal rule of George the Third in England. In 1784 young William Pitt had become the real head of the English Government, and Parliamentary reform was only a question of time.

George the Third fails to carry out his plans.

TO THE PUPIL

1. Review the attempt on the part of the British, first, to subdue Massachusetts in 1775, and second, to get control of the Hudson River and the Middle States in 1776 and 1777. You will remember that there was but little fighting in 1778 and 1779.

2. Why did the British in 1780 turn their attention to conquering the South? Take note of their first successes there.

3. Explain why the Battle of King's Mountain was important.

4. What was the character of partisan warfare in the South? Look up facts about the Swamp Fox and his men. Subject for essay: Partisan warfare in the South.

5. What were the results of Arnold's trial by court-martial? What reason did he assign for requesting that he might be placed in command of the troops at West Point?

6. How was his treasonable scheme to be carried out? What part did André take in this scheme? Discuss Arnold's disgrace and death. Subject for essay: Arnold the traitor.

7. What were the difficulties of Greene when he succeeded Gates in the South? How did Morgan's brilliant victory at Cowpens play havoc with the plans of Cornwallis?

8. What was the condition of the English army after the Battle of Guilford Court House? What had been Greene's main purpose and how had he carried it out?

9. Why did Cornwallis go to Yorktown? What direct aid did the Americans now receive from the French fleet? Before its arrival what plans of attack upon the British had Washington made? What changes did he make in his plans after the arrival of the fleet?

10. Outline the events leading to the surrender of Cornwallis. What were its results?

11. Study carefully these topics: George Rogers Clark and the West; George the Third fails to carry out his plans.

12. Subject for debate: Resolved, that Greene was a better general than Cornwallis. Subject for debate: Resolved, that the capture of Burgoyne was a greater achievement than the capture of Cornwallis.

13. Read Simms's Partisan and the chapter on Arnold's treason in Coffin's Boys of '76. Memorize Bryant's Song of Marion's Men.

State. Duties were levied on goods carried from one State into another. For example, New York laid a duty on chickens, vegetables, and dairy products from New Jersey, and on firewood from Connecticut. New Jersey retaliated by laying a tax of $1,800 a year upon a lighthouse which New York had erected on the New Jersey shore, and the merchants in Connecticut began to hold meetings for the purpose of stopping all trade with New York.

All such bickerings over inter-State trade made the States more jealous and unfriendly toward one another. And it is worthy of notice that all this increase of selfishness, the continuation of which could only result in civil war and the political ruin *Congress without power to regulate commerce.* of the Confederation, was brought about by the inability of Congress to regulate commerce. But there were other commercial difficulties of a serious nature.

178. Financial Difficulties of the Confederation.—After the Revolution our imports, which had to be paid for in specie, were so much more than our exports that the country was soon drained of nearly all its gold and silver. Congress was in great need of money, and there was financial distress throughout the country.

179. Shays's Rebellion.—Business depression steadily continued to grow worse. People were in debt, their taxes were heavy, and they could not get money for what they had to sell. The consequence was that nearly all the States began to issue paper promises, which they called money. Distress was especially great among the farmers in western Massachusetts. Their cattle and their farms were sold by the sheriff, and they themselves were sometimes thrown into prison for *Distress of farmers in western Massachusetts.* debt. When their State Legislature refused to issue paper promises in order that they might pay their debts, two thousand angry farmers in the region about Springfield and Worcester, under the leadership of Daniel Shays, surrounded the court-houses in those cities and put a stop for the time to all lawsuits against debtors. For a while (in the latter part of 1786 and early part of 1787) they had things their own way. They not only burned barns and carried off movable goods, but they tried to seize the arsenal at Springfield for the purpose of securing muskets and cannon. After about seven months the rebellion was put down by the State militia.

180. Conflicting Claims to the Northwest Territory.— Thus we see that, by reason of the inability of Congress to regulate commerce and to raise money by taxation, difficulties were growing day by day. There was still another vexing question. That was the conflicting claims to the territory between the Ohio and the Mississippi, known as the Northwest Territory. Four States claimed each a part or all of it. Massachusetts and Connecticut based their claims to the northern part upon their chartered rights. New York insisted that about all of it belonged to her by an agreement with the Iroquois Indians. Virginia claimed the whole of it not only by chartered right but by the conquest of George Rogers Clark during the Revolution.

Of course these conflicting claims led to bitter disputing, in which Maryland took a leading part. She objected to the

Maryland objects to these claims.

ownership of the Northwest Territory by a part of the States. She said that inasmuch as all the States had fought France and England to secure this territory, all ought to have a share in the ownership of it. Maryland therefore refused to agree to the Articles of Confederation until it was clear that these claims would be abandoned. The four States having yielded their claims, she signed the articles in 1781.

In taking this position Maryland was doing a great service to the whole country. The common possession of the

Results of common ownership.

Northwest Territory by the thirteen States helped to hold the States together. They all had an equal interest in this extensive region, whose land sales would enable the Confederation to get money enough to pay all its debts.

181. The Ordinance of 1787.—The outcome of the dispute concerning this common ownership was the ordinance of 1787, which was the most important measure passed by the Confederation. This ordinance provided for the government of the Northwest Territory, and for dividing it into five States. Education was to be encouraged, and there was to be religious freedom. Although runaway slaves were to be returned to their masters, slavery was to be forever prohibited. This ordinance was passed by Con-

CELEBRATING IN NEW YORK THE ADOPTION OF THE CONSTITUTION.

gress in 1787, the year of the formation of the Constitution.

182. Events Leading to the Constitutional Convention. —The many commercial and financial difficulties, ending in Shays's Rebellion, showed that the Confeder- The Confederation ation was breaking down. Shays's Rebellion breaking down. in Massachusetts might soon be followed by similar uprisings in other States. In the face of such dangers the Confederation was almost powerless. A better form of government had therefore become a necessity, and this the Constitutional Convention devised.

The question of the regulation of commerce led to the calling of the Constitutional Convention. Western settlement showed the need of connecting the East and the West by a system of canals. As the navigation of the Potomac River was concerned, commissioners from Maryland and Virginia met to adopt some regulations for the use of this river by the two States (1785). When the Virginia Legislature adopted the commissioners' report, they also voted to invite all the States to send delegates to a convention the following year. This convention was to consider commercial regulations for the whole country. As delegates **The conference at** from only five States met at this conference, **Annapolis.** held at Annapolis in 1786, it did not seem worth while to discuss the business for which they were called together. But before adjourning, they recommended that delegates from all the States should meet to consider the Articles of Confederation and make them adequate to the needs of the country.

All the States except Rhode Island appointed some of their ablest men as delegates to the convention, which met in Philadelphia (May 25, 1787) and remained in secret session almost four months. Washington was presiding officer of **The Constitution** this convention, which framed the Constitu-**ratified.** tion[1] for the New Federal Union. The adoption of the Constitution required its ratification by nine States. When the ninth State ratified it on June 21, 1788,

---

[1] *Slavery Compromises in the Constitution.*—In appointing representatives to Congress from each State, some of the Southern States wished all the slaves to be counted. The Northern States opposed the counting of any of the slaves. Finally, it was agreed that in deciding the number of representatives from any slave State three-fifths of the slaves should be counted. The North, or commercial part of the country, wished the national government to have power to regulate commerce, but the South feared this power might be used to prohibit the slave trade. At last it was voted that Congress should have full control of commerce, but that importation of slaves should not be stopped before 1808.

preparations were immediately made for the organization of the new government.

183. Supporters and Opponents of the Constitution.— There was much opposition to the Constitution from men who honestly believed that too much power was given to the national government. These men believed that the States should have most of the power, as under the Confederation.   Because they opposed the Federal Constitution they were called Anti-Federalists.   The brilliant orator, Patrick Henry, belonged to this political party.   Among the Federalists, or supporters of the Constitution, were Washington, Hamilton, and Franklin, who firmly believed in a strong central government to control all matters of national interest.   After a long struggle between these political parties throughout the country, the Constitution was ratified by the various States, and thus the New Federal Union was established.

The Federalists and the Anti-Federalists.

TO THE PUPIL

1. **The period** from the close of the Revolution to the adoption of the Constitution has rightly been called the Critical Period.   Ascertain the reason.
2. Why was there a delay in the adoption of the Articles of Confederation?   What is meant by saying that Congress was merely an advisory body?
3. What was the relation between Congress and the various States?
4. Be sure that you get clear ideas about the following topics: Commercial war between the States; Congress without power to regulate commerce.
5. What financial difficulties did the Confederation have after the close of the Revolution?   What caused Shays's Rebellion?
6. What claims were made by various States to the Northwest Territory?   Why did Maryland object to these claims?   Name the leading provisions in the Ordinance of 1787.
7. Can you now tell why the Confederation broke down?   Outline the events leading to the Constitutional Convention in Philadelphia. What was the position taken by those who opposed the Constitution?   By those who supported it?

CHRONOLOGY

1765. PASSAGE OF THE STAMP ACT.

1765. MEETING OF STAMP ACT CONGRESS.

1767. NEW TAXES ON GLASS, LEAD, PAPER, AND TEA.

1768. BRITISH TROOPS QUARTERED IN BOSTON.

1770. BOSTON MASSACRE.

1773. DESTRUCTION OF TEA IN BOSTON AND ELSEWHERE.

1774. BOSTON PORT BILL PASSED.

THE CONTINENTAL CONGRESS MEETS AT PHILADELPHIA.

1775. *April* 19, FIGHT AT LEXINGTON AND CONCORD.

May 10, CAPTURE OF TICONDEROGA AND CROWN POINT. SECOND MEETING OF THE CONTINENTAL CONGRESS.

1775. *June* 15, WASHINGTON APPOINTED COMMANDER-IN-CHIEF. *June* 17, BATTLE OF BUNKER HILL.

November 12, MONTREAL TAKEN BY MONTGOMERY—ARNOLD'S MARCH TO QUEBEC.

December 30, DANIEL BOONE SETTLES IN KENTUCKY.

1776. *January* 1, UNION FLAG RAISED AT CAMBRIDGE, MASS.

February 27, BATTLE OF MOORE'S CREEK BRIDGE.

June, ARRIVAL OF BRITISH FLEET IN NEW YORK BAY. *June* 28, ATTACK ON FORT SULLIVAN, CHARLESTON, S. C.

July 4, DECLARATION OF INDEPENDENCE BY CONGRESS.

August 27, BATTLE OF LONG ISLAND.

September 15, AMERICANS ABANDON NEW YORK.

October 28, BATTLE OF WHITE PLAINS.

November 16, SURRENDER OF FORT WASHINGTON.

December 26, BATTLE OF TRENTON.

1777. *January* 3, BATTLE OF PRINCETON.

June 14, FLAG OF STARS AND STRIPES ADOPTED BY CONGRESS.

July 6, BURGOYNE CAPTURES TICONDEROGA.

August 6, BATTLE OF ORISKANY. *August* 16, BATTLE OF BENNINGTON.

September 11, BATTLE OF BRANDYWINE.

October 4, BATTLE OF GERMANTOWN. *October* 17, SURRENDER OF BURGOYNE. HOWE OCCUPIES PHILADELPHIA.

1778. CONWAY CABAL.

ALLIANCE WITH FRANCE.

May, CLARK'S EXPEDITION TO ILLINOIS.

June, ATTACK ON WYOMING. *June* 18, BRITISH LEAVE PHILADELPHIA. *June* 28, BATTLE OF MONMOUTH.

July, ARRIVAL OF FRENCH FLEET UNDER D'ESTAING.

December 29, SAVANNAH TAKEN BY THE BRITISH.

1779. *September* 22, FIGHT BETWEEN THE *BONHOMME RICHARD* AND THE *SERAPIS*. SULLIVAN'S EXPEDITION AGAINST THE IROQUOIS.

1780. *May*, CAPTURE OF CHARLESTON BY THE BRITISH.

August 16, BATTLE OF CAMDEN.

September, ARNOLD'S TREASON.

1781. *January* 17, BATTLE OF COWPENS.

March 15, BATTLE OF GUILFORD COURTHOUSE.

September 8, BATTLE OF EUTAW SPRINGS.

October 19, CORNWALLIS'S SURRENDER AT YORKTOWN.

1782. *November* 30, PRELIMINARY TREATY OF PEACE SIGNED.

1783. *September* 3, FINAL TREATY OF PEACE WITH GREAT BRITAIN SIGNED.
    November 25, EVACUATION OF NEW YORK.
    December 4, WASHINGTON TAKES LEAVE OF HIS OFFICERS.

1784. JEFFERSON'S NORTHWEST ORDINANCE PROPOSED.

1786. SHAYS'S REBELLION.

1787. NORTHWEST TERRITORY ORGANIZED, AND ORDINANCE ADOPTED.
    May 25, CONSTITUTIONAL CONVENTION MET AT PHILADELPHIA.
    September 17, CONSTITUTION OF THE UNITED STATES SIGNED BY THE DEL-
    EGATES.

1788. *June* 21, CONSTITUTION RATIFIED BY NEW HAMPSHIRE, SECURING ITS
    ADOPTION.

CHAPTER XV

THE NEW STRUGGLE FOR POLITICAL INDEPENDENCE AND THE GROWTH OF NATIONAL FEELING (1789–1829)

REFERENCES: **Scribner's** Popular History of the United States, IV.; **Andrews's** United States, I.; **Walker's** Making of the Nation; **Richardson's** History of Our Country; **Wright's** Children's Stories of American Progress; **Hale's** Stories of Invention; **Coffin's** Building the Nation; **Hart's** Formation of the Union; **Channing's** United States; **Eggleston's** Household History; **Drake's** Making the Great West; **Drake's** Making the Ohio Valley States; **Barnes's** Popular History of the United States; **Burgess's** Middle Period.

OUTSIDE READINGS: **McMaster's** United States, I.–IV.; **Hildreth's** United States, IV.–VI.; **Schouler's** United States, I.; **Henry Adams's** United States, I.–IX.; **Brooks's** First Across the Continent; **Lossing's** Field-book of the War of 1812; **Roosevelt's** Winning of the West, IV.; **Roosevelt's** Naval War of 1812; **Spears's** History of Our Navy; **Wilson's** A History of the American People, III.; **Thwaites's** Rocky Mountain Exploration; **Hosmer's** A History of the Mississippi Valley; **Hart's** How Our Grandfathers Lived; **Gordy's** Political History of the United States, I.–II.; **Parton's** General Jackson; **Johnston's** American Politics; **Lodge's** George Washington; **Lodge's** Alexander Hamilton; **Morse's** Thomas Jefferson; **Wharton's** Martha Washington; **Bolton's** Famous Americans; **Gilman's** James Monroe; **Magruder's** John Marshall; **Gay's** James Madison; **Schurz's** Henry Clay; **Morse's** John Quincy Adams.

FICTION : **Martineau's** Peasant and Prince; **Dickens's** Tale of Two Cities; **Henty's** In the Reign of Terror; **Hale's** Philip Nolan's Friends; **Hale's** Man Without a Country; **Elggeston's** Signal Boys; **Eggleston's** Captain Sam; **Eggleston's** Big Brother; **Bynner's** Zachary Phips; **Seawell's** Little Jarvis; **Seawell's** Midshipman Paulding.

POETRY : **Holmes's** Ode for Washington's Birthday ; **Key's** Star Spangled Banner; **Drake's** American Flag; **Holmes's** God Save the Flag ; **Holmes's** Old Ironsides.

DOMESTIC AFFAIRS IN THE EARLY YEARS OF THE NEW GOVERNMENT

184. Washington the First President.—It was natural that the people should wish George Washington to be the first President.[1] He stood for no party but was the choice of all the people, and he received the unanimous vote of the Presidential electors.[2] John Adams, of Massachusetts, was elected Vice-President. The inauguration had been planned for the first Wednesday in March, but travelling was so slow in those days that it was impossible for Congress to meet and count the electoral votes in time to have the inauguration before April 30. New York City was the capital of the country.

The inauguration at Federal Hall was very impressive. The oath of office was solemnly taken, and the chancellor of New York, who had given it, then turned to the people and cried, "Long live George Washington, President of the United States!" The cry was taken up by the throng, who, amid their joyous shouts, had escorted Washington from his house in New York to Federal Hall on his way to deliver his first inaugural.

The Inauguration.

185. The Number and Distribution of the People.— According to the census of 1790 the population of the

[1] George Washington, first President of the United States (1789-1797), was born in Westmoreland County, Va., February 22, 1732, and died at Mount Vernon December 14, 1799. When he was eleven years old his father died, leaving the youth in care of a faithful and devoted mother. While at school George was painstaking and careful with his work and excelled in such athletic sports as running, leaping, and wrestling. He was so true to himself and to others that he often acted as a judge in deciding disputes between his young friends. In 1759 he married a rich young widow, Mrs. Martha Custis, whose property, added to his own large estates at Mount Vernon, made him a man of much wealth. His bravery, patriotism, and military skill, as shown in the Last French War, led to his being chosen by the Continental Congress as Commander-in Chief of the American troops during the Revolution. By reason of his modesty he shrank from this service, for which he was admirably fitted. He refused to receive any pay during the entire Revolution. It may indeed be truly said that he proved himself indispensable to the success of the Americans in that war. He was a man of commanding presence and dignified manner. His success lay not in intellectual brilliancy, but in a well-balanced judgment, in a belief that right made might, and in a rare power of winning men's confidence.

[2] Under Section I., Article II., of the Constitution, may be found the following:

" Each State shall appoint, in such manner as the Legislature thereof may direct, a number of *Electors* equal to the whole number of Senators and Representatives to which the State may be entitled in the Congress." The people in the various States vote for these Presidential electors. The latter, called when taken together the Electoral College, vote directly for President and Vice-President.

United States was nearly 4,000,000 souls, about one-fifth of whom were negroes. Most of the people resided in the thirteen original States, not more than five per cent. being found west of the Alleghanies. The belt of settlement extended from Maine to Florida, with an average width of two **Well-settled** hundred and fifty-five miles. The most densely **regions.** peopled regions were on the coast of Massachusetts, of southern New England, and of New York. Other well-settled regions included the Hudson River val-

WASHINGTON'S MANSION—SOUTH AND WEST FRONTS—MT. VERNON, VA.

ley as far as Albany, the Mohawk valley, the route now followed by the Pennsylvania Railroad from New York across New Jersey to Philadelphia, and the river valleys of eastern Virginia.

Virginia ranked first in population, having 532,000 inhabitants. Massachusetts and Pennsylvania, with about **Five principal** 330,000 each, stood next. There were no large **commercial** cities. The principal commercial centres **centres.** were Philadelphia, with about 31,000; New York, with 23,000; Boston, with 15,000; Baltimore, with

13,000, and Charleston, with nearly 11,000. All these five cities contained fewer people than Albany or Denver alone contains to-day.

186. Modes of Travel.—The people lived mainly along rivers or on the coast, because one of the easiest and most convenient methods of travel was by boat or   Simple conditions sailing packet. It is not easy for us to realize   of life. how simple the conditions of life were in those days. Imagine our being without steamboats, railroads, electric cars,

telegraphs, and telephones, and you will have an idea how slowly life moved in 1789.

The best method of conveying passengers and goods by land was the clumsy old stage-coach. In Washington's first administration two stage-coaches

WASHINGTON'S BEDROOM, MT. VERNON, VA.

and twelve horses were sufficient to accommodate all the people and carry all the goods passing between Boston and New York, two of the chief commercial cen-   The old tres in the country. It took about as long to   stage-coach. make the trip as it does now to travel from Boston to San Francisco, or from New York to Liverpool. In summer the stage could cover forty miles a day. In winter, when the snow lay upon the ground or the roads were heavy with mud, the distance was cut down to twenty-five miles a day. About ten o'clock at night the traveller reached the wayside inn, where he put up for the night. He was called at three o'clock the next morning in time to renew his journey for another eighteen hours.

187. Ferries.—There were no bridges spanning large rivers as there are now. In going by stage from Boston to Philadelphia the passenger had to be ferried across eight or ten rivers. In a high wind these crossings were very dangerous, owing to great blocks of floating ice. Not uncommonly the ferryboat was upset by a sudden gust of wind. The passage in winter from New York to Jersey City (then Paulus Hook) involved more risk than a trip from New York to Japan does now.

188. The Mails.—To-day a number of express trains daily carry mail in less than six hours from New York to Boston, but in Washington's time a postman carried the mail on horseback from New York to Boston three times a week in summer and twice in winter. It required six days

The post-rider.

SERVANTS' QUARTERS, MT. VERNON, VA.

to make the trip in summer and nine in winter. A pair of saddle-bags sufficed to carry all the mail between these two commercial centres. Postmen carried mail from New York to Philadelphia five times a week, and were two days in making the journey. In regions remote from business centres an old man was often made post-rider. While his horse jogged leisurely along he would while away the lonely hours in knitting socks and mittens or in opening and reading the letters in the mail-bag.

These clumsy methods of travel and communication kept the people ignorant of those parts of the country which were not near them. The Massachusetts citizen knew very little about the citizen of South Carolina, and neither un-

Lack of national patriotism.

derstood the other. Under such conditions there was much foolish prejudice in each State against people in other States, and but little attachment to the Union. We see, therefore, that the patriotism of those days was a State patriotism rather than a national patriotism.

189. Washington's Formality.—The Federalists included much the larger part of the wealthy and commercial classes, and were especially strong in the cities. They were aristocratic in their feelings and were inclined to imitate English social and official customs. Believing in a strong central government, they wished the Presidential office to be one of great dignity. **Aristocratic feelings of the Federalists.** Washington had seen something of the pomp and state of the royal governor's court in Virginia, and it seems to have appealed to his sense of fitness. He therefore surrounded himself with much ceremony. On state occasions he rode in a coach drawn by six horses, and on ordinary occasions in a coach drawn by four horses. When walking on the street he was followed at a respectful distance by a body servant in livery. Every Tuesday afternoon, from three

A MAIL CARRIER.

A FAST MAIL—1876.

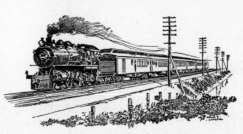

A TWENTIETH CENTURY FLYER.

to four o'clock, he held at the executive mansion a public reception, when he appeared in court dress, with powdered hair, a dress-sword at his side, and a cocked **Washington at public receptions.** hat under his arm. Standing with his right hand behind him, he bowed formally as his guests were presented. Moreover, he allowed his birthday to be celebrated.

These things greatly displeased many people, who charged Washington with the desire to become king. They wished the President to dress plainly and to live as simply as an ordinary citizen.

190. The New Government.—Washington's first duty was to organize the new government. John Jay was appointed first Chief Justice of the Supreme Court. The cabinet is most important, because its members are the

JOHN JAY.

heads of various executive departments and aid the President in doing his official work. Washington chose for his cabinet four eminent citizens who represented both political parties. Thomas Jefferson became Secretary of State; Alexander Hamilton, Secretary of the Treasury; General Henry Knox, Secretary of War; and Edmund Randolph, Attorney-General.

191. Hamilton and Jefferson the Two Great Political Leaders.— Hamilton was a stanch Federalist, but Jefferson was a bitter opponent

of the Federalists. They became the respective leaders of the two political parties, and were soon engaged in a long and bitter struggle to carry out their views of government. The struggle was not personal. It was a struggle of principles and did not end when Hamilton and Jefferson passed out of public life. It continued until it brought on the great Civil War. Shall the Federal Government be supreme over the State? Shall there be a liberal construction of the Constitution, so as to grant large powers to Congress and the President? Hamilton said "Yes;" Jefferson said "No." Jefferson feared that the Federal Government might become so strong as to rob the States of their powers and at last to drift into a monarchy. He believed that the general government had only such powers as were definitely

Shall the Federal or the State Government be supreme?

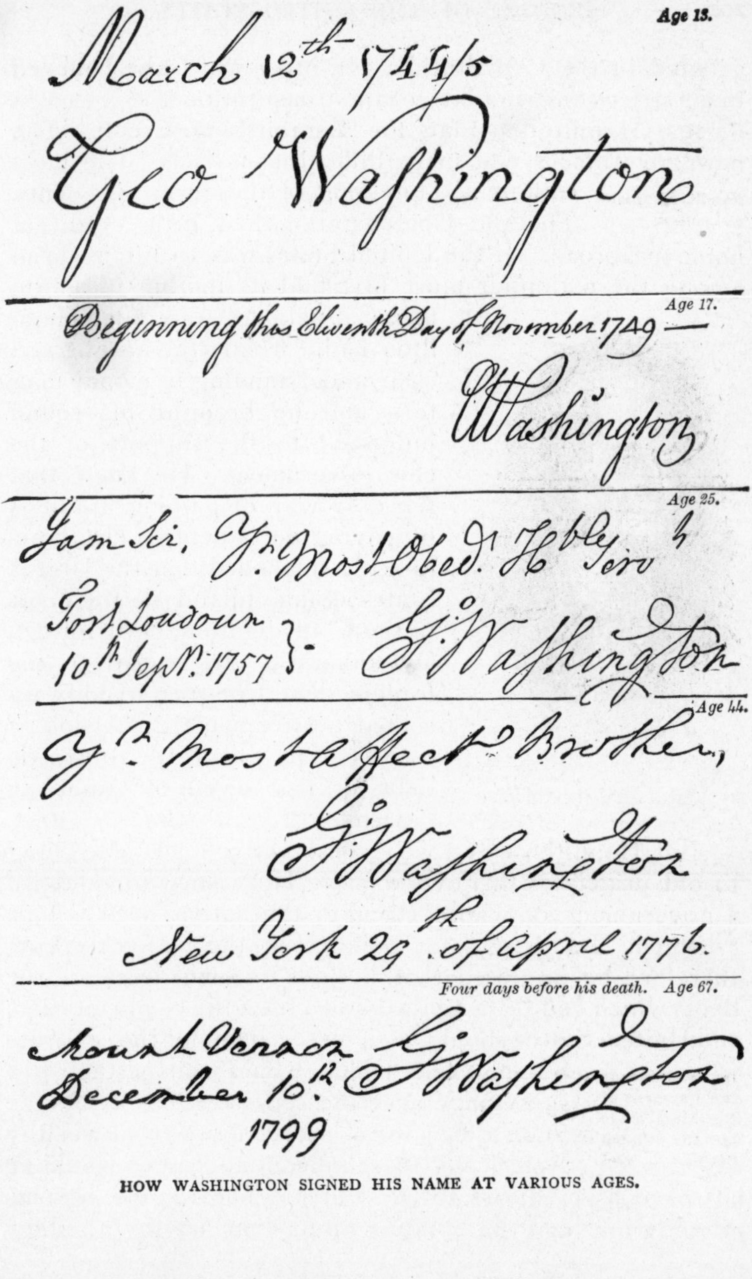
Age 13.
March 12th 1744/5
Geo Washington
Age 17.
Beginning this Eleventh Day of November 1749 —
Washington
Age 25.
Sam Sir, Yr. Most Obedt. Hble Servt.
Fort Loudoun 10th Septr. 1757 } — G:o Washington
Age 44.
Yr. Most affect.e Brother,
G:o Washington
New York 29th of April 1776.
Four days before his death. Age 67.
Mount Vernon December 10th 1799
G:o Washington

HOW WASHINGTON SIGNED HIS NAME AT VARIOUS AGES.

granted in the Constitution. In other words, he believed in a "strict construction" of the Constitution.

192. Hamilton's Plan for Establishing Credit.—The new government had many difficulties to face. The most *Hamilton's finan-* serious and pressing of these were its debts. *cial policy.* The old Confederation had little credit at home or abroad. If the United States was to lift its head among the nations it must first find its footing in a firm

ALEXANDER HAMILTON.

financial policy. Alexander Hamilton had a wonderful insight and clear understanding in money matters, and he brought his sound judgment to the support of the new government. He knew that the only way of gaining credit is by paying one's debts. He therefore recommended that the United States assume in full all the debts of the Confederation, both foreign and domestic. In regard to the foreign debt, Congress readily assented. After some discussion, it voted to pay also the domestic debt, or that owed to American citizens.

But Hamilton was a very conservative man. He clung to old principles of government. He wished to establish a government of whose strength the nation need not be ashamed. In his plan for building up the nation's credit, therefore, he proposed that, besides its own debts, or the debts which had been handed down from the Confederation, the United States should assume the debts of the separate *He recommends* States. The Union would thus establish a *the payment of* supremacy over the separate States. As the *the State debts* *by the United* State debts were mostly loans from wealthy *States.* Americans, these influential citizens would be attached as creditors to the Union. They would become directly interested in building up its financial credit. They would work to make the central government strong by giving it a large taxing power with which to obtain a revenue to pay its debts.

This part of the plan was novel and unexpected, and greatly alarmed the followers of Jefferson. They believed that the States should do a large part of the governing. They dreaded more than all else a strong central government, because they feared it might lead to a monarchy. They accused Hamilton of trying to rob the people of their rights by placing them under the rule of a king. Accordingly, the followers of Jefferson opposed the payment of the State debts by the United States, and after a bitter struggle defeated Hamilton's scheme by a narrow majority.

Jefferson's followers oppose the payment of the State debts.

Later, however, in return for an agreement to locate the new capital, Washington, upon the banks of the Potomac, the Jeffersonians conceded the assumption of the State debts to the followers of Hamilton. The measure proved one of the wisest policies ever adopted. It was a brilliant example of Hamilton's far-seeing statesmanship.

Washington made the capital.

193. A Tariff Laid on Foreign Trade.—How to raise the money to pay all these debts was a serious question. At its first session, Congress laid an indirect tax upon vessels and certain kinds of goods coming into this country from foreign ports. This tax, or tariff, was not only for the purpose of raising a revenue, but also for protecting the young manufactories springing up at various points in the United States. As this tariff did not yield revenue enough for the country's need, a direct tax was laid later on spirituous liquors (1794). Direct taxes are not generally popular, and this one was no exception. It was an unpleasant reminder of the Stamp Act. We need not be surprised, therefore, that resistance was offered to this direct tax imposed by the new government.

Tax on spirituous liquors.

194. The Whiskey Rebellion (1794).—The people of western Pennsylvania lived so far from business centres, which they could reach only by poor roads, that it was very expensive for them to transport their grain to market. There was more profit in making the grain into whiskey, which was much less bulky than the grain from which it was made. As the tax levied upon the whiskey lessened the profit of the farmers, they regarded this tax as unjust. They therefore refused to pay it, and severely handled officers sent by the Government to see that it was enforced. The people rose in arms to resist the law, but Washington promptly sent a body of troops, which easily put down the insurrection.

195. The Invention of the Cotton-gin (1793).—The Whiskey Rebellion had merely a passing interest. Whit-

A PRIMITIVE COTTON-GIN.

ney's cotton-gin had a permanent influence upon our history. Let us now consider that remarkable invention. In 1793 Eli Whitney, a Massachusetts man then living as a tutor at the home of General Greene's widow in Georgia, invented the cotton-gin. The influence of this invention upon cotton-growing, slavery, and the future history of the country cannot be measured. Before that time cotton was not raised to any great extent in the South. Without the cotton-gin a slave could separate, in a day, the seeds from only a single pound of cotton fibre, but now, with the aid of the cotton-gin, he could in the same time separate the seeds from a thousand pounds. The value of slave labor was thus greatly increased, and the planter could afford to sell his cotton much cheaper than before.

At once there was a great and increasing demand for cotton in English as well as Northern cotton-mills, and its culture became highly profitable. The general belief had been that slavery would gradually die out all over the country. It did not pay in the North, where there were no large plantations, and in that region it was already disappearing. But now the cotton-growers in the South and the owners of cotton-mills in the North had a selfish interest in the institution. For the owners of cotton-mills, like the planters, made money on the ever-increasing

Results of the invention of the cotton-gin.

WHITNEY'S FIRST COTTON-GIN.

demand for cotton, the price of which had been greatly lessened by the cotton-gin. They all thought that cotton-raising could not be carried on successfully without slave-labor. Hence the demand from this time forward for more and more slaves in the cotton States.

TO THE PUPIL

1. Note the fact that Washington was President for two terms, 1789–1797.
2. With your map before you, study carefully the distribution of the people in 1790. Why did the people live mainly along rivers or on the coast?
3. Try to form vivid mental pictures of travel by the old stage-coach. How was the mail carried in 1790? How did the clumsy methods of travel and communication affect the attitude of the people in one State toward the people of another State? On all these topics McMaster's History, I., will repay careful reading.
4. What classes of people were included in the Federalists? Discuss Washington's formality.
5. What is meant by the Cabinet?
6. "Shall the Federal Government be supreme over the States?" What answer did Hamilton give? Jefferson? You may well keep this great question in mind, for it will come up again and again in

the subsequent periods of our history. As you will find later, disagreement about the answer led at last to Civil War. What is
meant by "strict construction" of the Constitution?

7. What was Hamilton's financial policy? Why did he urge that the
United States should assume the debts of the separate States?
Why did Jefferson's followers oppose this part of Hamilton's plan?

8. Which do you think was right in his attitude toward the State debts,
Hamilton or Jefferson? Give reasons for your answer.

9. Review the difference between a direct and an indirect tax. What
indirect tax was levied? What was its purpose? What direct
tax was levied? Why was it unpopular?

10. What influence did the invention of the cotton-gin have upon the production of cotton by slave-labor? Explain why the Southern planters
and the Northern cotton-mill owners had, from the time the cotton-
gin was invented, a selfish interest in slavery.

11. For social life in New England and in other States read Coffin's
Building the Nation.

FOREIGN RELATIONS IN THE EARLY YEARS OF THE NEW
GOVERNMENT

**196. A Period of Trial and Uncertainty for the Young
Republic (1789–1815).**—When in 1789 Washington became
President, many intelligent people, both in Europe and
America, doubted whether the Federal Union would live
long. This was a reasonable doubt, for the young republic was yet weak and called forth little national feeling. A foreign traveller, visiting
the United States at this time, said that he
found no Americans; that the people were all English or
French in their sympathies and feelings. The English
party, or the Hamiltonians, and the French party, or the
Jeffersonians, were almost as intense in their dislike of each
other as were Englishmen and Frenchmen in Europe.

Soon after the outbreak of the French Revolution (1789),
war began between France and England and, with short
intervals of peace, continued until Napoleon's
downfall at Waterloo (1815). During this
great struggle many efforts were made to drag
the United States into the war. Both France and England were unwilling that this country should remain neu-

*Little national
feeling in the
United States.*

*War between
France and
England.*

tral.   When the United States refused to form an alliance with either country, both of them seriously injured our commerce.   They showed little respect for a people who seemed so lacking in national spirit.

The entire period from 1789 to the close of the War of 1812 was one of anxiety for the well-wishers of the republic. During all these years the American people were engaged in a struggle similar to the American Revo- *From 1789 to 1815* lution.   In the earlier struggle they were *the Americans* fighting to become independent of England; *struggle for in-* in the later they were striving to become *dependence of* *Europe.* independent of Europe.   This later period culminated in the War of 1812, which has been rightly called the Second War of Independence.   But from the beginning of Washington's administration the struggle over commercial or other difficulties was pressing.

197. Influence of the French Revolution upon American Affairs.—The same year that Washington became President was also the first year of the French Revolution. The people of France had been so oppres- *The French* sively taxed and otherwise misgoverned that *Revolution.* they were at last ready to resort to violence against the French monarchy.   They tore down the gloomy prison called the Bastile and afterward put to death the king and queen.   In the "reign of terror" that followed thousands of men and women were guillotined.   To add to the confusion, the French Republic was soon at war with neighboring countries.   She declared war with England in 1793.

Hamilton and his followers took the side of England; Jefferson and his supporters sympathized with the French revolutionists.   As France had helped us in the American Revolution, the French claimed that we ought *Washington* to help them in their struggle for freedom. *refuses to aid* *France.* At first Washington and the Hamiltonians, with gratitude to France for aid given us in the American Revolution, felt a warm interest; but later, when the revolutionists had resorted to extreme violence to carry out their plans, Hamilton began to regard them with great distrust.

Besides, Washington agreed with Hamilton in the belief that we were too weak to become involved in European wars, and he therefore issued a proclamation of neutrality.

198. Citizen Genet Defies Washington.—The new French Government, the Directory, knowing that many Americans were in sympathy with the French revolutionists, sent Citizen Genet as minister to the United States. In utter defiance of the President this indiscreet man tried to fit out American privateers to be used in destroying English commerce. In answer to objections from Washington, Genet threatened to appeal to the people, hoping they would approve his course and take his side against their own President. This threat was a striking bit of audacity and showed the contempt Genet felt for our government. But the people sustained Washington, and at his request Citizen Genet was recalled.

199. Jay's Fruitless Treaty with England.—The English would not give up Oswego, Niagara, Detroit, and other *Our difficulties with England.* Northwestern forts which, by the treaty of peace at the close of the Revolution, they had agreed to surrender. They also seriously interfered with our commerce by forcibly stopping and searching our vessels for deserters, and in many cases impressing our seamen into their service. Besides all this, they would not let us trade with the English West Indies. On the other hand, the English maintained that we had failed to keep our part of the same treaty by refusing to pay certain debts owed by Americans to English merchants, and by not making good the losses sustained by American Tories when they left their homes in this country during the Revolution.

To settle these difficulties John Jay was sent over to England. As a result a treaty was agreed upon which settled nothing about the impressment of American seamen. *Jay's treaty makes the Americans indignant.* England refused to discontinue this practice, but Jay felt that in our weak position among the nations of the world we must be satisfied with what we could get from a country so much stronger than our own. Washington, believing the treaty was the best we could arrange, urged its adoption. A large part of the American people were indignant. Hamilton was stoned while making a speech in New York in defence of the treaty, and Washington was so bitterly attacked and unjustly accused that he said he would rather be in his grave than be President.

200. Political Parties.—Originally, as we have seen, those supporting the Constitution were called Federalists, and those opposing it Anti-Feder-alists. After the Constitution went into effect, the Federalists, under the lead of Alexander Hamilton, favored a strong central government, while the Anti-Federalists, under the lead of Jefferson, wished the States to have most of the powers of government. The Jeffersonians called themselves Republicans, but since Jefferson's followers favored the French revolutionists, the Federalists called them Democrats, after the French Democrats. A little later they became known as Democratic-Republicans. In Andrew Jackson's administration

JOHN ADAMS.

they were called Democrats, and the name has remained till the present time.

201. The "X Y Z Papers."—Our trouble with France was by no means settled by the recall of Genet. When the Jay treaty with England was ratified, the French were so angry that they sent home our minister and recalled their own from the United States. French cruisers openly attacked our merchant vessels. The country was too weak for war, and President Adams[1] wished to avoid one if possible.

The French angry about the Jay treaty.

[1] John Adams, second President of the United States (1797–1801), was born at Braintree, Massachusetts, in 1735 and died July 4, 1826. After graduating from Harvard he became a lawyer. He was a prominent member of the Continental Con-

The French having promised to receive an embassy with honor, President Adams sent over three envoys, John Marshall, afterward Chief Justice, Charles Pinckney, and Elbridge Gerry to set things right. Upon their arrival they were not received with respect. They were boldly informed that peace with France could be secured only on two conditions: (1) That a large sum of money should be paid to members of the Directory, and (2) that an additional sum should be loaned to France for carrying on her wars. The papers reporting to Congress these shameful propositions were signed, not by the names of the secret agents representing the French Government, but by the letters X Y Z. Hence they were called the "X Y Z Papers." Pinckney's indignant reply was, "Millions for defence, but not one cent for tribute," and this became a rallying cry throughout the United States.

Congress organized an army and put Washington at the head of it. In the meantime, the French continued to capture our vessels and seized a thousand of them.

Serious trouble with France.

Soon a state of war existed on the sea, where Commodore Truxton defeated and captured two French frigates.[1] These defeats recalled France from her insolent attitude, and when President Adams again sent over envoys,

gress, and proposed Washington for commander-in-chief of the American troops. Being an eloquent advocate of independence, he did much to bring about a political separation from England. He was one of the three commissioners who negotiated a treaty of peace with Great Britain at the close of the Revolution and afterward became the first American minister to England. His honesty and courage won the admiration of his friends, but his obstinacy and lack of tact involved him in many quarrels.

John Adams was inaugurated at Philadelphia, which had taken the place of New York as the seat of government. During his term of office, in 1800, Washington became the capital.

[1] Out of the excitement that thrilled the people the song, "Hail, Columbia," sprang. The words were written by a lawyer of Philadelphia, Joseph Hopkinson, and set to the music of the march composed for Washington's inauguration. "Hail, Columbia" was first sung at a theatre in Philadelphia. The applause was tremendous. Men rose to their feet, throwing their hats into the air, and women vigorously waved their handkerchiefs. Again and again the audience called for the song until it had been sung nine times. In a few weeks "Hail, Columbia" was known by thousands of enthusiastic Americans.

Napoleon Bonaparte, who was then at the head of affairs, made things satisfactory to this country.

202. Alien and Sedition Laws (1798).—These difficulties with France stirred the patriotic feelings of our people and for a time strengthened the Federalist party. Its leaders went too far, however, when they passed the Alien and Sedition Laws. Many of the Democratic-Republican newspapers were under the influence of Frenchmen who had come to live in the United States. These men used their papers to make bitter and slanderous attacks upon President Adams and the government. Naturally the Federalists, with their leanings toward a strong central government, believed that such attacks weakened the Union by lessening the respect of the people for it. They therefore passed the Alien Law, which gave the President power to send out of the country any foreigner whom he might think dangerous to its peace. The Sedition Law gave him power to fine or imprison any one who might conspire against the government or publish anything evil against it.

This law violated the first Amendment to the Constitution by interfering with the freedom of the press, and aroused the Democratic-Republicans to a high state of indignation. They said such laws were tyrannical and proved the desire of the Federal leaders for something like a monarchy. The Virginia Resolutions, written by Madison, and the Kentucky Resolutions, written by Jefferson, expressed their dislike of the Alien and Sedition Laws. These Resolutions not only declared the laws to be unconstitutional, but the Kentucky Resolutions went so far as to say that a State might rightfully nullify any act passed by Congress that was not constitutional. Nullifying a law is declaring it not binding, and therefore nullification is a most dangerous doctrine; for if each State should reserve the right to refuse obedience to any law which in its judgment violates the Constitution, that document would in time be worth as little as the paper it is written on, and the Federal Union would fall to pieces.

The Virginia and the Kentucky Resolutions (1798-1799).

203. Chief Justice Marshall's Influence in Strengthening the Federal Union.—That this result was not brought about was largely due to the influence of one man. Just before going out of office in 1801, President Adams appointed John Marshall,[1] of Virginia, as Chief Justice of the Supreme Court. He heartily believed in the liberal construction of the Constitution, and for thirty-five years his decisions as Chief Justice of the Supreme Court had great influence in making the general government superior to the States in all questions affecting the common interests of the whole people. It has well been said of him: "He found the Constitution paper, and made it power; he found it a skeleton, and clothed it with flesh and blood."

TO THE PUPIL

1. Review the significance of the following dates: 1492, 1588, 1689. Now add to these 1789. Why is it significant? Can you think of any reason for the lack of national feeling among the Americans in 1789?

2. Look up in Coffin's Building the Nation the causes of the French Revolution.

3. Why was the entire period from 1789 to 1815 one of trial and anxiety for the Young Republic? Do not forget these dates.

4. Why did the French Revolutionists maintain that we should aid them in their war with England? What did Washington think of aiding them? Was he right or wrong? Give reasons for your answer.

5. What difficulties did we have with England? Why was Jay's treaty unsatisfactory to a large part of the American people? Do you like it or not? Give reasons for your answer.

6. Review the origin of the Federalist and the Anti-Federalist parties. What were these parties now called? What was the principal difference between them?

7. How did the French indicate their anger about the Jay treaty? Explain clearly the "X Y Z Papers." What recalled France from her insolent attitude toward the Americans? At this juncture John Adams, our second President, was in office. He served one term, 1797–1801.

[1] John Marshall was a great American and left his impress upon the government as few men have done. His personal appearance was striking. He was tall and slender, with black hair and small eyes. Simple in dress and modest in manner, his warm heart won the truest friendship of those who knew him. With rare grasp of mind and greatness of purpose, he labored to make the Union strong.

8. What facts led the Federalists to pass the Alien and Sedition laws? What were these laws? What were the Virginia and Kentucky Resolutions? Mark them well. They were a significant and dangerous step toward the nullification and secession movements of later years.

9. What kind of man was Chief Justice Marshall? Memorize the quotation which well indicates the work of this remarkable man, the greatest chief justice we have ever had.

10. If you will read Martineau's Peasant and Prince you will have clear ideas about the leading facts of the French Revolution.

SETTLEMENT OF THE MISSISSIPPI VALLEY

204. **Thomas Jefferson, the Democratic-Republican Leader, becomes President.**[1]—Before beginning to discuss the settlement of the Mississippi valley let us consider for a moment a statesman whose greatest act was the purchase of Louisiana, a large part of this valley. That statesman was Thomas Jefferson, of Virginia, who became the third President (March 4, 1801).[2] Up to that time the national government had been under the control of the Federalists, and many people believed that the election of the Demo-

[1] Thomas Jefferson, third President of the United States (1801–1809), was born at Shadwell, Virginia, in 1743 and died at Monticello, Virginia, July 4, 1826. At seventeen years of age he entered the College of William and Mary, where he was an earnest student. He afterward became one of the most learned men of his times, being known as the "Sage of Monticello." He was also a daring horseman and an excellent violinist. After graduating from college he studied law and soon exercised a large influence over the politics of his State and his country. He was elected a member of the Continental Congress and, as chairman of the committee to draft the Declaration of Independence, wrote practically all of that remarkable document. At the end of his Presidential term of office he retired to his beautiful home, Monticello, where he spent the remaining years of his life.

[2] The Presidential election for a successor to John Adams caused much bitter feeling between the two political parties. The Federalists cast their votes for John Adams and C. C. Pinckney; the Republicans, for Thomas Jefferson and Aaron Burr. As the two latter each received seventy-three electoral votes, neither was elected, and the election was thrown into the House of Representatives, which, according to the Constitution, was to choose one of them for President. The contest was prolonged and exciting, but ended, as above stated, in the choice of Jefferson as President. Burr became Vice-President. This unfortunate contest resulted in the Twelfth Amendment to the Constitution, in accordance with which the Presidential electors must vote separately for President and for Vice-President.

cratic-Republican President would lead to the country's ruin. In this, of course, they were greatly in error, for Jefferson, as President, moved slowly in changing the policy of the government, and did many things to make the general government stronger than it had been before.

205. Jefferson's " Republican Simplicity."—During the eight years of his Presidency Jefferson wielded a large personal influence over the people.   Form and ceremony were distasteful to him. He believed the President should be simple in dress and manner and mingle freely with the people. In his " red waistcoat, yarn stockings, and slippers down at the heel," he presented a striking contrast to the courtly appearance of Washington.

SCHOOL-HOUSE WHERE THOMAS JEFFERSON RECEIVED HIS EARLY EDUCATION.

On the day of his inauguration he went on foot to the Capitol, in his ordinary dress, escorted by a number of his political friends.[1] It became his custom, when visiting the Capitol, to ride on a horse, which he tied with his own hands before entering. He did not hold **Jefferson the idol** weekly receptions, but he entertained hospi-**of the masses.** tably and allowed persons wishing to see him to call at any time. Though the Federalists did not be-

[1] Henry Adams, in Vol. I., pp. 190, 191, of his History of the United States, denies the truth of the story that on the day of his inauguration " Jefferson rode on horseback to the Capitol and, after hitching his horse to the palings, went in to take his oath."

lieve it best for men of all classes and conditions to vote, Jefferson, because of his great faith in the people, was an advocate of universal manhood suffrage. We need not be surprised, then, to learn that he became the idol of the masses.

206. Pioneers in the Mississippi Valley before the Revolution.—We have seen how Boone, Clarke, Sevier,

MONTICELLO, THE HOME OF JEFFERSON.

and Robertson were leaders among the pioneers who went from Virginia and the Carolinas across the mountains before the Revolution and made settlements in Kentucky and Tennessee. Their only roads were the forest-trail and the river; their only means of travel and transportation the pack-horse and the canoe. Daring and full of the spirit of adventure, they relied quite as much upon the rifle as upon the axe and the hoe. Leading their pack-horses along the rough mountain pathways, they built log huts for dwellings, and with their rude tillage raised a few vegetables and a little corn for food.

The pack-horse and the forest-trail.

207. Life in the Backwoods of Kentucky and Tennessee in Pioneer Days.—Often the pioneer's cabin was built of rough logs and had only one room, with a ladder reaching to a loft above, where the children slept. Articles of clothing hung upon pegs that were thrust into the sides of the house. A rough piece of board resting upon four wooden legs served as a table, three-legged stools were used as chairs, and wooden bowls as dishes. Life was everywhere plain and simple, and society democratic. Land was plentiful, and every head of a household had his own farm, usually of about four hundred acres.

The cabin and its furniture.

THOMAS JEFFERSON.

The settler relied upon his rifle for meat. He dressed much like an Indian, often appearing in a fur cap, a fringed hunting-shirt of buck-skin, and moccasins and leggings made of the skins of wild animals. Amusements took a practical turn, the pioneers making them a pleasurable means of getting their work done. Hence, log-rollings, corn-huskings, and quiltings were common. After the work was out of the way the guests sat down at a table loaded with an abundance of such coarse foods as the backwoods afforded and such beverages as rum and whiskey. Then followed dancing, wrestling, racing, and various other sports calling for strength and skill.

The settler.

Amusements.

208. The Flatboat and the Ohio River.—Soon after the ordinance of 1787 was adopted, and the fertile region lying between the Ohio and the Mississippi was opened for settlement, population began to stream westward. Yankees from New England, Scotch from New York, and Germans from Pennsylvania formed the bulk of this second emigration to the West. This wave of

Westward emigration.

migration was greatly accelerated by the use of the flatboat, which could be employed as soon as the Ohio River was reached. By means of the flatboat the settler could carry many more goods than with the pack-horse. He could also travel much more rapidly, especially when

A PACK-HORSE.

going with the current. For this reason it was natural that this westward movement should follow the lines of the Ohio and the streams flowing into it from the north. Along their banks such towns as Marietta, Cincinnati, and Louisville rapidly sprang up.

209. Twofold Use of Rivers.—The rivers were valuable, not only for bringing the new settlers to their homes, but also as highways for their trade. The settlers could not profitably carry their bulky produce, such as corn-meal, flour, ham, and bacon, on pack-horses over the mountains to eastern business centres; but they could easily float their produce on rafts or flatboats down the currents of the Ohio and Mississippi Rivers to New Orleans. There, instead of attempting the slow and laborious return against the current, they disposed of their cargoes and sold their boats as lumber.

The goods received in exchange were put aboard

A HAND CORN-MILL.

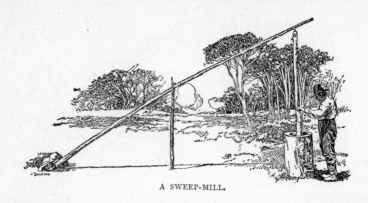

A SWEEP-MILL.

vessels sailing for Baltimore or some other Atlantic port, and from there taken over the mountains to the Ohio valley.

The roundabout trip the settler must make in trading.   Several months were required to make this roundabout trip. But this circuitous route was the only one by which the Westerners could get such home comforts as clothing, furniture, and other manufactured products. As the Mississippi was their outlet into the world, their prosperity depended upon its free use for navigation.

210. Napoleon's Scheme to Plant Colonies in the Mississippi Valley.—By the treaty of 1763 France had given

BREAKING FLAX.

up to Spain all claim to the Mississippi valley lying west of the river. The dreams of La Salle for establishing a New France in America had failed to be realized. But by 1800 Napoleon, who had become the all-powerful ruler of France, conceived a similar and equally brilliant plan. He determined to secure Louisiana—which included all the country from the Mississippi to the Rockies between Texas and Canada—and to people it with French colonists. New France in America would thus be revived, and the American Union would be hemmed in between the Mississippi and the Atlantic.

211. France Regains Louisiana from Spain (1800).— Napoleon forced Spain to cede Louisiana to France, and thus carried out the first part of his plan. He next sent an army to subdue the island of San Domingo. His purpose was to make this island a base for his extensive operations in the Mississippi valley. But in this attempt he met a mighty opposition. Toussaint L'Ouverture, a native black

AN OHIO RIVER FLATBOAT.

general, fought the French troops with desperate heroism. Although he was taken prisoner, yellow fever finished the work which he had begun. Many thousand French soldiers perished, and the island was not subdued. The army intended for the support of the colonists in Louisiana never reached New Orleans. War between France and England was again about to break out, and Napoleon was too busy in Europe to think of colonizing America.

French army for Louisiana detained at San Domingo.

212. Alarm in the United States.—When the Americans found that Louisiana had again passed into the hands of France they were alarmed. It was bad enough to have the territory colonized by feeble Spain. It was far worse to have for a neighbor a dangerous rival like France. This feeling was especially prevalent among the settlers west of the Alleghanies. Their alarm was increased when they learned that the Spanish authorities at New Orleans had refused to let them float their products to that town and there reship them. Closing the Mississippi to their trade meant their commercial ruin. Their indignation was at a white heat and they talked loudly of war. They urged Jefferson to get control of the island on which New Orleans stood, and of the territory including the east bank of the river to its mouth and extending some distance eastward. The free navigation of the Mississippi would thus be assured.

The indignant Westerners talk of war with Spain.

213. The United States Purchases Louisiana (1803).— President Jefferson therefore sent Monroe over to France as special envoy to aid Livingston, the American minister, in securing West Florida and New Orleans. It was an opportune time for the Americans. As Napoleon was greatly in need of money for his war with England, he was willing to sell much more territory than the envoys were instructed to buy. The result was that we purchased from France in 1803, for $15,000,000, the immense Louisiana territory, a larger area than the United States of that day contained.[1] By this purchase Jefferson was taking much greater liberties with the Constitution than the Federalists had ever done. His action was directly contrary to the teachings of his party. He realized this, but the purchase was so plainly for the interests of the people that he felt justified in making it.

The purchase proved to be the greatest act of his administration and had four important results : (1) It kept France from planting colonies which would be our near neighbors; (2) it prevented England from getting possession of the territory by treaty with France; (3) it gave us the control of the Mississippi River ; (4) it added much to the strength of the national government.

Results of the purchase.

[1] Before 1803 the area of the United States was 827,844 square miles. The Louisiana purchase added 1,171,931 square miles to this area.

EARLY SETTLERS CROSSING THE PLAINS.

Singularly enough, Jefferson, the writer of the Kentucky Resolutions, boldly did that for which the Constitution made no express provision. The Federalists declared the purchase to be unconstitutional, *Jefferson's bold action.* and many people opposed it on the ground that we already had territory enough. But the great majority, especially in the West, warmly applauded Jefferson's course.

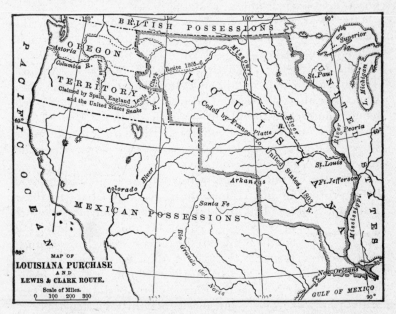

MAP OF
LOUISIANA PURCHASE
AND
LEWIS & CLARK ROUTE.
Scale of Miles.
0   100   200   300

214. Lewis and Clark's Expedition[1] through the Louisiana Territory to the Pacific (1804–1806.)

—Previous to the purchase of Louisiana, Jefferson sent to Congress a message recommending that an exploring party be sent to the Pacific Ocean. Accordingly a party of thirty men under Lewis and Clark started from St. Louis in 1804 and travelled in boats to the head-waters of the Missouri, nearly three thousand miles from its mouth. Here they procured horses from some Indians, made their way over the moun-

---

[1] In accordance with Jefferson's long cherished desire this expedition was designed *primarily* to explore the Missouri River to its source and then by the easiest route to reach and explore some river flowing into the Pacific Ocean.

tains, and again taking to boats, floated down the Columbia River to the Pacific. After nearly two years and a half, the party returned with a most interesting account of their experiences. Besides giving the American people some **Results of the expedition.** idea of the vast extent and great wealth of the Louisiana purchase, Lewis and Clark's expedition gave the United States a basis for claiming the Oregon Country some years later.

215. War with the Barbary States (1801–1815).—In the year 1801 the attention of the American people was suddenly drawn toward the East. The Barbary States included the petty Moorish powers of Morocco, Algiers, Tunis, and Tripoli, on the northern coast of Africa. For some time their pirates had been seriously disturbing American commerce in the Mediterranean. They captured and destroyed our vessels, confiscated the cargoes, and made slaves of the crews. In many cases large sums were paid to ransom Americans from slavery.

Like the various nations of Europe, the United States had been protecting her commerce by paying tribute to these Barbary States. But the pirates grew continually more **War with Tripoli.** aggressive. Tripoli became so insolent that finally the United States declared war against that country (1802). By 1805 Tripoli was forced by our navy to make peace and to stop interfering with our commerce. For some years the Barbary pirates did not interfere with American vessels, but it was not till 1815 that their at- **Results of war with the Barbary States.** tacks were entirely suppressed. The war with these states had two good results: (1) It forced Jefferson to increase the navy; (2) it was a training school by which our officers and seamen greatly profited in the War of 1812.

216. Fulton's Steamboat and River Navigation. — The war with the Barbary States brought the young republic into a more prominent position in the eyes of Europe, and showed that the American spirit would have to be reckoned with. But, important as the results were, they sank into comparative insignificance when placed beside an event

LEWIS'S FIRST GLIMPSE OF THE ROCKIES.
(Lewis and Clark Expedition, 1804.)

which, at the time, attracted no special attention. In the year 1807 Robert Fulton, after many trials and difficulties, succeeded in applying steam to boats as a motive power. The outcome of his efforts was the steamboat *Clermont*, a clumsy affair that people ridiculed by calling it " Fulton's Folly." On the day advertised for its trial trip from New York, a large crowd **The 'Clermont."** gathered on the river side, expecting to witness a failure. When the boat slowly moved off they began to jeer, but when finally the success of the experiment was no longer in doubt they were equally hearty in their applause. The *Clermont* steamed up the Hudson from New York to Albany, 150 miles, at the rate of nearly five miles an hour. At once the boat became a wonder to the people, and they came many miles to see it.

Four years later (1811) the first steamboat on Western rivers was launched on the Ohio at Pittsburg. As this strange-looking object passed down the Ohio at what was then regarded as wonderful speed, the people on the riverbanks were filled with awe and fear. The flying sparks, especially at night, and the unusual noise of the wheels, made some of the more ignorant onlookers believe the end of the world was near. This boat was soon **Use of the steam-** followed by others, and the great network of **boat on Western** rivers became thick with steam-driven craft, **rivers.** defying wind and current. The steamboat was a great advance upon the flatboat. Western settlers could now more easily and cheaply reach the fertile land in the great valley and send their produce to good markets. The steamboat gave a fresh impulse to Western migration also. Population increased and many new settlements sprang up.

217. Burr's Conspiracy.—While holding the office of Vice-President, Aaron Burr—a brilliant and villainous man —killed Alexander Hamilton in a duel, because Hamilton had prevented him from being made President of the United States, and later from being elected Governor of New York. Having failed to satisfy his political ambition in the East, Burr got together soldiers and adventurers from the Western States, and sailed down the Ohio and the Mississippi to carry out some schemes not yet fully understood. It is thought that his plan was to establish a personal government in the Southwest, possibly including the Spanish possessions in Mexico. In due time he was taken and tried for treason, but was acquitted for lack of evidence. He died many years later, disgraced by his own acts and despised by the American people.

TO THE PUPIL

1. How did Jefferson illustrate his republican simplicity? Compare his ideas of formality with those of Washington. Why would the Federalists naturally favor pomp and ceremony on the part of the President?

2. Prepare to write five minutes about any one of the following Western leaders: Boone, Clark, Sevier, and Robertson. Describe the life of the pioneer settlers.

3. What advantages had the flatboat over the pack-horse? What were the two uses of rivers? With your map before you, outline the roundabout trip the Western settler had to make in trading.

4. Napoleon is one of the most interesting men in all history. Can you not look up some facts about his life and his plans of conquest? Any short French History will give you all you need. Perhaps after you have read such a brief sketch you will wish to read what you can find about the great general in Henry Adams's History of the United States.

5. What was Napoleon's scheme to plant colonies in the Mississippi valley? Compare this scheme with La Salle's. In this connection review La Salle's work. In what respect was La Salle like Napoleon?

6. What country owned Louisiana at this time? What had the island of San Domingo and the black general Toussaint L'Ouverture to do with Napoleon's scheme for colonizing the Mississippi valley? Why did the cession of Louisiana to France alarm the people of the United States?

7. What steps did Jefferson take which finally led to the purchase of Louisiana? What were the results of this purchase?

8. Do not fail to get a clear idea of the territory that was included in Louisiana. How many States like your own did its area equal?

9. How did the steamboat aid Western migration?

10. Find out what you can about Burr's relations with Hamilton. Compare the two men. What was Burr's Conspiracy?

11. In connection with the study of Aaron Burr, read Hale's Man With-
    out a Country.   The chapter in Shaler's History of the United
    States, Vol. I., on the Mississippi valley, is worth careful reading.

THE WAR OF 1812, OR THE SECOND WAR OF INDEPENDENCE

218. England Claims the Right to Search American
Vessels and Impress American Seamen.—England still
continued to search our vessels and to impress into her
service American seamen.   She claimed that " Once an English-
English seamen, having once been English man, always an
subjects, always remained such; or, as the say- Englishman."
ing ran, " Once an Englishman, always an Englishman."
On the other hand, our government claimed that an English-
born subject could become an American by naturalization.

There was doubtless cause for annoyance on both sides.
Many English seamen, on reaching American ports, easily
procured fraudulent naturalization papers, and Fraudulent nat-
entered the American service.   As a result, an uralization.
English captain was often embarrassed to find that, after
making a port and visiting the town, he had no crew with
which to put to sea again.   And why was American service
preferred?   Because better treatment and higher pay were
received on American vessels.

The commanders of English war-ships therefore insisted
upon searching our vessels and taking off American seamen
on the charge that they were deserters.   English cruisers
hovered about the more important American ports, and in
their search for seamen boarded every vessel entering or
leaving the harbor.   Before the War of 1812 began nine
hundred American vessels had been searched, and more
than 4,000 Americans had been impressed into the English
service.

These insults and outrages reached their most irritating
stage in the attack made on the frigate *Chesapeake* by the
British man-of-war *Leopard*, off the coast of Virginia.   The
English captain made a demand for some English deserters
who, he claimed, were on the American frigate.   When

the American commander protested, the Englishman fired a broadside, killing or wounding twenty-one of the Ameri-

The "Leopard" fires upon the "Chesapeake." can crew. The *Chesapeake*, not being in a condition to make resistance, surrendered. She was boarded, and four of her crew were arrested for deserters and taken on board the *Leopard*. One of these was afterward hanged as a deserter and the other three, who were Americans, were released.

The people were deeply excited, and in some quarters there was a clamor for war. But as the country was ill prepared for war, Jefferson could go no further than to en-

Results. ter a protest, and warn English men-of-war to leave American waters. In return, the British Government made a tardy and half-hearted apology, but declared its purpose to continue the impressment of seamen.

219. England and France Greatly Injure American Commerce (1806–1807).—England and France, now at war, tried to starve each other into submission. Each country, in her efforts to injure the other's trade, seriously crippled American commerce. During the early years of the war our vessels had done much of the carrying trade of the world, and our merchants had been growing rich. But in 1806[1] and 1807 England issued her " Orders in Council,"

England's "Orders in Council" and Napoleon's "Decrees." which forbade neutral vessels to trade with France or her allies. Napoleon retaliated by issuing his " Decrees," which placed a prohibition upon all neutral trade with England. As nearly all American commerce was with England, France, and their respective allies, these restrictions threatened it with ruin. If an American vessel was bound for an English port she was liable to be seized by the French. If she risked a voyage to a French or other Continental port she was liable to be seized by an English man-of-war. Thus our

---

[1] "Orders in Council," issued in England in 1806, declared that all the ports between Brest and the Elbe were in a state of blockade. In 1807 a similar order declared all ports blockaded from which the British flag was excluded, and forbade all vessels to trade with France or any of her allies.

merchantmen were between two fires. They were pretty certain not to escape both.

220. Jefferson's Peace Policy and the Embargo (1807). —With all his greatness, Jefferson was not a model executive in time of serious foreign difficulties demanding firm and vigorous measures. He abhorred war and believed that the same results could be accomplished by peaceful means. He thought that by refusing to trade with England and France he could force them to a reasonable and just treatment of the United States. As an expression of his peace policy, he secured the passage of the Embargo Act (December, 1807). This prohibited all American vessels from leaving the United States for foreign ports and foreign vessels from taking cargoes out of American ports.

Jefferson thought that France and England stood in such need of our trade that they would soon come to terms when deprived of it. But they could do without our trade much better than we could do without theirs. Our ships rotted at the wharves. Our commerce was destroyed. New York and New England especially suffered, and business distress became very severe. A few hot-headed men in the Eastern States suggested withdrawing from the Union.[1] The farmers and planters also suffered greatly because they could not export their produce. Many of the Virginia planters, whose principal source of wealth was tobacco, were nearly ruined.

Disastrous results of the Embargo, and its repeal.

Dissatisfaction was so bitter that Jefferson, after considerable urging, consented to the repeal of the Embargo after a trial of fourteen months. The Non-intercourse Act, allowing American vessels to open trade with all the world except France and England, took the place of the Embargo (1809).[2]

Bitter dissatisfaction leads to the repeal of the Embargo.

[1] When New England commerce was ruined, the merchants of that part of the country invested their money in manufacturing.

[2] By act of Congress the Embargo was removed on March 4, the day when Jefferson's term of office expired and Madison succeeded him as President. James

221. Tecumseh's Conspiracy (1811).—From these commercial difficulties we may now turn our attention to Indian troubles, supposed to be incited by England. The rapid settlement north of the Ohio in the early part of the century made the Indians of that region restless and dissatisfied. General Harrison, who had been appointed Governor of Indiana Territory, bought from some of the tribes a tract of land on the Wabash River. Tecumseh, an able Indian chief, objected to the sale. A few tribes, he said, had no right to sell

Tecumseh and his plans. land belonging to the whole Indian race. It is quite likely that he was encouraged by the English in his unfriendly feelings against the Americans, for it is thought that the English supplied the Indians of the Northwest with arms and ammunition. Tecumseh's plan was similar to that of Pontiac. It was to unite the Southern and Northwestern Indians in one great conspiracy, in order to drive the whites back from the frontiers and make the Ohio River a permanent boundary between the red race and the whites.

JAMES MADISON.

When General Harrison became aware of Tecumseh's purpose, he marched with a body of troops against the Indian town on the Tippecanoe River, in Indiana. A battle

Madison, fourth President of the United States (1809–1817), was born in King George County, Virginia, in 1751, and died in 1836. After he was graduated from Princeton, at twenty-one years of age, he studied law. Few men of his time did so much to bring about the Federal convention of 1787. He was one of the ablest advocates of the Constitution, and was the author of many of its fundamental features. He was associated with Hamilton and Jay in writing the very able papers that appeared in the Federalist. After being Jefferson's Secretary of State, he was elected President. Like Jefferson, Madison was a man of scholarly attainments and constructive statesmanship, but was not adapted to the pressing emergencies that must be met by the President of the United States in time of war.

was fought in which the Indians were defeated. Their power between the Ohio and Mississippi was broken forever. It was at last decided that the Northwest Territory, so long in dispute between the English and the Indians on one side and the Americans on the other, was to remain in possession of the United States. Thus did a single battle dispose of Tecumseh's conspiracy. The troubles with England about commerce and the impressment of American seamen were much more serious.

Battle of Tippecanoe and its results.

222. Causes of the War of 1812; Political Parties.— Congress expressed a willingness to repeal the Non-intercourse Acts (May, 1810), provided France and England would revoke their decrees against American commerce. Napoleon, who had little regard for truth when it stood in the way of his ambition, then played a trick upon our government in the hope of bringing on war between the United States and England. He informed us that he would revoke his decrees, but at the same time he sent secret orders to the French Admiralty to continue seizing our vessels. When the French emperor made this promise, England was requested to do likewise. She, however, would not consent, because she knew that Napoleon was not acting in good faith. For a time American vessels were allowed to enter French ports without being seized. But when a goodly number were within reach, the French swooped down upon them and confiscated them and their cargoes.

Napoleon's trick.

England believed that Americans were favoring France, and therefore vexed and irritated them more than ever before. Her war-ships lay in wait along the entire eastern coast of the United States and captured many of our merchantmen. Bitterness toward England increased. It seems pretty clear that the United States had as much ground for going to war with the one country as with the other. But we were too weak to go to war with both of them, and the stronger of the two political parties, which had always sympathized with

Increasing trouble with England.

France, wished for war with England rather than with France.

The Federalist party included most of the commercial classes and the wealthy business men of the country. They were strong in New England and were closely **Attitude of the two political parties toward war with England.** allied in trade with England. They believed that the war was needless and wicked. They asserted that in making it the United States was really strengthening Napoleon in his ambitious schemes in Europe. This was true. On the other hand, the Democratic-Republicans were largely made up of the agricultural classes in the South and West. The Westerners in particular cherished bitter memories of England's Indian policy during the Revolution, and were eager for a war with that country. The young leaders, Henry Clay, of Kentucky, and John C. Calhoun, of South Carolina, thought that such a war would result in the speedy conquering of Canada. Later on, as we shall see, the attempt to conquer Canada became a leading feature of the war.

Finally, on June 18, 1812, war was declared, although New England hotly opposed it. This opposition led to great difficulty in securing the necessary loans for carrying **War declared.** on the war, because a large part of the money in the country was in the hands of New England business men, who refused to loan it to the government.

223. The British and the American Navies.—When the war began the United States was not prepared for it. The Democratic-Republicans had never favored a navy. Moreover, Jefferson had been so bent on paying off the national debt that he had used all his influence against building a strong navy. The land forces were without proper equipment, good discipline, or competent officers. England's navy contained about 1,000 vessels, many of them belonging to the largest and most powerful class. It was greater than the combined navies of the rest of the world. To match this, the United States navy contained only twelve war-vessels, none of them large, but all well built and the best of their class.   There was small hope that this little navy could do much when fighting against the " Mistress of the Seas." But as soon as war was declared, the American vessels gallantly started out in search of the enemy.

224. Fight Between the Constitution and the Guerrière (1812).—The first sea fight of importance was between the *Constitution*, commanded by Captain Isaac Hull, and the English man-of-war *Guerrière*, which were thought to be about equal in fighting strength.   Within a half-hour the Americans won a splendid victory.   They thoroughly disabled the English vessel, so that she had to be destroyed where she lay at the end of the fight.   The *Constitution* was practically unharmed, and lost in killed and wounded only fourteen men.   The *Guerrière* lost one hundred.   This naval duel took place (August 19, 1812) in less than three months after war was declared.   By reason of this and later victories, the people afterward proudly named the *Constitution* " Old Ironsides."

225. Superiority of Americans in Naval Battles.—In twenty years of fighting with France, England had lost only five vessels.   In about six months of fighting in the War of 1812 she lost every one of the six vessels that fought with the Americans.   Europe was amazed.   England was, of course, chagrined ; but Americans were carried away with enthusiasm.   Their gallantry on the sea showed that they had lost none of the national spirit shown by them in the days of the Revolution.   The British officers and seamen were so accustomed to winning victories that they had become careless in their training and discipline.   The marvellous success of the Americans was due to better seamanship, more accurate gunnery, and the superior construction of their vessels.

But our victories did not prevent the immense English navy from blockading our coast.   Smarting under repeated defeats when she had counted on certain victory, England transferred a good part of her navy to American waters.   Whenever one of our war-vessels entered a harbor, several British vessels

English war-vessels blockade our coast.

hovered near to prevent her escaping to sea again. As a consequence, during the last half of the war the larger American vessels, shut in by this blockade, could not engage **Privateers.** in fighting. But American privateers inflicted great loss on English commerce. During the war about 2,500 British merchant vessels were captured by American privateers. These privateers were New England vessels that were prevented by war from engaging in commerce. But while we were successful on the sea, we were not so successful on land.

226. War in the Northwest (1812–1813).—It will be remembered that one of the leading purposes of the war (see par. 222) was to invade and conquer Canada. With this aim in view General William Hull started from Detroit into Canada. He was soon driven back and forced to surrender at Detroit with his entire force (August 16, 1812).[1] A little later the English captured Fort Dearborn, now Chicago. Instead of our securing Canada it looked very much as if the British would get control of all the territory north of the Ohio. To prevent this, General Harrison was sent, early in the winter of 1813, to drive the British troops out of Detroit, but his advance force was obliged to surrender at the River Raisin, where the Indians cruelly massacred the wounded prisoners.

227. Perry Wins a Brilliant Victory on Lake Erie (September 10, 1813).—Before the English could come into effective control of the Northwest, it was necessary for them to command Lake Erie. To prevent this, Captain Oliver H. Perry, a naval officer twenty-eight years old, was sent there to build and man a fleet. With remarkable energy **Perry's remark-** energy and perseverance he cut down trees, **able energy.** constructed vessels of green timber, and got together men whom he trained for the severe struggle they were to engage in. Some of his best men were Rhode Island seamen and Kentucky riflemen.

---

[1] People were indignant at Hull for his surrender and accused him of cowardice. Although he was tried by court-martial and sentenced to be shot, the sentence was never executed. It now seems clear that General Hull was an innocent man.

AMERICAN SEAMEN BOARDING THE FROLIC.

The engagement between the Wasp and the Frolic—War of 1812.

On September 10, 1813, the British fleet, commanded by Captain Barclay, a veteran officer, hove in sight. There was little difference in the strength of the two fleets. The British had six vessels with sixty-three guns, and the Americans had nine vessels with fifty-four guns; but while the enemy's vessels were larger, their guns were smaller. By concentrating their fire upon Perry's flagship, *Lawrence*, the British completely disabled her. Only Perry and eight of his men were left unharmed. It was a supreme moment. Most men would have surrendered.

His bravery.

He boldly entered a rowboat and, standing up, flag in hand, rowed straight for the *Niagara*, another vessel of his fleet. Although the British directed their fire upon the little boat, Perry reached the *Niagara* without injury. He then renewed the battle with great vigor, and in fifteen minutes compelled the English captain to strike his colors.

This was the first time in history that an entire English fleet was captured. It was a brilliant victory. Taking out of his pocket an old letter, Perry wrote on the back of it his celebrated dispatch to General Harrison: " We have met the enemy and they are ours."   General Harrison at once attacked and defeated the land forces at the Thames River (October 5, 1813).   These two victories put the Americans in entire control of Lake Erie and saved the Northwest.

228. Threefold Attack of the British in 1814.—In the Northwest neither side had made any decided gain when invading the other's territory. This was equally true of the fighting farther east, where the Americans failed at Niagara River,[1] and the English at Fort Erie. Having defeated Napoleon in Europe, England now had more soldiers and seamen for the war in the United States. Accordingly, she decided to invade American territory from the north, on the old Burgoyne route, and to enter the Mississippi

[1] Under the lead of General Scott and General Brown, the bloody battles of Chippawa and Lundy's Lane were fought and won just west of Niagara River, on Canadian soil.   As the United States troops had to retreat across the Niagara River, these victories were of no immediate advantage.

on the south and capture New Orleans.   At the same time attacks were to be made at various points along the eastern coast, so as to keep the inhabitants in that quarter in a state of fear and doubt. By making this threefold attack, the English expected to prevent the Americans from concentrating at any point.

229. McDonough's Victory on Lake Champlain.—Toward off the attack from the north, the Americans had a squadron under Commodore McDonough on Lake Champlain, and a land force of 1,500 at Plattsburg on the lake shore. The English also had a fleet on the lake and an army of 14,000 on land. Although the English fleet was stronger in men and guns, McDonough, in about two hours, gained a decided victory, and captured all the larger vessels belonging to the English fleet. As soon as the news of the battle reached land, the English army beat a hasty retreat (September 11, 1814). This invasion, in its purpose and failure, recalls that of Burgoyne in 1777.

230. The British Capture Washington and Attack Baltimore (1814).—In August (1814) a British fleet sailed into Chesapeake Bay and landed an army which marched against Washington. They reached Bladensburg, six or seven miles from Washington, before they met with any opposition. Here General Winder, an incompetent commander, with a body of Americans composed largely of untrained and ill-supplied militia, made a short, feeble resistance and fled in confusion. The British then marched into Washington, almost capturing President Madison himself. Here they disgraced their victory by destroying the Capitol and other government buildings. After a few days they sailed for Baltimore, where they were bravely repulsed, with the loss of General Ross, their commander.[1]

---

[1] When the British were marching against Washington, they seized and carried off a friend of Francis S. Key. As soon as Key heard of the capture he took steps to secure the release of the prisoner. President Madison gave assistance by ordering that a vessel be placed at the disposal of Key. General Ross consented to the release of Key's friend, but insisted that Key should be detained until after the attack upon Baltimore. During the night of attack Key could see, by the glare of the firing guns, the "Star-Spangled Banner" waving over Fort McHenry. But

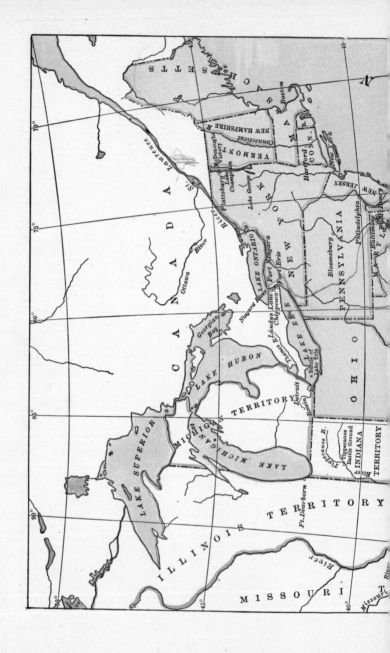

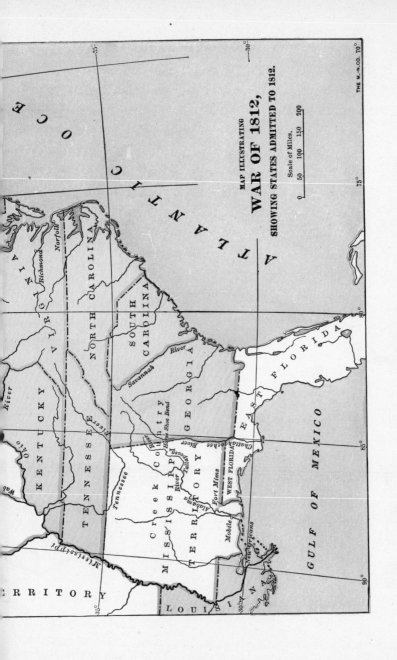

MAP ILLUSTRATING

WAR OF 1812,

SHOWING STATES ADMITTED TO 1812.

Scale of Miles.

0   50   100   150   200

THE M.·N. CO. 70°

The British fleet visited many points of the Virginia and Carolina coast, burning bridges, farm-houses and villages, and carrying off crops, stocks, and slaves belonging to the inhabitants. They also maintained a strict blockade all along the coast from Maine to Georgia.

231. War with the Creek Indians (1814).—Tecumseh, when planning his conspiracy in the Northwest, had aroused against the Americans the powerful Creek Indians, occupying territory now included in Georgia and Alabama. Like the Indians north of the Ohio, they saw the whites getting control of their hunting-grounds and killing their game. Believing this time of war to be a favorable opportunity for getting back their lands, the Creeks planned an attack. They captured Fort Mimms, near Mobile, and cruelly slaughtered some 400 men, women, and children in the garrison (summer of 1813). Andrew Jackson, with men from Tennessee, Georgia, and Mississippi, marched against the Creeks, and, after defeating them several times, won a decisive victory over them at Horseshoe Bend, on the Tallapoosa River, in eastern Alabama (March, 1814). This battle so broke the power of the Creeks that they were obliged to abandon much of their territory and go farther west.

232. Battle of New Orleans (1815).—The British wished to get possession of New Orleans, in order to control the trade of the Mississippi and the territory of Louisiana after the close of the war. As their success here would give them a great advantage over the Americans, they sent against New Orleans 12,000 veterans who had fought in Wellington's army.

The success of the expedition, which was in command of skilful generals, seemed well-nigh certain. **Andrew Jackson's** But Andrew Jackson, who was put in com- **preparations.** mand of the Americans at New Orleans, proved himself

toward morning, when the firing ceased, he was in an agony of suspense to learn whether or not our flag yet floated in triumph over the fort. After finding that the "flag was still there," he gave expression to his deep feeling in "The Star-Spangled Banner," a part of which he hastily penned on the back of a letter.

equal to the emergency. When he found that the enemy were close at hand, he began with unbounded energy to prepare for the defence of the city. After arming even free colored men and convicts, he could number only half as many men as the English.

But with his army strongly posted behind fortifications, he awaited the final assault, which was made January 8, 1815. The British gallantly advanced, but they were mowed down in hundreds by the terrible cannonade opposing them. It was chiefly an artillery battle, the main British column not arriving within fair musket range. The British lines could not advance in the face of such fearful slaughter. In twenty-five minutes they had lost their commander, General Pakenham, and 2,600 men killed and wounded, or more than one-fifth of their army. The Americans lost only twenty-one. Here, as in all the fighting on

Bloody repulse of the British. land and sea, the superiority of the American gunnery was noteworthy. In fact, throughout the war the Americans were unmistakably ahead of the English in intelligence and quickness of movement.

We more fully appreciate the telegraph and submarine cable when we learn that this battle, so terrible in loss of life, was fought two weeks after the treaty of peace had been agreed upon. Communication in those days was so slow that the news of Jackson's victory (January 8, 1815) did not reach Washington until February 4. News of the treaty of peace reached New York a week later. The

Result of the battle. battle, therefore, did not in any way affect this treaty. But it did revive the confidence of the American people in the military ability of their soldiery when under competent leadership.

233. **The Hartford Convention (December, 1814–January, 1815).**—From the outset New England Federalists had

New England's dissatisfaction. been much opposed to the war. As it progressed, their opposition became bitter. At first the government had not only appointed weak commanders, but all along it had poorly managed the finances. It had not protected the New England coasts from British attack, and to New England merchants it had seemed indifferent about furnishing such protection. Commerce was practically ruined, and there was much business distress.

New England had bravely done its part in carrying on the war, Massachusetts having furnished much more than its share of men and money, but the Federalists in New England had no confidence in President Madison and his

OLD STATE HOUSE, WHERE THE HARTFORD CONVENTION MET.

government. At length they called together the Hartford Convention, which met at Hartford, in December, 1814. All the meetings were secret, and the peo- **The people greatly** ple throughout the country were greatly ex- **excited.** cited about the possible outcome. Democratic-Republicans openly charged the members with plotting to break up the Union and to form a separate government.

As the proceedings were not published, nobody knows all that the Convention did. It did, however, take a bold and dangerous step toward the dissolution of **What the Hartford** the Union, by recommendiag that the pro- **Convention did.** ceeds of the national taxes, collected in each New England State, should be reserved by it to pay troops for its own defence. This recommendation was extremely unwise. It sounded much like the Virginia and Kentucky Resolutions of 1798 and 1799. The Hartford Convention was a great political blunder. It killed the Federalist party.

234. Treaty of Peace and Results of the War (December 24, 1814).—The treaty of peace was agreed upon December 24, 1814. No mention was made of impressment of seamen and the unjust interference with our commerce by the English navy. But the war put a stop to both evils, and had, in addition, three results: (1) It showed the superiority of American seamanship; (2) it gave the United States a position of respect and honor among the nations of the world; (3) it led the Americans, who had been for so many years cut off from the manufactured goods of Europe, to build mills and factories for themselves and thus become more independent of European manufactures than ever before. Well may this war be called the Second War of Independence. In the Revolution Americans fought for independence of England; in the War of 1812 they fought for independence of Europe.

TO THE PUPIL

1. What complaints did we make against England about searching American vessels and impressing American seamen? What complaints did England enter against us?

2. How did England and France injure American commerce? What was Jefferson's purpose in securing the passage of the Embargo Act? What was the Embargo? How did it affect American commerce?

3. Why was there more commerce carried on in New England than in the South? Why was the Embargo Act repealed?

4. James Madison, our fourth President, was inaugurated March 4, 1809, and served two terms, 1809-1817. Name in order the three Presidents who preceded him.

5. What led to Tecumseh's conspiracy? What were the results of the battle of Tippecanoe? What had Tecumseh's conspiracy to do with our trouble with England?

6. What was Napoleon's trick, and how did its success lead to increasing trouble with England? Why did the Federalists oppose a war with England? Why did the Democratic-Republicans favor such a war?

7. Subject for debate: Resolved that in 1812 we should have gone to war with France rather than with England.

8. Why had we so small a navy in 1812 ?   Compare it with the English navy at that time.

9. Give an account of the fight between the " Constitution " and the "Guerrière."   How great was the success of the American navy in the first six months of the war ?   How do you account for this success ?

10. What disasters fell upon our armies in the Northwest in 1812–13 ?   What led to the battle of Lake Erie ?   Imagine yourself with Perry during the battle, and write to a friend, giving an account of your experiences.   What were the results of Perry's victory ?

11. What was the threefold plan of attack made by the British in 1814 ?   Give the results of McDonough's victory on Lake Champlain.

12. What was the object of the British in trying to capture New Orleans ?   Give the results of the battle.   In what ways were the Americans superior to the English in this and in other battles of the war ?

13. Why were New England Federalists bitterly opposed to the Embargo ?   How was their dissatisfaction increased during the war ?   What recommendation did the Hartford Convention make ?   Compare this recommendation with the Kentucky and Virginia resolutions of 1798 and 1799.   You observe that even in 1814 true national feeling was not strong and deep in the United States.   Name three results of the war.

14. Learn well the story of The Star-Spangled Banner's origin and then memorize the poem.   Read again and again Drake's American Flag and Holmes's Old Ironsides.

DEVELOPMENT WEST OF THE ALLEGHANIES

235. Purchase of Florida.—At the close of the Revolution Florida had passed into the hands of Spain.   During the War of 1812 the Spaniards were in sympathy with the English, and allowed them to build forts in Florida and to arm the Seminole Indians living there.   This unfriendly attitude of the Spaniards embittered the Southern States.   Moreover, many slaves, escaping from Georgia and Alabama, fled into the swamps and morasses of Florida, and there found protection among the Seminole Indians, with whom they married and lived.

The Seminole Indians protect runaway slaves.

The slave-owners often followed in search of their slaves, and for years carried on a kind of border warfare.   As Spain did not set matters right, General Andrew Jackson was

sent down (1817) with a body of troops. Jackson acted
with his usual decision and energy. He hanged two Ind-
Jackson in Florida. ian chiefs, and two Englishmen whom he accused of inciting the Seminoles. He captured
Pensacola and established a garrison there. These acts
were open war against Spain, but trouble was avoided by
our buying Florida. The purchase was made in 1819, for
$5,000,000. The territory was more than twelve times the
size of Connecticut.[1]

236. The Monroe[2] Doctrine (1823).—Having watched
the United States win independence from England and
then become strong and prosperous, Mexico and the other
Spanish colonies in America rose in revolt against Spain.
One after another they declared their independence and
set up republics of their own. Spain was unable of herself
Spain and the to enforce authority, and looked for aid to the
"Holy Alliance." "Holy Alliance." This alliance had been
formed in 1815, after the downfall of Napoleon, by Russia,
Austria, and Prussia. Its purpose was to prevent the people of any European monarchy from overthrowing the gov-
ernment, as the French people had done during the French
Revolution. From the American standpoint, if the great
European powers should begin to interfere with the countries of America, they might, by obtaining a foothold here,
endanger the welfare of the United States.

The experiment of twenty-five years of struggle between
the United States on the one hand and England and France

---

[1] The area of Connecticut, being 4,990 or approximately 5,000 square miles,
makes a very convenient unit of measurement. It will hereafter be so used in
many cases.

[2] James Monroe, fifth President of the United States (1817–1825), was born
in Westmoreland County, Virginia, in 1758, and died in 1831. Soon after his
student life began at the College of William and Mary, he was called away to
active service in the Revolution. He fought bravely at Trenton, Brandywine,
Germantown, and Monmouth. He filled many high stations in his country's service, not only at home, where he was a member of the Continental Congress, and
later of the Senate under the Constitution, but abroad, where he was minister to
France, England, and Spain. After being Secretary of State under Madison, he
was elected President. In all his public service he proved himself a patriotic and
upright citizen.

on the other had culminated in the War of 1812. We had thus learned the wisdom of keeping out of European entanglements. We had learned, also, the wisdom of managing our own affairs without the intervention of England, France, or any other European country. President Monroe, therefore, in a message to Congress at **The " Monroe Doctrine."** this time, declared (1) that we would take no part in European wars; (2) that we would not interfere with any European colonies already established in America; (3) but that any attempt on the part of a European nation to interfere with the independence of an American state would be regarded as an unfriendly act.[1] This statement of our position gave expression to the general American sentiment which has since become known as the " Monroe Doctrine."

JAMES MONROE.

It was a strong position to take, but the valor of Perry on Lake Erie, of McDonough on Lake Champlain, of Jackson at New Orleans, and of **Results of the " Monroe Doctrine."** the American sailors on the sea, had won the respect and admiration of Europe. The Holy Alliance wisely refrained from meddling with American affairs; a precedent was established; and the Monroe Doctrine has ever since been the settled policy of the United States.

237. The National Road.—The Monroe Doctrine practically settled the foreign policy of the United States; but there remained a question at home which appeared almost to defy solution. From early colonial times two obstacles

---

[1] We find a similar sentiment expressed in Washington's Farewell Address, from which the following is quoted: " The great rule of conduct for us in regard to foreign nations is, in extending our commercial relations, to have with them as little political connection as possible. . . . It is our true policy to steer clear of permanent alliances with any portion of the foreign world."

had stood in the way of westward migration. These were the Indians and the natural barriers to travel and transporta-

Two obstacles to westward migration. tion. By the overthrow of Tecumseh's conspiracy in the Northwest and of the Creeks in the Southwest, the power of the Indians east of the Mississippi River had been broken.

This vast, fertile area was now open to migration. People from New England and the Northern States began to move westward in large and increasing numbers. The steamboat greatly aided this westward movement, but

The steamboat and the pack-horse. the steamboat was of use only on the rivers and lakes. It was necessary for men and all kinds of movable property to pass over wide stretches of country through which navigable rivers did not flow. The pack-horse of early days needed only a path through the woods, but the emigrant called for a roadway to connect the East and the West. Hence the "National Road," beginning on the banks of the Potomac, at Cumberland, Maryland, was undertaken at national expense.

The first contract was let in 1811. By 1820 the road was extended over the mountains to Wheeling, where it connected with the steamboats on the Ohio. The original purpose was to build this road to the Mississippi. But by the time it reached Illinois (1838) the coming of the railroad made its farther extension unnecessary. It helped much in furthering emigration and westward growth. For the construction and repair of this road Congress spent nearly seven million dollars.

238. The Natural Boundary Line Between Freedom and Slavery.— Nature had decreed that the large plantation should have no place in the North. Mason and Dixon's Line and the Ohio River formed the convenient and natural boundary line between the free and the slave States as far west as the Mississippi River.

North of that line slaves were of use mainly as household servants. It was thought that other kinds of work could be done with greater profit by white labor. In all this northern area, therefore, there were comparatively few slaves. But south of that line the soil and climate were favorable to the growth of cotton, rice, sugar, and tobacco. The successful cultivation of these great staples called for an abundance of cheap labor always at hand when needed. Slavery fulfilled these conditions. Moreover, it was assumed that the negroes, if set free, would not work, and hence slavery seemed to the Southern planter necessary for his highest prosperity. Since the freeing of the slaves, this assumption has been shown to be incorrect, but it was none the less believed in the South before the Civil War.

Slavery in the North and in the South.

239. The Question of the Extension of Slavery into the Louisiana Territory.—Before the Louisiana Purchase, then, soil and climate seem to have largely decided what should be the line separating freedom from slavery. Seven of the thirteen original States were free and six were slave, but the admission of new ones had been so planned that in 1819 there were eleven standing for freedom and the same number for slavery. In this way each section had an equal vote in the Senate. In the House of Representatives the North, having grown in population much faster than the South, had by 1819 a much larger vote.[1] If, however, the South could maintain an equality in the Senate, legislation unfriendly

The South eager to maintain an equality in the Senate.

[1] REPRESENTATION IN CONGRESS IN 1820.

No.	Free States.	Admitted.	Senate.	House of Rep.	No.	Slave States.	Admitted.	Senate.	House of Rep.
1	Pennsylvania...	1787	2	23	1	Delaware......	1787	2	2
2	New Jersey....	1787	2	6	2	Georgia........	1788	2	6
3	Connecticut....	1788	2	7	3	Maryland.....	1788	2	9
4	Massachusetts..	1788	2	13	4	South Carolina	1788	2	9
5	New Hampshire	1788	2	6	5	Virginia......	1788	2	23
6	New York.....	1788	2	27	6	North Carolina	1789	2	13
7	Rhode Island..	1790	2	2	7	Kentucky.....	1792	2	10
8	Vermont.......	1791	2	6	8	Tennessee....	1796	2	6
9	Ohio..........	1803	2	6	9	Louisiana ...	1812	2	1
10	Indiana	1816	2	1	10	Mississippi ...	1817	2	1
11	Illinois........	1818	2	1	11	Alabama	1818	2	1
12	Maine.........	1820	2	7	12	Missouri	1821	2	1
12	Free	......	24	105	12	Slave.........	......	24	82

to slavery could be prevented, and to this end the slave-holders were ready to put forth all their energy.

240. The Missouri Compromise (1820).—In 1818 Missouri, a part of the Louisiana Purchase, applied for admission into the Union. The first State admitted from this purchase, Louisiana, had come in as a slave State in 1812, but it was far south of the line dividing freedom and slavery as already established. Missouri, however, lay partly north of this dividing line and partly south. The Northern people claimed that as Congress had control of the Territories it had a constitutional right to decide whether they should be free or slave. The Southern people, on the other hand, insisted that each State had a constitutional right to decide this question for itself.

Attitude of the North and the South toward slavery in Missouri.

HENRY CLAY, "THE GREAT PEACEMAKER."

When applying for admission the people of Missouri had requested that they might have slavery. It happened that about the same time Maine wished to be admitted as a free State. The slaveholders, therefore, refused to allow Maine to enter the Union unless Missouri should be admitted as a slave State. The struggle was long and bitter. At last, largely through the influence of Henry Clay, an act known as the "Missouri Compromise" was passed, which, for the time, settled the difficulty.

This compromise had two provisions: (1) Missouri was to come into the Union as a slave State; (2) all the remaining territory in the Louisiana Purchase, north of the parallel of 36° 30', or the southern boundary of Missouri, was to be forever free. Maine was admitted as a free State in 1820, and Missouri as a slave State in 1821, making twelve free and twelve slave

The two provisions of the Missouri Compromise.

States. It was supposed that the slavery difficulty was forever settled. "Forever" in this case meant only about twenty-five years.

241. The Erie Canal (1817–1825).[1]—Transportation overland, from east to west, by means of wagons and draught animals was slow and expensive. Some better means of travel and communication between the Altantic coast and the Mississippi valley had therefore become a necessity. This necessity suggested to the thoughtful mind of DeWitt Clinton the building of a canal to connect the Great Lakes with the eastern seaboard. So in 1817, through his untiring energy, a large body of laborers began the task of digging the Erie Canal.

It extended from Buffalo, on Lake Erie, to Albany, on the Hudson, a distance of three hundred and sixty-three miles. As Lake Erie is nearly six hundred feet higher than the level of the Hudson, and as the canal had **Difficulties in** to pass through forests and over rivers, many **building the canal.** people looked upon the scheme as a foolish venture. By way of ridicule they called the canal "Clinton's Ditch." But Clinton's perseverance overcame all opposition, and the Erie Canal was ready for use in 1825. It was built at the expense of the State of New York, and was easily paid for by tolls levied on boats and goods passing through it.

242. Results of the Construction of the Erie Canal.— The results of constructing the Erie Canal surpassed the

[1] The Erie Canal was opened in the autumn of 1825, the first year of John Quincy Adams's administration. John Quincy Adams, the son of John Adams and the sixth President of the United States (1825–1829), was born at Braintree, Massachusetts, in 1767, and died in 1848. After graduating from Harvard he began the study of law. His public service was long and distinguished. He was not only American minister to Holland, Portugal, England, Prussia, and Russia, but was one of the American peace commissioners at the close of the War of 1812. After serving with signal ability as Monroe's Secretary of State, he was elected to the presidency. As President he was unpopular and made many enemies. But the greatest part of his career began when he entered the national House of Representatives in 1831. Here he became the anti-slavery statesman of his time. His fearlessness won the admiration of friend and foe alike. He remained a member of the House until 1848, when he fell dead in the Capitol. He was well called the "Old Man Eloquent."

highest expectations, even of Clinton. (1) Cost of transportation was reduced. Before the canal was in use $10 was paid for carrying a barrel of flour from Buffalo to Albany by wagon. By canal-boat the expense was reduced to thirty cents per barrel. (2) Since the canal made travel easier and less expensive, it increased migration westward. Before the building of the New York Central Railroad it carried thousands of emigrants. (3) All along the canal towns and cities rapidly grew up, so that New York soon became the most populous State in the Union. (4) It greatly stimulated the development of New York city, which shortly became, as it has since remained, the chief commercial city in the country. (5) By largely reducing the freight charges for transportation of goods it made the food produced on Western farms much cheaper in the East, and for the same reason it caused manufactured goods from the East and imported goods from Europe to sell for lower prices in the West. It therefore increased the wealth of both the East and the West.

JOHN QUINCY ADAMS, THE ANTI-SLAVERY STATESMAN.

243. Internal Improvements.—The National Road and the Erie Canal were a part of an extensive system of internal improvements which were of great service in developing the West and connecting it with the East. This system included not only the building of roads and canals, but the improvement of rivers and harbors. Some of these roads and canals were built by private enterprise and some by the separate States. The cost of building and keeping them in repair was met by toll charges. Many people believed that Congress had a right to make internal improvements at the expense of the whole people. Many others insisted that such improvements should be made by private companies or by

Two ways of making internal improvements.

the separate State governments. These last urged that the "general welfare"[1] of the people was not served by building roads and canals and by improving rivers and harbors, which directly benefited limited areas only. They therefore argued that such works should not be undertaken by the general government at national expense.

This was the view of those who gave a strict construction to all parts of the Constitution. Madison, Monroe, and Jackson were of this party. Those who gave a broad construction to the Constitution said that this power was implied in the following clause: "The Congress shall have power to make all laws which shall be necessary and proper for carrying into execution the foregoing powers, and all the powers vested by the Constitution in the government of the United States" (Article I., Section 8, Clause 18). This has rightly been called the "Elastic Clause." **The "Elastic Clause."** The "River and Harbor Bill," passed every year for the improvement of rivers and harbors in all parts of the country, shows that Congress to-day gives a liberal construction to the Constitution.

244. New Problems and a New Political Party.—The best way of making internal improvements was a new problem for the people to solve, but there were other problems equally difficult. The Alien and Sedition laws had seriously injured the Federalist party; the **The era of good feeling.** Hartford Convention had killed it, leaving the Democratic-Republicans as the only political party in the country. From 1817 to 1825, during Monroe's administration, this singular condition of affairs prevailed, and this period has ever since been known as the "Era of Good Feeling."

But the new problems that soon presented themselves led to the rise of a new political party and involved three pressing and vital questions: (1) Shall internal improvements be made by Congress at **Three pressing questions.** national expense? (2) Is the United States Bank constitutional? (3) Is the true policy of the country a tariff for

[1] See preamble of the Constitution.

revenue only or a high tariff for the protection of home industries? The Democrats, as the Democratic-Republicans now began to call themselves, believed in leaving internal improvements to private enterprise or to State governments. They regarded the Bank of the United States as unconstitutional. They favored a low tariff.

The new party wished internal improvements to be made at national expense, approved the United States **The National Republican party.** Bank, and urged that a high protective tariff was for the best interests of the people. Because this new party favored the strengthening of the national government in these three ways it was called the National Republican Party.

TO THE PUPIL

1. James Monroe was now President, serving two terms, 1817–1825.
2. What difficulties led to the purchase of Florida?
3. What was the Holy Alliance, and what was its connection with the Monroe Doctrine? Name the three main provisions of this Doctrine. Try to understand clearly the meaning of the Monroe Doctrine. It will come up again later.
4. Before the purchase of Louisiana, what was the natural boundary line between free and slave territory? Explain how soil and climate favored slavery south of Mason and Dixon's Line and the Ohio River.
5. Why was the South eager to maintain in the Senate an equality with the North? What difficulty was settled by the Missouri Compromise? What was this Compromise?
6. Review what has been said about the pack-horse, the flat boat, the steamboat, and the National Road. In what way did the Erie Canal supplement these? Do not be satisfied until you know well the results of constructing this canal, especially the last one named in the text.
7. John Quincy Adams, who served for one term, 1825–1829, was now President.
8. What was meant by internal improvements? Why were they greatly needed at this time? What two views were held as to the best way of making internal improvements?
9. You see you are again face to face with the two opposite views of the true meaning of the Constitution. What were these views? What is the "Elastic Clause"?

10. What were the new political problems, and what the pressing questions they involved? What was the new political party, and how did it answer each of these questions? How did the Democratic party answer them?

11. In this connection you might well review what you have already studied about political parties. You will recall two great mistakes made by the Federalist party. Make frequent use of the index.

12. Read Washington's Farewell Address and the message containing the Monroe Doctrine.

CHAPTER XVI

JACKSONIAN DEMOCRACY AND THE WEST (1829–1841)

REFERENCES: **Scribner's** Popular History of the United States, IV.; **Andrews's** United States, I.; **Burgess's** Middle Period; **Wright's** Children's Stories of American Progress; **Wilson's** Division and Reunion; **Coffin's** Building the Nation; **Richardson's** History of Our Country.

OUTSIDE READINGS: **Schouler's** United States, III. and IV.; **Rhodes's** The United States, I.; **Wilson's** A History of the American People, IV.; **Sumner's** Andrew Jackson; **Lodge's** Daniel Webster; **Von Holst's** John C. Calhoun; **Schurz's** Henry Clay; **Morse's** John Quincy Adams; **Johnston's** American Orations (Webster and Hayne); **Bolton's** Famous American Statesmen; **Teft's** Webster and His Masterpieces.

FICTION: **Eggleston's** Hoosier Schoolmaster; **Eggleston's** Graysons.

245. Character of Andrew Jackson.[1]—The six Presidents that preceded Jackson came from Virginia or Massachusetts. They were all men of culture and stood for what was best in the social life of New England and the South. Andrew Jackson was of a different type. He represented the frontier life of the West.

His education had been meagre, but he was a man of much ability and of strong and forceful character. He was a natural leader of men and had occupied many positions of trust in the community in which he lived. His unbounded

---

[1] Andrew Jackson, seventh President of the United States (1829–1837), was born in Union County, North Carolina, in 1767, and died at his home, "The Hermitage," near Nashville, in 1845. When only fourteen years old he joined the American force under Sumter. After the Revolution he began to study law. At the age of twenty-nine he removed to Nashville and soon became prominent in public life. He was elected to the national House of Representatives, and later to the Senate. In 1814 he was appointed major-general in the United States army and in this position won the brilliant victory at the battle of New Orleans. On account of his obstinate will his friends called him "Old Hickory."

faith in his own convictions caused him to commit some errors as President. But he was always sincere and intensely patriotic. He was loyal to his friends, but severe upon his enemies. His personal prejudices and his jealousy for the nation were so intense that he regarded those disagreeing with him as not only enemies to himself but to his country.

His genuine interest in the welfare of the people cannot be questioned. During the eight years of his Presidency (1829–1837) his influence upon the course of events was a **A man of the people.** personal one. He was in a true sense a man of the people, who cheerfully followed wherever he led.

246. The Spoils System.—When Jackson became President he desired to reward those political friends who had worked faithfully for his election. Moreover, he believed in the rights of the people, and did not deem it democratic to allow any set of men to remain long in office to the exclusion of others just as worthy.

ANDREW JACKSON.

"The Union! It must and shall be preserved!"

He therefore decided to adopt the more democratic principle of "rotation in office." "To the victors belong the spoils," was his motto. He accordingly turned out of office two thousand postmasters[1] and other officials, **Rotation in office.** although their work was in no way connected with politics. Jackson appointed his own followers to positions which he had made vacant by removal. He appointed them because they were his followers and not because they had a special fitness for the official work they were to do. This was the introduction into national

[1] During the forty years from 1789 to 1829, there had been only 74 removals, or, on an average, less than two a year. Of these, Washington had made 9; John Adams, 10; Jefferson, 39; Madison, 5; Monroe, 9; John Quincy Adams, 2.

politics of the "Spoils System." The system, until 1883, had full sway in the country, and has had a most demoralizing influence on the political life of the nation.

247. "A Tariff for Revenue with Incidental Protection."—It will be remembered that during the time of the Embargo and the War of 1812 the country, being cut off from foreign trade, was obliged to build its own mills and factories to produce whatever manufactured goods were needed for home use. As the streams flowing down New England hillsides furnished excellent water-power, the business men of that region gradually invested their capital in manufacturing instead of commerce. Until 1816 duties had been levied on goods from foreign countries mainly for revenue to pay the expenses of the national government. These duties furnished only incidental protection to American manufacturers. Such a system of duties is called "a tariff for revenue with incidental protection."

248. A Protective Tariff.—After the war closed, however, and trade was resumed with foreign countries, our

English goods in American markets. markets became flooded with foreign goods, especially from England. Labor was so much cheaper in England than in this country that her merchants could sell goods to the United States at a lower price than American manufacturers could afford to sell them.

Our manufacturers naturally called for a higher tariff on the goods that could be made to advantage in American mills and factories. These imported goods would then cost so much in the United States that the American manufacturer could afford to undersell the foreigner and still make a profit. Such a tariff is said to encourage home industries, or to protect American manufacturers from foreign competition. It is therefore called a protective tariff.

249. South Carolina Objects to a High Protective Tariff.—The first protective tariff was laid in 1816. It was too moderate. The duties were so low that foreign merchants could pay them and still fill our markets with their goods. The New England manufacturers could not thrive under such conditions and urged Congress to raise the duties. These were therefore gradually in- **The high tariff of** creased until the high tariff of 1828 was passed. **1828.**

The industrial conditions of the South were so different from those of the North that manufacturing had no place there. The people of the South were almost **Slavery and the** exclusively employed in raising on their plan- **four great staples** tations the four great staples: rice, sugar, cot- **of the South.** ton, and tobacco. The slaves were not intelligent enough to be employed in manufacturing. They were adapted only to agricultural labor. Such a difference in industrial conditions between the North and the South was decidedly unfortunate. The conflicting business interests of the two sections brought about a seri- ous disagreement in regard to the tariff system.

The Southern people had to buy all the manufactured goods they used, and naturally wished to buy them at as low prices as possible. They claimed the right **The South desires** to import foreign **free trade.** goods free from duty. In other words, they wished free trade, or freedom to seek, without govern-

JOHN C. CALHOUN, THE DE FENDER OF SLAVERY AND STATE RIGHTS.

ment restrictions, any foreign market. The people of South Carolina claimed that a protective tariff made them poorer and the New England manufacturers richer, and that it was therefore sectional and unfair.

250. Calhoun and Nullification (1831–1832).—John C. Calhoun, of South Carolina, Vice-President during most of Jackson's first term, and an able statesman, was the leader of his State in this memorable struggle over the tariff. He declared that inasmuch as the tariff enriched the Northern manufacturers at the expense of the South, it was sectional and, therefore, unconstitutional.

His theory was that of the Kentucky and Virginia Resolutions. It declared that the States were superior to the Union and that each was its own master, or practically a sovereign nation. According to his idea, the Union was only a loose-jointed confederacy, and South Carolina had a right to decide for itself whether or not laws passed by Congress were constitutional. This was the doctrine of State Rights. He believed, also, that the State could nullify, or declare not binding in its own territory, any law which it decided to be unconstitutional. This was the doctrine of Nullification.

Calhoun believes in State Rights and Nullification.

251. New England Manufacturers and the Protective Tariff.—On the other hand, the manufacturers of New England and of other Northern States vigorously maintained that a protective tariff would benefit the whole country in the following ways: (1) It would provide a revenue to defray the expenses of the Government; (2) it would, by making wages higher, better the condition of workingmen; (3) it would furnish a home market for the products of the farm; (4) it would cause a greater diversity of interests in the United States and would thus make the country more independent of foreign nations, especially in time of war.

252. Webster and the Union.—About the same time there was in the United States Senate a great debate between Daniel Webster, of Massachusetts, and Robert Y. Hayne, of South Carolina, over the public lands. This debate was a part of the controversy between the North and the South about the true meaning of the Constitution. Webster, like Hamilton, believed in a strong Federal Union, supreme in matters concerning the interests common to all the people. He saw clearly that a Union composed of States with the right to nullify at pleasure any laws passed by Congress must in time break down, just as the Confederation had after the close of the Revolution. He therefore insisted that, under the Constitution, the State governments were inferior to the Federal government. According to his idea, the United States was a nation with supreme authority over

Webster believes the Union to be supreme over the States.

the States, and he summed up his views in those glowing words that to-day should inspire us with lofty patriotism: "Liberty and Union, now and forever, one and inseparable."

253. Jackson's Feeling Toward Nullification.—In the meantime there was much excitement over the tariff agitation. The South Carolina people, knowing Jackson's opposition to a high protective tariff, were eager to find out the President's feeling about the position their State was taking. They invited him to a dinner in Washington, and called upon him for a speech on a toast of his own selection.

DANIEL WEBSTER.

"*Liberty and Union, now and forever, one and inseparable.*"

He startled them by proposing this toast: "Our Federal Union: it must be preserved." Although he did not like the tariff, yet as the head of the Federal Union he meant to enforce its laws. At another time, when asked by a member of Congress from South Carolina whether he had any message for his friends in that State, he said: "Please give my compliments to my friends in your State, and say to them that if a single drop of blood shall be shed in opposition to the laws of the United States, I will hang the first man I can lay my hands on engaged in such treasonable conduct." In this struggle for the Union, Jackson was nobly supported by Thomas H. Benton, a prominent Senator from Missouri.

254. South Carolina and State Rights.—In 1832 an attempt was made to pour oil upon the troubled waters by adopting a new protective tariff, lower and therefore less objectionable to the South than the tariff of 1828. But South Carolina, being opposed to the principle of protection, was still dissatisfied.

Accordingly, a State convention was called (1832) which

declared that the tariff acts of 1828 and 1832 were null and void, and prohibited the collection, after a certain date (February 1, 1833), of duties under these laws in the ports

South Carolina declares the tariff acts null and void. of South Carolina. It threatened that, in case the United States should try to enforce the tariff laws in South Carolina, she would withdraw from the Union and organize a separate government. When Jackson received the news of the action of the South Carolina Convention he was filled with indignation. Rais-

ing aloft his right arm, he exclaimed: "The Union! It must and shall be preserved! Send for General Scott!" Troops and war-vessels were at once sent to Charleston with orders to collect duties upon all imported goods entering the harbor.

Through Clay's influence, however, Congress enacted a compromise measure, gradually lowering

The compromise with South Carolina. the duties. Under this gradual reduction, the tariff, at the end of ten years, would not be far removed from a tariff for reve-

ROBERT Y. HAYNE

nue only. But the prompt, energetic action of the President was an object-lesson to the nation. We should remember with gratitude the unflinching devotion of Daniel Webster and Andrew Jackson to the Union at this critical time.

255. Jackson and the United States Bank.—The first United States Bank was planned and chartered by Alexander Hamilton[1] for twenty years (1791 to 1811); and the second one also received a charter for the same number of years (1816 to 1836). It was to receive all revenue and other public money and to pay this out as needed by the government. Its friends, the National Republicans, main-

---

[1] This bank was an important feature in Hamilton's scheme for giving the national government a firm financial footing.

tained that it made the paper currency safer and more uniform throughout the United States. Jackson declared it was unconstitutional: that it enriched its managers at the expense of the people, and was therefore not democratic: that its funds were used in politics to reward its friends and to injure its enemies.

256. Jackson's Removal of Deposits (1833).—Although the charter of the second United States Bank was not to expire until 1836, a bill to recharter was passed by Congress in 1832. It failed to become a law by reason of Jackson's veto. The next year the President decided upon the removal of the deposits. He therefore ordered that after that time all the money of the government should be deposited in various State banks. This was known as the "removal of deposits." Since in every case these banks were managed by Democrats, they were known as "pet banks." The effect of this **Pet Banks.** "removal of deposits" will be better understood if we observe how money was used at that time in the development and expansion of the West.

257. The Introduction of the Railroad.—Vast sums had been spent in the construction of better means of transportation. As already seen (see par. 216), the application of steam-power to boats made the people independent of wind and current. But methods of trade and travel overland were altogether too slow and meagre for the energetic American people. Roads, canals, and steam- **The new problem.** boats had promoted travel and transportation, but the great problem was to find some way of applying steam-power to travel and transportation by land. The railroad and the steam-driven locomotive-engine furnished a solution.

The first form of the railroad was the wooden rail used in the coal mines of England. The next step was to cover the wooden rail with a thin layer of iron for protection. This was the form in which the first railroad appeared in the United States at Quincy, Massachusetts (1826). This road was only five miles long, and its cars were drawn by horses. It was used to carry granite from the quarries to the place of shipping. In 1828 the first passenger railroad in the United States was begun in Baltimore. It extended westward about thirteen miles, and its cars were at first drawn by horses. This road was the beginning of the Baltimore & Ohio Railroad.

The first passenger railroad in the United States.

THE BALTIMORE & OHIO RAILROAD, 1830-35.

258. The Growth and Results of the Railroad. — The growth of the railroad in the United States has been wonderful. In 1828 there were only 3 miles; in 1837, 1,500 miles; and in 1840, 2,200 miles. From that time on the growth has been tremendous. The United States now has over 200,000 miles of railroad.

The railroad brought about great changes in the life of the people: (1) It stimulated Western migration; (2) it

THE BOSTON & WORCESTER RAILROAD IN 1835.

made Western lands more valuable; (3) by lowering cost of transportation, it cheapened Western food in the East and Eastern manufactured goods in the West; (4) it therefore added to the wealth of both parts of the country and brought the people into closer sympathy and union.

259. Rapid Growth of the West.—From 1821 to 1837 the country was highly prosperous. Crops were good, trade and manufacturing flourished, and cities grew rapidly. In 1821 the population of the whole country was ten millions; in 1837 it was sixteen millions. This remarkable growth in population was encouraged by the vast expanse of rich public land which the government was offering for very small sums, in order to increase Western migration and settlement.[1]

The growth was stimulated by the steamboat and the railroad. Before 1837 steamboats were in extensive use on

[1] An examination of the following two tables, one showing the number of foreign immigrants for the years 1829–1837, and the other the population of many of the States for 1821 and 1837, will give a better idea of the rapidity of this growth in the West:

IMMIGRATION TABLE, 1829-37.

Year.	Number of Immigrants.	Year.	Number of Immigrants.
1829..................	22,520	1834................	65,365
1830..................	23,322	1835................	45,374
1831..................	22,633	1836................	76,242
1832..................	60,482	1837................	79,340
1833..................	58,640		

	POPULATION IN 1821.		POPULATION IN 1837.
		Round Numbers.	Round Numbers.
New York.............................		1,400,000	2,200,000
Pennsylvania.........................		1,000,000	1,600,000
Ohio.................................		600,000	1,400,000
Tennessee............................		450,000	800,000
Indiana..............................		170,000	600,000
Mississippi..........................		80,000	320,000
Missouri.............................		70,000	350,000
Illinois.............................		60,000	400,000
Michigan.............................		10,000	200,000

the Great Lakes, the Ohio, the Mississippi, and the many smaller tributaries of those rivers. And now, with the invention of the railroad, settlement spread westward with ever-increasing rapidity. Towns and cities sprang into existence as if by magic. In 1830 Chicago consisted of a fort (Dearborn) and a small village. In 1833 it had 550 inhabitants; in 1837 it numbered 4,170; and at the last census the population was 2,185,283.

260. Speculation in Western Lands.—Extensive areas of Western public lands, offered at low prices, filled men with the fever of speculation. Plans were laid to buy up large tracts and connect them with the East by roads, canals, and railroads. It required a great amount of money to establish all these great lines of communication started up by the railroads, but the demand was easily met after the "removal of deposits," for then the public money was distributed among many State banks, and was more accessible to borrowers. Loans could now be obtained, and here and there cities were laid out in the West. Then by the sale of these lands, at an enormous advance in price, the speculators became suddenly wealthy. Fortune-making seemed so easy that men took great risks with borrowed money.

261. Wild-cat Banking.—The increasing demand for money led to "wild-cat" banking. A few men with little or no capital to make good the notes they issued, would start a bank by issuing cheaply printed bills (notes) which they circulated under the name of money. After buying public lands from the government at high prices and paying for them with these notes, they would sell their lands for gold and silver. When, however, their own notes returned to be redeemed in gold and silver, these dishonest bankers would fail, and, in some cases, go elsewhere and repeat their swindling operations.

262. The United States Free from Debt.—Of course this speculation in government lands made it easy for the United States to pay the public debt. Whereas, in 1830, the sum received for these lands was $2,300,000, six years later it reached nearly $25,000,000. We need not be surprised, then, that by the end of 1835 the public debt was paid. The apparent prosperity made foreigners eager to emigrate from Europe to this country, and they came in large numbers (see table, page 274).

263. State Speculation in Internal Improvements.— After the public debt was paid there was a large surplus, $28,000,000 of which was distributed among the various States. It was now very easy for State governments, especially where the "pet banks" were located, to get money for carrying out their extensive plans, and these governments invested large sums in internal improvements. Not satisfied with what their

A RAILWAY COACH OF 1830.

States supplied, they began to borrow largely from foreign countries. By 1837 these foreign debts amounted to nearly two hundred million dollars. Of course the loans from foreign countries made money all the more plentiful, and the fever of speculation raged more fiercely than ever.

264. The Specie Circular.— Such reckless speculation could not fail to bring disaster. The wild-cat banks had issued so many paper promises, based upon nothing more solid than the people's willingness to receive them, that, like the Continental currency, they became worthless. Jackson was alarmed at the amount of this worthless paper coming into the United States Treasury.

He therefore issued the famous Specie Circular, which declared that in the future nothing but specie, or gold and silver, should be received in payment for these lands. Wild-cat bank-notes were no longer of any use in buying and selling public lands. These notes went streaming back to the Eastern banks that had issued them, for redemption in gold and silver. Since the banks were without the gold and silver to make good these printed promises, the promises were worth nothing and could not be redeemed.

265. The Financial Panic of 1837.[1]—Of course there at once arose a great cry for money. Men tried to sell stocks, houses, lands—in fact every kind of property—to raise money to pay their debts. All wanted to sell. None cared to buy. As always happens under such conditions, prices went down with astonishing rapidity. There were extensive business failures, and rich men became poor. Mills and factories shut down because they could not sell their goods. Laboring men were thereby thrown out of work, and their families suffered for lack of food. Soon there were bread riots in the streets of New York. It was a terrible time and has always been known as the " Panic of 1837."

MARTIN VAN BUREN.

266. The Independent Treasury.—As mentioned above, many of the States had made extensive foreign loans for the purpose of building roads, canals, and railroads. When caught by the great financial panic of 1837, some States refused to pay the interest on these loans, and some went so far as to refuse **Repudiation of** to pay either principal or interest. Such a **State debts.** refusal on the part of a State to pay its debts is called repudiation. In the midst of this financial distress

[1] Martin Van Buren, eighth President of the United States, was born at Kinderhook, New York, in 1782, and died in 1862. After he had received his training as a lawyer he began, at only eighteen years of age, his long political career. He represented New York in the Senate and afterward served his State as Governor. When Jackson was elected President he made Van Buren his Secretary of State. During Jackson's second term Van Buren was Vice-President. In 1837 the latter became President, but owing to the unpopularity of his administration he failed to be re-elected. He was eminent not only as a lawyer but also as a political leader.

the "pet banks" were unable to pay the Federal Government the public money which it had deposited in them.

The government being greatly embarrassed, President Van Buren, Jackson's successor, was obliged to call a special session of Congress to adopt some plan for getting money to pay the running expenses of the government. Congress authorized the Treasury Department to issue $10,000,000 in notes. The wisdom of having an independent treasury instead of a number of State Banks for the safe-keeping of all the public money, was now evident. By 1846 it had become the settled policy of the United States to have a national treasury which should take care of all the money paid to the government. This independent treasury is at Washington, while there are nine branches known as subtreasuries distributed in various commercial centres.[1]

267. The Public School System and the Newspaper.— As life began to move at a quicker pace people began to think more actively, and to take a larger interest in things outside of their immediate surroundings. In the newer States there was such a democratic feeling that every man was made a voter.[2] Manhood suffrage, adopted in all the West, soon spread to the older communities of the East. All the people, coming into full control of public affairs, began to feel a deep interest in political life.

Manhood suffrage.

It thus became a necessity to educate men to an intelligent conception of their duties toward the State and society. This led to a great improvement in the public school systems, especially in the newer States. If the people were to be rulers they must have intelligence and virtue enough to rule wisely. In this period the modern newspaper may be said to have been born. The New York *Sun* (1833) and the New York *Herald* (1835) became more ener-

[1] These are located in New York, Chicago, San Francisco, Philadelphia, Boston, St. Louis, Cincinnati, New Orleans, and Baltimore.

[2] In the earlier years the suffrage was in many ways restricted in the older States.

getic than before in collecting news, were printed in a more convenient form, and were sold at lower prices. From that time the daily newspaper has had a great influence in moulding public opinion.

268. Other Aids to Progress.—Other aids to progress were furnished in the establishment of transatlantic steamship lines and in the invention of the McCormick reaping-machine. The *Savannah*, sailing from Savannah, Georgia, in 1819, was the first ocean steamship to cross the Atlantic. In 1838 two English steamships, the *Sirius* and the *Great Western*, sailed from England to New York. Two years later the first regular transatlantic steamship line, between New York and Liverpool, was established. This was the beginning of the well-known Cunard Line. Ocean steamship traffic greatly stimulated European immigration to this country.

The McCormick reaping machine, which came into use in 1834, was destined to have a large influence upon the development of the West. By making farm-work easier and more profitable, it stimulated emigration to the fertile Western lands.[1]

269. The Temperance Movement.—There was so much pauperism and general demoralization during the years following the War of 1812 that people became alarmed and began to inquire the cause. Investigating committees reported that drinking was the most fruitful source of the evil. Everybody drank—ministers, doctors, merchants, laborers, and even women and children. An occasion was never wanting; at funerals, weddings, dinners, and whenever friends met, the social glass flowed.

In 1824 there began in Boston a great national movement which swept through the Union. Its principle was abstinence from strong drink. By 1830 a thousand temperance societies had been formed and hundreds of merchants had given up the sale of liquor. Temperance societies increased in number and influence, saving hundreds of thou-

[1] In 1838, matches, adding much to the comfort and convenience of household life, came into successful use.

sands of men from the curse of the drinking habit.   From
that time the cause of temperance has steadily gained
ground.

TO THE PUPIL

1. You have now reached an important chapter in your nation's history.
   Study it carefully.   Since 1829 the influence of the West has been
   very great.   You will therefore add 1829 to the following land-
   marks: 1789, 1803, 1812–1814, 1820.   Review the meaning of these
   dates.

2. Are you still grouping less important events about the more important ?

3. Andrew Jackson was President for two terms, 1829–1837.   Name in
   order the Presidents who preceded him.   What was the secret of
   Jackson's large influence over the people ?   Name his most striking
   characteristics.

4. What was the "Spoils System"?   What did Jackson mean by saying
   that it was democratic ?   How did he apply this system to the national civil service ?   What is the civil service ?   Do you think
   Jackson was wise, or unwise, in introducing the "Spoils System"
   into national politics ?   Give reasons for your answer.

5. Review the tariff measure enacted when Washington was President.
   What was its double purpose ?   What is meant by "a tariff for
   revenue, with incidental protection"?

6. Recall the effect which the Embargo and the War of 1812 had upon
   the growth of manufacturing in New England.   Why could English
   goods be sold at a lower price than American ?   What is a protective
   tariff?

7. Why did South Carolina object to a high protective tariff?   What
   difference was there in the industrial conditions of the North and
   the South ?

8. On what ground did Calhoun declare that the protective tariff was
   unconstitutional ?   What was his idea of the Union ?   Define nullification and State rights.

9. What arguments did Northern manufacturers advance in favor of a
   protective tariff?   What was Webster's idea of the Union ?   Find
   out all you can about the personality of these noted statesmen.

10. What was Jackson's feeling toward nullification ?   How did he ex-
    press this feeling in a toast and in a message he sent to friends in
    South Carolina ?

11. What action was taken by the State Convention in South Carolina ?
    What did Jackson do when he heard of South Carolina's bold step ?

12. Subject for debate : Resolved, that a protective tariff was for the best
    interests of the country as a whole.

13. What was the purpose of the United States Bank? What three charges did Jackson bring against it? What is meant by his "removal of deposits" and by "pet banks"?

14. What results followed the building of railroads? Discuss the rapid growth of the West. Why was there extensive speculation in Western lands, and how did the "removal of deposits" make such speculation easier?

15. What was wild-cat banking? How did speculation affect the payment of the public debt? What effect did the payment of the public debt have upon foreign immigration? Can you now explain the relation of the railroad to Western development and to speculation in Western lands?

16. What led Jackson to issue the specie circular? How did it help to bring on the financial panic of 1837?

17. What is the independent treasury?

18. Prepare yourself to write from three to five minutes on any of the following topics: The public schools, the newspaper, and the temperance movement.

19. Read Webster's famous "Reply to Hayne" and memorize some of the most eloquent passages.

CHAPTER XVII

THE SLAVERY QUESTION (1841[1]–1859)[2]

REFERENCES: **Scribner's** Popular History of the United States, IV.; **Andrews's** United States, II.; **Wright's** Children's Stories of American Progress; **Burgess's** Middle Period; **Wilson's** Division and Reunion; **Richardson's** History of Our Country; **Coffin's** Building the Nation.

OUTSIDE READINGS: **Rhodes's** United States, I. and II.; **Schouler's** United States, IV. and V.; **Wilson's** A History of the American People, IV.; **Draper's** Civil War, I.; **Ropes's** Story of the Civil War; **Hart's** Romance of the Civil War; **Brigham's** Geographic Influence in American History; **Goldwin Smith's** United States; **Johnston's** American Orations, II. and III.; **Bolton's** Famous American Statesmen; **Trent's** William Gilmore Simms; **Grant's** Personal Memoirs; **Olmstead's** Seaboard Slave States; **Olmstead's** Texas Journey; **Olmstead's** Journey in the Back Country; **Page's** Old South.

FICTION: **Stowe's** Uncle Tom's Cabin; **Stowe's** Minister's Wooing; **Munroe's** Golden Days of '49; **Harris's** Uncle Remus; **Brooks's** Boy Settlers; **Brooks's** Boy Emigrants.

POETRY: **Whittier's** Slave Ships; **Whittier's** Our Countrymen in Chains; **Longfellow's** Slave's Dreams.

THE RISE OF THE ABOLITION MOVEMENT

270. Morse and the Electric Telegraph (1844).—Before we consider the slavery question, let us briefly refer

---

[1] William Henry Harrison, ninth President of the United States, was born in Charles City County, Virginia, in 1773, and died in Washington, District of Columbia, in 1841. After attending Hampden Sidney College, Virginia, he began to study medicine, but being drawn toward military life he soon entered the army at nineteen years of age. In the War of 1812 he served as major-general with distinguished success. Later he represented his State in both Houses of Congress. He was the Whig candidate for the Presidency in 1840, and after an exciting canvass in what has been called the "log-cabin and hard-cider campaign" was elected. He died just one month after his inauguration.

[2] John Tyler, tenth President of the United States (1841–1845), was born in Charles City County, Virginia, in 1790, and died in 1862. After he was graduated

to a few other events.   After twelve years of patient effort, Samuel F. B. Morse succeeded in bringing the electric telegraph into practical use (1844).   Being poor, he had tried for four years to get an appropriation from Congress for testing his invention.   At length Congress reluctantly voted him $30,000 for constructing a line from Baltimore to Washington, a distance of forty miles.

Morse himself sent the first message from the Supreme Court room, in Washington, to Baltimore.   " What hath God wrought!" was the message. Fitting words were these, since the

What the telegraph has done for the world. telegraph has brought great changes into the world.   By means of it trade and commerce have been much increased.   Business men can keep themselves acquainted with the quotations of the world's great markets every hour in the day. They can transact more business in five or six hours now than could have been transacted in as many months a hundred years ago.

WILLIAM HENRY HARRISON.

Another wonderful discovery of untold value to mankind was made in 1844 by Horace Wells, a dentist of Hartford, Connecticut.   He tried an ex-

Horace Wells and anæsthetics. periment upon himself.   He caused one of his teeth to be extracted after he had inhaled nitrous oxide, or " laughing-gas," and found that while under the influence of the " laughing-gas" he was insensible to pain.   About two years later William T. G. Morton and Charles T. Jackson, both of Boston, made a similar appli-

from the College of William and Mary he studied law and entered upon his long political career.   He served his State as governor and represented it in both Houses of Congress.   He was elected Vice-President by the Whigs in 1840, and on the death of Harrison became President.   He was soon engaged in a bitter struggle with the Whig leaders, with whom he became extremely unpopular.   As a warm advocate of State sovereignty, he gave his cordial support to the secession movement in 1861, when he was elected a member of the Confederate Congress.

cation of sulphuric ether to render surgical operations painless. When sulphuric ether and "laughing-gas" are thus used they are called anæsthetics.

271. **"Fifty-four Forty or Fight"** (1844).—In the same year that Morse's electric telegraph came into successful use, there was much excitement in the United States over the dispute between our country and England about the Northwest Boundary. *Conflicting claims to the Oregon Country.* Our government claimed the country west of the Rockies from the northern boundary of California, then a part of Mexico, to the southern boundary of Alaska, or the parallel of 54° 40'. Great Britain claimed the region as far south as the Columbia River in latitude 46°. By 1818 the dispute over these conflicting claims had grown serious, but the two countries agreed to a joint occupation of the Oregon Country for ten years, and at the end of that period they renewed their agreement for an indefinite time. Why the United States at length laid vigorous claim to it and became so eager for

JOHN TYLER.

it that the Democratic party in the presidential campaign of 1844 was shouting "Fifty-four forty or fight," can be told in a few words.

272. **American Settlers Strengthen Our Claims to Oregon.**—We had several reasons for claiming Oregon. In 1792 Captain Gray, of Boston, discovered the Columbia River, which he named in honor of his ship; in 1805 Lewis and Clark explored this river, and in 1811 an American company established at its mouth the trading post, Astoria. But we made a yet stronger claim by reason of the actual settlements which Americans planted there before 1845. These settlements began in a small way as early as 1832, missionaries being among the first Americans to find their way to the Oregon Country. *Reasons for our claims to Oregon.*

Now in this matter of planting settlements we had the advantage of England, because we were nearer the disputed territory. For a long time, to be sure, the English Hudson Bay Company had been out there making money in fur-trading, but this company had planted no settlements.

The Americans, too, were for many years little inclined to seek homes in Oregon. Although small parties of Amer-

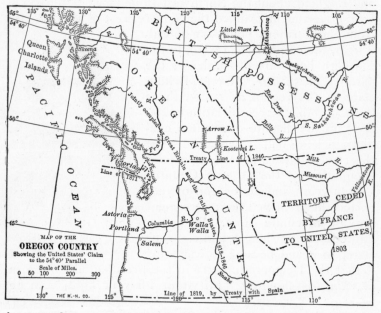

MAP OF THE
OREGON COUNTRY
Showing the United States' Claim
to the 54° 40′ Parallel
Scale of Miles.
0   50   100   200   300

ican settlers started for the Columbia River after 1832, no large settlements were made until 1843. In that year one

American emigration in 1843 and 1844.

thousand emigrants made the journey of more than two thousand miles, braving many dangers and enduring much hardship. The next year two thousand more went out, and by 1845 about seven thousand American settlers had made their homes in Oregon. The English Hudson Bay Company held only a small number of military posts and trading stations. The United States could therefore claim the country by right of actual possession.

By a treaty agreed upon in 1846 both England and the United States gave up a part of their claims. The boundary determined upon was neither 54° 40′ as desired by the United States, nor 46° as desired by England, but 49°, as at present. The whole Oregon Country included what is now the States of Oregon, Idaho, and Washington, or an area equal to more then fifty States like Connecticut.

The Oregon boundary dispute settled by treaty.

273. The Anti-Slavery Movement.—Hitherto we have not had occasion to refer to a movement which was destined to overthrow the most cherished institution of the South. In order to understand this movement we must notice for a moment the new spirit which was gaining ground among the plain people of the country. It has been rightly said that when Andrew Jackson went to Washington as President he took the people with him. It is certainly true that at that time the common people began to feel a sense of their power such as they had not felt before. Jackson supported them in this feeling by standing up for their rights and by encouraging them to have faith in themselves as controlling the affairs of the nation. There had been various limitations on suffrage in the Eastern States, but now manhood suffrage spread from the West to the East. Government by the people and for the people had become a reality.

The rights of the common people.

The anti-slavery movement, led by the abolitionists, was partly the product of this democratic spirit, but was mainly due to the gradual recognition of the dignity and worth of man as man, regardless of race or color. It was felt that slavery was out of place in a country where the people are the rulers. This sentiment, at first limited to a despised few who were called fanatics, rapidly spread through all classes of society.

274. William Lloyd Garrison and The Liberator.— In 1831 William Lloyd Garrison, a young man of slender means and little education, began to publish a paper called *The Liberator*. In it he urged that all the slaves in the United States should be immediately set free. He went so

far as to declare that it would be better to have no
Union at all than to have a Union with slavery in one
section of it. He boldly asserted that slavery was a " sin
against God and a crime against man," and that the Constitution, by giving it support, " was a covenant with death
and an agreement with hell."

275. Southern Opposition.—The Southern people, however, believed that the immediate abolition of slavery would

FAC-SIMILE OF THE HEADING OF GARRISON'S PAPER.

bring about their financial ruin. Inasmuch as the whole
industrial system of the South rested on slavery, they regarded the advocates of immediate abolition as nothing
less than public enemies of that section. Therefore governors and State legislators in the South were so eager
to punish the abolitionists that large rewards were offered for their capture. But the abolitionists were in
earnest, and by means of lectures, pamphlets, books, and
newspapers scattered their anti-slavery ideas among the
people.

276. Northern Opposition.—Very few people, even in
the North, had any sympathy at that time with Garrison's
extreme views about immediate abolition. Northern people
thought that such agitation could only result in stirring up
sectional feeling and might end in breaking up the Union.
To them a Union with slavery seemed better than no Union
at all. So the abolitionists were for a time disliked in the
North quite as much as in the South, and in various parts

of the North anti-slavery mobs and riots were common for some years.

The opposition to Garrison's teachings became so intense that he was mobbed in the streets of Boston (1835). The mob in its fury had almost torn the clothing from his body and was dragging him through the streets with a rope around his waist, when he was saved from death by the police. Elijah P. Lovejoy was mobbed and murdered in Illinois for printing an abolition newspaper (1837), and abolition speakers became accustomed to showers of eggs and stones at public meetings.

Garrison mobbed in the streets of Boston.

277. Growth of the Abolition Movement.—But in spite of all the scorn and contempt heaped upon them, in the North and in the South, the heroic William Lloyd Garrison and his brave followers would not be silenced. They were, like most reformers, extreme in their views and unwise in their methods, but they were right in their leading idea that slavery was wrong. Their sincerity of purpose had its influence, and won the sympathy of many who joined them in forming abolition societies, which by 1837 included probably 150,000 members. Among them were two of the ablest defenders of the anti-slavery crusade, Wendell Phillips, the anti-slavery orator, and John Quincy Adams, the anti-slavery statesman.

278. John Quincy Adams Defends the Right of Petition. —John Quincy Adams was the champion of the sacred right of petition. For many years he stood almost alone in the national House of Representatives in his opposition to slavery. He presented on the floor of the House hundreds of petitions that slavery be abolished in the District of Columbia, and that the slave-trade between the States be stopped.

As these petitions were very displeasing to Southern members, Congress unwisely voted not to receive them. This was not fair play and aroused much sympathy in the North for the abolition movement. The "gag-law," by which the House refused to receive these petitions, continued in effect for many years (1836–1844), but the heroic efforts of the "old man eloquent,"

"Gag - law" in the House of Representatives.

as Adams was rightly called, at last gained for these anti-
slavery petitions a respectful consideration (1844).

TO THE PUPIL

1. What has the telegraph done for the world?
2. Upon what did we base our claim to Oregon?
3. What reason is assigned in the text for the origin of the anti-slavery
   movement? What position did William Lloyd Garrison take upon
   the slavery question?
4. How did Southern opposition to the abolitionists express itself? How
   did Northern opposition? What do you admire in William Lloyd
   Garrison and his anti-slavery friends? What connection did John
   Quincy Adams have with the abolition movement?
5. Read the account of his untiring efforts as described in Morse's "John
   Quincy Adams."

TEXAS AND THE MEXICAN WAR

279. The Annexation of Texas.—About 1820 Southern
people began to migrate to Texas, which was then a part
of Mexico. By the year 1835 several colonies had been
planted by these settlers from the Southern States. Being
dissatisfied with Mexican rule the Texans revolted (1835),
defeated the Mexicans, and drove them out of Texas. They
then declared their independence and sought annexation to
the United States.

The South was eager for this annexation, because Texas
lay south of the slavery line established by the Missouri
Why the South   Compromise in 1820. If Texas, which was as
favored the   large as fifty States like Connecticut, could be
annexation of Texas. added to the slave territory of the South, the
cause of slavery would be materially strengthened. In time,
four or five slave States would be made out of this vast area,
and the South would thereby have a larger number of senators. This increase of voting power in the Senate would
enable her to maintain, for some years at least, the balance
between the slave States and the free States. The North
entered a vigorous protest against annexation, but the South
won, and Texas entered the Union as a slave State in 1845.

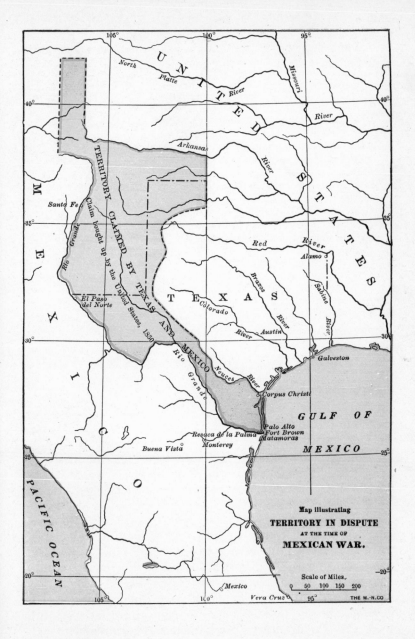

Map illustrating
TERRITORY IN DISPUTE
AT THE TIME OF
MEXICAN WAR.

Scale of Miles.
0   50   100   150   200

280. Attitude of the North and the South Toward the Mexican War.—One of the reasons urged by the North against annexation was, that it would cause trouble with the Mexicans, who refused to acknowledge the independence of Texas. But this objection had no weight with the Southern slaveholders. A war with Mexico might result in the acquisition of more slave territory, and hence such a war was not, from their stand-point, undesirable. The North, however, earnestly opposed the acquisition of any more slave territory, and just as earnestly opposed a war with Mexico.

JAMES K. POLK.

281. The Causes of the Mexican War.—Mexico wished to avoid serious trouble with the United States about the annexation of Texas. But before the question could be settled there arose a dispute about the boundary line between Texas and Mexico. Texas claimed the territory to the Rio Grande; Mexico claimed it to the Nueces River. The territory in dispute was large and therefore desirable both to the South and to Mexico. While the difficulty was still under discussion, however, our government took steps that were almost certain to bring on war.

General Taylor had been sent down in command of American troops to support the cause of Texas, and was ordered to advance into the disputed territory. He did so, taking a position on the Rio Grande at Fort Brown, opposite Matamoras.[1] *General Taylor advances into the disputed territory.* The Mexicans justly considered this an invasion of their territory and therefore an act of war. It certainly looked

[1] Before this time President Polk had sent an envoy to Mexico, whose government refused to receive him. This action of Mexico aroused the resentment of our government.

James K. Polk, eleventh President of the United States (1845–1849), was born

THE STORMING OF CHAPULTEPEC.
An incident in one of the important battles of the Mexican War.

like an attempt to provoke them to make an attack on the American troops. At all events, this was the result of General Taylor's movement. A Mexican force crossed the Rio Grande and killed some American dragoons belonging to a reconnoitring party.

At once President Polk sent to Congress a message in

in Mecklenburg County, North Carolina, in 1795, and died in 1849. In 1806 he removed to Tennessee. After being graduated with distinguished honors from the University of North Carolina he entered upon the study of law. He served the State of Tennessee not only as governor but as member of the national House of Representatives. His manners were simple, and his private life sincere and blameless.

which he declared, " War exists notwithstanding all our efforts to avoid it—exists by the act of Mexico herself. Mexico has invaded our territory and shed Amer- Congress declares
ican blood upon American soil." Congress war.
therefore declared that war existed " by the act of Mexico,"
and at once sent troops and supplies to invade Mexican territory (1846).

282. **The Character of the Struggle.**—The American
plan of campaign was comprehensive. It indicated that the
purpose of the war was the conquest of new territory. Although the Americans met with stout opposition from
Mexico, the American commanders easily carried out their
plans. The war was one-sided. The battles were all won
by the Americans, even in cases where the Mexicans greatly outnumbered our troops.

There were many reasons for the defeat of the Mexicans.
Their government was weak and poor ; their generals were
inefficient ; and their troops were without discipline and
proper equipment. Although the Mexicans were spirited
and brave, they were greatly inferior to the Americans in
intelligence, dash, and endurance.

283. **Results of the War.**—In less than two years
Mexico was conquered, and her entire territory was at the
mercy of the United States. But however unfair our government may have been in bringing on the war with this
weak country, it was willing to pay for any territory it
might secure. Mexico received more than eighteen million
dollars[1] for the cession it made to the United States. Nevertheless, we cannot but regret that our people, distinguished
for their keen sense of justice, should have consented to
wage this war in the interests of slavery. But the results
of the war seemed decidedly favorable to the slaveholders, who thought they had gained a vast region adapted to
the use of slave labor.

If we include in the territory acquired by the Mexican
war the State of Texas and the parts of Arizona and New

[1] The sum paid to Mexico was $15,000,000. The United States also satisfied
claims of American citizens against Mexico to the amount of about $3,500,000.

Mexico secured by the Gadsden Purchase [1] a little later, the whole area is equal to more than one hundred and ninety States like Connecticut.

284. The Wilmot Proviso.—But there was another result which made the war a costly one to the United States, and that was the increased bitterness between the two sections over the slavery question. The South insisted that slavery should go into the new territory, and the North insisted that it should not. In fact, this quarrel over the question of slavery in the new territory began even before the war was over. For when in 1846 it seemed pretty evident what the result of the fighting would be, David Wilmot, a representative in Congress from Pennsylvania, proposed that slavery should be forever prohibited in all the territory which should be acquired from Mexico. This was called the Wilmot Proviso. It failed of enactment by Congress, but it expressed a policy which was soon to be made a guiding principle by a great political party. Two years later this principle became the political watchword of the Free Soil Party and later of the Republican Party. The Wilmot Proviso marked the swift approach of the downfall of slavery in the United States.

TO THE PUPIL

1. Why did the South favor the annexation of Texas? What was the attitude of the North and the South toward the Mexican War?
2. What were the causes of this war? How did it begin? Give three reasons why the Mexicans were defeated in every battle.
3. What were the principal results of the war? Including Texas and the Gadsden Purchase, how many States like your own would the whole territory acquired by the Mexican War equal? What was the Wilmot Proviso?
4. Read Thomas Nelson Page's "Old South."

[1] In 1853 a treaty was negotiated through James Gadsden which settled the disputed boundary with Mexico. The United States paid $10,000,000 and gained the Mesilla Valley, an area of about twenty million acres. It formed the southern part of what is now New Mexico and Arizona, and became known as the Gadsden Purchase.

THE MEXICAN CESSION AND THE COMPROMISE OF 1850

285. Discovery of Gold in California and Its Results (1848).—California had been valued for its fertile soil and its delightful climate. It had also the fine harbor of San Francisco. These attractions drew a few settlers, who in 1848 made a great discovery. Some workmen, in digging a mill-

SUTTER'S MILL, WHERE GOLD WAS FIRST FOUND IN CALIFORNIA.

race for Captain Sutter, a Swiss immigrant, discovered shining particles of gold in a stream flowing into the Sacramento River, about 100 miles northeast of San Francisco. Upon examination of the surrounding country, the soil, the river-beds, and the rocks were found to be rich with gold. It was a wonderful discovery. Before the close of 1861 these mines had yielded more than $500,000,000.

As soon as the news spread abroad people were almost beside themselves with excitement, and at once rushed for the gold region from all the settled parts of **Excitement of the** the United States. Farmers, carpenters, store- **people.** keepers, and professional men were seized with a desire for sudden wealth, and left their work to seek the golden treasure. Vessels coming into the harbors of San Fran-

cisco were deserted by their crews, who, with the rest, wildly rushed with pickaxe and shovel to the mines.

There were three routes to California from the Eastern
States: the first and longest was by vessel around Cape
Horn, the trip from New York to San Francisco in 1848
taking about one hundred and thirty days; the second was
down to the Isthmus of Panama, across it, and up along
the western coast to San Francisco; the third was by

slowly moving trains of wagons
The three routes and ox-carts overland
to California. across the country.
By this last route it took one hundred days to travel to the valleys of
California after reaching the plains
west of the Mississippi.

The difficulties and dangers in
crossing the plains and the desert
region on the journey were many.
The Indians often attacked the emigrants, and in one instance they
were encouraged to do so by a few
white settlers of southern Utah,
who pleaded in palliation that these
emigrants had exasperated them

ZACHARY TAYLOR.

beyond endurance. Thousands died on the way, and the
bones of human beings, horses, and oxen were strewn along
The dangers of the route. The gold-seekers found the Mor-
the overland mon settlements near the Great Salt Lake of
route. much convenience, as they could there rest
in safety and secure fresh supplies to enable them to reach
their journey's end.

Large numbers of men flocked to the gold regions. In
less than eighteen months after the discovery, California
Results of the dis- had a population of not less than 100,000. In
covery of gold in the meantime, San Francisco increased from
California. 2,000 to 20,000 people, and Sacramento from
a little cluster of houses to a place of 10,000 inhabitants.
The discovery of gold in California had important results:

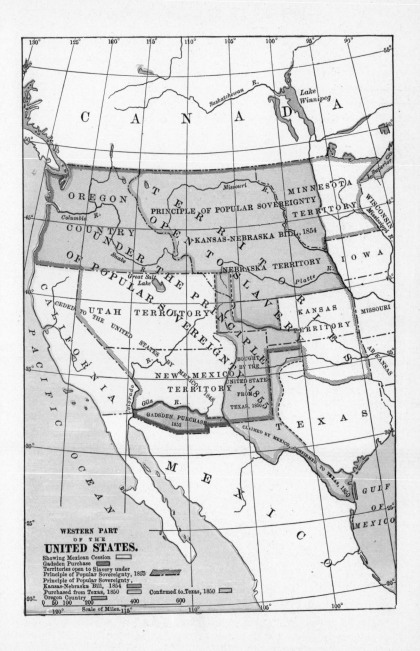

WESTERN PART
OF THE
UNITED STATES.

Showing Mexican Cession
Gadsden Purchase
Territories open to Slavery under
Principle of Popular Sovereignty, 1855
Principle of Popular Sovereignty,
Kansas-Nebraska Bill, 1854
Purchased from Texas, 1850   Confirmed to Texas, 1850
Oregon Country
0 50 100   200   400   600
Scale of Miles.

(1) By greatly increasing the gold in circulation, it stimulated trade and commerce; (2) by developing the Pacific
coast it led about twenty years later to the building of the
first Pacific railroad; (3) it had, as we shall now see, an
important bearing upon the slavery question.

**286. California Seeks Admission into the Union as a
Free State (1849).**[1]—In about a year after the discovery of
gold there were people enough in California for a State.
But Congress had been so busy discussing the slavery question that it had not established any government at all there.
This was most unfortunate, for among the gold-diggers
there were many thieves and ruffians, who were very disorderly and lawless. Hence the better class of citizens
were forced to act without waiting for Congress. They
organized a government of their own, established order,
and applied for admission into the Union in 1849. As a
large majority of the people were from the North, they
wished California to be made a free State.

287. Difficult Slavery Questions in 1850.—It will be remembered that the Missouri compromise was called forth

---

[1] Zachary Taylor, twelfth President of the United States (1849-1850), was
born in Orange County, Virginia, in 1784, and died in 1850. While he was yet
an infant his parents removed to Kentucky, which continued to be his adopted
State until 1841, when he made his family home in Baton Rouge, Louisiana. Although his opportunities for education were very limited, his keen desire for
knowledge led him to study with care ancient and modern history. He became a
daring and skilful soldier, serving his country with great distinction as brigadier-
general in the Mexican War. "Old Rough and Ready," as he was fondly called
by his many admirers, indicates that he was a popular hero. He died in the second year of his Presidency.

Millard Fillmore, thirteenth President of the United States (1850-1853), was
born in Cayuga County, New York, in 1800, and died in 1874. In early youth he
learned the meaning of a life of struggle. Like Lincoln and Garfield, he was a
poor boy, and like them he overcame, by invincible determination, almost insur-
mountable difficulties. Until fourteen years of age he worked on a farm nine
months of the year, and attended the primitive schools of those times the remaining three. At fourteen he was apprenticed to a trade, but managed to find some
time for hard study. Later he studied law, and won for himself an enviable position at the bar. Having been elected Vice-President in 1848, he became President
on the death of Zachary Taylor in 1850. His kindly manner and never-failing
courtesy made him very popular.

by the purchase of the Louisiana Territory. The whole
question was opened afresh by the Mexican cession.
Should the territory acquired from Mexico be slave, or
free? The North argued that inasmuch as this territory
had been free, it should continue to be so. The South was
divided in opinion. Some of the Southerners wished to
extend the line of the Missouri Compromise, 36° 30', as a
boundary to the Pacific. Others claimed, as in 1820, that

MODES OF TRAVEL IN THE WEST.   AN OLD STAGE-COACH AND PRAIRIE SCHOONER.

Congress had no constitutional right to interfere with
slavery; and that the people in the territories ought to be
allowed to decide for themselves whether they should come
into the Union as free or slave States.

The settlement of the dispute was one of extreme importance. It involved several points of issue: (1) California
wished to come in as a free State, but in that case the balance of power in the Senate would be disturbed. Hence
there were strong objections from the South. (2) The anti-
slavery men continued to urge upon Congress legislation
that would abolish slavery, or, at least, the slave-trade in

the District of Columbia. Whether or not Congress had a right to meddle with slavery in the territories, it clearly had a right to enact a measure against slavery in the District of Columbia, which was under the direct control of Congress. We have Slavery in California and the District of Columbia. already seen how John Quincy Adams bravely struggled for years in behalf of legislative action against slavery in this district. (3) The South bitterly complained that the North was violating the Fugitive Slave Law, by aiding the escape of slaves from their masters to Canada.

All these difficult slavery questions were pressing for satisfactory answers, and many people began to fear a dissolution of the Union. Threats of secession were freely made by Threats of secession. some of the more hot-headed pro-slavery men. It was evident that prompt and wise measures must be taken to quiet the violent feelings among people in both sections.

MILLARD FILLMORE.

288. The Compromise of 1850.—Henry Clay had already fairly gained the title of "Peace-maker" by taking a leading part in securing the Missouri Compromise in 1820, and the compromise in 1833 settling the Henry Clay the "Peace-maker." difficulties brought about by the tariff and nullification in South Carolina. In his old age he was again called upon to help meet these new difficulties in 1850. He therefore prepared what was called the Omnibus Bill, because it made provision for settling many questions.

This famous Omnibus Bill, or Compromise of 1850, contained four essential clauses, two of which favored the North and two the South. They were as follows: (1) California was to be admitted as a free State (for the North) ; (2) but in the rest of the The four essential clauses of the Omnibus Bill. Mexican cession, divided into the two territories of Utah and New Mexico, the people were to decide for themselves whether or not they would have slaves (for the South); (3) the slave-*trade*, not slavery, was to be abolished in the District of Columbia (for the North); (4) but a vigorous and exacting fugitive slave law was to be passed (for the South). Many people thought that this compromise would bring peace and good-will throughout the country.

289. The Fugitive Slave Law and Its Results in the North.—Congress had directed that the Fugitive Slave Law

enacted in 1793 should be carried out by the various State governments. As the South charged that the Northern States were neglecting to enforce this law in a proper manner, the fugitive slave clause was inserted in the

FUGITIVE SLAVE ADVERTISEMENTS.

Compromise of 1850, as has just been stated. In accordance with this clause Congress passed a rigid Fugitive Slave Law, which was to be enforced not by State but by Federal officers.

By the provisions of this law fugitive slaves, or negroes claimed as fugitive slaves, were to have no trial by jury and were not to be permitted to testify in their own defence. All citizens, if called upon, were required to aid the United States marshal in capturing runaway slaves. Many cases of cruelty, injustice, and violence followed.

The indignation of the North rose to fever heat, and soon the "higher law" of right and justice was openly proclaimed. Some people in the North were ready to defy a law that was in their view cruel and inhuman. They took the same attitude toward the law that South Carolina took in the Nullification Act.

290. Personal Liberty Bills and Their Results in the South.—The outcome of this intense opposition to the Fugitive Slave Law was the passage, by many Northern States, of the Personal Liberty Bills. These laws granted trial by jury to runaway slaves and in other ways protected them from the severity of the Fugitive Slave Law. Naturally these Personal Liberty Laws embittered the Southern slave-holders, who accused the North of a desire to break up slavery. They further asserted that in passing these Personal Liberty Bills the Northern States were nullifying an act of Congress and violating the Constitution.

291. The Underground Railroad.—Some people in the North secretly aided the runaway slaves in escaping to Canada. The fugitives made their way to freedom by means of the so-called "Underground Railroad." The "stations" were the houses of persons who received the negroes at any hour, night or day, giving them food and shelter and keeping them in a safe hiding-place until they could be sent on to the next "station." In this way they were fed and cared for until they reached Canada, the northern end of this strange railroad. It is estimated that over 30,000 fugitive slaves escaped to Canada between 1830 and 1860.

292. Uncle Tom's Cabin (1852).—In the midst of the stirring discussion about slavery "Uncle Tom's Cabin," by Harriet Beecher Stowe, appeared. During the first year after its publication more than 200,000 copies were sold. It was read in all parts of Europe as well as in the United States. It not only appealed to the imagination, but it also touched the heart and conscience. It rapidly caused people to feel that slavery was more than a political question. Through its influence many men and women now joined the abolitionists in the conviction that slavery was a great moral evil.

293. Commodore Perry Secures a Treaty with Japan (1854).—While all this discussion of slavery was going on, Commodore Perry sailed into the ports of Japan with a fleet of steamers. Previous to that time the Japanese had been suspicious of all foreign nations and had refused to

trade with them.   Commodore Perry won the good-will of
these people, and they entered into a treaty of commerce
with our country.   From that time Japan has been on a
most friendly footing with the United States.   Through
her trade relations with this country and Europe she has
come into touch with Western civilization, and has surprised the world by the eagerness with which she has
adopted it.

294. **Filibustering Expeditions (1851–1860); The Ostend Manifesto (1854).** — By the admission of California as

FRANKLIN PIERCE.

a free State in 1850 the balance between the free and the slave States
was destroyed, for now there were
sixteen free to fifteen slave States.
The outlook for slavery was so
gloomy that the Southerners turned
their eyes toward Cuba, as they had
turned them, a few years before,
toward Texas.   Slavery
already existed in Cuba,
and if the island could be secured to
the Union it would furnish two more
slave States.   Our government was
on friendly terms with Spain, and no
pretext for war existed when, in 1851,

The slaveholders
eager for Cuba.

the first filibustering expedition started out from New Orleans.   The scheme ended in disaster, but there were still
many greedy eyes turned toward Cuba.

Some people thought that Spain might be induced by
treaty to give it up, and even advocated seizure if it could
not be got by cession.   In 1854, therefore, the United States
ministers to England, France, and Spain, acting under in-
struction from President Pierce,[1] met at Ostend, Belgium,

[1] Franklin Pierce, fourteenth President of the United States (1853–1857), was
born in Hillsborough, New Hampshire, in 1804, and died in 1869.   In his class
at Bowdoin College, from which he was graduated, were Henry W. Longfellow
and Nathaniel Hawthorne, the latter being a life-long friend.   Entering the army
at the outbreak of the Mexican War, he was so brave that he was promoted to the
rank of brigadier-general.   After serving in both Houses of Congress he was elected

to discuss the situation. They declared, in the Ostend Manifesto, that Cuba ought to belong to the United States, and that if Spain should refuse to sell it we should secure it by force. It is perhaps unnecessary to say that the United States did not adopt any such policy.

TO THE PUPIL

1. Trace on your map the three routes to California from the Eastern States. What were the results of the discovery of gold?
2. Explain why California sought admission into the Union as a free State. What were the three difficult slavery questions in 1850?
3. In what way was the Missouri Compromise called forth by the Louisiana Purchase? What question was asked about the Mexican cession? How did the North answer the question? How did the South?
4. What two clauses in the Compromise of 1850 favored the North? What two the South?
5. What was the Fugitive Slave Law, and what were its results? Explain the Personal Liberty Bills and the Underground Railroad. What effect had "Uncle Tom's Cabin" upon the slavery question?
6. What was the purpose of the filibustering expedition? What do you think of the Ostend Manifesto?
7. Read the chapters on slavery in Coffin's "Building the Nation."

THE FIGHT FOR SLAVERY IN THE TERRITORIES

295. The Kansas-Nebraska Bill (1854.)—By the Compromise of 1850 the people in all the territory acquired from Mexico, except California, were to decide for themselves whether or not they would have slavery. But this act was not enough. The South desires a further extension of slave territory.

The need of the South for a still further extension of slave territory to offset the rapidly growing power of the free North became more pressing every year.

By the Missouri Compromise of 1820 slavery was forever prohibited in the Louisiana Purchase north and west

to the Presidency in 1852. Although he believed in "State Rights" and opposed all anti-slavery movements, he urged the people of New Hampshire, in the stormy days following the attack upon Fort Sumter in 1861, to stand by the Union.

of Missouri, or north of the parallel of 36° 30′. In 1854 Stephen A. Douglas, a Democratic Senator from Illinois, claimed that the Compromise of 1850 had repealed the Missouri Compromise; moreover, that Congress had no Constitutional right in 1820 to shut out slavery from the Louisiana Purchase. He therefore proposed the erection of the two territories of Kansas and Nebraska, in which the settlers should decide whether they would have slavery or not. This measure, known as the Kansas-Nebraska Bill, became a law in 1854.

It had many important results: (1) It took from Congress all authority over slavery in the territories, and gave this authority to the people; (2) it opened to slavery all the territories belonging to the United States; (3) it led to a bitter struggle over Kansas; (4) and it reopened with renewed bitterness the slavery controversy, which could never again be settled by peaceable means.

Results of the Kansas-Nebraska Bill.

296. The Struggle for the Control of Kansas.—Since the people now had authority to decide the question of freedom or slavery in Kansas, both the North and the South made a desperate effort to gain control of the territory. Emigration was no longer a matter of private or personal interests. There were now urgent political reasons why emigration to Kansas should be encouraged from both sections. Meetings were therefore held in many leading Northern cities, and money was raised for the support of emigrant aid societies to send settlers to Kansas. Soon long trains of emigrant wagons were winding their way across the prairies. As Southern sympathizers refused to let them pass across Missouri, they were obliged to go north through Iowa.

Emigrant aid societies in the North.

The South now hastened its preparations to get control of Kansas. But in this struggle it was at a disadvantage, because slave-holders were afraid to risk taking their slaves into a territory that might, by vote of the people, become free. The South, therefore, did not make such an organized effort to settle Kansas as was made in the North.

The pro-slavery men, however, made hasty preparations to do all they could. Arming themselves, Bloodshed in Kansas. they crossed the border and began to plant colonies. Both sides were aroused, and both took part in the plundering, burning, and murdering.

297. Triumph for the Free-State Men.—On election days Southern sympathizers who came to be called "border ruffians," went over to Kansas in large numbers and cast fraudulent votes in the interests of slavery. By false voting and false counting of ballots the pro-slavery party was for some time ahead. Two rival governments were established. Although the Two rival governments in Kansas. anti-slavery men were clearly in the majority, President Pierce supported the pro-slavery faction and used the influence of the administration to secure the admission of Kansas into the Union as a slave State. But in

CHARLES SUMNER.

spite of all that could be done by President Pierce and the pro-slavery leaders, the cause of freedom triumphed. After three years (1855–1858) of this civil war, in what was truly called "Bleeding Kansas," the free-State men won a victory, and Kansas was admitted to the Union in 1861 with an antislavery constitution.

298. Assault on Charles Sumner (1856).—During the fiery debating in Congress over the difficulties in Kansas, the distinguished anti-slavery leader, Charles Sumner, of Massachusetts, made in the Senate a vigorous speech on the "Crime against Kansas." In this speech he severely attacked Senator Butler, from South Carolina. Sumner's Southern enemies became more intense in their hatred of him than ever before. In the midst of the exciting days which followed, Senator Butler's nephew, Preston S. Brooks, who was a representative in Congress from South Carolina, came suddenly upon Mr. Sumner while writing at his desk in the Senate Chamber and assaulted him. Again and again Brooks struck Sumner over the head with a cane until he **Results of the assault.** reeled and fell senseless to the floor. Sumner did not recover from the shock for over three years. This assault increased the bitterness of feeling and made both sections more determined in their actions.

299. New Political Parties (1854).—Slavery had brought about in political parties great changes, which we will now **The Whigs.** briefly consider. In 1833 the National Republican Party (see par. 244) was succeeded by the Whig Party, of which Henry Clay became the leader. This party opposed the Mexican War. At the close of this war many Northern Whigs and Democrats believed in the principle of the Wilmot Proviso—that slavery should be prohibited in all the Mexican cession. They became anti-slavery men and, joining the Abolitionists, formed the Free Soil Party. But while many Northern Whigs became anti-slavery men, many pro-slavery Whigs in the South joined the Democrats. The result was the breaking into fragments of the Whig Party after 1852.

The passage of the Kansas-Nebraska Bill (1854) caused still another split in parties. By reason of this measure all **The Republican Party.** voters in the North who opposed the further extension of slavery, whether they had been previously known as Democrats or Free Soilers, called themselves Anti-Nebraska Men. In the following year the " Anti-Nebraska Men " began to be called the Republican Party, which has ever since been known by that name. The corner-stone of the Republican Party was the principle contained in the Wilmot Proviso.

TABLE OF IMMIGRATION FROM EUROPE FOR THE YEARS 1845–1856.

Year.	Number of Immigrants.	Year.	Number of Immigrants.
1845	114,371	1851	379,466
1846	154,416	1852	371,603
1847	234,968	1853	368,645
1848	226,527	1854	427,833
1849	297,024	1855	200,877
1850	310,004	1856	200,436

300. Immigration from Europe.—Before 1840 the total number of foreign immigrants into the United States during any one year never exceeded 100,000. A reference to the immigration table given .above will show that from 1845 onward, especially after 1848, the increase was surprisingly great. During almost the whole decade from 1840 to 1850 there was in Europe much unrest, and this led to political disturbances extending through many European countries. In 1846 and 1847 a terrible famine in Ireland caused thousands to seek homes in the United States. The discovery of gold in California, also, had a great influence in stimulating the desire to seek a land where the working man could have prosperity, political freedom, and happiness. As can be seen by noting the rapid increase of population in many of our Western States and Territories, a large number of these immigrants joined the westward movement.

The reasons for the great increase in immigration from Europe.

TABLE OF POPULATION IN WESTERN STATES AND TERRITORIES IN 1840, 1850, AND 1860.

STATES.	POPULATION.		
	1840.	1850.	1860.
Illinois..........................	472,254	846,034	1,704,323
Indiana	478,698	977,154	1,339,000
Iowa	42,924	191,881	673,844
Michigan........................	211,560	395,071	742,314
Wisconsin.......................	30,749	304,756	774,710
California.......................	......	91,636	361,353
Minnesota.......................	......	6,038	171,864
Utah	......	11,354	40,214
Colorado........................	......	......	34,231
Kansas	......	......	106,579
Nebraska	......	......	28,759
Oregon	......	......	52,337

It is significant that nearly all of them sought the North. They avoided making their homes in the South, because there labor was servile and degrading. In fact, the slave-holders did not encourage European immigrants to come South because

Why immigrants would not settle in the South.

they thought the presence of free white laborers might dissatisfy the slaves with their condition and lead them to rise in insurrection. The slave-holders even guarded against the spread of intelligence among their slaves, on account of the discontent intelligence was sure to bring about among the blacks.

301. Economic and Social Conditions in the South.— We see, then, that slavery in the South prevented the increase of population there by immigration, and thus hin-

OLD PLANTATION DAYS.

dered the most rapid development of its resources. There were reasons, also, within the South's own boundaries, which explain why it did not keep pace with the North in indus-

Three reasons why the South fell behind the North in prosperity.

trial prosperity: (1) The negroes were so lazy and ignorant that they did not work so effectively as they would have done if they had been free and intelligent white men. (2) Since slavery degraded labor, the large class of people in the South known as "poor whites" would work but little. (3) The planters themselves spent most of their time in leisure, leaving their business in charge of overseers.

When we bear in mind that of the three great classes of people in the South—the planters, the poor whites, and the slaves—the planters did nothing, the poor whites as little as they could, and the slaves not more than half as much as the same number of intelligent free laborers would have done, we cannot be surprised that the South was so rapidly out-stripped by the North in productive power and therefore in wealth and prosperity.

302. Economic and Social Conditions in the North.— While there were three great classes in the South, there was in the North, so far as production was concerned, but one. In this section nearly all belonged to the working, producing class. In the North, there was the busy hum of industry. A spirit of enterprise, manifesting itself in agri-culture, manufacture, trade, and commerce, was everywhere present. All labor was honorable and idlers were few. Such being the industrial conditions, the North was soon far ahead of the South in population, in productive power, and in political influence.

303. Influence of the West in Favor of Nationalism.— Again glancing over the tables of population in some of the Western States and territories from 1840 to 1850 and from 1850 to 1860, we shall see that the increase was very great. Nor was it all due to foreign immigration. Much of it was the result of the large movement of population from the Eastern States. The prairie lands, so fertile and so easily brought under cultivation, invited The prairies and the laborer to begin life anew where indus- the railroad. trial conditions highly favored prosperity. The railroad encouraged the movement by making the transportation of emigrants and goods rapid, easy, and inexpensive.

It is worth while to notice that only a small part of this westward emigration was from the South. Friendly relations The West was being rapidly occupied by men between the North who were not in sympathy with the slave- and the West. holding planter. Moreover, when these people in the West began to find a market for their corn, wheat, and other produce, they traded with the North because the North had what they needed. The North and the West found mutual profit in trade. With common interests they soon found themselves having common sympathies and common political aims and purposes.

Year by year the West became more and more like the North. Her loyalty to the Union was unquestioned. Having received statehood from the national government, the Western States had very little of that State Rights feeling **National feeling** so common in the South. They were first of **in the West.** all Americans, ready to stand up for the preservation of the Union whenever it should be in danger. When the inevitable clash of arms between the North and

JAMES BUCHANAN.

the South came in 1861, the Westerner was on the side of the North, and shouldered his musket in behalf of a Union which he had unwittingly helped to weld into a solid, indivisible nation.

304. The Financial Panic of 1857.—The great financial panics of the last century occurred at intervals of about twenty years. You will recall that the panic of 1837 was preceded by unusual business prosperity. The same condition existed before the panic of 1857. It was easy to get money, and men were seized with the desire to make fortunes by speculating in Western lands. Railroads were built faster than they could get business support. The discovery of gold in California and Australia had increased the money in circulation **Causes of the** and thus contributed to the general feeling of **panic.** prosperity. Extravagance in living followed. Trade was greatly stimulated, and soon there was an over-production of goods. There had been too much credit, and that brought on the panic. In August, 1857, the crash came and everywhere there was great business distress.

305. The Dred Scott Decision (1857).[1]—The Kansas-Nebraska Bill (1854) deprived Congress of all authority over

[1] This noted decision was made public in the first year of Buchanan's administration. James Buchanan, fifteenth President of the United States (1857–1861), was

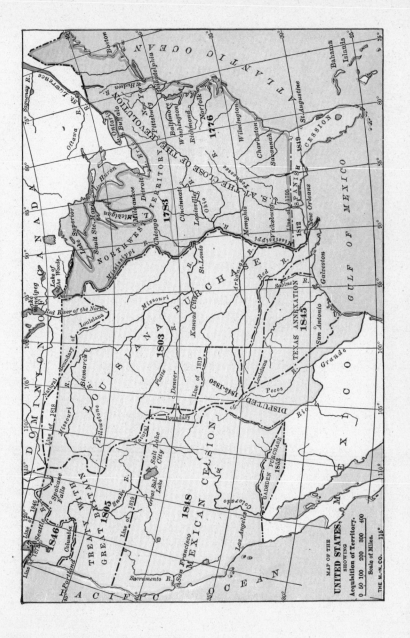

MAP OF THE
UNITED STATES,
SHOWING
Acquisition of Territory.
Scale of Miles.
0 50 100 200 300 400

THE M. M. CO.

the question of slavery in the Territories and left it wholly in the hands of the people. Then began the The principle of struggle between the two sections for control. popular sover- eignty applied to It was soon evident that the North, with all the Territories. greatly superior resources, must win the other Territories just as it had won in Kansas.

The South was dismayed at the prospect and looked about for some means of escaping from the apparently hopeless situation. The means was found in the Dred Scott Decision (1857). Dred Scott was a slave belonging to an army surgeon. In 1834 this surgeon went with his slave from Missouri to Illinois, and some years afterward to Minnesota Territory. On the return of master and slave to Missouri, Dred Scott claimed that, inasmuch as he had been taken by his owner into free territory, he himself was a free man. The case was finally tried in the Supreme Court of the United States. The decision supported the position the pro-slavery men had taken.

It declared, in effect, (1) that a slave, according to the Constitution, was not a person but a chattel or mere piece of property; (2) that the Missouri Compromise, forbidding slavery in a part of the Louisiana Purchase, was unconstitutional, since Congress had no right to interfere with slavery in the Territories; (3) and that a master had as much right to take his slave with him into a free State as he had to take his horse, his cow, or any other kind of personal property.

This decision was far-reaching. It meant nothing less than the extension of slavery all over the Union. It intensified the anti-slavery feeling in the North, where many threatened that they would not obey the decision.

306. John Brown's Raid at Harper's Ferry (1859).—John Brown was a thorough-going abolitionist, who had taken a

born near Mercersburg, Pennsylvania, in 1791, and died in 1868. After his graduation from Dickinson College he studied law. He filled many public positions of great responsibility. Besides serving in both Houses of Congress, he became Secretary of State under President Polk and minister to England in Pierce's administration. As President of the United States during the trying years just preceding the Civil War, he was severely blamed by the Unionists because he did not take a firm stand in opposition to the secession movement.

ENGINE HOUSE, HARPER'S FERRY, WHERE JOHN BROWN WAS
CAPTURED BY UNITED STATES MARINES.

prominent part in the struggle for Kansas. He had a strong
will, a rugged, intense nature, and was deeply
religious. He believed that slavery was a
curse to the nation, and that he himself was an instrument
in God's hands to put an end to it in this country. The
only way to carry out his purpose was, as he thought, to
make slave-property insecure. His plan was to aid the
slaves in rising and then escaping to the mountains of Virginia, which would become a rallying-place for the negroes.
Having this aim in view, in the autumn of 1859, with about
twenty followers, he seized the arsenal at Harper's Ferry.

His plan met with disastrous failure. He was captured,
brought to a speedy trial, and hanged. Throughout his
trial he was calm and dignified, and he died
bravely. The South was alarmed and angered
by this deliberate plan to stir up a general uprising of

John Brown and his plan.

Results of the raid.

slaves. A large majority of the Northern people also bitterly condemned it. John Brown's raid increased the misunderstanding and widened the breach between the two sections. The irrepressible conflict was now at hand.

TO THE PUPIL

1. How did the Kansas-Nebraska bill differ from the Missouri Compromise? What important results did it have? What struggle did the North and and South make to get control of Kansas?

2. You can easily see how such a struggle would stir up bitter feelings in the people of the North and of the South. The assault on Charles Sumner illustrates well the intensity and depth of this feeling.

3. You will do well to note that the "Anti-Nebraska Men" banded together on the one issue—that there should be no further extension of slavery. The members of the Republican Party did the same. The fight all along, except in the case of the Abolitionists, was about the extension of slavery into new States.

4. Why did European immigrants refuse to settle in the South? Give three reasons why the South fell behind the North in prosperity.

5. Account for the friendly relations between the North and the West, and for the national feeling in the West.

6. Before taking up the Dred Scott decision review the following topics: Natural boundary between the free and the slave States before the purchase of Louisiana; the Missouri Compromise (1820); the Compromise of 1850; the Kansas-Nebraska Bill (1854).

7. What extreme ground was taken by the slave-holders in the Dred Scott Decision? What were the far-reaching results of this decision?

8. What was John Brown's plan? What were the results of his raid?

CHAPTER XVIII

SECESSION AND THE CIVIL WAR (1860–1865)

REFERENCES: **Scribner's** Popular History of the United States, IV.; **Andrew's** United States, II.; **Burgess's** Civil War and Reconstruction; **Wilson's** Division and Reunion; **Coffin's** Building the Nation; **Richardson's** History of Our Country; **Champlin's** Young Folks' History of the War for the Union; **Barnes's** Popular History of the United States.

OUTSIDE READINGS: **Wilson's** A History of the American People, IV.; **Comte de Paris's** Civil War; **Draper's** Civil War; **Rhodes's** United States, III. and IV.; **Ropes's** Story of the Civil War, I. and II.; **Greeley's** American Conflict; **Alexander H. Stephens's** War Between the States; **Jefferson Davis's** Rise and Fall of the Confederate Government; **Goldwin Smith's** United States; **Pollard's** Lost Cause; **Spear's** The History of Our Navy, IV.; **Morris's** Half Hours with American History, II.; **Ropes's** Army Under Pope; **Doubleday's** Chancellorsville and Gettysburg; **Fiske's** The Mississippi Valley in the Civil War; **Cox's** March to the Sea; **Pond's** Shenandoah Valley; **Coffin's** Drum-Beat of the Nation; **Coffin's** Freedom Triumphant; **Coffin's** Marching to Victory; **Soley's** Sailor Boys of '61; **Soley's** Blockade and Cruisers; **Parker's** Recollections of a Naval Officer; **Hague's** Blockaded Family; **Maury's** Recollections of a Virginian; **Dodge's** Bird's-Eye View of the Civil War; **Johnson's** Short History of the War; **Nicolay** and **Hay's** Abraham Lincoln; **Morse's** Abraham Lincoln; **Brooks's** Abraham Lincoln; **Pratt's** Lincoln in Story; **Tarbell's** Abraham Lincoln; **Grant's** Personal Memoirs; **Adams's** Charles Francis Adams; **Lothrop's** William H. Seward; **Davies's** General Sheridan; **Mahan's** Admiral Farragut; **Lee's** General Lee; **Sherman's** Memoirs; **Sheridan's** Memoirs; **Horne's** General Thomas; **McClellan's** Own Story; **Cooke's** Robert E. Lee; **Cooke's** "Stonewall" Jackson; **Hughes's** Joseph E. Johnston; **Church's** Ericsson; **Goss's** Recollections of a Private; **Trumbull's** War Memories of an Army Chaplain; **Gordon's** Reminiscences of the Civil War; **Hart's** Romance of the Civil War; **Alcott's** Hospital Sketches; **Livermore's** My Story of the War.

FICTION: **Page's** In Ole Virginia; **Page's** Among the Camps; **Page's** Two Little Confederates; **Henty's** With Lee in Virginia; **Trowbridge's** Cudjoe's Cave; **Trowbridge's** Three Scouts; **Trowbridge's** Drummer Boy; **Butterworth's** In the Boyhood of Lincoln; **Goss's** Tom Clifton; **Stoddard's** Battle of New York; **Churchill's** The Crisis.

POETRY: **Holmes's** View of the Loyal North; **Holmes's** Our Country; **Whittier's** Barbara Frietchie; **Harte's** John Burns of Gettysburg; **Read's** Sheridan's Ride; **Work's** Marching through Georgia; Tenting on the Old Camp Ground; **Stoddard's** Burial of Lincoln; **Longfellow's** Decoration Day.

THE WAR BEGINS

307. Slavery Splits the Democratic Party (1860).—By 1860 the question of slavery caused a split in the Democratic Party. The Northern Democrats believed in the principle of *popular sovereignty*, which allowed the people in the territories to decide for themselves whether or not they would have slaves. The Southern Democrats declared that the Constitution imposed upon Congress the duty of *protecting* slavery in the territories, and they supported their view by the Dred Scott Decision. The Republican Party declared that the Constitution imposed upon Congress the duty of *forbidding* slavery in the territories and repudiated the Dred Scott Decision. This party did not at that time favor the abolition of slavery. The great political issue, therefore, in the campaign of 1860 was the extension of slavery into the territories. The Northern Democrats nominated for President Stephen A. Douglas; the Southern Democrats, John C. Breckinridge; and the Republicans, Abraham Lincoln. As the Democratic vote was divided the Republicans elected their candidate.

308. Abraham Lincoln.[1]—The new President was one of the most remarkable men that the country has produced. While Lincoln was still young, his parents, who were of very humble origin, moved to Indiana. His home surroundings were such as a log hut in the backwoods could

[1] Abraham Lincoln, sixteenth President of the United States (1861–1865), was born in Hardin County, Kentucky, February 12, 1809, and died at the hands of an assassin in 1865. His father, who could neither read nor write, removed to Indiana when his son was only seven years of age, and later to Illinois. After serving as captain in the war with the Black Hawk Indians Lincoln was elected as a member of the Illinois State Legislature. In 1837 he began to practise law and soon became distinguished for his ability as a lawyer. In 1847–1849 he served as Rep-

furnish, and his advantages were few.   He had less than a year's training in the rude schools of the region; yet despite his rough exterior he developed into a youth of manly character.   He became known as "Honest Abe."   His clear head and good judgment caused him to be selected as a judge to settle disputes among his friends and neighbors.   He was six feet four inches in height and a giant in strength.

His opportunities for reading were so limited that it was hard work for him to make much headway with even the

few books he could get. But he was patient and persevering in the face of difficulties, and gradually won a great reputation as a debater and public speaker. He had a keen sense of humor, was a good story-teller, and possessed a rare power in winning men over to his views. His magnetic influence, joined to his clear judgment and sincerity of purpose, thus made him a great leader in the affairs of the nation.

Patient and persevering.

ABRAHAM LINCOLN.

309. The Southern Point of View.—Soon after Lincoln's election, South Carolina, the leader in the attempt to dissolve the Union, passed the Ordinance of Secession (December 20, 1860). The Southern leaders did not closely discriminate between Abolitionists like William Lloyd Garrison and John Brown, and Republicans like Seward and Lincoln. Therefore, when the Republican candidate was elected, these leaders naturally thought that

resentative in Congress.   He first attracted special attention, however, by his able speech in reply to Stephen A. Douglas on the repeal of the Missouri Compromise. This speech and his great reputation led to his nomination by the Republicans in 1858 for the United States senatorship.   Douglas was nominated by the Democrats.   The contest was a memorable one.   Although Douglas secured the election, Lincoln's brilliant debating with Douglas led to his nomination for the Presidency in 1860.

5

slavery would thrive better out of the Union than in it. Like Calhoun, Southern leaders in general were more attached to their States than to the Union. And, since they believed that the separate States were possessed of sovereign power, they also believed that any State could withdraw, or secede, from the Union whenever it pleased.

The State first in the South.

310. The Northern Point of View.—The North believed, as Webster had declared (1830), that the Constitution was

LINCOLN'S BIRTHPLACE.

not a compact between sovereign States but the fundamental law of the nation; that the Union was "now and forever, one and inseparable." With the South the State was first and the Union second: with the North the Union stood first, and no State had a right to secede from the Union against the consent of the other States. According to the latter view, peaceable secession, as Webster said (1850), was impossible. When, therefore, South Carolina passed the Ordinance of Secession, she gave the signal for a terrible struggle in which the life of the nation was threatened.

The Union first in the North.

311. The Principal Steps toward the Civil War.—The following were the principal steps in the disagreement[1]

---

[1] Of course the two sections had long disagreed on the tariff question also. But we have already seen how slavery led to this disagreement.

resulting in Civil War between the North and the South. By reason of an unfavorable soil and climate, slavery did not pay in the North, while it seemed to pay in the South. As the moral sentiment against slavery increased in the North, Steps toward the the South saw that the interests of the slave-Civil War. holder demanded an extension of slavery into new States. The North objected. This disagreement arrayed the sections against each other.

Finally the Southern slave-holders declared that, since the States were nations with sovereign power, they had a perfect right to secede from the Union and erect a Confederacy. When eleven of the fifteen slave States tried to break up the Union by secession, the free States were determined to preserve the Union, and the result was the Civil War. Before taking up the study of the war, let us notice a few of the conditions under which it was carried on.

312. Secession of the Remaining Cotton States and Organization of the Confederacy.—Within six weeks after the secession of South Carolina, the six other cotton States, Georgia, Florida, Alabama, Mississippi, Louisiana, and Texas, had likewise seceded. The cotton States naturally seceded first, because there slave labor was more profitable than in other parts of the South. On February 4, 1861, delegates from all these[1] States except Texas met at Montgomery, Alabama, and proceeded to the organization of the "Confederate States of America."[2] Jefferson Davis,[3] of

---

[1] The South was disappointed because some of the slave States did not secede and because the Northern people were so united. The Secessionists did not expect the cause to meet with such firm opposition throughout the North.

[2] The Confederate capital was removed from Montgomery, Alabama, to Richmond, Virginia, on May 20, 1861.

[3] Jefferson Davis was born in Kentucky in 1808, and died in 1889. After graduating from West Point (1828) he served in the army for some years and then became a cotton-planter in Mississippi. He took his seat in Congress in 1845, but again entered the army on the outbreak of the Mexican War. He distinguished himself for bravery in this war, receiving a severe wound at the battle of Buena Vista. He represented his State (Mississippi) in the United States Senate in 1847–51, and was Secretary of War under President Pierce. He again entered the Senate in 1857 and there remained until the beginning of the Civil War, when he resigned. He was elected President of the Southern Confederacy and remained in that office until the end of the war.

Mississippi, was elected President, and Alexander H. Stephens,[1] of Georgia, Vice-President.

313. Advantages of the North.—In this great struggle the North and the South were more evenly matched than is sometimes supposed. The North had many advantages: (1) She had a population of twenty-three millions, while the seceding States had but nine millions, three and a half millions of whom were slaves. (2) She had many factories, by means of which the necessary military supplies could be furnished to her armies. The South had to get her supplies from abroad.[2] (3) The North had a navy that gave her command of the sea, while the South, having put nearly all her energies into the cultivation of rice, cotton, sugar, and tobacco, had few sailors and no navy. Her extensive seacoast and large rivers were therefore open to attack from Northern vessels. (4) The North had also a greater number of able business men and far more wealth than the South. The industrial system of the North had developed men of the highest business ability.

JEFFERSON DAVIS.

314. Advantages of the South.—The South had the following advantages: (1) Fighting on the defensive, on her

[1] Alexander H. Stephens was born near Crawfordsville, Georgia, in 1812, and died in 1883. After graduating from the State University at the head of his class, he studied law and soon began his long political career by securing an election to the State Legislature. As a representative in Congress for sixteen years, 1843–59, he proved himself to be a statesman of conspicuous ability. In 1860 he vigorously opposed secession, but when Georgia seceded "he went with his State." He was elected Vice-President of the Southern Confederacy and continued in that position throughout the Civil War. The year before his death he was elected governor of Georgia. He was a man of very slight, frail body, and toward the end of his life had to be wheeled about in a chair.

[2] Not until the war was half over did the Confederates succeed in building and equipping the factories necessary for supplying their troops with guns and ammunition.

own soil, she needed fewer soldiers. Generally she could select her own positions behind breastworks and could fight near her base of supplies. On the other hand, many Northern troops were required to garrison strategic points that had been captured in the South. Before the war had closed a large proportion of the Union soldiers were guarding conquered territory. (2) At the beginning of the war the South had most of the experienced generals. (3) Moreover, the Southern people, almost exclusively devoted to the out-door life of agricultural pursuits, were well prepared to endure the severe physical strain demanded of a soldier in time of war. (4) The Southern troops, accustomed to the woods of the South, had a great advantage also in that considerable part of the fighting took place in the woods and wild regions.

315. The South Seizes National Property; the Star of the West.—Throughout the area of secession the South at once began to seize custom-houses, forts, arsenals, and all other property belonging to the United States. Some of President Buchanan's Cabinet were Southern men in full sympathy with the secession movement, and they took active measures to aid the South by sending arms and military supplies to Southern forts. ·

Buchanan did not believe in the right of secession, but neither did he believe that the National government had a right to use coercion. As he was in sympathy with the Southerners on the slavery question, he was unwilling to oppose them by preventing secession. The seceding States were therefore allowed to do much in preparation for war before Lincoln came into office. If the iron-willed Andrew Jackson had been President, in place of Buchanan, secession would probably have been put down before gaining much headway. Buchanan, with unfortunate indecision, let things drift, and by this let-alone policy brought disaster upon the Union.

Buchanan's indecision brings disaster upon the Union.

Before Lincoln's inauguration the South was ready for a terrible struggle. Early in January (1861) President Bu-

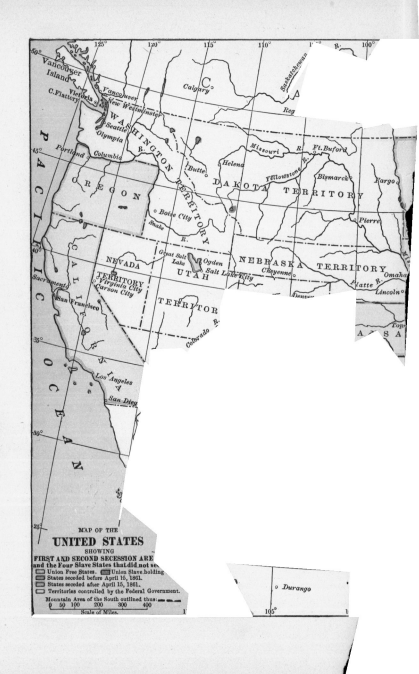

MAP OF THE

UNITED STATES

SHOWING

FIRST AND SECOND SECESSION ARE
and the Four Slave States that did not se

☐ Union Free States. ☐ Union Slave holding
☐ States seceded before April 15, 1861.
☐ States seceded after April 15, 1861.
☐ Territories controlled by the Federal Government.

Mountain Area of the South outlined thus: ▄▄ ▄▄

0   50 100   200   300   400
Scale of Miles.

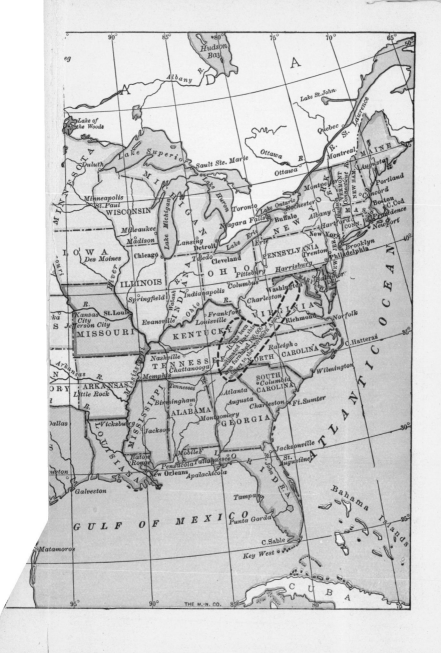

chanan sent the merchant steamer *Star of the West* with men
and supplies for Major Anderson of the United States army,
who had command at Fort Sumter in Charleston Harbor,
but the South Carolina army in Charleston fired upon the
steamer and prevented her reaching the fort.

316. Lincoln's Inaugural Address.—The time for decisive action had at last come. In the midst of intense excitement all over the Union Lincoln started from his home
in Illinois for Washington. Before reaching Baltimore he
was informed that a plan had been laid to assassinate him
as he passed through that city. He therefore changed his
plans and went to Washington at night on a special train.
In his inaugural address (March 4, 1861) he said he had no
intention of interfering with slavery, because he thought
the Constitution had given him no such authority. But he
declared that he would do everything in his power to preserve, protect, and defend the Union. President Lincoln's
address was free from bitterness, but left no doubt of the
firmness of his purpose to uphold the Constitution.

317. The Confederates Capture Fort Sumter.—Neither
the North nor the South wished to strike the first blow, but
the South was eager to get possession of Fort Sumter.
Major Anderson was in command here with a small force of
about eighty fighting men. The Confederates had an opposing army of between 5,000 and 6,000 men. Moreover,
Major Anderson had only a small supply of provisions on
hand. About one month after the inauguration of Lincoln
the latter decided to send supplies to the garrison.

Two days after this decision reached South Carolina
General Beauregard, who commanded the Confederate
troops in Charleston, demanded the surrender of the fort.
When Major Anderson refused, Beauregard opened fire at
4.30 on the morning of April 12, 1861. For thirty-four hours
the brave garrison, with little to eat, held out <small>The brave little</small>
against the overwhelming forces of the enemy. <small>garrison makes a</small>
On the morning of the second day the Con- <small>stubborn defense.</small>
federates, firing hot shot, set on fire the barracks and other
wood-work in the fort. The flames were dangerously near

the powder magazine, and the smoke almost suffocated the soldiers. Falling flat upon the ground, they covered their faces with wet cloths for protection, but would not give up. At last, seeing that there was no hope of supplies reaching the garrison, Major Anderson was compelled to surrender. On Sunday afternoon, the 14th, the Union soldiers saluted the Stars and Stripes with fifty guns, and, with drums beating "Yankee Doodle," marched out of the

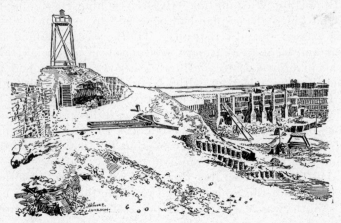

INTERIOR OF FORT SUMTER AFTER THE BOMBARDMENT IN 1863.

fort to embark for New York. In this bombardment no one was killed on either side.

The North was ablaze with indignation at the attack on Fort Sumter. Lincoln issued a proclamation calling for 75,000 volunteers (April 15), and declared Southern ports to be in a state of blockade (April 19). Troops flocked to Washington. The North thrilled with martial enthusiasm. The South was surprised. The secessionists had looked for compromise, but war had begun. In the North and in the South alike armies were promptly organized.

Results of the attack on Fort Sumter.

318. Secession of Four More States.—When Virginia, North Carolina, Tennessee, and Arkansas were called upon to furnish their quota of troops to the National army, they refused. Although these States had not wished to secede, they believed in the right of secession, and therefore when it became certain that the government meant to coerce their sister States to remain in the Union, they voted to secede. The secession area was thus extended over eleven States.[1]

319. Battle of Bull Run.—When, early in July, the Northern army had driven the Confederate forces out of West Virginia, the people in the North became impatient for an advance upon Richmond. General McDowell was in command, in Washington, of a Union army (of about 30,000 men). General Patterson (with about 18,000) was in the Shenandoah Valley watching General Joseph E. Johnston[2] (with 9,000), and the Confederate army, commanded by General Beauregard, with 22,000, was posted at Manassas Junction, about thirty-five miles from Washington, on a little stream called Bull Run. This position was selected by the Confederates because it could be easily reached by rail with men and supplies, and because an advance upon Washington from this point would be easy.

The opposing forces.

Here, on July 21, McDowell made an attack upon the Confederates, in which he seemed at first to be winning a

[1] The remaining slave States, Delaware, Maryland, Kentucky, and Missouri, did not secede. The mountainous parts of western Virginia, not being adapted to the cultivation of rice, cotton, sugar, or tobacco, had no large plantations, and there was not a large ownership of slaves in that part of the State. The people, therefore, did not sympathize with secession, and early in 1861 withdrew from Virginia and organized a separate State government under the name of West Virginia. In June, 1863, West Virginia was admitted to the Union. The attitude of this State toward the war is an interesting illustration of the intimate connection between soil and climate and slavery, and between slavery and secession. In the mountainous regions still farther south many of the people were loyal to the Union. It is estimated that 100,000 of these mountain whites fought in the Northern armies.

[2] Joseph E. Johnston was born in Longwood, Virginia, in 1807, and died in 1891. He was graduated from West Point in the same class with Robert E. Lee, who was ever after his warm, personal friend. Like Lee, he did not favor secession, but "went with his State" when it seceded. Next to Lee he was probably the ablest Confederate general. After his success at the battle of Bull Run he fell into a serious disagreement with Jefferson Davis, the effect of which was to injure the Southern cause. Johnston's defensive campaign in Georgia in 1864, when Sherman was advancing upon Atlanta, showed military ability of a high order.

victory by forcing back a part of the Confederates a distance of a mile and a half. At the critical moment, how-
The Northern   ever, the Confederates were reinforced by
army, at first   fresh troops from the Shenandoah, where John-
successful, re-
treats in a panic. ston had eluded Patterson with his entire
army, most of which had joined Beauregard on July 20th.
The Federal army fled in a panic toward Washington, but

LONG BRIDGE ACROSS THE POTOMAC AT WASHINGTON, D. C.

the Southern army, by reason of its crippled condition,
made no attempt at pursuit.

320. **Results of the Battle of Bull Run.**—This battle
probably benefited the North more than it did the South.
The Confederates seemed to think the war was over and
began to seek their homes. But the defeat caused the
North to appreciate the need of putting forth all her energies in preparation for the great struggle which, it was now
evident, could not be avoided. General McClellan, who
had been very successful in driving the Confederates out of
West Virginia, was called from his victories there to organize and drill the army. During the autumn and winter
the warring forces were busy fortifying their respective

capitals, Washington and Richmond, and gathering all possible strength for the campaigns of 1862.

321. The Trent Affair.—To secure aid for the Southern cause Mason and Slidell had been selected by the Confederate government as commissioners to England and France.   In November, 1861, they escaped the blockade at Charleston and took passage at Havana on the British mail steamer *Trent*.   Captain Wilkes, of the United States war-vessel *San Jacinto*, stopped the *Trent* not far from the Bahama Islands, took off Mason and Slidell, and confined them in Fort Warren, in Boston Harbor.

322. England Resents the Capture of Mason and Slidell.—For this act Captain Wilkes was greatly applauded by Northern people, but England was highly indignant and at once began to make preparations for war.   She sent troops and war-vessels to Canada and was unnecessarily harsh in her demands that the prisoners be given up.

GEORGE B. McCLELLAN.

President Lincoln, knowing that the War of 1812 was brought about mainly because England claimed the right to stop and search neutral American vessels at sea, wisely refused to approve the course taken by Captain Wilkes. Accordingly he at once gave up the prisoners to England, with the statement that Captain Wilkes had acted without any authority from **President Lincoln gives up Mason and Slidell.** the United States Government.   But the North could not help thinking that England was not only insolent in her demands, but over-hasty in her preparations to make war upon us.   Ill-feeling between the two countries was thus aroused and was a source of more or less irritation throughout the war.

TO THE PUPIL

1. You are now ready to study the Civil War. Only a few of the great battles are described in this history, but these will enable you to understand the character of the terrible conflict. You do not need to know the details of military movements, but you do need to know what kind of men your country sent to the camp and battle field. Were they brave men? Were they manly, vigorous, and true? Find out as you study the war.

2. How did slavery split the Democratic Party? What did the Republicans think of slavery? Learn all you can about the life and character of Abraham Lincoln.

3. What was the Southern point of view of the Constitution? The Northern point of view? Recall the liberal construction and the strict construction theories of the Constitution in the time of Hamilton and Jefferson. What were the principal steps in the disagreement which resulted in Civil War?

4. Why were the cotton States the first to secede? Name the advantages of the North and of the South in the war.

5. What was President Buchanan's attitude toward the secession movement? Contrast this attitude with that of Andrew Jackson toward nullification. What was the result of Buchanan's attitude?

6. Why did the Confederates attack Fort Sumter? Imagine yourself to have been in the fort with the brave little garrison and describe your experience there. What were the results of the attack on Fort Sumter?

7. Why did Virginia, North Carolina, Tennessee, and Arkansas secede? Account for the refusal of the people in the western part of Virginia to join their State in the secession movement.

8. Locate on your map the position of the opposing forces just before the Battle of Bull Run. What were the results of this battle?

9. What was the " Trent affair "? Do you think President Lincoln acted wisely in giving up Mason and Slidell? Give reasons for your answer.

10. By reading the opening chapter of Ropes's " Story of the Civil War " you will get a clear idea of the difference between the Northern and the Southern point of view of the Union.

THE NATION IN PERIL

323. **Union Plan of the War.**—Not until the opening of 1862 was a plan of operations matured by the North. This plan, at the outset, was threefold: (1) To blockade

Southern ports; (2) to open the Mississippi; (3) to capture Richmond. The successful carrying out of this plan led also to Sherman's campaign in Georgia in 1864.

324. England and King Cotton.—At the outbreak of the war people at the North supposed they had only the South to deal with. They soon found, however, that they had to contend with an insidious influence from abroad. When Jefferson Davis said, " Cotton is king," [1] he doubtless thought that England's money and friendship could be secured by her need of cotton. In 1860 the cotton exports, most of which went to English factories, amounted to more than $202,000,000. Many English manufacturers and merchants and 4,000,000 English working people were dependent upon Southern cotton for their means of support. The Southern leaders naturally thought that these English manufacturers and working people would never submit to any action on the part of the North which would cripple their industries. It was therefore expected by the Confederates that the need of cotton in England would win for them the sympathy of the English people.

325. The Blockade.—But from the beginning of the struggle the North was determined to blockade the South so effectually that the latter could neither send cotton to England nor receive in return the much-needed supplies for her soldiers and homes. In the end, as the world knows, the South was forced to give up the struggle because of a lack of the very supplies which cotton alone could procure; in other words, the Confederacy was starved into submission by the blockade. Although, as stated above, the cotton exports in 1860 had amounted to $202,000,000, in 1861 the exports fell in value to $42,000,000, and in 1862 to $4,000,000. In the remaining years of the war the blockade was so effectual that the value of the cotton exports was not worth consideration.

326. The Merrimac and the Monitor.—It was to break the blockade that the *Merrimac* was set afloat. When the

[1] At the beginning of the war the cotton States in the South furnished nearly two thirds of all the cotton used in the world.

Norfolk navy-yard was abandoned by the United States
Government at the outbreak of the war, among the ships

The Confederates burned and sunk was the frigate *Merrimac.*
make an iron-clad
of the Merri- This had been one of the largest and finest
mac. ships in the navy. The Confederates raised
her and converted her into an iron-clad. Up to this time
very few iron-clad frigates had been built, and none had
been tested in war. The Confederate naval officers

DECK OF THE *MONITOR.*

thought, however, that one iron-clad would be much more
effective in reducing the Union navy and raising the
blockade than a whole fleet of wooden craft to match those
generally in use. The history of the naval duel between
the *Merrimac* and the *Monitor* shows how wisely the Confederates planned. The hull of the *Merrimac* was razed to
the water's level. The vessel was rebuilt with sloping
sides, plated with iron four inches thick, and was furnished
with a cast-iron beak and a formidable battery. The *Merrimac* had been many months in construction, and when,
about noon of March 8, 1862, she steamed into Hampton
Roads, where the United States had a fleet of five powerful
war-vessels, she was not wholly unexpected.

In advancing to meet her, three of the blockading squadron ran aground on account of low water. But the *Congress* and the *Cumberland*, supported by the batteries on the shore, made ready for the attack. They poured broadside after broadside into the *Merrimac* as she approached. The balls rebounded from her iron sides with no effect. The *Merrimac* steered straight for the *Cumberland*, discharging a broadside into the *Congress* in passing. Continuing her fire she rammed her iron beak into the *Cumberland's* side, making a great hole, into which the water rushed. The crew of the *Cumberland* continued firing until they reached the water's edge, and when they went down their colors were still flying. The *Merrimac* then turned to the *Congress*, poured hot shot into her, set her afire, and forced her to surrender. At nightfall the *Merrimac* steamed back to her landing, expecting to complete her work of destruction the following day.

The Merrimac plays havoc with the blockading squadron.

Great was the joy in the South that night, and great was the consternation in the North. Statesmen were grave, the people terrified. The blockade was broken at Norfolk. Soon it might be broken at other ports, and Northern commerce might be ruined by the ravages of this invulnerable sea-monster.

Consternation in the North.

But in history, as in fiction, it is the unexpected that often happens. That night a strange-looking craft came into the harbor. It was Ericsson's *Monitor*, which had been completed in New York two days before. The *Monitor* was an experiment, and her construction had been pushed with desperate energy, that she might be ready as soon as the *Merrimac*. She was built with an iron-plated deck almost level with the water, and had a revolving iron turret with two powerful guns. The purpose of this peculiar construction was to present as little resisting surface as possible to the enemy's guns. The Confederates well described her appearance when they said she looked like a Yankee cheese-box on a raft. She had arrived just in time.

The Monitor arrives just in time.

The following morning the *Merrimac* steamed out of

Norfolk confident of a victory over the other three frigates. She steered for the *Minnesota*, by the side of which the *Monitor* was lying, and soon found that she had a new adversary to deal with. The *Monitor* steered straight for the *Merrimac*, and one of the strangest naval battles ever fought began. The duel continued over three hours. At points the *Merrimac's* armor was crushed but not pierced. Captain Worden of the *Monitor* received a wound which delayed the action for a little, and the *Merrimac* withdrew. Neither side cared to continue the struggle. The *Merrimac* had met her match and made no further attempt to break the blockade. The sturdy little *Monitor* had saved the Union.

The sturdy little Monitor saves the Union.

This fight revolutionized naval warfare, for it showed that the days of wooden war-vessels were at an end. Against such iron-clads as the *Monitor* and the *Merrimac* wooden vessels of the finest type were useless.[1]

327. The Importance of the Mississippi.—In order to cut off the South from communication with the rest of the world, it was necessary not only to maintain the blockade but to gain possession of the Mississippi River. For by way of Mexico trade was kept up with European countries to some extent. Other advantages would be secured to the North by getting control of this river: (1) Such control would cut the Confederacy in two, making Texas, Arkansas, and Louisiana of little use to the Southern cause; (2) it would prevent the South from getting supplies of any sort from the region west of the Mississippi; (3) it would enable the North to use her navy to great advantage in concentrating troops in the rear of the Confederacy and in getting supplies to her armies in that region; (4) it would open the Mississippi to the trade of the West and the Northwest.

Why the North desired to get control of the Mississippi.

---

[1] Neither of these famous iron-clads ever again took part in a battle. When, two months later, McClellan forced the Confederates to evacuate Norfolk, they destroyed the *Merrimac*, which drew so much water that she could not steam up the James River to Richmond. In December of the same year the *Monitor* went down, with most of her crew, in a storm off Cape Hatteras, North Carolina.

THE BATTLE BETWEEN THE MONITOR AND THE MERRIMAC.

328. Capture of Forts Henry and Donelson.—It was one thing to cut off the South from the rest of the world; it was quite another to get possession of her vast territory. But this last was necessary also. Early in the war the Confederates had been driven from West Virginia and from Missouri. In the winter and spring of 1862 the Federal generals began a series of movements whose twofold purpose was to open the Mississippi to the North and gain possession of Tennessee.

To defend Tennessee, the Confederates had built Fort Henry on the Tennessee and Fort Donelson on the Cumberland. Their line of defence, as will be seen **The Confederate** by consulting the map, extended from Colum- **line of defence.** bus through Forts Henry and Donelson, Bowling Green, and Mill Springs, to Cumberland Gap. To break this line of defence, it was necessary for the North to capture Forts Henry and Donelson. By capturing the two forts the two important rivers would be under the control of Northern vessels, and Nashville would have to be abandoned by the Confederates. Columbus, when cut off from support, would also have to be given up without a struggle.

With all these things in view, General Grant, with the aid of Commodore Foote, moved upon the two forts. Commodore Foote soon captured Fort Henry (February 6); and General Grant,[1] after a hard fight, received the surrender of Fort Donelson with nearly 15,000 prisoners (February 16). By this important victory the first Southern line of defence in the West was thus broken, and Columbus and Nashville fell into the hands of the Federals.

329. The Battle of Pittsburg Landing (or Shiloh).— The Confederates now fell back upon another line of defence, extending from Memphis, through Cor- **General Grant at** inth, an important railroad centre, to Chatta- **Pittsburg Landing** nooga. Under General Albert Sidney John- **waits for General** **Buell.** ston, the Confederate army, 40,000 strong, took position at

[1] When General Buckner sent to Grant for terms of surrender the following answer was sent: " No terms except unconditional and immediate surrender can be accepted. I propose to move immediately upon your works."

Corinth.   General Grant, with 33,000 men, advanced as far
as Pittsburg Landing on the Tennessee River, about twenty-
four miles from Corinth.   Here he waited for Buell, who
was hastening from Nashville to join him with an army of
27,000 men.   On Buell's arrival the Federal army was to
attack Johnston's forces at Corinth.

Before Buell could reach Pittsburg Landing, however,
Johnston attacked Grant early on Sunday morning, April 6.

PARAPET AT FORTRESS MONROE.

It was a terrible day.   By nightfall the Confederates had
driven Grant's troops back a mile and a half toward the

Grant wins a victory. river.   But before morning Buell's fresh troops
had come up, and they assisted Grant in driv-
ing the Confederates from the field.   In this battle about
20,000 men were killed or wounded.   Among the killed was
General Albert Sidney Johnston, whose death was a serious
loss to the South.

330. Capture of New Orleans.—New Orleans was important to the South because it controlled the lower Mississippi.   Thirty miles from the mouth of the river were two
forts nearly opposite each other.   Between them were

Confederate defences. stretched across the river immense chains
fastened to the hulks of old vessels.   A little
farther up the river was a strong fleet, which included a
formidable iron-clad ram like the *Merrimac* and a floating
battery covered with railroad iron.   There were also fire-
rafts ready to be turned loose upon the Federal vessels.

Farragut runs by the forts.

Commodore Farragut, who was in command of a fleet of nearly fifty wooden vessels that was to attack these forts, advanced up the river to New Orleans. There General Butler, with an army of 15,000 men,

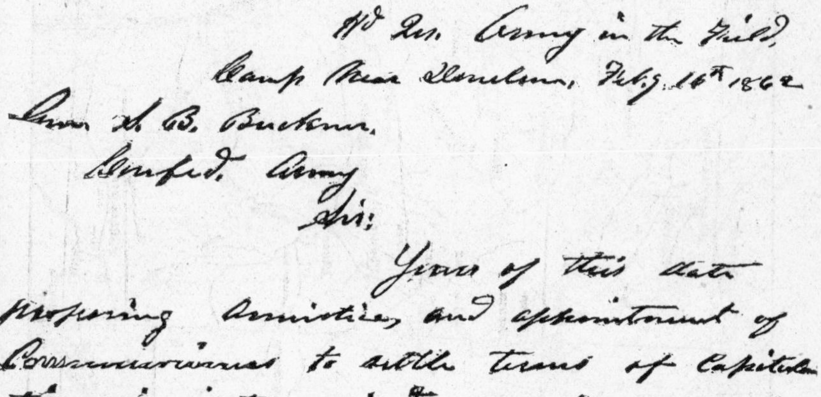

Hd Qrs. Army in the Field,
Camp near Donelson, Feby 16th 1862

Gen. S. B. Buckner,
Confed. Army

Sir:

Yours of this date proposing Armistice, and appointment of Commissioners to settle terms of Capitulation, is just received. No terms except an unconditional and immediate surrender can be accepted.

I propose to move immediately upon your works.

I am sir, very respectfully
Your obt. svt.
U. S. Grant
Brig. Gen.

GRANT'S "UNCONDITIONAL SURRENDER" LETTER.

By permission of General James Grant Wilson.

was to aid in getting possession of the city. After bombarding the forts for six days without making much impression, Farragut determined to run by them at night. It was a desperate undertaking, but it succeeded, and easily

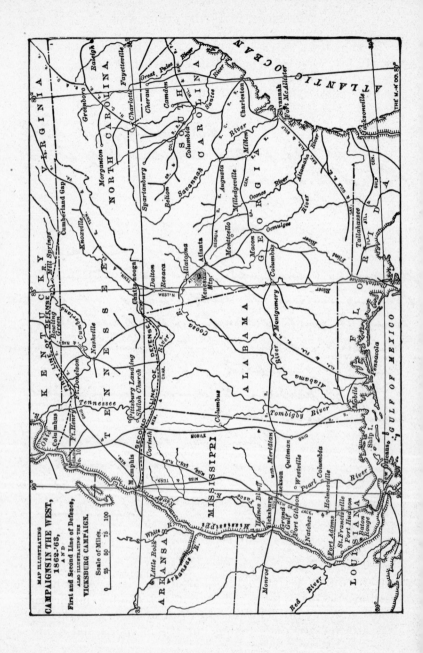

MAP ILLUSTRATING
CAMPAIGNS IN THE WEST,
1862-'63,
AND
First and Second Line of Defense,
ALSO ILLUSTRATING THE
VICKSBURG CAMPAIGN.

Scale of Miles.
0   25   50   75   100

brought New Orleans into the possession of the Union forces (April 25). With the aid of the river gunboats the Federals had, before the close of 1862, opened the river as far down as Vicksburg. This city and Port Hudson alone remained in possession of the Confederacy.

331. The Peninsular Campaign (1862).—These brilliant victories were in marked contrast with the failure of the army under General McClellan. As we have already seen, he was placed in command of the Army of the Potomac, which was intended for the defence of Washington and the capture of Richmond. Before the opening of the spring campaign in 1862, he had, by thorough organization and drill, created a splendid army. *McClellan creates a splendid army.*

His original plan was to approach Richmond by the James River. Lincoln opposed this because he thought that Washington would thus be exposed to attack. He therefore urged the wisdom of approaching Richmond overland from the north, in order to keep the Federal army between the Confederates and Washington. McClellan objected because there were so many rivers to be crossed, every one of which could, for defensive purposes, be made a Confederate stronghold. *McClellan objects to Lincoln's plan.* The swampy forests of this region were also in the same way of great value to the South. It is no exaggeration to say that these natural advantages were worth many thousand troops to the Confederate army, and it is unfair to McClellan and Grant not to take them into account. McClellan adopted neither Lincoln's plan nor his own, but compromised by approaching Richmond by way of the peninsula between the James and the York Rivers, making his base of supplies on the latter.

McDowell was stationed near Fredericksburg, between the main Confederate army and Washington. In this position he could protect Washington or unite with McClellan, as occasion required. To prevent an attack upon the capital by way of the Shenandoah, well known during the war as the " back *McDowell stationed at Fredericksburg.*

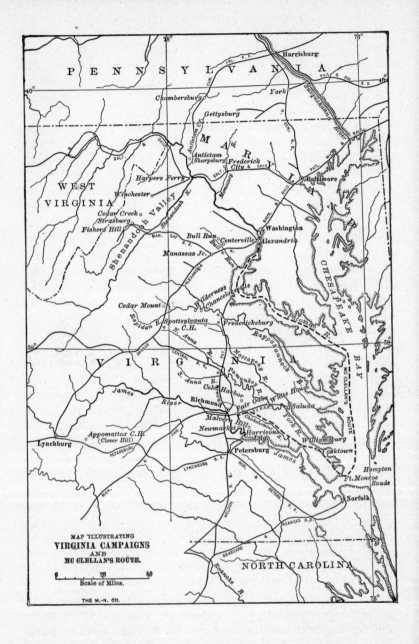

MAP ILLUSTRATING
VIRGINIA CAMPAIGNS
AND
McCLELLAN'S ROUTE.

0   25   50
Scale of Miles.

THE M.-N. CO.

door to Washington," Union forces were stationed there under Banks and Frémont.

332. McClellan Advances up the Peninsula.—Starting at Fortress Monroe on April 4, 1862, McClellan, with 120,000 troops, advanced along the York River to Yorktown. Here, instead of storming the town, he laid siege to it. When he was ready *McClellan stops for a month at Yorktown.* for an assault, the Confederates, having held him in check for a month, withdrew, and thus gained time to strengthen

A MORTAR BATTERY IN FRONT OF YORKTOWN.

their defences about Richmond. McClellan hurried after them and fought an indecisive battle at Williamsburg, from which the Confederates retired toward their capital. McClellan then advanced slowly, and by the end of May found himself within ten miles of Richmond. By that time the Confederates defending Richmond numbered 70,000.

Dividing his army, McClellan encamped upon both sides of the Chickahominy. He made this arrangement so as to establish easy connection between his north wing and McDowell, who (with 45,000 men) was near Fredericksburg with orders to be in readiness to unite with McClellan. **Heavy rains** caused the Chickahominy to swell, thus separating the two wings. General Johnston took advantage of the

Battle of Fair Oaks. situation to attack the division south of the river at Fair Oaks (Seven Pines), and threatened to overwhelm it, but McClellan got reinforcements across and stayed the retreat.

333. **"Stonewall" Jackson in the Shenandoah Valley; McClellan Changes his Base of Supplies.**—In order to prevent McDowell from joining McClellan, General Robert E. Lee, who was now in command of the Confederates,[1] sent "Stonewall" Jackson down the Shenandoah Valley to threaten Washington. Jackson defeated Banks and Frémont, and so thoroughly alarmed Lincoln that the latter ordered McDowell to return to the defence of Washington. After playing havoc with the Union forces in the Shenandoah Jackson hastily joined Lee.

Now that McDowell was prevented from joining the attack upon Richmond, McClellan changed his base of supplies to the James River. During the week that he was

The "Seven Days' Battles." transferring the army to the new base of supplies the terrible "Seven Days' Battles," in which McClellan lost 15,000 men, were fought. At Malvern Hill, the field of the last of these engagements, Lee repeat-

---

[1] Lee had succeeded General Joseph E. Johnston, who was wounded in the battle of Fair Oaks (May 31).

Robert E. Lee, son of Henry Lee, or "Light-Horse Harry," of Revolutionary fame, was born in Westmoreland County, Virginia, in 1807, and died in 1870. He was graduated from West Point in 1829, ranking second in a class of forty-six. He distinguished himself for bravery in the Mexican War and rose to the rank of colonel. After Virginia seceded in 1861 Lee decided "to go with his State." He therefore resigned his commission in the army of the United States, and a little later took command of the Virginia State troops. When, at the battle of Seven Pines, or Fair Oaks (1862), General Joseph E. Johnston received a serious wound that temporarily unfitted him for active service, Lee was put at the head of the Confederate army. From that time to the end of the war he was the leading Confederate general and handled his troops with consummate ability. Military critics rank him and Grant as two of the foremost commanders of this century. Lee won the confidence of the Southern people, who regarded him with unbounded admiration and affection. At the close of the war he became president of what is now Washington and Lee University, where he spent the remaining years of his life.

edly charged but was driven back with fearful slaughter. The Army of the Potomac fought here with magnificent heroism. Had McClellan taken immediate advantage of this victory he might, by a vigorous attack, have captured Richmond. As a whole, the Peninsular Campaign failed and caused bitter disappointment in the North.

334. **Lee's First Invasion of the North (1862).**—McClellan made no further attempt upon Richmond. In the

A FEDERAL BATTERY IN THE FIELD.

meantime Halleck had been put in chief command of the Union armies. Pope was appointed to take command of the forces in northern Virginia and McClellan was ordered to join him. Before McClellan could reach Pope, however, Lee pushed north. He united his forces with "Stonewall" Jackson's, which had been sent to surprise Pope's rear. After defeating Pope in the second battle of Bull Run he marched across the Potomac **Second Battle of Bull Run.** into Maryland, where he thought he would receive large recruits. In this he was disappointed. The great majority of the Maryland people were loyal to the Union, and

plainly showed this in their attitude toward the invasion.
When Lee's men marched into the State singing "My
Maryland people   Maryland" there was not a word of welcome
loyal to the Union. from the people. On reaching Frederick, Lee
was surprised to find not only places of business shut, but
even the doors closed and the blinds drawn. The North,
however, fearing an attack upon Baltimore, Washington, or
Philadelphia, was greatly alarmed.

ROBERT E. LEE.

335. Battle of Antietam (September 17, 1862).—After Pope's defeat in the second battle of Bull Run, McClellan, having united Pope's army with the Army of the Potomac, started in pursuit of Lee. On September 17, with an army of 70,000, he attacked Lee, who, with about 40,000, had taken his position at Sharpsburg, behind Antietam Creek. This battle was one of the bloodiest of the war. Although Lee
Lee retreats   successfully defended
into Virginia.   himself against the attack of the Union army, he had to retreat into Virginia without having gained anything by his first invasion of the North.

Some people thought McClellan ought to have routed
or captured Lee's army. As he did not follow the Con-
Burnside, who su- federates he was severely criticised for being
persedes McClel-
lan, is defeated at   slow and overcautious, and was superseded
Fredericksburg. by Burnside. Burnside was as rash as Mc-
Clellan was cautious, and later in the autumn met a crushing defeat when he attacked Lee, who was intrenched in a
strong position at Fredericksburg. The year's operations
had been successful for the Union cause in the West, but
unsuccessful in the East.[1]

[1] One of the bloodiest battles of the war was fought at the end of this year
at Murfreesboro, Tennessee. Beginning December 31 (1862), it lasted three days,
and resulted in the retreat of the Confederates after the most stubborn fighting.

TO THE PUPIL

1. What was the Union plan of the war? In what way did Jefferson Davis think that the cotton trade would secure the friendship of England for the Southern cause? Why was it extremely important for the North to blockade the South?

2. What did the Merrimac accomplish on the first day she attacked the blockading squadron? What were the results of the fight between the Merrimac and the Monitor?

3. Name four or five advantages to the North in securing control of the Mississippi. What purpose had the Confederates in building Forts Henry and Donelson? What effect did the capture of these forts by the Federals have upon the Confederate line of defence?

4. What was the second Confederate line of defence? What were the causes and results of the Battle of Shiloh? Why was New Orleans of importance to the South?

5. Are you making constant use of your map?

6. What was McClellan's plan of approaching Richmond? What was Lincoln's? Which do you think was the better plan? Give reasons for your answer. For defensive purposes, what natural advantages had the Confederates in Virginia? Why was General McDowell left at Fredericksburg?

7. Point out on the map Yorktown and Williamsburg, and show their connection with McClellan's advance upon Richmond. What was the purpose of " Stonewall " Jackson's movements in the Shenandoah? What was the result?

8. After reading as much as you can on the Peninsular Campaign, give reasons for McClellan's failure to capture Richmond.

9. Why did Lee decide to invade the North? How was he disappointed? What were the results of the Battle of Antietam?

THE TIDE TURNS

336. Lee's Second Invasion of the North; Battle of Gettysburg (1863).—After Burnside's repulse at Fredericksburg in December, 1862, he retired to winter quarters. Before the campaign of 1863 opened Hooker was put in command. In April he advanced to Chancellorsville with 113,000 men, and attacked Lee, who had 62,000.[1] Lee again badly defeated the Army

Hooker's defeat at Chancellorsville.

[1] In this battle the Confederates met with a grievous loss in the death of " Stonewall " Jackson. Through a mistake he was fired upon by some of his own men. Thomas J. Jackson, often called " Stonewall " Jackson, was born in 1824, in Har-

of the Potomac.   These two victories made the South jubi-
lant, but depressed the North.

   With an exultant and confident army Lee planned to
invade the North a second time.   Early in June he marched
down the Shenandoah, crossed the Potomac, and advanced
into Pennsylvania.   The whole country was wild with excitement.   Lee hoped to win a decisive victory, capture Baltimore or some other great
Northern city, and dictate terms of peace.
He had reason to believe that a victory on Northern soil

Lee's reasons for invading the North in 1863.

FUGITIVE NEGROES FORDING THE RAPPAHANNOCK.

would lead England and France to recognize the independence of the South.   These two countries were only waiting until some pronounced success on the part of the South
should afford them a reasonable excuse for giving such
recognition.

rison County, Virginia (now West Virginia), and was graduated from West Point in
1846.   He took part in the Mexican War, where he was promoted for good conduct.   He resigned from the army in 1851, on receiving an appointment as profess-
or in the Virginia Military Institute, at Lexington, Virginia.   He was so eccentric
that he became unpopular with the students, who did not regard him as a man of
ability.   Although he was opposed to secession he thoroughly believed in State
rights, and therefore "went with his State" when it seceded.   As soon as he took
command of troops on the battle field he showed himself to be a splendid soldier.
By his stubborn bravery at Bull Run he won the name of "Stonewall" Jackson,
and rose at once to the rank of major-general.   He was Lee's ablest subordinate,
and, next to Lee, was probably the most popular Confederate general.

Lee advanced his army toward Chambersburg and encamped in that vicinity. Hooker crossed the Potomac east of the mountains, marched north to Frederick, and sent a detachment west through the mountains to menace Lee's line of supplies. In order to draw off the Union forces from his rear, Lee marched eastward to threaten Washington. On the very same **Lee's advance.** morning Meade, who had superseded Hooker, started north from Frederick, keeping east of the mountains to protect Washington. The two armies were thus marching toward each other, and each was ignorant of the other's movements. **The two armies meet at Gettysburg.** They unexpectedly met at Gettysburg and fought a three-days' battle (July 1, 2, and 3).

THOMAS J. (" STONEWALL") JACKSON.

On the first day the advance forces of the Union army, being greatly outnumbered, were driven through Gettysburg **The first day.** with a loss of 5,000 prisoners. The Confederates also suffered heavy loss in killed and wounded. That night the Union army took a strong position on Cemetery Ridge, just south of the town. This ridge, three miles in length, is in the shape of a fishhook, with Culp's Hill for the barb and Round Top at the extreme southern end. Just north of Round Top was Little Round Top. Lee's army took position on Seminary Ridge, lying about a mile west of Cemetery Ridge and nearly parallel with it.

On the second day of the battle the Confederates made two vigorous assaults, one at Culp's Hill on **The second day.** the right wing of the Union army and the other in front of Little Round Top on the left wing. Although the Confederates gained some slight advantage, there was no definite result on either side.

Having failed to break the Union flanks and having received Pickett's fresh division, Lee spent the next morning in preparation for a grand assault on the Union centre, where he hoped to be more successful. By one o'clock in the afternoon he had placed in position on Seminary Ridge **The furious can-** more than a hundred guns. The Federals **nonade.** could find room for only eighty on Cemetery Ridge. At one o'clock the Confederate guns opened fire, and until three the furious cannonade continued. At that

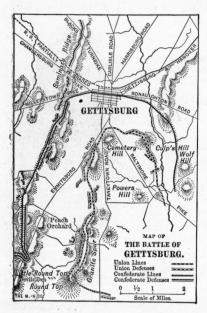

MAP OF
**THE BATTLE OF
GETTYSBURG.**

Union Lines
Union Defenses
Confederate Lines
Confederate Defenses

0   ½   1   2
Scale of Miles.

time the fire slackened on Cemetery Ridge in order to let the guns cool in time for the expected attack. The Confederates thought they had silenced the Union batteries, and that the moment for the South to make one mighty effort had come.

General Pickett, who was to lead this assault at the head of some of the best Virginia troops, was **Pickett's charge.** ordered to advance. In three magnificent lines, with a front a mile long, 15,000 Confederates charged across the field. The sight was thrilling, but soon the murderous fire from the Northern guns began to cut them down by hundreds. The fearful slaughter thinned the advancing lines. Still they pressed on. As they neared the first line of Northern troops, Lieutenant Cushing, a Union officer, although mortally wounded, pushed the only remaining gun of his battery to the fence and shouted to his commander, " Webb, I will give them one more shot." As he fired he fell, saying " Good-by." Pickett's men broke through the first line. Armistead, one of Pickett's generals, leaped over the fence, raised aloft his sword, upon the point of which he swung his hat, and shouted, "Give them the cold steel, boys!" Just as he laid his hand upon a Union gun to capture it, he was shot down. From every side the Union men came rushing headlong upon the enemy. The struggle that followed was terrific. Men and officers were mingled together in one seething mass, each man fighting for himself.

Pickett's men were soon repulsed, and with their lines broken into fragments they were driven back with disastrous loss. The failure of Pickett's charge insured Lee's defeat at Gettysburg, and with **Defeat of** that defeat the tide **Pickett's men.** turned. Next day, while Grant was receiving the surrender of Vicksburg, Lee began his retreat toward the Potomac. After this failure the South was unable to secure a foothold in the North.[1]

GEORGE G. MEADE.

337. **Capture of Vicksburg; Opening of the Mississippi River.** —At the close of 1862 Vicksburg and Port Hudson were the only Confederate strongholds left on the Mississippi. After months of unsuccessful effort to take Vicksburg from the north, General Grant moved his army down on the west bank of the river and, crossing over to the east bank, **Grant attacks** made an attack from the south. Pemberton, **Vicksburg from** who was in command of the Confederates in **the south.** Vicksburg, marched out to meet Grant, hoping to unite with Johnston, who was hastening to join him. Before the union of the two Confederate armies could be effected, Grant drove Pemberton into Vicksburg and compelled Johnston to retreat. Grant's bold plan was brilliantly executed.

[1] In this battle Meade's army (infantry and artillery) numbered about 82,000; Lee's about 74,000. Each army had in addition about 11,000 cavalry. Meade lost in all about 23,000; Lee 30,000, or more than one-third of his entire force.

He then laid siege to the city (May 19), cutting it off from supplies of all kinds. Flour sold for $1,000 a barrel (Confederate money). Provisions became so scarce that even rats and mule-flesh were used as food. So many thousand shells were thrown into the city daily that many people abandoned their homes. They lived in caves which

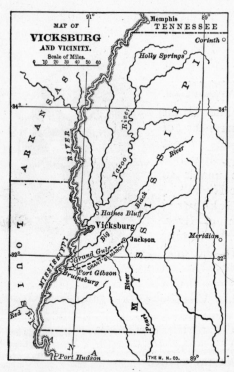

they dug in banks where the streets had been cut through the hills. In about seven weeks the Confederates were starved into surrender. On July 4, 1863, the day after Lee's defeat at Gettysburg, Pemberton surrendered Vicksburg with 32,000 men. When, four days later, Port Hudson was captured, the Mississippi River, to its mouth, was under the control of the North.

The Confederates starved into surrender.

338. **Slavery and the Emancipation Proclamation** (January 1, 1863).—In his inaugural address President Lincoln had declared that he would not interfere with slavery where it already existed because he had no constitutional right to do so. But as the war proceeded it became evident that the blacks in the South were a great source of strength to the Confederate cause; for while masters enlisted in the army, slaves by their labor supplied food not only for Southern families but for the

The slaves aid the cause of the South.

support of the Southern army. In this way they were aiding the cause of the South about as much as if they had been able to bear arms. Moreover, the sentiment in regard to slavery was changing in the North. People had come to look upon it as the cause of the war, and many desired the government to attack it as a war measure.

As commander-in-chief of the armies of the United States, President Lincoln had authority to set free all slaves

THE FIRST READING OF THE EMANCIPATION PROCLAMATION.

in territory conquered by the Union armies. Just after the Battle of Antietam, therefore, he warned the seceded States (September 22, 1862) that unless they returned to the Union before January 1, 1863, he would set their slaves free. As none of these States returned, the emancipation proclamation was issued on January 1, 1863. From that time the North fought not only for the Union but for the abolition of slavery.[1]

339. Employment of Emancipated Blacks in Northern Army Stops Exchange of Prisoners.—It was but one step further to arm the blacks and make them soldiers. If the

[1] General Butler, early in the war, confiscated the negroes whom he found employed in throwing up earthworks for the Confederates near Fortress Monroe. He fed and protected them, regarding them as contraband of war.

Emancipation Proclamation was issued as a military necessity in order to weaken the South and to make the issue of the war perfectly plain to the world, the same military necessity would call for the arming of these emancipated slaves. Before the end of the war there were enlisted in the Union armies 180,000 blacks, who made good soldiers. The Confederates bitterly resented the employment of their former slaves in the Union armies and refused to recognize

A FEDERAL CAVALRY CAMP—WINTER QUARTERS.

the negro soldiers or their officers in exchanging prisoners. This led to mutual misunderstanding and ended in stopping all exchange of prisoners. As a result, thousands of soldiers languished in prisons and suffered much from disease and famine.[1]

340. Conscription in the North; Draft Riots.—In 1863 the North found it advisable to resort to a conscription or draft. All able-bodied men between the ages of eighteen and forty-five were enrolled, and from the enrollment a certain proportion was chosen by lot. The draft was very unpopular, and in New York City, on July 13, 1863, a serious riot took place, lasting four days and resulting in the de-

[1] Some of the noted Southern prisons were Libby Prison and Belle Isle in Richmond, Virginia, and Andersonville, in Georgia.

struction of much property. The mobs showed especial
hatred toward colored people, brutally killing many. The
riot was finally put down by the aid of troops sent from
Gettysburg.

341. Conscription in the South.—In April, 1862, by an
act of the Confederate Congress, all able-bodied white men
between the ages of eighteen and thirty-five were required
to enter the Confederate army. In the autumn of the same

year all white men between the ages
of eighteen and forty-five were included in the conscription law, and
before the close of the war even boys
of sixteen and seventeen and old men
were included. So hard pressed for
men were the Confederates that just
before the war came to an end their
Congress had decided to enlist some
of the slaves in the Confederate army.
When all exchange of prisoners was
stopped, the South, by reason of the
scarcity of fighting men, was much
more seriously crippled than the
North. The whole number of men

GEORGE H. THOMAS, "THE
ROCK OF CHICKAMAUGA."

captured from the armies of the North and the South in
the entire war amounted to a half-million.

342. Battle of Chickamauga (1863).—After the loss of
Vicksburg and Port Hudson, the strongest and most important position held by the Confederates in   *The importance*
the West was Chattanooga,[1] which was not   *of Chattanooga.*
only a great railroad centre, but the key to eastern Tennessee and the gateway to Georgia. General Rosecrans, in

[1] From the outbreak of the war the Confederates had made a strenuous effort
to get control of Kentucky and Tennessee. The outcome was the remarkable
middle Tennessee campaign in 1862. On the last day of the year the battle of
Stone's River, or Murfreesboro, was fought, Rosecrans being the commander of the
Northern army and Bragg of the Southern. The result was the retreat of Bragg
with his army greatly weakened. This battle kept the South from capturing
Nashville, and made easier the movement of the Northern army against Chattanooga in 1863.

command of the Union army in Tennessee, advanced with 55,000 troops upon Chattanooga, which was occupied by Bragg. By moving to the south of this place, Rosecrans threatened Bragg's line of supplies and compelled him to withdraw from Chattanooga and take position at Lafayette (September 19–20), twenty-six miles to the south.

Here Bragg received a strong body of reinforcements and vigorously attacked the Union army, now outnumbered.

He overwhelmed and routed the right wing, **General Thomas saves the Union army from ruinous defeat.** and would have put to rout the entire army but for the unflinching courage of General Thomas, the "Rock of Chickamauga," who coolly held his position on the left until the rest of the army could make a safe retreat to Rossville on Missionary Ridge.

GENERAL GRANT AND STAFF ON POINT LOOKOUT, 1863.

343. Siege of Chattanooga. — Although Bragg defeated the Union army in the battle of Chickamauga, he did not secure what he greatly desired—Chattanooga itself. He therefore strongly fortified himself on Missionary Ridge and Lookout Mountain, overlooking Chattanooga, and tried to cut off the Union army from its supplies. The situation **Critical situation of the Union army.** became serious. For weeks all the Union supplies had to be brought over a single mountain road for a distance of sixty miles. When Grant, who had superseded Rosecrans, reached Chattanooga about the middle of November, the number of horses and mules had been so reduced by starvation that

the artillery could not be moved.[1] The soldiers were living on half-rations, and had not enough ammunition left
for a single day's battle. But in five days after reaching
Chattanooga Grant[2] got control of the river line of supplies. From that time the army, which had been cooped
up in Chattanooga for months, had an abundance of food.

**344. Battle of Chatta-
nooga.** — Having received
reinforcements, Grant now
decided to attack Bragg,
who occupied   **Bragg's strong**
a very strong   **position.**
position, with his right flank
resting on the northern end
of Missionary Ridge, his
left flank on the northern
end of Lookout Mountain,
and his centre stretching
across Chattanooga Valley.
His line was twelve miles
long and on the flanks appeared to be almost im-
pregnable. On November
24 Grant sent the gallant
Hooker and his men to
charge up the rocky heights
of Lookout Mountain. This

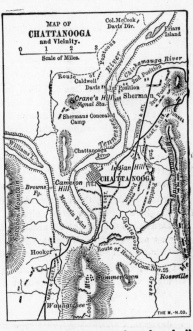

charge resulted in desperate fighting " above the clouds,"
and in driving Bragg's left flank from its mountain strong-

[1] Ten thousand horses and mules had starved to death.

[2] When seventeen years of age (see par. 371) Ulysses S. Grant received an appointment to a cadetship in the Military Academy at West Point. Although he
did not take high rank in scholarship, he became the finest horseman in his class,
and showed a marked aptitude for mathematical studies. Entering the army after
graduation, he distinguished himself for bravery in many important battles of the
Mexican War. He remained in the army until 1854, when he resigned his commission, and continued in private life until the beginning of the Civil War. During these years he tried farming, store-keeping, and selling real estate, but did not
have much success. In 1861 he received a commission as colonel of an Illinois
regiment, and, by his extraordinary military skill and ability, rose to the rank of

hold. Early next morning Sherman vigorously assaulted the north end of Missionary Ridge. Until three o'clock in
Two heroic
charges by the
Union troops.
the afternoon he struggled to drive the enemy from the heights, but in vain. Then Thomas's men were ordered to join the attack. Like a mighty whirlwind they swept away all opposition in their grand charge up the hill. Bragg's army, overwhelmed and defeated, fled from the battle-field in confusion.

TO THE PUPIL

1. Observe that after Lee's retreat from Antietam he defeated the Army of the Potomac in two battles, the first at Fredericksburg (December, 1862), and the second at Chancellorsville (May, 1863). What reason had Lee for a second invasion of the North in 1863?

2. Trace with care upon your map the location of the two armies on the second day of the battle of Gettysburg. As this is one of the world's great battles you will do well to understand it. Describe Pickett's charge. What were the most striking results of the battle?

3. Before studying the capture of Vicksburg review the following battles fought to open the Mississippi in 1862: Capture of Forts Henry and Donelson, the battle of Shiloh, and the capture of New Orleans. Now you are ready to describe the capture of Vicksburg. Read General Grant's excellent account of it in his "Personal Memoirs."

4. Why was it natural for the North, after emancipating the blacks, to employ them as soldiers? What effect did such employment have upon the exchange of prisoners?

5. Why was Chattanooga an important military position? What led to the battle of Chickamauga, and how did General Thomas save the Union army from rout? Describe the critical situation of the Union army when Grant reached Chattanooga. What were the results of the battle of Chattanooga?

6. You will find Coffin's books on the Civil War very interesting.

lieutenant-general (1864) in command of the Union armies. His brilliant strategy at Vicksburg and Chattanooga in 1863, and his advance upon Richmond in 1864-65, proved him to be one of the greatest military leaders of all time. His iron will, resolute purpose, cool judgment, and unflinching courage never failed him in the hour of trial and danger. He was also a man of singularly pure and gentle spirit, with a high sense of public duty.

THE HAMMERING CAMPAIGN

345. The Union Plan of 1864.—In March, 1864, Grant, who had won the confidence of the people by his campaigns in the West, was raised to a military rank second only to that of the President, with the title of lieutenant-general.[1] In reality he was placed in command of all the Northern armies. By the close of 1863 the Confederacy had been cut down to Virginia, North Carolina, South Carolina, and Georgia. The Union armies had now to get control of these four States.

General Grant placed in command of all the Union armies.

GENERAL U. S. GRANT.

Grant was to attempt the capture of Richmond, which was defended by Lee; Sherman was to get control of Georgia by defeating Johnston, who had command of the Confederates there. The watchword in the East was "On to Richmond;" in the West, "On to Atlanta." These two movements were planned to begin at the same time, early in May, so that, if possible, the Confederate armies might be prevented from aiding each other.

346. "On to Richmond."—Grant's advance upon Richmond began (May 4) by crossing the Rapidan and entering the Wilderness. He had 120,000[2] men against Lee's 62,000. For two days in the thick, gloomy woods, where the enemy could not be seen twenty feet away, a terrible struggle ensued. Grant's loss was severe, but he pressed on, writing to Lincoln, "I propose to fight it out on this line if it takes all summer." As Grant moved forward, terrible battles were fought at Spottsylvania Court House (May 8-18) and at Cold Harbor

In the Wilderness.

---

[1] Before that time only Washington and Scott had been made lieutenant-generals.

[2] Grant's army, arranged in ranks of four, the ranks being five feet apart, would extend a distance of more than twenty-eight miles.

(June 3). Before the close of June he had lost more than 60,000 men, and Lee, 40,000.

Realizing after this great loss of life that he could not capture Richmond by attacking it from the north, Grant **Grant transfers his army across the James.** transferred his army across the James in order to attack the city from the south. Here an attempt was made to capture Petersburg (July 30) by exploding a mine under the outer Confederate defences. The explosion was followed by a vigorous assault, but the plan failed.

347. Early's Raid in the Shenandoah.—It will be remembered that in 1862, when McClellan was near Richmond,

BUILDING A PONTOON BRIDGE.

"Stonewall" Jackson was sent into the Shenandoah to threaten Washington and prevent McDowell from reinforcing McClellan. In 1864 L e tried in the same way to weaken the attack upon Richmond. Toward the last of June he sent Early with 20,000 men to threaten Washington **Early threatens Washington and burns Chambersburg.** by way of the Shenandoah. Early swept on until he met General Lew Wallace with a much smaller force on the Monocacy River, not far from Washington. Here Wallace fought a losing battle in order to detain Early long enough for Grant to get a part of his army into Washington. These troops reached the city just in time to prevent its capture. A little later Early again pushed down the Shenandoah across

the Potomac into Pennsylvania, where he burned Chambers‑
burg.

348. Sheridan in the Shenandoah.—To put an end to
such raids in the North, General Sheridan[1] was sent with
30,000 men to watch General Early and to lay waste the
fruitful Shenandoah Valley. After defeating Early and
chasing him up the valley, Sheridan
destroyed 2,000 barns filled with
grain and farming implements and
seventy mills filled with flour and
wheat, besides driving off thousands
of sheep and cattle. A few days
later, while Sheridan[2] was away,
Early surprised the Union army at
Cedar Creek, and drove it back
seven miles. This was the occasion
of " Sheridan's Ride "   " Sheridan's
from Winchester,   Ride."
about fourteen (not " twenty ")
miles away. On Sheridan's arrival

PHILIP H. SHERIDAN.

he found that the Union forces had been formed in battle
array. Early's army was totally defeated (October 19) and
driven in confusion from the field.

[1] Philip H. Sheridan was born in Ohio in 1831, and died in 1888. He was
graduated from West Point in 1853. Upon the outbreak of the Civil War he was
made chief quartermaster of the army in the southwestern part of Missouri. He
handled his troops so ably at the battle of Murfreesboro that he was promoted to the
rank of major-general. He gave further striking evidence of military skill and daring at Chickamauga and Chattanooga. In 1864 Grant had Sheridan put in command of all the cavalry in the Army of the Potomac. His campaign in the Shenandoah was one of the great military achievements of the war. He was so popular that
he was called by his men " Little Phil." Some years before his death he became
lieutenant-general, and on his death-bed was promoted to the rank of general-in-chief.

[2] In the early morning of the battle, General Sheridan, who was at Winchester
on his return from Washington, was informed of the firing in the direction of Cedar
Creek. Mounting his handsome coal-black horse, he rode at full speed toward the
scene of battle. When he met the retreating soldiers he shouted, " Turn back,
men—turn back! Face the other way! " His inspiring presence heartened the
soldiers. With waving hats they cried, " Sheridan! Sheridan! " and cheerfully
followed their leader as he dashed forward. Sheridan's ride changed defeat into
overwhelming victory.

349. " On to Atlanta."—Early in May, 1864, Sherman,[1] with 100,000 men, was at Chattanooga, facing Johnston, with

Importance of Atlanta and Georgia.

64,000, at Dalton. It was desirable to get possession of Georgia because it was the workshop, the arsenal, and the storehouse of the Confederacy. Sherman's plan was to capture Atlanta, an important railroad and manufacturing centre, and then

DESTROYING A RAILROAD AT ATLANTA, GA.

to pass on to the sea and destroy the supplies necessary to sustain the Confederate armies.[2]

Sherman had great difficulties to face. In

Sherman's difficulties.

the first place, an able general, Joseph E. Johnston, opposed him; in the second place, every mile of advance took him farther away from his base of supplies at Nashville. He soon had to protect a long line of communication which the enemy was constantly trying to

[1] William T. Sherman was born in Lancaster, Ohio, in 1820, and died in 1891. Having graduated from West Point in 1840, he remained in the army until 1853 and then resigned his commission to engage in business. At the outbreak of the Civil War he became a colonel and took part in the battle of Bull Run. Soon after that battle he was raised to the rank of brigadier-general and transferred to Halleck's command in the Department of the West. His great military skill was shown at Shiloh and in the memorable Vicksburg campaign. When, therefore, Grant was placed in command of all the Union armies in 1864, he secured the appointment of Sherman as commander of the armies of the West. The " March to the Sea," one of the notable military achievements of modern history, followed. Sherman was among the ablest generals of the Civil War. When Grant became general-in-chief of the army in 1866, Sherman was made lieutenant-general, and when Grant was elected President, Sherman was promoted to the rank of general-in-chief.

[2] Such a course may seem cruel, but it is just as good generalship to starve an army into submission as to kill with firearms. Its effect is to shorten war and save life.

destroy. Johnston's plan was to draw him as far as possible from Nashville, always avoiding a pitched battle. Sherman's plan was to flank Johnston and threaten his line of communication with Atlanta. By a series of flank movements Sherman compelled Johnston to retreat. Battles were fought at Resaca, New Hope Church, and Kenesaw Mountain.

Both generals were skilful, but Johnston, by his cautious movements, failed to satisfy the Confederate authorities. He was superseded by Hood, who was as rash and impetuous as Johnston was careful and **Capture of Atlanta.** cautious. Hood at once made desperate attacks upon Sherman and was soon defeated. By cutting the railroad connections on the south Sherman captured Atlanta (September 2, 1864).

WILLIAM T. SHERMAN.

350. Sherman's " March to the Sea."—A little later Sherman, cutting loose from all communication with the North, started through Georgia on his famous march to the sea, which was some two hundred miles away. Hood, by moving northward, tried to draw Sherman after him, but Sherman sent Thomas to look after Hood, while he himself moved southward from Atlanta. After destroying three hundred miles of railroad and laying waste the country over a belt sixty miles wide, "from Atlanta to the sea," Sherman, with the loss of less than a thousand men, reached Savannah just before Christmas. He presented Savannah as a "Christmas gift" to the government.[1] In the mean-

---

[1] The following was Sherman's message to the President:

SAVANNAH, GEORGIA, *December 22, 1864.*
To His Excellency, President Lincoln, Washington, D. C.:

I beg to present you, as a Christmas gift, the city of Savannah, with one hundred and fifty heavy guns and plenty of ammunition; also about twenty-five thousand bales of cotton. W. T. SHERMAN, Major-General.

time Thomas so thoroughly routed Hood's army at Nashville that it could not be brought together again.

351. **Capture of Mobile.**—As we have seen, one of the
leading purposes of the North was to prevent, by blockade,
the export of Southern cotton.   By the middle of 1864
Union war-vessels had closed to foreign trade nearly all
the Southern ports.   One of the most important of these
was Mobile, which Admiral Farragut, in co-operation with

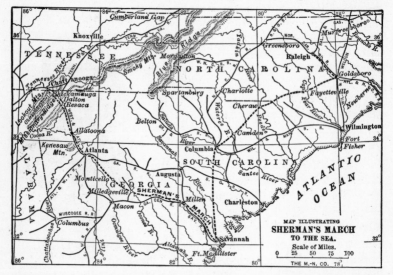

MAP ILLUSTRATING
SHERMAN'S MARCH
TO THE SEA.
Scale of Miles.
0   25   50   75   100
THE M.-N. CO. 78°.

a land force of 5,000 men, was sent to capture.   Realizing
the great value of Mobile, the Confederates had prepared

The defences   for a vigorous defence.   Two strong forts
of Mobile.   stood on opposite sides of the entrance of the
bay, the channel of which was obstructed by torpedoes.
Within the bay were three gun-boats and the powerful iron-
clad ram, *Tennessee.*

At six o'clock on the morning of August 5, 1864, the
Union fleet, consisting of fourteen wooden vessels and four
monitors, was under way.   In order that he might see over
the smoke, Admiral Farragut,[1] then sixty-three years old,

[1] David Glasgow Farragut was born near Knoxville, Tennessee, in 1801, and
died in 1870.   The night before the terrible struggle in Mobile Bay he wrote to his

took his position in the rigging of the flagship *Hartford*. One of the monitors was sunk by a torpedo, but the remainder of the fleet passed into the bay and engaged the *Tennessee*, the strongest of the Confederate iron-clads. By ten o'clock the fight was over and the capture of Mobile assured. In a few days the forts surrendered to the land force. This signal victory was due to the unflinching courage of Admiral Farragut.

352. Sympathy of English Workingmen with the North. —We may now leave the armies for a while and consider how England and France were look-ing upon the war. Jefferson Davis and the South greatly erred when they counted upon the sympathy of the working classes in England, for when English workingmen understood that the war was a struggle between freedom and slavery, their sympathies were with the North. Although the cotton famine in England, produced by the blockade of the South, forced hundreds of thousands out of employment, these starving laborers prayed for the success of the North. On the other

DAVID GLASGOW FARRAGUT.

hand, the aristocracy, with a few exceptions, and the English Government, being more in sympathy with the aristocratic Southern planter and perhaps jealous of American commerce, favored the South.

353. England and the Confederate Navy.—The South was in great need of a navy, and had no facilities for building one. English shipbuilders, therefore, with the knowledge of the English Government, responded to the need of the South, and built formidable Confederate cruisers in British dock-yards. These cruisers drove our merchant marine from the sea.

wife: "I am going into Mobile Bay in the morning, if God is my leader, as I hope He is, and in Him I place my trust. God bless and preserve you, my darling, and my dear boy, if anything should happen to me."

The most famous cruiser was the *Alabama*,[1] commanded by Captain Semmes. This vessel was built with English

The Alabama.

money in an English port, was manned by an English crew, carried English gunners, and hoisted an English flag. In a word, with the exception of her officers, she was an English vessel built for the special purpose of destroying Northern commerce. Charles Francis Adams, our able minister to England at that time, protested, but in vain. The United States, in the midst of a civil war, no longer commanded the respect of the English Government. Our country was not in a position to demand justice and satisfaction. But it resented England's attitude none the less keenly, and the time came when England was wise enough to listen.

The *Alabama* (1862–64) captured over sixty Northern vessels, amounting in value, with their cargoes, to over $7,-

The Kearsarge sinks the Alabama.

000,000. The duel between the *Alabama* and the *Kearsarge*, which had gone out in search of her, was fought off the coast of France (June 19, 1864). The *Alabama*, in about one hour, was shattered and sunk. The sinking of the *Alabama* put an end to the destructive work of Confederate cruisers. After the war England paid more than $15,000,000 for damages done by

The Alabama Claims.

Confederate cruisers. As the first of these claims made by our government for redress grew out of acts committed by the *Alabama*, all the claims growing out of the acts of all the vessels became known as the "Alabama Claims."

354. Napoleon III. and the Confederate Navy.—But the English Government did not stand alone in its unfriendly attitude. The French Government was equally

[1] " A score of other Confederate cruisers roamed the seas to prey upon United States commerce, but none of them became quite so famous as the *Sumter* and the *Alabama*. They included the *Shenandoah*, which made thirty-eight captures; the *Florida*, which made thirty-six ; the *Tallahassee*, which made twenty-seven; the *Tacony*, which made fifteen ; and the *Georgia*, which made ten. Most of these cruisers were built in British ship-yards."—R. JOHNSON.

The attitude of the English government toward the Confederate navy was most unfortunate, naturally causing in the North much bitter feeling toward England.

FARRAGUT IN MOBILE BAY.

The deck of the flagship Hartford.

hostile to the North.   Napoleon III., for personal reasons, was eager for the success of the Confederate cause, and urged England to acknowledge the independence of the South. He wished to see the Union dissolved, **Napoleon's desire** because it was his desire to establish an em- **to establish an** pire upon the ruins of the republic of Mexico, **empire in Mexico.** and he knew that so long as the Union remained unbroken he would not be permitted to carry out his plans.   He also, during the later years of the war, with contemptible duplicity equal to that of Napoleon I. just before the War of 1812, allowed formidable iron-clads for the Southern navy to be built in France.   One of these was finally launched, but the war was at an end before it could reach our coast.

Napoleon sent a French army to invade Mexico in 1861. By 1863 it had established an empire there, and Napoleon offered the throne to Maximilian, Archduke **Maximilian in** of Austria.   The United States protested, but **Mexico.** in vain.   After the close of the war, however, in response to the threatening attitude of this country, Napoleon withdrew the French troops.   Maximilian was then taken prisoner by the Mexican authorities, tried by court-martial, and shot.

TO THE PUPIL

1. What part of the Confederacy remained unconquered at the close of 1863?   Describe the Union plan of campaign in 1864.   Outline the "On to Richmond" movement.

2. Compare Early's raid in the Shenandoah in 1864 with Jackson's movement in that valley in 1862.   What did Jackson accomplish?   What did Early accomplish?   Why was Sheridan sent into the Shenandoah?   What did he accomplish there?   Why was the Shenandoah of importance to the Confederates?

3. Why was it desirable for the North to get possession of Atlanta? What difficulties did Sherman meet in his advance upon Atlanta? What was Johnston's plan of defence?

4. Outline Sherman's "March to the Sea."   Which do you think was the abler general, Sherman or Johnston?   Give reasons for your answer.

5. What did Jefferson Davis mean by speaking of cotton as "king"? At this point review the "Trent Affair," the importance of the blockade, the attempt on the part of the South to break the blockade by

means of the " Merrimac," and the effect the blockade had upon cotton export.

6. Why did English workingmen sympathize with the North? Why did the English aristocracy and the English Government favor the South? In what way did English shipbuilders aid the South?

7. What was the "Alabama," and what was the attitude of the English Government toward Southern cruisers built in English dockyards? What became of the " Alabama "? What were the " Alabama Claims "?

8. How did Napoleon III. show his sympathy with the South? What was his scheme in sending Maximilian to Mexico? In this connection review the Monroe Doctrine, and find out whether or not Napoleon III. violated this doctrine by supporting Maximilian with a French army? Why were the French troops withdrawn from Mexico after the Civil War?

APPOMATTOX COURT HOUSE

355. Fall of Richmond.—By the various disasters which we have recounted the Southern cause was brought into desperate straits. Careful observers could see that the end was near.[1] Sherman, after remaining about a month in Savannah, started through the Carolinas northward (February 1). Lee, with 40,000 men, still held Richmond, which Grant, with 100,000 men, was trying to capture. In order to join Johnston's force in North Carolina, Lee made one last effort to break through the Union army lying south of Petersburg. This plan was defeated by Sheridan in the battle of Five Forks, where 5,000 Confederates were captured.

Lee fails to break through Grant's army.

The next day (April 2) Lee evacuated Richmond and started on a retreat westward. The pursuit was hot. Hundreds of the Confederates, having little to eat and believing that their cause was hopeless, deserted, and thousands threw away their arms. Their condition was pitiable. For five or six days they lived on

Lee retreats.

---

[1] In the spring of this year General Wilson, in a brilliant cavalry movement, captured the five fortified cities of Selma, Montgomery, West Point, Columbus, and Macon. These places had important railroad connections, contained valuable supplies for the Confederate army, and manufactured for it war material.

A COUNCIL OF WAR AT MASSAPONAX CHURCH.

parched corn and the shoots of trees. One week after leaving Richmond (April 9), Lee, finding that every avenue of escape was cut off, agreed to hold a conference with Grant at Appomattox Court House, about seventy-five miles west of Richmond, to consider terms of surrender.

356. **Lee's Surrender.**—It was a notable meeting. The result of the interview was the surrender of Lee with 26,000 men, only 8,000 of whom had arms. The terms of surrender were very generous to the Confederates, who were to lay down their arms and were not, unless properly exchanged, to take them up again. With rare delicacy of feeling Grant ordered that all the Confederates owning horses or mules should be allowed to

Grant's delicacy of feeling.

take them home. "They will need them for the spring ploughing," he said. But consideration for the Confederate soldiers did not stop here, for when they marched in front of the Union soldiers to stack arms in token of surrender the Union soldiers saluted them. The Confederates promptly returned the salute.

Grant's attitude toward the Confederates, which won the hearts of the Southern people, was like that of the United States Government as a whole. Only one Confederate—the keeper of Andersonville Prison—was put to death at the close of the war. The death-penalty in this case was inflicted, not at all for connection with the Confederate movement, but because of inhuman cruelty. No government ever showed so great mercy to those who had tried to break it in pieces. The great struggle ended when Johnston surrendered to Sherman near Raleigh, North Carolina (April 26, 1865).

The generous attitude of the Government.

357. Flight and Capture of Jefferson Davis.—On Sunday morning, April 2, Jefferson Davis was attending service at St. Paul's Episcopal Church in Richmond when an officer walked quietly up the aisle with a telegram from Lee announcing the retreat of the latter from Petersburg. Davis at once left the church and prepared to leave the city. In a vain endeavor to escape capture he fled through the Carolinas into Georgia. While encamped 'n the woods near Irwinsville, Georgia, in the early morning he was surprised and captured (May 10). He was taken to Fortress Monroe and confined there for two years. At the end of that time many well-known men—among whom was Horace Greeley, a Republican leader of great prominence—used their influence to secure his release. Davis was never brought to trial.

358. The Assassination of Lincoln.—The rejoicing of the people over the return of peace soon gave place to mourning for the loss of the one who had safely piloted the nation through the storm of war. On the evening of April 14, 1865, while President Lincoln was at Ford's Thea-

THE SURRENDER OF LEE TO GRANT AT APPOMATTOX.

tre in Washington, an obscure actor, half-crazed over what
he believed to be the wrongs of the South, entered the President's box from the rear and shot him through the head.
He then leaped upon the stage, and shouting "*Sic semper
tyrannis !*" (So be it always to tyrants), rushed out of the
stage-door amid the wildest excitement of the people and
escaped.   In a few days he was hunted to his hiding-place
in Virginia and shot dead while resisting capture.

Lincoln's assassin was at the head of a conspiracy whose
aim was to bring confusion to the government by killing
some of the leading men and thus creating a   **The aim of the**
panic.   On the same evening one of these con-   **conspirators.**
spirators forced his way to the bedside of Secretary Seward, who was lying ill in his home, and vainly tried to stab
him to death.   Four of these conspirators were hanged and
three imprisoned for life.

Lincoln, who was shot a little after ten o'clock in the
evening, lingered, unconscious, until early next morning.
When Lincoln's spirit passed away, Secretary   **The grief of the**
Stanton was the first to break the silence by   **people.**
saying, "Now he belongs to the ages."   The grief of the
people for the nation's hero was well-nigh universal.   On
Friday, April 21, the train that was to take his body to
Springfield, Illinois, moved slowly out of Washington on its
mournful journey.   In order that the people might have
opportunity to express their love and grief for the departed
leader, it stopped at many large cities along the route.
The unbroken silence amid which the vast throngs filed
past the open coffin as the body lay in state indicated a feeling too deep for words.

The spirit of his noble service is well illustrated in the
closing words of his second inaugural address, March 4,
1865 : [1] "With malice toward none, with charity for all,
with firmness in the right, as God gives us to see the right,
let us strive on to finish the work we are in, to bind up the
nation's wounds, to care for him who shall have borne the

---

[1] It seems fitting to introduce here the memorable Gettysburg speech, made at
Gettysburg, November 19, 1863, on the occasion of the dedication of the National

battle, and for his widow, and his orphan—to do all which may achieve and cherish a just and lasting peace among ourselves and with all nations."

359. The Sanitary and Christian Commissions.—Early in the war the Sanitary Commission was organized by good men and women to supplement the work of the government in aiding needy and distressed soldiers. Recognized by the government and supported by all classes of the people, its career was one of extraordinary usefulness. It had its own physicians, nurses, and attendants, its own transports and methods of work. It ministered to the wounded on the battle-field and carried the wounded soldiers by easy methods of conveyance to the hospital. Furthermore, it gave special relief to men on sick-leave, collected and distributed supplies, and in every possible way cared for the suffering and needy soldiers.

The Christian Commission cared for the souls as well as the bodies of the soldiers. It distributed tracts, held prayer-meetings in improvised chapels, comforted the dying, and, where possible, gave Christian burial. This commission

Cemetery there. The speech well exemplifies, in its brevity, simplicity, and tenderness of feeling, the character of President Lincoln:

LINCOLN'S GETTYSBURG SPEECH

Four score and seven years ago our fathers brought forth upon this continent a new nation, conceived in liberty, and dedicated to the proposition that all men are created equal. Now we are engaged in a great civil war, testing whether that nation, or any nation so conceived and so dedicated, can long endure. We are met on a great battle-field of that war. We are come to dedicate a portion of that field as a final resting-place for those who here gave their lives that that nation might live. It is altogether fitting and proper that we should do this. But in a larger sense we cannot dedicate, we cannot consecrate, we cannot hallow this ground. The brave men, living and dead, who struggled here, have consecrated it far above our power to add or detract. The world will little note, nor long remember, what we say here; but it can never forget what they did here. It is for us, the living, rather to be dedicated here to the unfinished work which they, who fought here, have thus far so nobly advanced. It is rather for us to be here dedicated to the great task remaining before us; that from these honored dead we take increased devotion to that cause for which they gave the last full measure of devotion; that we here highly resolve that these dead shall not have died in vain; that this nation, under God, shall have a new birth of freedom, and that government of the people, by the people, and for the people, shall not perish from the earth.

also received the recognition and support of the govern‑
ment.   Thousands of noble women at home, in hospitals,
and near the scenes of battles expressed in   **The work of**
their service through these commissions not   **noble women.**
only a tender love and sympathy, but a patriotism as
faithful and true as that of the brave soldiers whom they
attended.

360. **The Results of the War.**—The Civil War was one
of gigantic proportions.   At its close the South was pros-

A SANITARY COMMISSION LODGE NEAR ALEXANDRIA, VA.

trated, the North was under severe strain.   About 600,000
men had been killed, and several hundred thousand more
permanently injured.   The loss of wealth can never be told,
but, including the expenditure of the government and
the States, the destruction of property by both armies, and
the value of slaves to the South, the war cost not far from
eight thousand millions of dollars.

The most important result of the Civil War was that
slavery was forever abolished throughout the Union.[1]   The
Emancipation Proclamation had set free only the slaves in

[1] See Thirteenth Amendment to the Constitution.

those States and parts of States conquered by Union armies; but now slavery was entirely swept away, and with it the attendant evils of State rights, nullification, and secession. The supremacy of the Union was established, and the United States, " one nation, indivisible, with liberty and justice for all," turned her energies to the new struggle of building up what had been torn down by four years of frightful havoc —the industries and wealth of her people.

TO THE PUPIL

1. Before studying the fall of Richmond review the various attempts made by the Army of the Potomac to capture that city. Your review will include Bull Run, the Peninsular Campaign, and the " On to Richmond " movement in 1864.
2. Describe Lee's retreat and his memorable surrender.
3. Read Lincoln's second inaugural, and memorize his Gettysburg speech.
4. Subject for debate : Resolved, that the army did more effective work than the navy in the Civil War.
5. What were the Sanitary and Christian Commissions? What were the most important results of the war ? Are you sure you know its causes ?
6. If you will read Alcott's Hospital Sketches you will get a sad picture of suffering in the hospitals during the war.

CHRONOLOGY

1789. *March* 4, FIRST CONGRESS ASSEMBLED IN NEW YORK.
    April 30, WASHINGTON INAUGURATED PRESIDENT.
1790. THE FIRST CENSUS, SHOWING A POPULATION OF 3,929,214.
1791. VERMONT ADMITTED TO THE UNION—FIRST NATIONAL BANK ESTABLISHED.
1792. KENTUCKY ADMITTED TO THE UNION.
1793. WAYNE'S CAMPAIGN AGAINST THE INDIANS.
    COTTON-GIN INVENTED BY ELI WHITNEY.
1794. THE WHISKEY INSURRECTION.
1795. JAY'S TREATY RATIFIED.
1796. TENNESSEE ADMITTED TO THE UNION.
1797. *March* 4, JOHN ADAMS INAUGURATED PRESIDENT.
1798. DEPARTMENT OF THE NAVY CREATED BY ACT OF CONGRESS.
    ALIEN AND SEDITION LAWS ENACTED BY CONGRESS.
1800. THE SECOND CENSUS, SHOWING A POPULATION OF 5,308,483.
1801. JOHN MARSHALL MADE CHIEF JUSTICE OF THE SUPREME COURT.
    March 4, JEFFERSON INAUGURATED PRESIDENT.
1802. OHIO ADMITTED TO THE UNION.
1803. LOUISIANA PURCHASED FROM FRANCE.

1804. LEWIS AND CLARK STARTED ON THEIR EXPEDITION

1805. TREATY OF PEACE WITH TRIPOLI.

1806. AARON BURR'S EXPEDITION TO THE SOUTHWEST.

November 20, THE BERLIN DECREE ISSUED.

1807. TRIAL TRIP OF FULTON'S FIRST STEAMBOAT.

November, THE ORDERS IN COUNCIL.

December, THE EMBARGO ACT PASSED BY CONGRESS.

1809. *March* 4, MADISON INAUGURATED PRESIDENT.

1810. THE THIRD CENSUS, SHOWING A POPULATION OF 7,239,881.

1811. THE FIRST STEAMBOAT STARTS DOWN THE OHIO FROM PITTSBURG FOR NEW ORLEANS.

November 7, BATTLE OF TIPPECANOE.

1812. LOUISIANA ADMITTED TO THE UNION.

June 18, WAR DECLARED AGAINST ENGLAND.

August 16, HULL'S SURRENDER OF DETROIT.

August 19, NAVAL FIGHT BETWEEN THE UNITED STATES VESSEL CONSTITU-TION AND THE BRITISH FRIGATE GUERRIÈRE.

1813. *March* 4, MADISON'S SECOND INAUGURATION.

September 10, PERRY'S VICTORY ON LAKE ERIE.

October 5, BATTLE OF THE THAMES.

JACKSON'S CAMPAIGN AGAINST THE SOUTHERN INDIANS.

1814. CAMPAIGN ON THE NIAGARA; BATTLES OF CHIPPEWA AND LUNDY'S LANE.

August 25, CAPTURE OF WASHINGTON BY THE BRITISH.

September 11, BATTLE OF PLATTSBURG.

December 15, HARTFORD CONVENTION MET.

December 24, TREATY OF PEACE SIGNED AT GHENT.

1815. *January* 8, BATTLE OF NEW ORLEANS.

1816. THE SECOND UNITED STATES BANK CHARTERED.

INDIANA ADMITTED TO THE UNION.

1817. *March* 4, MONROE INAUGURATED PRESIDENT.

July 4, CONSTRUCTION OF THE ERIE CANAL BEGUN.

MISSISSIPPI ADMITTED TO THE UNION.

1818. STEAM NAVIGATION BEGUN ON THE GREAT LAKES.

ILLINOIS ADMITTED TO THE UNION.

1819. ALABAMA ADMITTED TO THE UNION.

THE STEAMSHIP SAVANNAH MADE THE FIRST TRIP ACROSS THE ATLANTIC FROM SAVANNAH TO LIVERPOOL.

1820. MAINE ADMITTED TO THE UNION.

THE FOURTH CENSUS, SHOWING A POPULATION OF 9,633,822.

1821. RATIFICATION OF TREATY OF 1819, CEDING FLORIDA TO THE UNITED STATES.

MISSOURI COMPROMISE ADOPTED BY CONGRESS.

MISSOURI ADMITTED TO THE UNION.

1825. *March* 4, JOHN QUINCY ADAMS INAUGURATED PRESIDENT.

CORNER-STONE OF BUNKER HILL MONUMENT LAID IN BOSTON BY LAFAYETTE.

ERIE CANAL OPENED.

1826. FIRST RAILROAD BUILT IN THE UNITED STATES (AT QUINCY, MASS.).

1828. FIRST PASSENGER RAILROAD IN THE UNITED STATES BEGUN (AT BALTIMORE, MD.).

1829. *March* 4, JACKSON INAUGURATED PRESIDENT.

1830. THE FIFTH CENSUS, SHOWING A POPULATION OF 12,866,020.

1831. GARRISON ESTABLISHED "THE LIBERATOR."

1832. NULLIFICATION IN SOUTH CAROLINA.

1833. REMOVAL OF DEPOSITS FROM THE UNITED STATES BANK.

1835. TEXAS DECLARED HER INDEPENDENCE OF MEXICO.

1836. *June* 15, ARKANSAS ADMITTED TO THE UNION.
1837. *January* 26, MICHIGAN ADMITTED TO THE UNION.
    March 4, VAN BUREN INAUGURATED PRESIDENT.
1840. THE FIRST CUNARD STEAMER SAILS FROM LIVERPOOL TO NEW YORK.
    THE SIXTH CENSUS, SHOWING A POPULATION OF 17,069,453.
1841. *March* 4, HARRISON INAUGURATED PRESIDENT.
1842. THE DORR REBELLION IN RHODE ISLAND.
    THE ASHBURTON TREATY CONCLUDED.
1844. ELECTRIC TELEGRAPH LINE ESTABLISHED BETWEEN BALTIMORE AND WASHING-
    TON.
1845. TEXAS ANNEXED BY JOINT RESOLUTION.
    March 3, FLORIDA ADMITTED TO THE UNION.
    March 4, POLK INAUGURATED PRESIDENT.
    December 29, TEXAS ADMITTED TO THE UNION.
1846. *May* 8, BATTLE OF PALO ALTO, BEGINNING OF THE MEXICAN WAR.
    August 8, DAVID WILMOT INTRODUCED HIS PROVISO IN CONGRESS.
    December 28, IOWA ADMITTED TO THE UNION.
1847. *February* 22, 23, BATTLE OF BUENA VISTA.
    March 27, SURRENDER OF VERA CRUZ.
    September 14, CITY OF MEXICO OCCUPIED BY THE AMERICAN FORCES.
1848. *February*, TREATY OF PEACE WITH MEXICO CONCLUDED.
    GOLD DISCOVERED IN CALIFORNIA.
    May 29, WISCONSIN ADMITTED TO THE UNION.
1849. *March* 4, TAYLOR INAUGURATED PRESIDENT.
1850. THE CLAY COMPROMISE PASSED.
    THE SEVENTH CENSUS, SHOWING A POPULATION OF 23,191,876.
    September 9, CALIFORNIA ADMITTED TO THE UNION.
1853. *March* 4, PIERCE INAUGURATED PRESIDENT.
1854. *May* 30, THE KANSAS-NEBRASKA BILL PASSED.
1857. *March* 4, BUCHANAN INAUGURATED PRESIDENT.
    March 6, THE DRED SCOTT DECISION.
1858. *May* 11, MINNESOTA ADMITTED TO THE UNION.
1859. *February* 14, OREGON ADMITTED TO THE UNION.
    October, JOHN BROWN'S RAID ON HARPER'S FERRY.
1860. THE EIGHTH CENSUS, SHOWING A POPULATION OF 31,443,321.
    December 20, SOUTH CAROLINA SECEDED.
1861. *January*, MISSISSIPPI, ALABAMA, FLORIDA, GEORGIA, AND LOUISIANA SECEDED.
    January 29, KANSAS ADMITTED TO THE UNION.
    February, TEXAS SECEDED; PROVISIONAL CONFEDERATE GOVERNMENT ORGAN-
    IZED.
    March 4, LINCOLN INAUGURATED PRESIDENT.
    April 12, 13, BOMBARDMENT OF FORT SUMTER.
    April 17, VIRGINIA SECEDED.
    April 19, FIRST BLOOD SHED, IN BALTIMORE.
    May, ARKANSAS AND NORTH CAROLINA SECEDED.
    July 21, FIRST BATTLE OF BULL RUN.
    November 8, MASON AND SLIDELL TAKEN FROM THE TRENT.
1862. *February* 16, SURRENDER OF FORT DONELSON.
    March 9, FIGHT BETWEEN THE MERRIMAC AND THE MONITOR.
    April 6, 7, BATTLE OF PITTSBURG LANDING (SHILOH).
    April 25, CAPTURE OF NEW ORLEANS BY FARRAGUT.
    June 25, THE SEVEN DAYS' BATTLES BEFORE RICHMOND BEGUN.
    August 29, 30, SECOND BATTLES OF BULL RUN.

1862. *September* 17, BATTLE OF ANTIETAM.
 December 13, BATTLE OF FREDERICKSBURG.
1863. *January* 1, EMANCIPATION PROCLAMATION ISSUED.
 May 2, 3, BATTLE OF CHANCELLORSVILLE.
 June 20, WEST VIRGINIA ADMITTED TO THE UNION.
 July 1–3, BATTLE OF GETTYSBURG.
 July 4, SURRENDER OF VICKSBURG.
 July 8; SURRENDER OF PORT HUDSON.
 September 19, 20, BATTLE OF CHICKAMAUGA.
 November 24, 25, BATTLE OF CHATTANOOGA.
 May 4, SHERMAN'S ATLANTA CAMPAIGN BEGUN.
1864. *May* 5, 6, GRANT'S ADVANCE ON LEE, BATTLE OF THE WILDERNESS.
 June 14, GRANT CROSSES THE JAMES; SIEGE OF PETERSBURG BEGUN.
 June 19, THE ALABAMA SUNK BY THE KEARSARGE.
 August 5, BATTLE OF MOBILE BAY.
 September 2, FALL OF ATLANTA.
 September and *October*, SHERIDAN'S CAMPAIGN IN THE SHENANDOAH VALLEY.
 October 19, BATTLE OF CEDAR CREEK.
 October 31, NEVADA ADMITTED TO THE UNION.
 November 15, SHERMAN'S MARCH TO THE SEA BEGUN.
 December 15, 16, BATTLE OF NASHVILLE.
 December 21, SHERMAN ENTERS SAVANNAH.
1865. *January* 15, FORT FISHER CAPTURED BY GENERAL TERRY.
 March 4, ABRAHAM LINCOLN'S SECOND INAUGURATION.
 April 1, BATTLE OF FIVE FORKS.
 April 2, RICHMOND EVACUATED.
 April 9, SURRENDER OF LEE'S ARMY.
 April 14, PRESIDENT LINCOLN ASSASSINATED.
 April 26, SURRENDER OF JOHNSTON'S ARMY.
 May 10, CAPTURE OF JEFFERSON DAVIS.
 May 23, 24, REVIEW OF THE ARMY AT WASHINGTON.

Reconstruction and the New Union

CHAPTER XIX

RECONSTRUCTION DAYS (1865–1871)

REFERENCES: **Scribner's** Popular History of the United States, **V.**; **Andrews's** United States, II.; **Andrews's** Last Quarter Century, I.; **Burgess's** Civil War and Reconstruction; **Wilson's** Division and Reunion; **Richardson's** History of Our Country.

OUTSIDE READINGS: **Wilson's** A History of the American People; **Goldwin Smith's** United States; **Alexander H. Stephens's** War between the States; **Jefferson Davis's** Rise and Fall of the Confederate Government; **Blaine's** Twenty Years in Congress; **McPherson's** Political History of Reconstruction; **McCulloch's** Men and Measures of Half a Century.

361. Condition of the South when Johnson became President.—If all the wisdom and tact of Lincoln had been required during the war, much more were they needed in the trying days of reconstruction. The public debt was enormous, and the whole country was suffering from the strain of war. Fortunes had been lost, family circles broken, and thousands of brave fathers, husbands, and brothers slain in battle. Conditions were hardest in the South, where wasted plantations and ruined homes bore evidence of the terrible havoc of war. Bodies of Union cavalry were scouring the country in search of Confederate leaders who, when captured, were sent to forts and imprisoned until the nation should decide their fate.

"What shall be done with the leading Confederates?" "How shall the millions of Southern negroes be cared for?" **Perplexing questions.** "In what way shall the seceded States be treated?" These were a few of the perplexing questions of those trying times. It was hard to know

356

what was best to do—so hard that men soon realized that Lee's surrender presented new troubles as difficult to settle as the problems that brought on the war itself.

362. Andrew Johnson.[1]—Andrew Johnson, who succeeded Lincoln, was rash, hot-tempered, and self-willed, utterly without the delicate tact and persuasive power that gave Lincoln such a remarkable influence over men. In politics he was a strict constructionist, but was devoted to the Union. At the beginning of the war he was the only senator from the secession States who refused to resign his office. At this time he was an ardent believer in the doctrine of State rights, but he had no sympathy with the secession movement. This was accounted for by the fact that he was a man of humble birth and had little sympathy for men who belonged to the higher classes of society. We need not be surprised, then, to find him ready to put to death Jefferson Davis and other distinguished

ANDREW JOHNSON.

Confederates, and to show no special concern about the protection of the freedmen.

363. President Johnson's Plan of Restoring the Seceded States.—By the middle of July, 1865, President Johnson took steps to restore the eleven Confederate States to their places in the Union. Congress would not meet until

[1] Andrew Johnson, the seventeenth President of the United States (1865–1869) was born in Raleigh, North Carolina, in 1808, and died in 1875. His parents belonged to the class of people known as the "poor whites," and therefore his early advantages were extremely limited; but he was fearless, honest, energetic, and ambitious. He taught himself to read while apprenticed to a tailor, and after his marriage his wife taught him to write and cipher. While a young man he removed to Tennessee with his mother and sister, who were dependent upon him. There he gained the confidence of the people, and occupied one public office after another until his election to the Senate of the United States. He was governor of Tennessee when he was elected Vice-President, and after Lincoln's assassination he became President.

December, and up to that time he could carry out his own ideas in regard to the South. He appointed provisional governors, who were to call upon the white voters in their respective States to elect delegates to State conventions. These conventions were to pass three votes : (1) To declare the Ordinances of Secession to be null and void ; (2) to repudiate the Confederate war-debt; (3) and to ratify the Thirteenth Amendment, which forever abolished slavery in the United States.[1] The votes having been passed by all the seceded States, the President recognized the State governments[2] and declared them ready to be represented in Congress (December, 1865).

364. The Freedmen and Southern Legislation.—It was believed in the South that the freedmen, having so long been accustomed as slaves to the direction of masters and overseers, would not work unless compelled by law, and that the safety of the South was threatened by the presence of several million ignorant and shiftless beings. Southern Legislatures, therefore, began to enact laws whose results would have been to reduce the negroes to a condition little short of actual slavery. These laws aroused indignation in the North and had great influence in shaping the work of reconstruction.

365. The Congressional Plan of Reconstruction in the Seceded States (1867).—When Congress met in December, 1865, the Republicans refused to admit the representatives and senators from the seceded States until something President John-son's bitter feel-ing toward Con-gress. should be done to protect the freedmen in their civil rights. This action made President Johnson furious against Congress. He declared that it had no more right to keep a State out of the Union than the States had to secede from the Union. His bitterness increased until it led him to lose all sense of dignity and propriety as he gave expression to his violent

---

[1] This amendment did for the whole United States what the Emancipation Proclamation did for the seceded States.

[2] Johnson's plan of restoring the seceded States was similar to that outlined by Lincoln in his "Presidential Theory" of reconstruction.

feelings. In a short time he turned his party in Congress against him. As they numbered two-thirds of both the Senate and the House they could enact any laws they pleased, in spite of the President's veto. Johnson soon accused them of keeping out the Southern representation for this specific purpose. But the more he accused, the more solid became the ranks of the Republicans opposed to him.

By 1867 Congress had worked out a simple and thorough plan of reconstruction which it boldly proceeded to execute. By this plan, (1) the Confederate leaders were excluded from voting or holding office until pardoned by Congress, and (2) the freedmen were given the ballot. In other words, those who a few years before had been slaves were given large influence in public affairs, while many of their former masters were left without any political power whatever. No seceded State could be represented in Congress until it should submit to these two conditions. To indicate its submission each State was to ratify the Fourteenth Amendment.[1]

Two essential features of the Congressional plan.

366. The Work of Reconstruction Complete.—It is needless to say that the Southern people indignantly opposed these laws. They thought Congress unjust to deny the right of suffrage to the most intelligent and influential whites, and at the same time to give it to the ignorant blacks. But in June, 1868, seven[2] of the States had submitted, and their representatives were admitted again to Congress. By January 30, 1871, the work of reconstruction had been completed, and all the States were again represented in Congress.

367. Bitter Struggle Between President Johnson and Congress (1867–1868).—The President, as we have seen, had

[1] This made the freedman a citizen, declared that the Confederate leaders should not fill any public office until pardoned by Congress, and that while the debt of the Union should be paid, the debt of the Confederacy should not be paid. Tennessee was the first of the Confederate States to accept the Thirteenth and Fourteenth Amendments, and Congress voted, July 24, 1866, that she was entitled to representation.

[2] These States were Tennessee, North Carolina, South Carolina, Florida, Alabama, Louisiana, and Arkansas.

not agreed with Congress about the plan of reconstruction. The quarrel between them grew more bitter. Congress continued to pass measures over his veto, and he continued fiercely to attack that body in his speeches. This most unfortunate and undignified contest was brought to a climax by the Tenure of Office Act. Up to

The Tenure of Office Act.

that time it had been held that, while the President could appoint no high officials without the Senate's approval, he could remove them at his pleasure. But in March, 1867, Congress passed the Tenure of Office Act, providing that the President should not, without the consent of the Senate, remove any office-holder whose appointment required the consent of the Senate. In August, during the Congressional recess, Johnson removed from his Cabinet Mr. Stanton, Secretary of War, and appointed General Grant to fill the position. When the Senate again met, it refused to sanction Stanton's removal, and General Grant withdrew.

368. The Impeachment of President Johnson.—The President, believing that the Tenure of Office Act was unconstitutional, refused to obey it, and again removed Secretary Stanton, putting General Thomas in his place. The House then impeached the President; that is, it accused him of failing to do his duty as the executive head of the nation. He was tried before the Senate, Chief-Justice Chase presiding. As in all cases of impeachment, the Senate acted as a high court, a two-thirds vote being necessary to secure conviction. More than two-thirds of the Senators were Republicans, but seven of them voted for acquittal, making the vote stand thirty-five for conviction and nineteen for acquittal. The President had won by a single vote.

369. Negro Suffrage and Carpet-bag Rule (1868–1871). —Before the work of reconstruction was completed, the

The negro a freedman, a citizen, and a voter.

Fifteenth Amendment had become a part of the Constitution. The Thirteenth Amendment (1865) made the negro a freedman, the Fourteenth Amendment (1868) made him a citizen, and the Fifteenth Amendment (1870) made him a voter. With the right of suffrage in his grasp, his friends hoped that he might protect himself against oppression. But he was too ignorant to become a voter or lawmaker. As a slave he had not only been kept in ignorance, but, by his master's care for his wants, had been deprived of all sense of responsibility. One could hardly expect that all at once he would become an intelligent voter.

The whites tried by bribes and other means to keep the negroes away from the polls. When mild means failed, violence was used. As a natural result there was great disorder. The negroes were joined by a small number of white men, some of whom were adventurers from the North, called "carpet-baggers" because they were said to have brought all their possessions in their carpet-bags, and others were Southern men, called "scalawags" and despised as traitors by the South. It was a bad situation and was one of the unfortunate results of that long and cruel war which cost our country so much in money and human life. The Legislatures made bad laws and levied heavy taxes upon property owned mostly by the whites, who could not vote. Vast sums of money were wasted or stolen, and State debts were enormously increased.

Great disorder, heavy taxes, and bad laws.

370. The Ku-Klux Klan (1868-1871).—Naturally, men of property and intelligence resented these unjust practices and determined to put a stop to them. At first the whites used peaceable means, and soon got control in some of the States. But in others, especially where the blacks were in a majority, the whites were not so successful. In those States attempts were made to terrify the freedmen. Much of this terrorizing was done under the name of a secret society called the Ku-Klux Klan, which existed throughout the South.

It was at first a sort of police organized by the young men of Tennessee as a pleasurable means of keeping the negroes under control by working upon their superstitions. Its members wore hideous masks and disguises, and did much of their work at night. As disorder increased, "dens," or Ku-Klux societies, multiplied, especially in those States where the blacks were in a majority. Usually the

Brutal methods of the Ku=Klux Klan. knowledge that a "den" was organized in the vicinity was enough to terrify the negroes into submission. When that was not sufficient the Ku-Klux Klan, or men who pretended to belong to the society, began to whip, maim, and even murder the freedmen and their white Republican friends. Finally, law-abiding

The Horrible *Sepulchre* and Bloody Moon has at last arrived.

Some live to-day to-morrow "*Die.*" We the undersigned understand through our Grand "*Cyclops*" that you have recommended a big Black Nigger for Male agent on our nu rode; wel, sir, Jest you understand in time if he gets on the rode you can make up your mind to pull roape. If you have any thing to say in regard to the Matter, meet the Grand Cyclops and Conclave at Den No. 4 at 12 o'clock midnight, Oct. 1st, 1871.

"When you are in Calera we warn you to hold your tounge and not speak so much with your mouth or otherwise you will be taken on supprise and led out by the Klan, and learnt to stretch hemp. Beware. Beware. Beware. Beware. (Signed)

"PHILLIP ISENBAUM,
          "*Grand Cyclops*
"JOHN BANKSTOWN.
"ESAU DAVES.
"MARCUS THOMAS.
"BLOODY BONES.

"You know who. And all others of the Klan."

A KU-KLUX "WARNING" IN MISSISSIPPI.

citizens of both parties, aided by the National Government, united to put down the disorder, and by the close of 1871 had succeeded.

371. President Grant Sends Troops to the South.— The reconstructed governments, which were in the hands of the negroes, assisted by their white friends, appealed to President Grant[1] for national troops to help them secure

[1] Ulysses S. Grant, eighteenth President of the United States (1869–1877), was born at Point Pleasant, Ohio, in 1822, and died at Mount McGregor, near Saratoga, New York, in 1885. He was the oldest of six children, and in his boyhood helped his father in the work of the farm. The name given him by his parents was Hiram Ulysses. On receiving his cadetship at West Point, however, he found that his name had been inserted in the official appointment as Ulysses S. Although Cadet Grant informed the authorities at West Point of the mistake, they did not rectify it.

order. These were sent, but before 1877 the whites had gained control in all but three States, South Carolina, Florida, and Louisiana. The presence of bayonets Unsatisfactory Results of Reconstruction. in aid of the reconstructed governments had greatly irritated the Southern whites, who had thus been prevented from getting complete political control. The North did not clearly understand the situation, and the South found it hard to yield to the changed conditions. There was a great effort made on each side to do the best thing under the circumstances, but the obstacles were unusually great.

TO THE PUPIL

1. What perplexing questions called for answers at the close of the war? It was a trying time for the new President. Can you tell what his peculiar political views were?
2. What steps did he take to restore the seceded States? What three votes were the State conventions required to pass before the seceded States could be restored to their places in the Union? Remember that these things were done between the time when Johnson became President (April 15, 1865) and the meeting of Congress in December of the same year.
3. Before the meeting, however, what laws were passed by Southern Legislatures, and with what effect? Why, then, did Congress refuse to admit representatives and senators from the seceded States?
4. What were the two essential features of the Congressional plan of reconstruction?
5. You will observe the increasing bitterness of the disagreement between Johnson and Congress. What was the Tenure of Office Act? Why did Congress impeach the President? Which do you think had the right attitude toward the Tenure of Office Act, the President or Congress? Give reasons for your answer.
6. What effect did the Thirteenth, Fourteenth, and Fifteenth Amendments have upon the political condition of the negro? What kind of voter and law-maker did he make? What was the Ku-Klux Klan?
7. Note the dates, 1865-1871, of this reconstruction period and bear in mind the fact that Andrew Johnson was President nearly four of

His name ever after remained Ulysses S. He was inaugurated as President March 4, 1869. At the close of his first term he was re-elected. After retiring from public life he made a tour of the globe, and received distinguished attention wherever he went.

these years. His administration was, in some ways, as critical as that of President Lincoln during the Civil War, 1861–1865. These two groups of dates are important enough for you to know them accurately.

8. Read the pages of McCulloch's Men and Measures of Half a Century that refer to the difficult problem of reconstruction.

CHAPTER XX

THE NEW SOUTH (1877–   )

REFERENCES: **Scribner's** Popular History of the United States, V.; **Andrews's** United States, II.; **Andrews'** Last Quarter Century, I.; **Wilson's** Division and Reunion; **Richardson's** History of Our Country.

OUTSIDE READINGS: **Wilson's** A History of the American People, V.; **Grady's** New South; **Appleton's** Annual Cyclopædia; Cyclopædic Review of Current History; various magazine articles; the *World* and the *Tribune* almanacs, each issued annually.

372. President Hayes Withdraws the Troops from the South (1877).—When Hayes[1] became President many of the problems of reconstruction remained still unsolved. He nevertheless withdrew the Federal troops from the South, leaving the Southern people to settle their difficulties alone. This was a wise measure, for, as long as Federal bayonets were employed in the South, Southern men were kept in a state of irritation against the Federal government. The Republican governments in the South had been supported by Federal troops, but as soon as they were withdrawn the Democrats got control. The South was now "solid"; that is, the solid white[2] vote was in control and was Democratic.

[1] Rutherford B. Hayes, nineteenth President of the United States (1877–1881), was born in Delaware, Ohio, in 1822, and died in Fremont, Ohio, 1893. After graduating from Kenyon College he studied law at Harvard University. Entering the Union army during the Civil War, his gallantry and meritorious service led to his promotion to the rank of brigadier-general. In 1865 he resigned his commission because he had been elected to represent his district in Congress. Three times he was elected governor of Ohio. His popularity in that great State had a large influence in securing his nomination by the Republicans for the Presidency.

[2] Only a small fraction of the whites joined the negroes in voting the Republican ticket.

373. Eads and the Mississippi Jetties (1879).—Hayes's administration was fortunate enough to accomplish a great engineering achievement of vast importance to the South. The Mississippi River brings down large quantities of mud which, in its natural course, it deposits when its current becomes slower on reaching the Gulf of Mex-
The mud bars at the mouth of the Mississippi. ico. These deposits fill up the channel at the mouth of the river, thereby preventing the passage of heavy ships. Formerly these mud bars were a great hindrance to the shipping industry of this great sea-

port of the Southwest, and many millions were expended both by the United States Government and Louisiana for the removal of the bars and the deepening of the channel; but the work was not successful.

In 1874 Captain James B. Eads, an engineer who had built the magnificent steel bridge spanning the Mississippi River at St. Louis, proposed a different plan. He had noticed that where the river was narrow and the current swift the channel was also deep. He be-

RUTHERFORD B. HAYES.

lieved, therefore, that by narrowing the river at the mouth a deeper, swifter current could be secured, which by its natural force would
Captain Eads proposes the "jetty system." make and keep the channel free from obstructing deposits. Hence he proposed the "jetty system," which had been in use in Europe for more than a century.

Captain Eads met with great opposition, but Congress finally allowed him (1875) to make a trial of his plan on one
Success of the plan. of the smaller mouths. In the contract time, four years, he succeeded in all he had planned to do, and made the channel deep enough to float the heaviest steamships as far up the river as New Orleans. This was a gigantic undertaking, but its success has brought great increase of wealth both to New Orleans and the country at large.

374. The New South.—As the South became politically peaceful her industries took a new start. We have already noted that before the war the Southern people believed that slavery was necessary for the cultivation of their staples, especially cotton. Statistics since   Cotton. the war show us how greatly they erred in this belief. The largest cotton crop under slavery was about four and a half million bales (1860); in 1900 it was more than ten million bales. The South furnishes about five-sevenths of the world's supply of cotton. The United States exported during the fiscal year ending June 30, 1903, raw cotton valued at more than $316,000,- 000, and supplied our own mills with nearly two-sevenths as much. We must remember, too, that this is in spite of the fact that much labor has been turned in other directions.

EADS BRIDGE OVER THE MISSISSIPPI AT ST. LOUIS.
Copyright, 1903, by Underwood & Underwood, New York.

The South is no longer exclusively devoted to agriculture. There is scarcely an industry common to other parts of the country which has not been taken up there. Before the war there were very few   Railroads. railroads, the great network of rivers forming natural highways for trade, except in mountainous regions. But since the war railroads have spread in every direction, and hundreds of mills and factories have sprung up.

It is not too much to say that the South promises to become unsurpassed in the production of manufactured goods. It has been predicted that the mountainous area including

southern Tennessee, northern Alabama, and northern Georgia, may in time take the lead of the world in the produc-
Manufacturing.   tion of iron and steel. It is of great advantage to the factories in this region that their
raw materials, cotton, iron, coal, and lumber, are close to
the manufacturing centres.

The mountains of Tennessee, Alabama, and Georgia
Natural mineral   furnish rich mineral products, including the
resources.   finest marble in the country and extensive
coal-fields. It is estimated that at the present rate of con-

A COTTON PRESS YARD, NEW ORLEANS.

sumption these coal-fields could supply the world for one
hundred and fifty years.

Since 1880 the development of the new South has been
almost as remarkable as that of the West. Northern capi-
Prosperity in   tal has flowed in; the energies of Southern
the South.   men, held in check under the system of slavery, have been directed to new industries; and the better
class of negroes, forced to depend upon themselves, have
worked harder and to better advantage. The South is no
longer sectional. Her industries are varied; her interests
and feelings are national. Nowhere does loyalty to the
Union find more sincere expression than in the South.

375. The New Orleans Cotton Centennial (1884).—The
improved state of the South, under the new conditions, was

particularly evidenced in 1884 by a great exhibition. In that year a Cotton Centennial was held at New Orleans, to commemorate the first shipment of cotton from the United States. In 1784 eight bags were shipped from Charleston, South Carolina; in 1884 nearly four million bales were exported from our country. Two millions of these were sent from New Orleans, which had become the most important cotton port in the world.

This Centennial Exposition was a striking revelation of the vast changes that had been taking place in New Orleans

A SUGAR PLANTATION.

since the close of the war. In 1860 it was mainly a commercial city. Twenty-four years later it had not only become a great railroad centre, but had an immense capital invested in various kinds of manufac- **New Orleans in 1884.** turing and an export trade ranking second only to that of New York city. Its trade with foreign countries has been vastly increased by the construction of the Mississippi jetties.

376. The Atlanta Exposition (1895).—Another evidence of the changes wrought in the industries of the South was the Cotton States and International Exposition, held at Atlanta, Georgia, in the autumn of 1895. To make a successful exhibit so soon after the World's Columbian Exposition (1893) was a daring enterprise, but in beauty, extent,

STATE BUILDINGS, ATLANTA, GA.

and significance, the result fully justified the attempt. The Exposition at Atlanta was a great object-lesson to the country at large of the wonderful natural resources of the South, the variety of its manufactured products, the skill of its workmanship, and the surprising advance made by the negroes.

377. The Freedmen and Education (1865-   ).—We hear much said about the race problem in the South, but education is slowly finding a way out of the difficulty. Since the war the South has spent about $125,000,000 upon negro education, the Southern whites having cheerfully taxed themselves to give the blacks a start in life. The North, also, has contributed generously for the same purpose. The fund of $3,500,000 given by George Peabody for education in the South, and $1,000,000 given by John F. Slater for educating the freedmen in the South, aided by the immense work done by various religious denominations of the North, are causing rapid changes in the social and political conditions of that region.

Then, too, such institutions as Hampton School (Hampton, Virginia), Fiske University (Nashville), and Tuskegee

Normal and Industrial Institute (Tuskegee, Alabama) are giving young colored men and women the training best suited to make them leaders among their people in all parts of the South. In 1865 the freedmen had no property; the colored people in the whole country now have over $500,000,000 worth. This fact shows that the former slaves have made marvellous progress industrially. And the industrial training· that the normal schools for the colored people are now giving will still better prepare the freedmen to make intelligent use of their opportunities.

Industrial progress of the freedmen.

TO THE PUPIL

1. Note the dates of the period you are now beginning to study, 1877–1913. Grant was President in 1869–1877. Can you give in order the Presidents and the dates of their administrations, up to the time of Hayes's administration? Do not fail to learn them.
2. Why did President Hayes withdraw the Federal troops from the South? Do you think his action was wise? Give reasons for your answer. What is meant by the "solid South"?
3. What changes have been wrought in New Orleans since the war?
4. In studying the important paragraph headed The New South, note the sub-topics—cotton, railroads, manufacturing, natural mineral resources. By a careful study of these sub-topics you will see clearly how different is the New South without slavery from the Old South with slavery. What has been done for the education of the freedmen, and with what results?

CHAPTER XXI

THE NEW WEST (1865-   )

REFERENCES: **Scribner's** Popular History of the United States, **V.;** **Andrews's** United States, II.; **Andrews's** Last Quarter Century, I. and II.; **Wilson's** Division and Reunion ; **Richardson's** History of our Country.

OUTSIDE READINGS: **Appleton's** Annual Cyclopædia ; Cyclopædic Review of Current History ; various magazine articles ; the *World* and the *Tribune* almanacs, each issued annually.

378. Population and Immigration.—A reference to the table of population for the United States,[1] according to the census taken every ten years, from 1790 to 1910, will show that the increase has been exceedingly rapid. In 1900 the population was 75,568,686. In 1910 it was 91,972,266, making the rate of increase since 1900 more than one and one-half millions a year.

A comparison of the table of population with the table of immigration will show that since 1860 a large part of the increase has been due to immigration. From 1820 to

[1] POPULATION, 1790–1910

1790	3,929,214	1860	3²,443,321
1800	5,308,483	1870	38,558,371
1810	7,239,881	1880	50,155,783
1820	9,633,822	1890	62,622,250
1830	12,866,020	1900	75,568,686
1840	17,069,453	1910	*91,972,266
1850	23,191,876		

IMMIGRATION, 1820–1910

1820–1840	750,949	1881–1890...	5,238,728	
1841–1850	1,713,251	1891–1900...	3,687,564	
1851–1860	2,598,214	1901–1910...	8,796,308	17,722,600
1861–1870	2,466,752			
1871–1880	2,944,695	Total, 1820–1910..		28,196,461
	10,473,861			

*Total population of the U. S. and possessions is estimated to be about 101,100,000.

1910 more than 28,000,000 foreign immigrants came to the
United States. In the decade preceding the last census
(1901–1910) the number reached over eight   Immigration
and a half millions, and during the years 1881–   since 1880.
1910 immigrants swarmed into the United States at an average rate of nearly 600,000 a year; that is, nearly two-thirds
of all the foreign immigration since 1820 came into this
country during the last three census decades.

It is estimated that the better classes of immigrants
brought with them an average of at least $80 apiece, mak-
ing a very large sum in the aggregate. If we add to this
sum their power to produce wealth by their   Value of immi-
work, their contribution to the nation's wealth   grants to the
will be found to be enormous. Without for-   United States.
eign immigrants, a large part of whom were skilled laborers when they came and have made valuable citizens, it
would have been impossible to develop the resources and
increase the wealth of the country so rapidly.

But within the past thirty years the general character of the immigrants has not been so good as formerly,
the average of intelligence and morals being much lower
than it was before that time. The worst elements among
them, including paupers and criminals, become a burden
upon society and seriously tax the strength of our republican institutions.

**379. Influence of the Public Lands on our National
Growth.**—The foundation for our extraordinary national
growth and increase in population has been the vast area
of the public lands. These have been sold for very small
sums in order to get them into the hands of the people,
who have speedily brought them under cultivation.

At first it was the policy of the government to sell
these lands in order to increase the public revenue, but it
was afterward thought wiser to use them for the purpose
of developing the wealth and increasing the population of
the country. In 1841, by what is called the pre-emption[1]

[1] Pre-emption gives the settler the first right of purchase as against the investor
or speculator.

system, Congress began to sell farms on the public lands
The pre-emption   at the low price of $1.25 an acre. This was
system.   upon condition that the purchaser would occupy and cultivate the land.

Easy as these terms were, more liberal ones were desired. The growing sentiment in the West was that the
The Homestead   land belonged to the people and that the
Bill.   United States should grant free homes on the
public domain. Finally, after much debate, Congress passed
in 1862 the Homestead Bill, which is still in operation.

A CRIPPLE CREEK MINE.

This enables settlers to secure farms of one hundred and
sixty acres free of payment, except a small fee for legal expenses, on condition of settlement. This method has proved
very successful in establishing homes and communities,
thus increasing the value of the lands and the strength of
the nation.

380. **Westward Expansion.**—American history has been
largely the history of westward movement from the Atlantic to the Pacific. At the close of the Revolution (1783) the
area of settlement was confined, for the most part, between
the Alleghanies and the Atlantic. By 1825 it had reached
the Mississippi, by 1850 the Missouri,[1] and by 1890 the

[1] The gold-mining region of California is not here taken into account.

Pacific coast.[1] We thus see that the westward movement was at first slow. requiring about one hundred and fifty years to reach the Alleghanies.

But after 1825 it was wonderfully rapid. This marvellous expansion was in a large measure due to the opening of the prairies, which were easily brought under   The opening of cultivation because they were almost free from   the prairies. trees. In the forest-covered regions farther east, from forty to fifty days' labor was required to clear an acre of land for

A REAPER.

tillage, but only three or four days per acre were required in the prairie region. Moreover, the soil was rich and fertile and needed little cultivation.

Another reason why people flocked to the West was because of the great improvement in farm machinery. The McCormick Reaper (p. 264), which came into use about 1860, had a large influence. Drawn by two   Reaping and horses, it could do as much as twenty men   threshing using the "cradle." Yet it was but a beginning.   machines. The reaper was followed by the self-binder, which not only cut the grain but bound it into sheaves. The self-binder gave place to the steam-driven thresher, and that in turn to the combined reaper and thresher. This complex machine, which is in general use on the vast wheat farms[2] of the Northwest, is either drawn by horses to the number of thirty or more, or propelled by steam. It cuts, threshes, cleans;

[1] In 1889 North Dakota, South Dakota, Montana, and Washington were admitted to the Union, in 1890 Idaho and Wyoming, in 1896 Utah, and in 1907 Oklahoma, making the number of States in the Union forty-six.

[2] The wheat farms in the Red River Valley vary in size from 4,000 to 12,000 acres, but in recent years the tendency has been to cut up these large farms into smaller ones.

and measures the grain, and puts it into bags. Tended by four men, it will cut 3,000 bushels in a day.

Almost equally noteworthy was the change of method in breaking up the soil before planting or sowing the grain. The cast-iron plow, which could be drawn by a single horse, The steam-driven gang-plow. was an advance upon the wooden mold-board of colonial days. But the pressing need for something better on the large farms of the West led to the invention of the steam-driven gang-plow. The one commonly used will turn twelve furrows at one time and will plow in a ten-hour day from thirty-five to forty-five acres.

A STEAM-DRIVEN GANG-PLOW.

These various causes explain the great waves of migration westward, which in turn produced two important results: (1) They made labor scarce, and therefore wages Results of west-ward migration. high, in the East; (2) they led to an enormous increase in food products, and therefore lowered the cost of food. Both of these conditions were of immense advantage to the workingmen, and they help us to realize how much the general welfare of the people has been increased by the settlement and cultivation of the western part of the country.

381. The Mormons.—Among the many settlers of the West was a religious people who wished to enjoy their forms of worship and social customs without hindrance.

In 1839 the main body of these people, under the leadership of Joseph Smith, a native of Vermont, settled at Commerce, Illinois, and built up the city of
Nauvoo. Smith claimed to receive revela-   Joseph Smith.
tions from God, and to have discovered the Book of
Mormon, which, according to his teaching, is a religious
record of prehistoric America, containing the pure Gospel
of Christ. He was the founder of the Church of the Latter-
day Saints, otherwise known as Mormons. They prospered
at Nauvoo, but had trouble with some of the other people
of Illinois, and their leader fell a victim to mob violence.
Owing to these troubles with their neighbors, the Mormons

A THRESHER.

went into the wilderness to find a place where they could live
in peace and safety and in accordance with their own beliefs.
     Under their new prophet, Brigham Young, they soon
after emigrated to the desert region of Salt Lake valley.
There the Mormons prospered. With com-   Thrift of the Mor-
mendable industry and thrift they transformed   mons in Utah.
the desert, by irrigation, into fertile land, and soon built Salt
Lake City. Much credit is due to them for the rich cultivation under which they brought the surrounding land.
     382. The Pacific Coast and Chinese Immigration.—
A less desirable increase of population came from the far
East, at first in comparatively small numbers, but at length

in such large bodies as to cause a general demand for repressive measures. These people were the Chinese. In 1888 the Chinese Exclusion Act was passed to prevent the further immigration into the United States of Chinese laborers. Although at that time not more than 100,000 Chinese were in the United States, 75,000 of whom were in California, the American people, especially those on the Pacific coast, were bitterly opposed to any further Chinese immigration. For this opposition there were several reasons. (1) The Chinese brought no families with them, because they did not intend to remain and become citizens; they showed little interest in American affairs and almost no inclination to adopt our customs. (2) As they lived more meanly than the whites, eating little but rice, they could work for lower wages, and in this way they greatly injured our laboring men. (3) It was feared that in time they might come over in such vast hordes as seriously to endanger our institutions.

Three reasons for opposition to Chinese immigration.

383. The Pacific Railroads Furnish the Short Northwest Passage to China, Japan, and the Indies.—It is well to remember that the westward growth of population has depended much on easy, cheap, and rapid transportation, in which the railroad has played a most important part. The first trans-continental railroad, the Union and Central Pacific, was completed in 1869. It extended from Omaha, Nebraska, to San Francisco, California. Work had been progressing upon this road for six years, one party working east from San Francisco, the other west from Omaha. The parties met at Ogden, Utah. Since that time four other Pacific railroads have been built, so that there are now five great trunk lines connecting the Atlantic with the Pacific coast. The value of these Pacific railroads to the United States can hardly be estimated, for they have brought into service immense areas of land otherwise of trifling value. Without these roads and their network of branches running in all directions through the agricultural and mining regions of

The five Pacific railroads and Western settlement.

INDIAN WARFARE IN THE WEST.

Indians surrounding and attacking a detachment of United States troops.

the West, the rapid settlements made in the last fifty years would have been impossible.

At the close of the Revolution, Frederick of Prussia declared that no single republic could be held together in a territory so vast as that stretching from Maine to Georgia. He believed it would break into sections or give place to a monarchy. A like argument was made by a United States senator when the Oregon country came under discussion in 1843. This senator urged that such a far-off land could never become an integral part of the United States: that it would require ten months out of every twelve for the representatives in Congress from a State so remote to go to and from Washington. But we can now go from Oregon to Washington in less time than John Adams could go from Boston to Philadelphia in the days of the Continental Congress. Steam and electricity, applied to the transportation of men and

The railroad and the telegraph help to maintain the Union.

ARTESIAN WELL SYSTEM, RIVERSIDE, CAL.   AN ÆRATOR IN THE FOREGROUND.

goods and the transmission of thought, enable us to maintain a republic over an area of vast extent. It is difficult to see how the North, the South, the East, and the West, with their widely differing interests, could be held together in one great Union without the railroad and the telegraph.

But the effects of the Pacific railroads on international

trade, also, have been striking.   Americans in the nineteenth century have found what Europeans so eagerly sought in the fifteenth, sixteenth, and seventeenth centuries—a short northwest passage to China, Japan, and the **A short route to China and Japan.** East Indies.   Formerly, vessels with tea from China and spices from the East Indies sailed around Cape Horn and reached our eastern coast after a five or six months' voyage.   Now cargoes of these products are brought to San Francisco and reshipped by rail to New York, the whole distance being covered in five or six weeks.   The Pacific railroads have thus not only shortened the journey between Asia and the United States, but have reduced the cost of goods by diminishing freight charges.

384. **The Arid Region and the Problem of Irrigation.—** With the extension of facilities for transportation the

AN IRRIGATED ORANGE GROVE, RIVERSIDE, CAL.

rapidly increasing population of the country began to turn to the districts that yet remained unoccupied.   Under the Homestead Law nearly all the fertile land of the West, in regions of sufficient rainfall for agriculture, has been taken up by settlers.[1] But there is a great district which is barren until it is improved by irrigation. This arid and semi-arid region extends from the 100th meridian westward to a belt of country lying within about two hundred miles from the Pacific coast. It includes the whole of Idaho, Wyoming, Nevada, Utah, Colorado, Arizona, and New Mexico, and parts of Washington, Oregon, California, Montana, North Dakota, South Dakota, Nebraska, Kansas, and Texas. This vast region contains at least 1,000,000 square miles, or an area equal to more than two hundred States like Connecticut. The soil is of great depth, and is exceedingly fertile when watered by irrigating canals and ditches.[2] Professor Shaler estimates that the area of this immense arid region which may be won to tillage by irrigation is probably not less than ten States like Connecticut.

385. Forest Reservations.—Under authority from Congress President Harrison withdrew from public sale 18,000,000 acres of forest-covered public lands. The movement in the direction of forest preservation is exceedingly important, because forests hold water in the ground and let it drain off gradually. They thus influence the volume of water in rivers, and therefore greatly aid irrigation.

TO THE PUPIL

1. Why did our government, from the first, sell the public lands at very low prices? What was the Homestead Bill?

2. Trace on your map the advance of Western settlement and note the marvellous expansion due to the opening of the prairies.

3. What objections have been urged against Chinese immigration? What do you think of these objections? What influence has the building of the Pacific railroads had upon trade with China, Japan, and the Indies? Upon Western settlement? In this connection review the pack-horse, the flat-boat, the steamboat, the national road, and the Erie Canal.

4. Trace on your map the arid region and show what connection irrigation has with it. How many States like your own could be included in this region?

[1] Areas of fertile land still open to settlement are found in the forest regions of northern Wisconsin and Minnesota, and in those west of the Cascade Mountains in Oregon and Washington.

[2] Irrigation has been successfully introduced into many of the States of this region.

CHAPTER XXII

THE NEW UNION (1865)

REFERENCES: **Scribner's** Popular History of the United States, V.; **Andrews's** United States, II.; **Andrews's** Last Quarter Century, I. and II.; **Wilson's** Division and Reunion; **Richardson's** History of Our Country.

OUTSIDE READINGS: **Wilson's** A History of the American People, V.; **Appleton's** Annual Cyclopædia; Cyclopædic Review of Current History; **Field's** Story of the Atlantic Telegraph; **Elliott's** Our Arctic Province; **McCulloch's** Men and Measures of Half a Century; **Bourke's** On the Border with Crook; **Walker's** Indian Question; **Blaine's** Twenty Years in Congress; **Stanwood's** History of Presidential Elections; **Woodburn's** Political Parties and Party Problems in the United States; various magazine articles; the *World* and the *Tribune* almanacs, each issued annually.

386. The Atlantic Cable (1866).—We have considered in some detail the development of the South and of the West. We have now to glance rapidly at some matters that concern the nation as a whole. One of the most important facts in the history of the country since the close of the Civil War is the invention that has made possible the instant transmission of thought to the most distant parts of the world. In 1858, after several unsuccessful efforts, the two continents were connected by a wire cable extending from Newfoundland to Ireland. Two ships, each containing a section of the cable, met in mid-ocean, and, having

The wire cable of 1858 is not successful.

spliced the sections, returned, the one toward Newfoundland and the other toward Ireland, laying the cable as they went. The two ships reached land on the same day, and very soon afterward (August 16) the Queen of England sent to the President of the United States this message: "Glory to God in the highest, peace on earth and good-will to men." But within

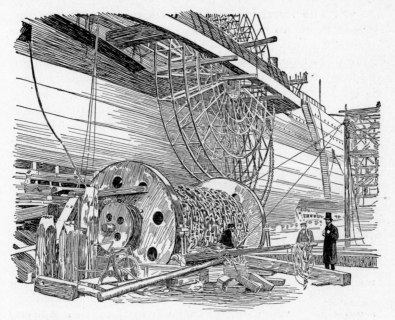

A MIDSHIP VIEW OF THE *GREAT EASTERN*, SHOWING ONE OF THE PADDLE-
WHEELS AND THE LAUNCHING GEAR.

Redrawn by permission from a copyrighted picture in Cassier's Magazine.

a month the cable failed to work, and not until 1866 did ocean cabling become permanently successful.

Since that time communication between Europe and America has not been interrupted, and now ten lines cross the Northern Atlantic. The cable has largely **Results of the** affected commerce, because the market prices **Atlantic cable.** in the great trade centres of America and Europe are reported every day, and large business transactions can easily be made in a few hours between American and European business houses. It has also brought the various parts of the civilized world into closer and more sympathetic relations, because the news of what is going on is so readily sent across the ocean. Our daily papers easily report European events a few hours after they have occurred.

387. The Purchase of Alaska (1867).—In 1867 our government gave to Russia $7,200,000 for Alaska, an immense territory equal in area to about one hundred and twenty States like Connecticut. The purchase was then thought by many to be an extravagant waste of the public money, because Alaska appeared to be almost worthless. But the investment has proved to be a good one, the seal-fur trade alone being worth $2,500,000 a year. Alaska furnishes beautiful white marble, and

SAMUEL F. B. MORSE'S ORIGINAL MODEL OF THE TELEGRAPH INSTRUMENT.

From the model in the Patent Office, Washington.

has mines of coal, iron, and gold of great value. Along many of the streams are found rich forests, consisting mainly of pine and cedar. The fisheries, which include salmon in the rivers and cod and halibut on the coast, are extensive. Besides all these natural resources Alaska has a coast well supplied with good harbors. By consulting the table below it will be seen that the entire area of the United States, exclusive of our island possessions, is now about 3,600,000 square miles, or nearly the size of all Europe.[1]

Natural resources of Alaska.

388. Grant's Indian Peace Policy (1869).—The Indians had always been more or less troublesome on the frontier, and during the Civil War the Sioux had committed shock-

	Square Miles.
[1] United States, in 1783	827,844
Louisiana, 1803	1,171,931
Florida, 1819	59,268
Texas, 1845	376,133
Mexican cession, 1848	545,783
Gadsden purchase, 1853	45,535
Alaska, 1867	577,390
Total	3,603,884

ing outrages in Minnesota. Half of the expenses of our War
Department, exclusive of those incurred by the Civil War,
had been occasioned by Indian wars, and yet   **Failure of the**
the Indians were not subdued. The war policy   **war policy.**
had failed, and therefore President Grant wisely adopted a
peace policy. He had observed that the Cherokees[1] had
developed by themselves a good degree of civilization, and
he believed that by kind
treatment and education
the more barbarous
tribes might be trained
into good citizenship.
He therefore entrusted
the management of a
few reservations to the
Society of Friends, with
whom the Indians had
always held peaceful re-
lations. No Indian agent
was to be appointed for
these reservations with-
out the approval of both
the President and the

R. F. T. ALLEN'S ORIGINAL MODEL OF THE
TYPEWRITER.

From a model in the Patent Office, Washington.

Society. The system gradually extended to other reservations and to other religious denominations, with some
success.

The Indian could not immediately appreciate this new
policy, however, and within a few years the Modocs (1872)
and the Sioux (1876) both made outbreaks. There is no
doubt that the Indian had grievances. He   **Grievances of**
could not understand why the Great Father   **the Indians.**
in Washington should allow the white man to invade his
reservations, as the white man did when he saw in them
fertile soil and unworked gold mines. But a more crying
evil was the dishonesty of Indian contractors, who were
making money by cheating both the government and the

---

[1] The five civilized tribes were the Cherokees, Chickasaws, Choctaws, Creeks,
and Seminoles. They all lived on reservations in the Indian Territory.

Indians, and were ready to oppose any plan likely to inter-fere with their schemes.

The government method of reservation was by treaty with the various tribes, the government agreeing to give yearly, for land yielded by the Indians, a quantity of **The Indian reser-** food, ammunition, and other supplies. The **vation.** food-supplies were to compensate for the loss of hunting-grounds, because hunting was the Indian's only means of support. Ammunition was to help them in secur-ing such game as their reservations supplied. The govern-ment made liberal promises for the comfort, education, and civilization of these Indians.

The reservation system was, however, not successful, because under it the Indians were placed by themselves, out of contact with **Why the reserva-** the civil-**tion system failed.** izing in-fluence of the whites. Moreover, it was im-possible for them to develop a spirit of manly independence when so much was done for them. The reservation plan made the Indian a pauper.

ALEXANDER GRAHAM BELL'S ORIGINAL MODEL OF THE TELEPHONE RECEIVER AND TRANS-MITTER.

From the model in the Patent Office, Washington.

The "Dawes Act," passed in 1887, provided for indi-vidual ownership of land by the Indians. In the course of **The Dawes Act.** time it is hoped that the individual Indian, like the white man, will have his own farm and reap the fruits of his own toil. Individual ownership, along with industrial training and general education, will aid in making him a useful citizen.

389. The Financial Panic of 1873.—The Indian prob-lem, serious as it was, affected a comparatively small part of the population. Far different was the trouble that attended the financial crash of the year 1873. This panic was much like the panics of 1837 and 1857. It was preceded by a period of general prosperity, and was brought on by rash speculations in Western railroads. For five years railroad building had been going on to such an extent that the railroad mileage in the United States had increased one-half.[1] This excessive railroad building, which was in the West, increased more rapidly than it could receive support from the population.

Speculation in railroad-building and Western lands.

Fortunes were made by some and lost by others in buying up tracts of lands in unsettled regions and increasing the value of that land by extending railroads through them. The speculative fever became so high that railroads were built much faster than they were needed.

As in 1857, the failure of a single great banking-house suddenly brought this panic upon the country. Financial ruin fell upon business firms and individuals, and want and suffering came into thousands of homes. It was six years before the country fully recovered.

ELIAS HOWE'S ORIGINAL MODEL OF THE SEWING MACHINE.

From the model in the Patent Office, Washington.

390. Railroad Strikes (1877).—During the years of financial distress following the panic of 1873, the earnings of the railroads were much reduced. In 1877 some of the railroads in the Middle and Western States lowered the wages of their men. Brakemen and other trainmen on the Baltimore & Ohio Railroad and on the Pennsylvania Railroad refused

[1] In 1861 only 651 miles of railroad were built; in 1871 7,779 miles were built. The Northern Pacific, extending from Duluth to Puget Sound, was the most important of these roads. During the five years preceding the panic, about $1,700,000,-000 were spent in railroad building.

OPENING DAY AT THE PHILADELPHIA CENTENNIAL, 1876.

to work. Then men on other roads followed their example. Soon there were bloody riots at Baltimore and Pittsburg, and large mobs in Chicago, St. Louis, and other cities. In Pittsburg a mob of 20,000 men had control of the city for two days, one hundred lives being lost. The State militia and the United States troops united to stop violence, but it continued about two weeks. During that time 100,000 men took part in the strike, which resulted in the destruction of ten million dollars' worth of property.

391. The Centennial Exhibition (1876).—But during these years of financial depression and industrial discontent the country gave striking evidence of its vast resources by holding the Centennial Exhibition of 1876 in honor of the hundredth anniversary of the founding of the nation. The place chosen was Philadelphia, the city in which the Declaration of Independence was given to the world. This exhibition taught the people many things. It showed them the wonderful results that had been brought about by

machinery and invention in all countries. It quickened
their sympathies and turned their attention toward art.
But education, especially, received such an
impetus that the good results have steadily
increased. The Centennial Exhibition also revealed to America, as well as to the rest of the world, the
richness and the variety of our natural productions and the
superiority of this country over all others in useful inventions.   Two of the most wonderful of these were the
telephone [1] and the application of electricity to lighting purposes.

**392. The Electoral Commission and
the Presidency (1877).**—In the Presidential election of 1876 there were disputes about the election returns made
in South Carolina, Florida, and Louisiana.[2] Hayes, the Republican candidate,
needed all the electoral   *A close election.*
votes from these States to
secure his election, while Tilden, the
Democratic candidate, needed only one.
Florida and Louisiana had given Democratic majorities, but the "returning
boards," who received the election returns as they came in
from various parts of the State, were Republican, and threw
out enough votes, on the charge of intimidation, to make a
Republican majority.   The people were much disturbed,
and feared there might be serious results.

*What the Cen-
tennial taught
the people.*

SAMUEL J. TILDEN.

The excitement increased as the time drew near for the
new President to be inaugurated.   The Senate being Republican and the House Democratic, they could not unite upon
any plan of seating either of the rival candidates.   Finally
a bill passed both Houses providing that a " Joint High
Commission " should be appointed, whose decision should

---

[1] The inventor of the telephone, which came at once into practical use, was
Alexander Graham Bell, of Massachusetts.   The American Bell Telephone Company was soon incorporated, and lines rapidly multiplied.

[2] There was some dispute about the election in Oregon also.

be final. The commission included five senators, five representatives, and five justices of the Supreme Court. The
The "Joint High Commission." fifth justice was appointed by the other four named in the bill. Before the fifth justice was appointed, seven of the commission were Republicans and seven were Democrats. It was expected that the fifth justice would be an independent, but circumstances caused a Republican to be selected, thus giving the Republicans a majority of one on the commission.

JAMES A. GARFIELD.

On March 2, just two days before the time set by the Constitution for **Decision in favor of Hayes.** inauguration, the decision in favor of Hayes was published. Opinions were divided as to the correctness of the returns, but whichever candidate was elected, the decision of the uncertain question was final. The people throughout the land, Democrats and Republicans alike, had shown remarkable wisdom and self-control during all the months of the trying situation.[1]

393. Resumption of Specie Payment (1879).—The financial disturbance of 1873 and subsequent years was partly caused by the instability of the currency and the undue encouragement thereby given to speculation. Nobody knew exactly how much a dollar was worth or how much it was likely to be worth. This condition was unavoidable during the Civil War, but it was intolerable in a time of peace. During the Civil War so much money was needed to carry on the extensive military operations that the government and the banks could not furnish gold and silver enough for the unusual demands. Congress, therefore, like

[1] To provide for possible contested elections in the future the Electoral Count Bill was passed in 1887. This measure threw the responsibility of Presidential elections upon the States, and provided that electoral certificates sent to the national capital by the various States should be opened by the president of the Senate in the presence of both Houses, and that four tellers, two from each House, should read aloud and make record of the votes.

the Continental Congress of the Revolution, issued millions of dollars of paper currency, which the people used instead of gold and silver. These paper notes were called greenbacks. As they were "legal tender"—that is, the law declared that they might be used in paying debts—everybody was willing to make free use of them. Gold, however, remained the standard of value, and the value of the greenbacks depended

Greenbacks during the Civil War.

SUPREME COURT ROOM, CAPITOL, WASHINGTON, D. C.

upon the defeats and victories on the battle-field. When the Northern armies won a great victory, the greenbacks rose in value; when they met with a severe defeat, the greenbacks fell in value. While the war was most threatening they were worth, in gold, little more than one-third of their face value, because the prospect of Northern success was very gloomy.

After the war, when the government began to pay the national debt rapidly, people began to have more and more confidence in these paper promises issued by Congress, and the greenbacks steadily rose in value. In 1879 the Secre-

**Greenbacks be-
come as good as
gold.**

tary of the Treasury announced that he would give gold for paper currency if it were presented at the Treasury. This action of the Secretary of the Treasury meant the resumption of specie payment by the government, and from that time on a paper dollar was worth as much as a gold dollar.

CHESTER A. ARTHUR.[2]

394. Assassination of President Garfield[1] (1881); Civil Service Reform (1883-1886).—When this important question of the currency was settled, the new administration of Garfield, who was elected in 1880, seemed to be opening a new era of prosperity. But only a few months after his inauguration the country was shocked by the announcement of his assassination (July 2, 1881). The assassin being a disappointed office-seeker, the tragedy brought forcibly to the minds of the people the great need of civil service reform. President Jackson had introduced the spoils system into the civil service in order to reward his political friends. Appointments were not made

---

[1] James A. Garfield, twentieth President of the United States, was born at Orange, Ohio in 1831, and died September 19, 1881, from a wound inflicted by a disappointed office-seeker. In early childhood Garfield's path was beset with difficulties. He was but two years of age when his father died, and his home, in a lonely log-cabin of the backwoods, was one of poverty and hardship. But the boy cheerfully helped his mother in supporting the family. After being graduated from Williams College he was for a time a college professor, and afterward studied law. Owing to his gallantry and daring on the battle-field in the Civil War he was promoted to the rank of major-general. His term of service in Congress (1863-1880) was so successful that he was elected to the Senate of the United States in 1880. Before taking his seat, however, he was nominated by the Republicans for the Presidency. He was the second President who was assassinated and the fourth who died in office.

[2] Chester A. Arthur, twenty-first President of the United States (1881-1885), was born in Fairfield, Vermont, in 1830, and died in 1886. After being graduated from

by reason of fitness for the work, but were distributed as rewards for political services.

In 1883 an act was passed by Congress authorizing the President to appoint civil service examiners, who should test by fair examinations, without regard to **Reform in the** party, the fitness of applicants for office. **civil service.** From the list of those passing the civil service examinations appointments and promotions were to be made. In accordance with this act, during the next twenty years about 110,000 office-holders were put under **Rapid growth of** civil service rules. As **the reform.**
a result all Federal officers are now under civil service reform rules, except two classes: (1) The higher officers, including the heads of departments, and (2) postmasters in fourth-class offices.[1]

These 110,000 positions are now filled by those who have successfully passed the civil service examinations without any reference to changes in Presidential administrations. The

GROVER CLEVELAND.[2]

spoils system in the Federal civil service has become largely a thing of the past. Experience, training, ability—in a

Union College he studied law and became a successful lawyer. In 1871 President Grant appointed him Collector of the Port of New York. Having been elected Vice-President by the Republicans in 1880, he succeeded to the Presidency on the death of Garfield. He was the fourth Vice-President who thus became the executive head of the nation.

[1] Of those not yet classified, over 72,000 are postmasters of the fourth class. These include postmasters receiving salaries of $1,000 or less a year.

[2] Grover Cleveland, twenty-second and twenty-fourth President of the United States (1885–1889 and 1893–1897), was born in Caldwell, New Jersey, in 1837. In his early childhood the family removed to New York State. Later, he became a lawyer and took high rank in his profession. After filling the offices of assistant district attorney and sheriff of the county he was elected Mayor of Buffalo. In this position he so fearlessly used his veto power that he was called the "veto mayor."

His success as mayor led to his nomination by the Democrats, in 1882, for gov-

word, personal fitness to perform the duties of the office—
are now demanded in our civil service.

395. **The Brooklyn Bridge (1883).**—In the same year
that Congress passed the act for civil service reform, another
great work affecting the public good was accomplished.
This was the completion of the Suspension Bridge spanning
East River and connecting Brooklyn with New York. The
bridge was sixteen years in building, and cost $16,000,000.

It is 85 feet wide, and
is more than a mile
long, its centre being
supported by four
main cables made of
steel wire nearly 16
inches in diameter.
There are five passage-
ways—two for cable-
cars, two for drive-
ways, and a middle
one for foot-passen-
gers. In design and
construction it is a
most stupendous work
of engineering.

BROOKLYN BRIDGE. ONE OF THE LARGEST
SUSPENSION BRIDGES IN THE WORLD.

*Copyright, 1901, by Underwood & Underwood,
New York.*

396. **Presidential
Succession Act (1886).**
—A great nation like
this should not be left for a single day without a President. Congress had already passed a law that in case of
the death or disability of both President and Vice-President, the temporary president of the Senate and, following
him, the Speaker of the House, should become President.
But in case either of the last named should be of the oppo-

ernor of the State of New York, to which office he was elected by an overwhelming
majority. Owing to his popularity in New York the Democrats nominated him
for the Presidency in 1884. James G. Blaine was nominated by the Republicans.
The political campaign was exciting and resulted in Cleveland's election. At the
close of his first term he was defeated by Benjamin Harrison, but in 1892 he in
turn defeated President Harrison and became President for a second term.

site party, their succession would not represent the choice
of the people, and the plan was therefore not considered
satisfactory. In 1886 an act was passed providing that in
case of the death or disability of both the President and
Vice-President, members of the Cabinet should, one after
another, be made Acting President as long as the disability
existed, or until the next election of a President by the people. The duty would fall first upon the Secretary of State,
and then upon the other members of the Cabinet in the
order of establishment of the various departments.[1] Such
members as might in any way be disqualified would be
passed over. There is scarcely an emergency now in which
the country could be left without a President.[2]

397. **Knights of Labor.**—We have already noted (see
par. 390) the great railroad strike of 1877. Within ten
years there were many similar troubles between workingmen and their employers. In order to strengthen themselves for a struggle with employers the workingmen
formed large organizations, one of which, the Knights of
Labor, contained many thousand members and exerted a
large influence all over the country. The members of the
organization, calling themselves union men, would suddenly
quit work, or strike, when they wished to force their employers to grant them higher wages or shorter hours. The
employers, in turn, united against the work-   Black lists and
ingmen by making out " black lists," contain-   boycotting.
ing the names of the more influential union men, whom
the employers would, from that time forward, refuse to employ. The workingmen sometimes resorted to "boycotting," which was refusing to have any business relations

[1] The order in which the various Cabinet positions were created was: (1) Secretary of State, 1789; (2) Secretary of the Treasury, 1789; (3) Secretary of War,
1789; (4) Attorney-General, 1789; (5) Postmaster-General, 1789; (6) Secretary
of the Navy, 1798; (7) Secretary of the Interior, 1849; (8) Secretary of Agriculture, 1889; (9) Secretary of Commerce and Labor, 1903.

[2] President Garfield died in September, nearly three months before Congress assembled, and during the intervening period President Arthur was critically ill.
Had he died at that time there might have been some confusion in the administration of the government.

with the man they wished to injure, either by using any goods he had manufactured or by handling them even for transportation. In most cases both parties gained little by their unfortunate attempts to injure each other.

398. The Statue of Liberty (1886).—In pleasing contrast with these serious labor troubles was an international

THE STATUE OF LIBERTY IN NEW YORK HARBOR.

event that took place in New York City in 1886. This was the unveiling of the enormous statue of "Liberty Enlightening the World," which was given by Frenchmen to the people of the United States as an expression of friendly feeling toward our country. The statue cost more than $200,000 and was paid for by 100,000 Frenchmen. It was placed on Bedloe's Island—now called Liberty Island—in New York Bay. The height of the statue is 151 feet and of the pedestal 155 feet.

399. Oklahoma Opened to Settlement (1889).—The rapid growth of population westward began at last to press upon the Indian reservation. That part of Indian Territory called Oklahoma was a large and fertile stretch of country especially coveted by white settlers. The United States therefore finally purchased it from the Indians in 1889, and President Harrison, by proclamation, declared it open to settlement. By nightfall of the day of occupation (April 22, 1889) several thousand persons had staked out their claims in Guthrie and had taken steps to form a city government. Before the year came to a close the territory had nearly or quite 60,000 people, 8,000 of whom were in Guthrie and 5,000 in Oklahoma City. The population of Oklahoma in 1900 was 398,331. In 1907 this territory and Indian Territory were admitted into the Union as one State, Oklahoma.

Rapid growth of Oklahoma.

400. Pension Bill (1890).—In 1890 Congress passed a Pension Bill which was very liberal to the soldiers and sailors injured in defending the Union during the Civil War. In accordance with this measure the government paid in pensions, to the close of 1903, more than $137,000,000 a year, on an average. This sum will be diminished gradually as our veterans pass away. No other nation has ever before been so liberal to its soldiers and sailors, nor has any other nation, with the possible exception of Germany, ever had in its service an army and navy ranking so high in intelligence and fighting ability. Well may we be proud of American manhood as it was seen on the battle-fields of this war.

401. The Pan-American Congress (1889-1890).—The attention of the people of this country during the past generation has naturally been given, for the most part, to questions of internal polity and development. But questions of wider import have now and then been brought to the front. The relations of this country to the countries of South America present a still unsettled problem. More than one American statesman has cherished the hope of bringing about closer relations and more friendly feelings between the United States and the leading independent countries of North and South America. Hence our government invited these countries to send representatives to a congress to meet at Washington.

The invitation was accepted, and the Pan-American Congress was held in the autumn of 1889. Seventeen countries were represented by sixty-six members. Questions concerning closer business relations and better means of communication between the various countries represented in the Congress were discussed. But by far the most important work of the Pan-American Congress was its recommendation

What the Pan-American Congress did.

SENATE CHAMBER, WASHINGTON, D. C.

that the republics of North, Central, and South America should settle by arbitration all disputes and difficulties that might arise among them.

402. Trouble with Italy (1890) and with Chili (1891).— The desirability of a system of arbitration with foreign

Assassination of the New Orleans Chief of Police. countries was made suddenly and painfully evident. In 1890, on the failure of the jury to convict some Italians on trial for assassinating the New Orleans Chief of Police, a party of lynchers, indignant at this failure of justice, broke into the jail and

Three Italian citizens lynched. put to death eleven Italian prisoners. As three of these men were Italian citizens there was serious trouble with Italy over the lynching; but through our able Secretary of State, James G. Blaine, a satisfactory settlement was reached when our government agreed to pay $25,000 to the families of the murdered men.

Equally unexpected and unwelcome was the complication with Chili. In 1891, in the streets of Valparaiso, a mob

HALL OF THE HOUSE OF REPRESENTATIVES, WASHINGTON, D. C.

attacked[1] some sailors from the American warship *Baltimore*, killing two of them and wounding eighteen others. When the United States demanded satisfaction, Chili disavowed the act and agreed to pay damages to our government.

403. Our New Navy (1883–   ).—These various difficulties with foreign nations showed the need of a more powerful navy. During the twenty years succeeding the Civil War nothing was done to build up or maintain our navy. The ships that had served **Need of a new navy.** during the war had either been disposed of or had gradually become useless through age. Such a navy could afford but small protection to our commerce and extensive sea-coast, and was unworthy of a great nation like the United States.

[1] A revolution having broken out in Chili, our Minister there took sides with the Chilian president. Moreover, a Chilian cruiser had been seized in a port of California because she was thought to be on the point of sailing with a supply of arms for the revolutionists. Hence the anger of the Chilian mob.

Finally, people began to realize its worthlessness and took measures to improve its condition. Accordingly, in 1883 Congress authorized the building of four steel cruis-

The strength of our navy. ers. This was a beginning. Since that time other cruisers of great strength and speed, and battle-ships of immense power, have been brought into use. The cruisers are for the protection of our commerce and the destruction of the enemy's commerce in case of war.

JAMES G. BLAINE.

404. The Australian Ballot System Introduced into Most of the States (1888–1892).—By the year 1888 public opinion demanded a sweeping reform in the methods of voting at State and national elections. Votes **Demoralizing effect of buying votes.** were so easily bought and sold that the results of the election in some cases seemed to depend in a large measure upon the amount of money spent in buying votes. This was a serious menace to our institutions and was highly demoralizing. The feeling of the people against this corruption of American manhood soon expressed itself in an emphatic way. State after State passed ballot-reform laws, the purpose of which was to lessen vote-buying and to give voters a better opportunity to cast a secret ballot. These laws provided for a method of voting called the Australian ballot system. By this plan every voter could shut himself in a stall and there prepare and fold his ballot, so that no one could know how he voted or interfere in any way with his choice. By 1892 thirty-seven of the States, with the aid of both of the great political parties, had passed such ballot-reform laws.

405. The Bering Sea Trouble Settled by Arbitration (1886–1893).—This movement, important as it was, aroused no great attention abroad. But an international question that had remained long unsettled threatened for a time to embroil us with Great Britain. After the purchase of

THE NEW BATTLESHIP *MAINE*.

Alaska (1867) the United States claimed entire control of the seal-fisheries in Bering Sea. England insisted that the jurisdiction of our government could not extend beyond three miles from the shore, and she therefore encouraged Canadian sailors in seal-catching outside the three-mile limit. So great had become the destruction of seals that their extermination **England and the United States disagree.** seemed only a matter of a few years. In 1886, when our cruisers seized Canadian vessels and confiscated all their cargoes of seal-furs, the dispute between the United States and England became serious.

After a warm diplomatic correspondence the matter was referred to a tribunal of arbitration, which decided (1893) that the United States had no right to control the seal-fisheries beyond the three-mile **The decision.** limit. But in making careful provision for the protection of the seals, the decision was satisfactory to the United States, whose main purpose was to prevent the destruction of the seals. The settlement of this dispute without an appeal to arms was, like the settlement of the Alabama Claims (1871), another triumph for arbitration.

406. The United States and the Hawaiian Revolution (1893-1894).—In 1893 a revolution broke out in Hawaii.[1] The revolutionists at once appointed a committee of safety

[1] Hawaii was annexed to the United States in 1898, and was made a Territory in 1900.

which organized a provisional government and sent commissioners to Washington to secure a treaty of annexation. The treaty was arranged and sent by President Harrison[1] to the Senate for confirmation. But before the Senate could act upon it President Harrison's term of office had expired (March 3). Five days after taking his seat, President Cleveland withdrew the treaty from the Senate and sent to Hawaii a minister who recommended that the queen be restored to her throne. Congress, however, refused to take any action.

BENJAMIN HARRISON.

407. The World's Columbian Exposition (1893).—Our history opened with the discovery of America by Columbus in 1492. Four hundred years later the great Columbian Exposition in Chicago celebrated that event. This exhibition surpassed all previous international exhibitions, being regarded as one of the marvels of the world. The location on the lake front was most fortunate, and the buildings were wonderful in their grandeur and beauty. The dedication exercises were held October 21, 1892, and the fair was formally opened in May, 1893. Foreigners were greatly impressed by the evidence of the growth of our people in higher than industrial lines; and Americans were justly proud of the intellectual and artistic advance of their country.

[1] Benjamin Harrison, twenty-third President of the United States (1889–1893), was born in North Bend, Ohio, in 1833, and died in 1901. After being graduated from Miami University, he studied law in Cincinnati, removed two years later to Indianapolis, and soon won much success in his chosen profession. In 1862 he entered the Union army as a lieutenant, and a little later, having organized a company of an Indiana regiment, received the commission of colonel of the regiment. He remained in the army throughout the war and rose to the rank of brigadier-general. He became a United States Senator in 1881 and ably represented the State of Indiana. He was elected President in 1888.

AT THE WORLD'S FAIR.
The Administration Building on Chicago Day.

408. Financial Panic of 1893.—While the country was still celebrating the great achievement of Columbus, there came, almost without warning to ordinary observers, one of the worst financial panics the United States has ever passed through. It was called the panic of 1893. There were business failures and financial distress everywhere. As great manufacturing establishments could not sell their goods, many of them shut down their factories altogether or ran them on shorter hours. Soon there were hundreds of thousands of workingmen out of work, with suffering and want in their families. President Cleveland, believing that silver legislation was one of the principal causes of the panic, summoned Congress to repeal the Sherman Act, which it did (November, 1893) after a long and bitter struggle.

409. Silver Legislation (1873-1893).—By 1873 the silver dollar, having become worth more than the gold dollar, had practically passed out of circulation. Very little silver had been coined in the United States since 1834, and for more than twenty years the yield from newly discovered gold mines had been so abundant that it was gener- *Silver demonetized in 1873.* ally supposed, both here and abroad, that the supply of gold would be sufficient to provide all the specie the world needed. Congress therefore passed a coinage act (1873) which demonetized silver by declaring that it should no longer be a legal tender for debts.

But many people desired to have more gold and silver money in circulation. Accordingly, in 1878, the Bland Silver Bill was passed, which not only made silver a legal tender for debts, but also directed that the *The Bland Silver Bill.* mints should coin not less than two, nor more than four, million silver dollars a month. In spite of this extensive purchase of silver by the government, however, there was a demand for a still larger purchase.

Congress, therefore, passed the Sherman Act (1890), which modified the Bland Bill by providing *The Sherman Act.* that the Secretary of the Treasury should purchase not less than $4,000,000 worth of silver bullion each month and pay for it by issuing Treasury notes which were a legal tender for all debts, and redeemable in gold or silver coin at the discretion of the Secretary of the Treasury. The purchase of silver was therefore increased, but its coinage was no longer compulsory.

410. The Tariff Question.—During the Civil War duties on foreign goods were raised repeatedly for increased revenue to meet the enormous expenses of maintaining the army and navy. After the war no change worthy of mention was made for about twenty-five years. During Mr. Cleveland's first administration (1885–1889) it was found that the

internal revenue on tobacco and spirituous liquors, and the duties on foreign goods, piled up in the national treasury $100,000,000 every year, after all the expenses of the government were paid. President Cleveland therefore recommended such a reduction in the tariff as would make the revenue and the expenses more nearly equal. The Mills Bill, representing the policy of the President, was passed in the House but failed in the Senate.

$100,000,000 piled up in the Treasury every year.

WILLIAM McKINLEY.

In the election of a President and a Congress in 1888 the tariff was the main issue between the two great parties, the Democrats and the Republicans. The Democrats demanded a tariff for revenue only, and the Republicans a high tariff for the protection of American manufactures. The Republicans were successful not only in electing the President, Benjamin Harrison, but in getting control of both Houses of Congress. The outcome was the passage of the McKinley Bill in the interests of a high tariff to protect and stimulate American manufactures.

The McKinley Bill.

In the Presidential election of 1892 the tariff plank was the principal difference between the platforms of the Republicans and the Democrats. As in 1888, the Republican policy was a high protective tariff, while the Democratic policy was a tariff for revenue only. The Democrats were successful, electing the President and an overwhelming majority in the House of Representatives. As soon as they came into office they set about a revision of the tariff by passing the Wilson Bill, which, **The Wilson Bill.** in its final form, differed from the McKinley Bill mainly in the degree of protection it called for.[1] In other words, the Wilson Bill stood for a moderately low protective tariff; the McKinley Bill for a high protective tariff.

411. The Pullman Boycott and the Great Railroad Strike (1894).—The financial depression of 1893 caused such a decrease in travel that there was little demand for the sleeping-cars furnished to numerous railroads by the Pullman Car Company, located at Pullman, Illinois, near Chicago. Its income being greatly lessened, the Pullman Company decided upon a reduction of wages. When, on receiving notice of this reduction, 3,000 of the workmen went out on strike, the company shut down its works.

The outcome was a strike which soon spread to twenty-two railroads running out of Chicago. Business in Chicago was prostrate, and travel became dangerous. The usual large supplies of meat and provisions going out to various parts of the country from that city were cut off, and a meat famine was threatened. Various kinds of trade and industry throughout the land were thrown into confusion. To aid the local authorities in putting an end to the disorder in Chicago, 2,000 United States troops and 4,000 state militia were sent there. During the strike, the worst of which was over at the end of three weeks, the money losses to workingmen, railroads, and the United States Government were not less than $7,000,000.

412. The Anglo-Venezuelan Difficulty and the Monroe Doctrine (1895–1897).—For a long time there had been a dispute between Venezuela and England about the boun-

---

[1] As an amendment to the Wilson Bill, an Income Tax of two per cent. on all incomes of more than $4,000 a year was proposed, but the Supreme Court decided by a vote of five to four that such a national tax was unconstitutional.

THE INAUGURATION OF WILLIAM McKINLEY.

dary line separating Venezuela from British Guiana. By
1895 the dispute had become serious, and our government
tried—as it had for years been trying—to induce England
to submit the whole question to arbitration. The English
Government declared, however, that England and Venezuela could settle their own disputes, without aid or interference from the United States. Our government answered
that if, in this controversy, England insisted upon enforcing
her claims to territory not shown to be rightfully her own,
she was violating the Monroe Doctrine. In the high-
spirited diplomatic correspondence between the two govern-

ments, our Secretary of State, Richard Olney, argued the American side with great vigor and ability. There was, for a short time, talk of war; but this war feeling quickly subsided, and England and Venezuela agreed to settle their boundary dispute by arbitration. A most fortunate outcome of the Anglo-Venezuelan dispute was a growing feeling on the part of a large number of people in both the United States and England in favor of the settlement of difficulties between the two countries by arbitration.

413. The Presidential Campaign of 1896.—Scarcely had the excitement over the Anglo-Venezuelan difficulty passed when the United States entered upon an experience which can never be forgotten. This was the Presidential campaign of 1896. The two leading political questions to be answered by the people were as follows: *Free silver and the tariff.* (1) "Shall we have free and unlimited coinage of silver, or shall we maintain a gold standard?" (2) "Shall we have a protective tariff, or a tariff for revenue only?"

When the Republicans met in their National Convention to make nominations for President and for Vice-President they declared in their platform that they were in favor of a protective tariff, and that they were "opposed to the free coinage of silver, except by international agreement with the leading commercial nations of the world." The convention nominated William McKinley, of Ohio, for President, and Garrett A. Hobart, of New Jersey, for Vice-President. The Democratic Nominating Convention "demanded," in its platform, "the free and unlimited coinage of both silver and gold at the present legal rate of 16 to 1, without waiting for the aid or consent of any other nation." This Convention also declared itself in favor of a tariff for revenue only, and nominated William J. Bryan, of Nebraska, for President. *The Republicans nominate McKinley and the Democrats Bryan.*

Some Democrats, believing in a gold standard, would not join the silver movement, and nominated their own candidates for President and Vice-President; while many voters, who were called Populists, believing that the government should own and manage all railroads and telegraph lines, just as it owns and manages the post-office, nominated still other candidates.

After an intensely earnest and serious campaign McKinley was elected, and was inaugurated President, March 4, 1897.[1] He at once set about the revision of the tariff by calling a special session of Congress. The result was the passage of the "Dingley Tariff" (July 24, 1897), which raised the duties on foreign goods in accordance with the promises made by the Republicans in the Presidential campaign of 1896.

TO THE PUPIL

1. Although the events discussed under "The New Union" are important, their connection is not always easily traced. They require all the more careful study.

2. Discuss the difficulties and results of the Atlantic Cable. Of what value is Alaska to the United States? How many States like your own does its area equal?

3. What grievances had the Indians even after the adoption of Grant's peace policy? What is the reservation system, and why has it failed? What was the Dawes Act?

4. Subject for debate: Resolved, that the Indian has been unjustly treated by the whites.

5. Name the causes of the financial panic of 1873, and show the connection between it and Western settlement. What did the Centennial Exhibition teach the people?

6. What difficulty was there about the Presidential election of 1876, and how was it settled? Observe that Rutherford B. Hayes was President in 1877-1881. Name all the Presidents in order up to this time.

---

[1] William McKinley, twenty-fifth President of the United States (1897), was born at Niles, Trumbull County, Ohio, in 1844, and died in 1901. When the Civil War began he was a teacher in a country school. Although only seventeen years old he enlisted as a private in the 23d Ohio Regiment, which was commanded later by Rutherford B. Hayes. Young McKinley fought so gallantly in the battles of Antietam, Opequan, Fisher's Hill, and Cedar Creek, that he was advanced to the grade of major. After the war was over he studied law and began the successful practice of it in Canton, Ohio. In 1877 he entered Congress as a Republican representative from Ohio, and served almost continuously until 1891. During his last term, as Chairman of the Committee of Ways and Means, he became the author of the McKinley Bill. In 1891, and again in 1893, the Republicans elected him Governor of Ohio, and he gave evidence of rare tact and executive ability. President McKinley was a very effective public speaker.

7. Why was so much paper currency issued during the Civil War? Upon what did the value of the greenbacks depend? What is meant by resumption of specie payment?

8. Review Jackson's introduction of the spoils system and rotation in office. What are the demoralizing influences of this system? What is civil service reform?

9. Observe that James A. Garfield was inaugurated as a Republican President in 1881, and that after his death Chester A. Arthur became President, continuing in office in 1881-1885. Grover Cleveland, elected by the Democrats, was President in 1885-1889. Benjamin Harrison, elected by the Republicans, was President in 1889-1893. For the next four years, 1893-1897, Cleveland was again President, and gave place to William McKinley, who was inaugurated March 4, 1897. What was the Presidential Act of 1886?

10. Prepare to write from three to five minutes on any of the following topics: Oklahoma, the Pan-American Congress, the trouble with Italy, the Pension Bill, and the trouble with Chili.

11. Why do we need a strong navy?

12. What is the Australian ballot system, and why has it been introduced into most of our States?

13. What was the Bering Sea trouble? What was the decision reached in regard to it by the tribunal of arbitration? What is arbitration?

14. Write an outline of the silver legislation, 1873-1893.

15. Before taking up the tariff question here review the difficulties about the tariff which resulted in nullification in South Carolina in Jackson's administration. What were the Mill's Bill, the Wilson Bill, and the McKinley Bill?

16. Review the Monroe Doctrine and Maximilian in Mexico. What was the trouble between Venezuela and England? What attitude did our government take toward this trouble?

17. What were the leading political questions before the people in the Presidential campaign of 1896? What answers did the Republicans propose? the Democrats?

CHAPTER XXIII

THE SPANISH–AMERICAN WAR AND RECENT EVENTS
(1898–   )

OUTSIDE READINGS: **Watterson's** History of the Spanish-American War; **Kennan's** Campaigning in Cuba; **Spear's** Our Navy in the War with Spain; **Russell's** History of Our War with Spain; **Roosevelt's** Rough Riders; **Lodge's** War with Spain; **Foster's** American Diplomacy in the Orient; **Woolsey's** America's Foreign Policy; **Griffis's** America in the East; **Andrews's** United States in Our Own Times; **Wilson's** History of the American People, V.

414. The Cubans Rise against Spain (February, 1895). —Tariff revision and the financial policy of the government were serious questions, but there soon arose an international complication of overshadowing interest, which absorbed much of the thought and energy of the nation. From the beginning of her control in Cuba the rule of Spain was cruel and unjust. The Cubans tried several times to throw off the galling yoke, but in vain. In February, 1895, however, they organized in eastern Cuba an insurrection that within a year spread to the western end of the island.

THE WRECK OF CERVERA'S FLAGSHIP *COLON*.

Copyright, 1899, by Strohmeyer & Wyman.

In alarm the Spanish Government decided upon severe measures, and appointed General Weyler as governor-general. He drove the country people into **The brutal policy** towns and cities, burned their dwellings, and **of concentration.** destroyed everything that might furnish support to the fighting Cubans. Such was the brutal policy of concentration. By this policy General Weyler hoped to starve the people into submission, but he failed. Blanco succeeded him as governor-general and tried by a milder policy to win the Cubans back to Spain. The Cubans' cry, however, was, "Independence or death!" At the end of three years, with an army of more than 200,000, Spain had made little headway in putting down the insurrection.

W. S. SCHLEY.

415. Blowing up the Maine.—As the war went on American indignation grew bitter. In the midst of a period of deep feeling aroused by the inhuman methods of conducting the war, the people of the United States were shocked by an awful event. On the night of February 15, 1898, the American battle-ship *Maine*, lying in the harbor of Havana, was blown up, two hundred and **The Maine and** sixty-six of her sailors being killed by the ex- **the submarine** plosion. Great excitement swept over the **mine.** country. The President at once appointed a naval court of inquiry, which, after four weeks of investigation, reported that the *Maine* was blown up by the explosion of a submarine mine. The American people, holding Spanish officials responsible for the destruction of the *Maine*, were more than ever inclined to insist that Spain should end the war. President McKinley did all in his power to bring about a settlement of the trouble, but without success.

416. War Declared (April, 1898).—In the meantime affairs in Cuba were becoming worse every day. The President, urged by an impatient Congress to decisive action, declared, in a message sent to that body: "In the name of humanity, in the name of civilization, in behalf of endangered American interests which give us the right and the duty to speak and to act, the war in Cuba must stop."

Congress responded by passing a joint resolution to the following effect: (1) The Cubans are free and independent; (2) Spain must give up all authority in Cuba and withdraw her troops; (3) The United States will exercise control over Cuba long enough to restore peace and good order, and will then leave the island under the control of the Cubans. A little later Congress declared that war had existed since April 21st, and in due time the President called for 200,000 volunteers from the various States and Territories. Congress voted that the regular army also should be increased to 62,000.

Spain must give up Cuba.

GEORGE DEWEY.

417. Dewey's Brilliant Victory at Manila.—Commodore Dewey, the commander of the American fleet in Asiatic waters, was ordered to sail at once for the Philippine Islands and capture or destroy the Spanish fleet. He hastened to Manila, where he found (May 1st) the Spanish fleet lying under the protection of strong shore batteries. With a daring unsurpassed he headed his ships for the enemy. While his flagship was steaming boldly into action, two submarine mines exploded just in front of her, but Commodore Dewey did not falter. The skilful seamanship of the Americans and the rapid and accurate handling of their guns made the battle short and decisive. The entire Spanish fleet of ten war-vessels was destroyed, and 1,200 Spaniards were killed or wounded. Not one American was killed and only eight were wounded, and not one American vessel received serious injury. It was one of the most brilliant naval victories in history.

The Spanish fleet destroyed.

SHIPPING AND DOCKS, PASIG RIVER, MANILA.

Admiral Dewey[1] could have captured Manila, but, not having men enough to hold it, he had to wait for reinforcements. As soon as possible over 15,000 soldiers were sent under General Merritt to co-operate with the American fleet. After a combined attack was made upon Manila by the army and the fleet, the city surrendered (August 13th).

418. The Coming of Cervera's Fleet.—Until the Spanish fleet at Manila had been destroyed, there was fear of an attack upon our Pacific coast. And there was still grave fear that an attack might be made upon the great Atlantic seaports by the Spanish fleet under the command of Admiral Cervera. At the outbreak of the war this fleet was at the Cape Verde Islands, whence it soon steamed away toward Cuban waters.

What were Cervera's plans? Would he try to reach Havana by attacking the American fleet which, under the

[1] On the news of the victory the President appointed Dewey as acting admiral

command of Admiral Sampson, was blockading the northern coast of Cuba? Would he steer directly for some
Cervera's plans.   great city on the Atlantic coast? Or would
he try to intercept the *Oregon*[1] on her way up
the eastern coast of South America? Events soon answered these questions.

Cervera arrived at Martinique and then sailed for the
Dutch island Curaçao off the coast of Venezuela, where he

CUBA.

got much-needed coal. He was then ordered to Santiago,
which, on account of the highlands and the narrow mouth
of its protected harbor, was thought to be a good hiding-
Cervera "bottled   place while taking on coal and other supplies.
up" at Santiago.   Soon after his arrival the fleet under Commodore Schley discovered and blockaded the harbor. The
Spanish fleet was now " bottled up."

Still there was fear that Cervera might on some dark,
stormy night succeed in getting away. To prevent this, a

[1] This great battle-ship had, on March 19, begun her remarkable journey of
some 15,000 miles from San Francisco around Cape Horn. On May 24th the
Oregon arrived safely and soon joined the blockading squadron.

UNITED STATES TROOPS LANDING AT BAIQUIRI, CUBA.

daring plan was laid to sink the collier *Merrimac* directly across the very narrow entrance to the harbor. Lieutenant Hobson and seven other heroic men tried to carry out this plan; but a Spanish shot having carried away the rudder of the *Mer-* **Lieutenant Hobson's daring exploit.** *rimac* before she could be blown up, Hobson did not succeed in sinking her directly across but only along the channel, and thus but partly obstructed it.

419. On to Santiago.—A plan of campaign in Cuba was quickly organized, and an army of 15,000 men was soon on its way to unite with Admiral Sampson's squadron for the capture of Santiago and Cervera's fleet. A little later the troops were on Cuban soil, pressing on toward Santiago. The advance had hardly begun when a battle took place at Las Guasimas[1] between about 1,000 Americans, among whom were the **Roosevelt Rough Riders at Las Guasimas.** famous Roosevelt Rough Riders, and a force of Spaniards considerably larger. This battle was fought in a tropical forest, where the dense undergrowth often made it impossible to see the enemy a few yards away. The Americans

[1] The first engagement was at Guantanamo, where 600 American marines gallantly held their ground against an attack of greatly superior numbers.

advanced in a series of short, desperate rushes, by which they steadily drove the Spaniards before them and won a signal victory.

420. The Battle of Santiago.—Yet in spite of this victory it was evident that the Spaniards would make a stout resistance. Moreover, the Americans had to face unusual difficulties. The so-called roads were rough paths frequently crossed by rushing torrents without bridges.

THE PALACE AT SANTIAGO ON WHICH THE AMERICAN FLAG WAS RAISED WHEN THE AMERICAN TROOPS TOOK POSSESSION.

Under such conditions heavy siege-guns could not be moved forward promptly. But delay meant something worse than Spanish bullets. The intense heat and the extreme dampness threatened the American ranks with deadly disease. General Shafter therefore decided to move on without delay, and on July 1st made a vigorous attack upon the outworks of Santiago at El Caney on the Spanish left *A glorious American* and the strong position of San Juan, com-*can victory.* manding the city. Both these places were stoutly defended. The battle was hotly contested, but ended in glorious victory for the Americans, who by brilliant charges swept the enemy before them and captured the two strongholds.

421. Cervera's Fleet Destroyed.—On the morning of July 3d the Spanish fleet dashed boldly out of the harbor in a desperate attempt to escape. When (about half past nine) it was seen coming out, every American sailor eagerly leaped to his post of duty. The battle was on. As at Manila, the Americans showed themselves superior to the Spaniards in gunnery, and won a victory as brilliant as that of Admiral Dewey. The entire Spanish fleet of six war-vessels was destroyed, 600 Spaniards were killed and 1,300 captured. Only one American was killed and one severely wounded, and not one of our ships was seriously harmed. About two weeks afterward Santiago and the eastern end of Cuba, with 22,000 Spanish soldiers, surrendered.

THEODORE ROOSEVELT.
From a photograph copyright 1904, by Arthur Hewitt.

422. Results of the War.—A large American force under General Miles was then sent to Porto Rico, and was rapidly getting control of the island, when Spain expressed a desire for peace. President McKinley, therefore, appointed a special commission to arrange a treaty. The terms of the treaty were as follows: (1) Spain gave up Cuba and ceded to the United States Porto Rico and the island of Guam in the Ladrones. (2) She also ceded to the United States the Philippines, the United States agreeing to pay her $20,000,000. But there was marked difference of opinion in regard to the clause relating to the Philippine Islands. Some people objected to their annexation to the United States. Others declared that such annexation would aid us in securing trade in China and other parts of the Far East. In the Senate, where a two-thirds vote is necessary before a treaty can become effective, there was prolonged discussion. But the treaty was ratified February 6, 1899.

There was another important result of the struggle besides those set forth in the treaty. The war helped to bring all parts of the country into closer and deeper sympathy. The various sections were united as they had never been before.

423. Porto Rico under the Control of the United States (1900).—The people of Porto Rico were glad to come under the control of the United States. But they did not get rid of all their troubles when they got rid of Spanish rule. They were in great financial distress. The war had par-alyzed their trade, and a fierce hur-ricane had swept over the island in

Americans relieve financial distress in Porto Rico.

1899, destroying prop-erty worth $22,000,000. The Americans gener-ously came to their aid by distrib-uting immense quantities of food. But to relieve the distress some-thing more was necessary. In the spring of 1900, therefore, Congress returned to Porto Rico more than $2,000,000 that had come into our treasury in the form of duties laid upon imports from the island. Later, all tariff rates between Porto Rico and the United States were removed.

W. T. SAMPSON.

In April, 1900, Congress passed a law providing for a territorial government. Under this law the President of the United States appoints a governor and the people of the island elect a legislature.

424. The Re-election and Assassination of President McKinley (1900-1901).—Scarcely had the question of civil government in Porto Rico been settled when the country was astir with the excitement of another Presidential cam-pain. The Republicans again nominated William McKinley for President, and the Democrats William J. Bryan. As in 1896, the leading issue before the country was whether there should be a free and unlimited coinage of silver at the rate of 16 to 1 or a gold standard. The people voted in favor of William McKinley and the gold standard.

Six months after his inauguration, during a visit to the Pan-American Exposition [1] at Buffalo, President McKinley was assassinated. While receiving in line a great number of people in the Temple of Music on the afternoon of September 6th, he was shot by an anarchist who concealed a pistol under a handkerchief wrapped about his hand. This

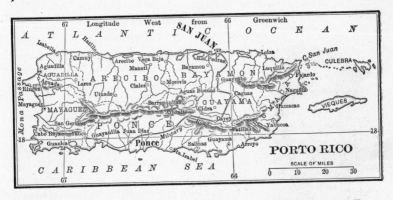

PORTO RICO

dastardly act sent a thrill of horror through the land. During eight days the nation was held in anxious suspense. Then the President died, deeply mourned by the people. The Vice-President, Theodore Roosevelt,[2] at once took the oath of office as President of the United States.

[1] This was called the Pan-American Exposition because all the countries of North America, Central America, and South America were represented there.

[2] Theodore Roosevelt, twenty-sixth President of the United States (1901), was born in New York City, October 27, 1858. He was graduated from Harvard College in 1882, and two years afterwards was elected a member of the New York legislature. In later years he rendered valuable service as a member of the National Civil Service Commission, as president of the New York Police Board, and as Assistant Secretary of the Navy. At the outbreak of the Spanish-American War he resigned his position as Assistant Secretary of the Navy in order to help organize the First United States Cavalry Volunteers (popularly known as the "Roosevelt Rough Riders"), a regiment that distinguished itself in the Cuban campaign. By reason of his gallantry on the battle-field Roosevelt was promoted from the rank of lieutenant-colonel to that of colonel. The year after the war he was elected Governor of New York, and in 1901 Vice-President of the United

425. Military and Civil Government in the Philippine Islands (1899–1901).—Before the treaty of peace at the end of the Spanish-American War could be ratified, some of the Filipinos, led by Aguinaldo, rebelled against the authority of the United States (February, 1899). After hard fighting,

Aguinaldo, the leader of a rebellion.

Aguinaldo's forces were driven from their position near Manila and then out of Malolos, the rebel leader's capital. But the rebels continued their desperate struggle against a large American army[1] until Aguinaldo was captured in April, 1900. From that time the rebellion offered no serious resistance.

NELSON A. MILES.

The islands remained under military rule until July 1, 1901, when civil government was established, a special

Civil government in the Philippine Islands.

effort being made to give the people as large a share in their government as they had capacity to exercise. William H. Taft was appointed governor. For ten months he had worked zealously as chairman of the civil commission appointed for the purpose of organizing the best attainable government for the Filipinos. Governor Taft's administration was successful in securing good order and popular content.

426. China and the "Open Door" (1900).—Our presence in the Philippine Islands and our rapidly increasing foreign commerce brought us into close touch with affairs in the Far East. After the war between Japan and China in

The scramble for Chinese territory.

1894–95, some of the European powers began to vie with each other in seizing large areas of Chinese territory—known as "spheres of influence"— in order to bring them under their own control. In 1899

States. In the midst of his busy public life he has also written many books, most of them in the field of history or biography. In all his work he has labored with earnestness, vigor, and sincerity of purpose.

[1] In October, 1900, the army there contained 71,000 men.

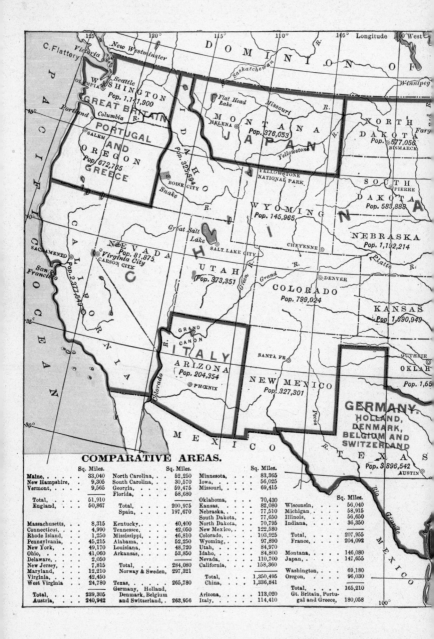

COMPARATIVE AREAS.

	Sq. Miles.		Sq. Miles.		Sq. Miles.		Sq. Miles.
Maine,	33,040	North Carolina,	52,250	Minnesota,	83,365		
New Hampshire,	9,305	South Carolina,	30,570	Iowa,	56,025		
Vermont,	9,565	Georgia,	59,475	Missouri,	69,415		
		Florida,	58,680				
Total,	51,910			Oklahoma,	70,430	Wisconsin,	56,040
England,	50,867	Total,	200,975	Kansas,	82,080	Michigan,	58,915
		Spain,	197,670	Nebraska,	77,510	Illinois,	56,650
				South Dakota,	77,650	Indiana,	36,350
Masssachusetts,	8,315	Kentucky,	40,400	North Dakota,	70,795		
Connecticut,	4,990	Tennessee,	42,050	New Mexico,	122,580	Total,	207,955
Rhode Island,	1,250	Mississippi,	46,810	Colorado,	103,925	France,	204,092
Pennsylvania,	45,215	Alabama,	52,250	Wyoming,	97,890		
New York,	49,170	Louisiana,	48,720	Utah,	84,970		
Ohio,	41,060	Arkansas,	53,850	Idaho,	84,800	Montana,	146,080
Delaware,	2,050			Nevada,	110,700	Japan,	147,655
New Jersey,	7,815	Total,	284,080	California,	158,360		
Maryland,	12,210	Norway & Sweden,	297,321			Washington,	69,180
Virginia,	42,450			Total,	1,350,495	Oregon,	96,030
West Virginia,	24,780	Texas,	265,780	China,	1,336,841		
		Germany, Holland,				Total,	165,210
Total,	239,305	Denmark, Belgium		Arizona,	113,020	Gt. Britain, Portu-	
Austria,	240,942	and Switzerland,	263,956	Italy,	114,410	gal and Greece,	180,058

Secretary Hay urged these powers to unite in guaranteeing to all nations equal rights of trade in China. The powers agreed to carry out his wishes, and thus established the policy of the "open door." By securing an agreement to this policy Secretary Hay did much to prevent the break-up or "partition" of the Chinese Empire for the benefit of those European powers that coveted her territory for their own enrichment.

The unseemly scramble for her territory developed in China a bitter anti-foreign sentiment, which culminated in

NATIVE TAGALO CHILDREN, MALABON.

1900 in a serious outbreak. Some foreigners were killed, and even the lives of foreign ministers in Peking were in danger. In order to put down the uprising and rescue the legations, the European powers, Japan, and the United States found it necessary to send troops to Peking. In the settlement of the difficulties in China our government exercised a pre-dominating influence in favor of fair treatment of the Chinese. This was an incident in the persistent policy of the United States to preserve the territorial integrity of China.

The Chinese uprising against foreigners.

427. **The Republic of Cuba (1902).**—While these events were taking place in the Far East, others of deep concern to

us were taking place at our very doors.   When Spain gave
us Cuba, the island came under the military authority of
the United States.   According to a joint resolution passed
by Congress before the outbreak of the war, this military
control was to continue until order should be restored and
the Cubans should
organize a govern-

The Cubans organ- ment
ize a government. satisfactory to Con-
gress.   Early in
November, 1900, a
convention of Cu-
bans met at Ha-
vana, and before
the middle of Feb-
ruary, 1901, com-
pleted a constitu-
tion modelled after
that of the United
States.   On Janu-
ary 1, 1902, a presi-
dent and members
of congress were
appointed in ac-
cordance with the
provisions of the
Cuban Constitu-
tion, and on May
20, 1902, the new
Cuban govern-
ment was formally
inaugurated.   True

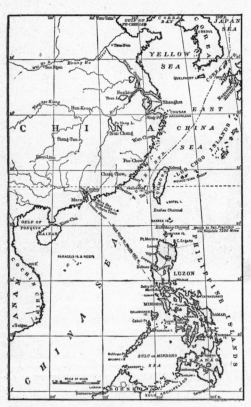

PHILIPPINE ISLANDS.

to its pledges, the United States handed over the control
of affairs to the recognized official, and the people of the
young republic entered upon their full independence.

In Cuba, as in Porto Rico and the Philippine Islands,
the United States greatly improved sanitary conditions

and rapidly organized an effective system of public schools.

In December, 1903, the Cuban Reciprocity Act was passed. This provided for a reduction of twenty per cent. of the Dingley Tariff rates on Cuban imports into the United States, and thus greatly increased Cuban trade.

428. The Isthmian Canal (1901–1904).—For some time our growing commercial interests had led many people to believe that we should be benefited by the construction of a canal across the Isthmus of Panama or some narrow part of Central America. But public opinion in the United States demanded that such a canal should be owned and controlled by our government. In accordance with this sentiment, therefore, the Hay-Pauncefote treaty between England and the United States was signed in November, 1901. By the terms of this treaty the United States was to have sole power to construct, control, and defend an Isthmian Canal for the benefit of the commerce of the world. *The Hay-Pauncefote Treaty.*

The next step toward the construction of such a canal was the passage by Congress in June, 1902, of the Isthmian Canal Act. This act empowered the President to secure the unfinished Panama Canal *The Isthmian Canal Act.* at a cost not to exceed $40,000,000, and also to secure from the Republic of Colombia a strip of land, at least six miles wide, extending across the Isthmus of Panama. Within this strip of land the United States was to construct, operate, and protect a canal with control of its terminal ports. If, however, the unfinished Panama Canal and the land from Colombia could not be secured in a reasonable time and on reasonable terms, the President was empowered to secure a canal route from Costa Rica and Nicaragua.

When the Colombian government rejected the treaty containing the conditions expressed in the Isthmian Canal Act, the people of the State of Panama, feeling that their interests had been disregarded, *The revolution in Panama.* planned a revolution, which broke out on November 3, 1903. They quickly organized a provisional government and proclaimed their political independence as the Republic of Panama. The new republic was recognized by the United States, November 6th.

On November 18th a new canal treaty was signed by Secretary Hay and the representatives of Panama. By the

The treaty with Panama. terms of this treaty Panama granted to the United States " in perpetuity the use, occupation, and control " of a zone of land ten miles wide on the margins of the canal. In return the United States guaranteed the independence of Panama, the payment of $10,000,000

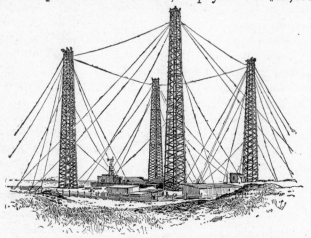

WIRELESS TELEGRAPH STATION AT WELLFLEET, CAPE COD.

when the treaty should become active, and at the end of nine years an annual payment of $250,000.

The Senate of the United States adopted this treaty on February 23, 1904.

429. The Pacific Cable and Wireless Telegraphy (1903). —Another link in the chain of communication which is drawing the nations of the earth more closely together is the Pacific Cable. This was completed in 1903 and extends from San Francisco to Hong Kong by way of Hawaii and Manila. On July 4, 1903, President Roosevelt sent the first message, which flashed around the world in four minutes.

Of less importance to commerce, but of unmeasured value in other ways, is the wonderful invention of the Marconi wireless telegraph, by which messages are sent through the air. On January 18, 1903, from the station at Wellfleet on Cape Cod, President Roosevelt sent to King Edward of England the first wireless message to cross the Atlantic.

430. The Louisiana Purchase Exposition at St. Louis (1904).—Long before these events took place the people of the United States had been intent upon carrying out a great enterprise. This was the Louisiana Purchase Exposition, planned to commemorate the centennial of the purchase of the Louisiana territory in 1803. It opened April 30, 1904, and closed December 1st. Like other international expositions on a large scale, it had a great educational influence. Its architecture, its sculpture, and its landscape-gardening were of a high order of excellence, and so were its exhibits of industry and commerce. The latest scientific discoveries were among the remarkable features of this exposition. It is especially worthy of note, however, that for the first time in the history of international expositions, the educational exhibit had a building exclusively for itself.

431. Theodore Roosevelt Elected President (1904).—While interest in the Louisiana Purchase Exposition was still at its height, the public mind was earnestly engaged in considering the Presidential nominations that were to be made in the summer of 1904. When the national conventions of the two great parties met, the Republicans nominated Theodore Roosevelt, and the Democrats Alton B. Parker.

The principal point of difference between the two party platforms related to tariff reform, but the issue was largely one of the personal popularity of the candidates. As the sentiment of the people was with Mr. Roosevelt, he was elected by a very large popular majority.

432. President Roosevelt as Peacemaker (1905).—From these questions of national interest and importance we turn to one which involved the welfare of the whole civilized world.

On February 6, 1904, nine months before the election of President Roosevelt, a terrible war broke out between Russia and Japan.   All the Western nations, shocked by the

War between Russia and Japan. frightful loss of life, watched the struggle with great concern.   Finally, when the progress of the war and the condition of the opposing forces seemed to warrant it, President Roosevelt addressed a note to the Governments of Russia and Japan (June 8, 1905).   In this note he urged the warring nations, not only in their own interests, but in the interests of the civilized world, to try to agree upon terms of peace.

The outcome was a conference at Portsmouth, New Hampshire, between commissioners from each of the two

THE ATLANTIC FLEET STARTING ON ITS VOYAGE AROUND THE WORLD, DEC., 1907.
From a photograph, copyright, 1907, by Underwood & Underwood, New York.

countries.   The people in this and in other lands looked on with anxious suspense as the commissioners continued, week after week, to discuss the question of peace or war.   At last, when it seemed likely that the conference had come to a point of deadlock and was about to break up in failure, President Roosevelt, with well-timed decision and tact, brought about a delay until he could communicate with the Czar of Russia and the Emperor of Japan. The result was the sending by the home Governments of such instructions to the commissioners at Portsmouth as enabled them speedily to agree to a treaty of peace. The successful outcome of President Roosevelt's efforts showed the immense influence of the United States in the affairs of the world.

Immense influence of our country in world affairs.

433. **The Atlantic Fleet Sails Around the World (1907–1909).**—In December, 1907, the battle fleet of the United States Navy, including sixteen battleships, started from Hampton Roads, Virginia, on a voyage around the world. The route was by way of South America and the Pacific coast to San Francisco, then westward to Australia, the Philippine Islands, Japan, and China, passing through the Indian Ocean, the Suez Canal, the Mediterranean Sea, and the Straits of Gibraltar. The voyage was completed on Washington's Birthday, 1909, at Hampton Roads, where the fleet arrived after having travelled more than 30,000 miles. Everywhere it was received with great enthusiasm.

This cruise was a noteworthy event in naval history. It not only tested and proved the expert seamanship of our navy, but it called into expression the friendly feeling of foreign powers.

434. **The Second Peace Conference (1907).**—In marked contrast with this cruise of warships was the second Peace Conference[1] held in the same year at The Hague. The first Peace Conference had met there in 1899. These meetings, which included distinguished men from the various civilized nations of the world, were held in the interests of international peace and goodwill. In both conferences our country took a leading part in advancing the peaceful settlement of disagreements between nations.

The old method of barbarous warfare, with its cost of maintaining vast armies and navies, is a great strain upon the people. But even this burden is not to be compared

[1] At the first, 26 of the powers of the world were represented; at the second, 44.

with the frightful suffering and loss of life which is caused by war. Although the United States is a peaceful nation, **War and arbitration.** its wars have cost an enormous sum. More than two-thirds of the national revenue is paid out in pensions, in interest on war debts, and in the support of the army and navy.

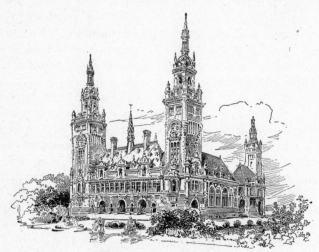

PEACE PALACE, THE HAGUE.
From a photograph by Underwood & Underwood, New York.

It is to be hoped that the day will soon come when all disagreements between nations will be settled by arbitration, just as those between individual men are now settled by courts of law. Already a number of such disputes have been settled in the Court of Arbitration at The Hague, which was established by the First Peace Conference in 1899. **The Court of Arbitration at The Hague.**

Each nation is represented in this Court by four men who may be called upon to serve as judges in international disputes. When any two nations have a disagreement and refer the matter to the Court they select from among the judges a small number to try their case and settle the disagreement. Many believe this to be a step toward a Supreme Court of the world, which will decide issues between nations as our Supreme Court does between separate States.

435. The United States a World-Power.—Our prominence in the two peace conferences held at The Hague calls attention, in a striking way, to far-reaching changes that have taken place during the last hundred years in this country's relation to the great powers of Europe.

You will remember that the American Revolution was fought to secure our independence from England. But at the end of that war there was no strong spirit of union among the people of the various States. Even after we organized a new plan of government under the Constitution, our country was so weak from lack of union that it did not command the respect of Europe. *Independence from England.*

In fact, England and France treated the United States as if it were a vassal. The outcome was the War of 1812, which has well been called the second war of independence; this time it was independence from Europe. In less than ten years after this war, we gave expression to our feeling of independence and national strength by setting forth what is known as the Monroe Doctrine. Its central idea was "America for Americans," and supplemented Washington's Farewell Address, which had for one of its central ideas "Europe for Europeans." *Independence from Europe.*

These two maxims stand roughly for the traditional attitude of our nation toward Europe until the time of the Spanish-American War of 1898. When that war closed, Spain had lost the West Indies and the Philippines and we ourselves were in control of extensive territory overseas.

In fact, by this expansion the United States had become "Greater America." Our nation was now a world-power because our interests were world-wide, and our wishes received consideration in any part of the globe. Our people felt the change. They were *Greater America.*

conscious of new strength. They were ready to solve new problems and had the courage to face new responsibilities. Henceforth the United States stood prepared to take an active and leading part in the affairs of the world.

Moreover, for many years before the Spanish War, we had been wonderfully prosperous. We had amassed al-

The chief manufacturing nation. most untold wealth, and had become the chief manufacturing nation of the world. All this, combined with our new prominence as a world-power, made the United States an important rival of England, France, and Germany.

436. The World-Powers of Europe.—But these countries, as well as some others of Europe, had been undergoing a transformation. Let us briefly note how there came to be a Greater Britain, a Greater France, a Greater Germany, and a Greater Russia.

After the overthrow of Napoleon in 1815, there were five great powers in Europe—Great Britain, France, Austria, Prussia, and Russia. This situation remained without much change, though with some difference in

Two movements. relative strength, for nearly sixty years. Then followed two movements which altered the entire balance of the European world. The first of these movements was toward national unity and the second toward national expansion.

Italy had been for ages a mere "geographical expression." It was not a single kingdom like Spain, but was made up of several kingdoms and other states, some ruled

United Italy. by Austria and others by the Roman Pontiff. For many years patriots had striven to make of these a united Italy. In 1859 began an armed contest for this ideal. It ended in 1870 with the complete union of all parts of Italy into a single kingdom, with a constitution and a national parliament. Victor Emmanuel was made King.

The next country to form a union of its many states was Germany. Austria and Prussia, the most important

ones, had long been rivals for leadership. But in 1866, in a "seven weeks' war," Prussia defeated Austria, and then forced many other states into a new North German Confederation, with the King of Prussia at its head. United Germany.

This sudden rise of Prussia to a leading position among the great powers of Europe stirred the envy and alarm of the French Emperor, Louis Napoleon, and he welcomed an opportunity to humble the pride of his neighbor. This occurred in the Franco-Prussian War, which began in 1870. But the war did not end as Napoleon had expected, for, within six weeks, he was overwhelmingly defeated by the Germans. They captured the French Emperor, whose people at once deposed him, and at the end of seven months they were in possession of Paris and had conquered France. The Franco-Prussian War.

Then the Germans compelled France to pay one billion dollars as a war indemnity and give up Alsace and Lorraine. But the most marked result of the war was in Germany herself, where a new Germanic Empire was created. All the German states except those of the Austrian Empire—Austria had by this time united with Hungary to form Austro-Hungary—were now united (1871) in one federal empire, with a written constitution, and with the King of Prussia at the head of the whole. He was also called the German Emperor. A new Germanic Empire.

Somewhat later, years after this spirit of national union had made itself felt in Italy and Germany, there suddenly began among the European countries a wild scramble for territory in foreign lands. This was the beginning of a fresh era of expansion. "Spheres of influence" were sought in new lands, because of a keen desire for new markets to increase commerce and enrich the people. Wild scramble for territory.

Of all these countries England had been the most successful colonizing nation. But she had lost her chief

American colonies because she had governed them selfishly and for her own interests. In course of time she found

England.

out that she had more to gain by allowing some of her colonies, such as Canada, New Zealand, and Australia, to manage their own affairs, and they remained loyal to her. Although she still held these and others in various parts of the world, she now wanted more.

Germany, having become a strong military power with a large and ever-increasing population, had great need for an outlet to her industries and commerce, which had grown

Germany, France, and Russia.

enormously. So she also was stubbornly resolved to gain new territory beyond the seas. France likewise, not wishing to be left behind, was seized with a feverish desire for expansion. She had the old belief that colonies by themselves would bring national riches. Russia alone was able to expand along her borders instead of across the sea; but she needed additional seaports, and these the other powers were determined to prevent her from getting.

By the time the First Hague Conference was held (1899) almost all of Africa and more than half of the

Result of expansion.

great continent of Asia were under control of European powers. Thus you can easily see how, in this era of expansion, there came to be not only a Greater America, but also a Greater England, a Greater Germany, a Greater France, and a Greater Russia. Moreover, in this gigantic struggle for control of new territory all these countries were engaged in world-wide competition for world trade.

437. **The Spirit of Union and of Nationalism in Canada.**—The first colony to profit by England's change in

Dissatisfaction in Upper and Lower Canada.

colonial policy was Canada. The people in Upper Canada, or the province of Ontario, and of Lower Canada, or the province of Quebec, had been growing more and more dissatisfied because their legislatures did not have a larger control over their executives and over the expenditure of money. As a consequence of the popular discontent, there was a rebellion in 1837 in both Upper and Lower Canada. Although this rebellion was easily put down, to satisfy the Canadian people England allowed the two provinces to unite into one, called Canada, and govern themselves as they desired.

In 1867 a broader union was organized to include other provinces. At first only four—Ontario, Quebec, Nova Scotia, and New Brunswick—joined the union; but not many years later British Columbia and Prince Edward's Island became members of the *A broader union in Canada.* federation. This desire for union on the part of the Canadians was doubtless quickened by the groundless fear that the United States might attempt to seize and annex their country.

438. The Spirit of Co-operation Among the Nations. —From the foregoing you can easily see that along with the development of the spirit of union and nationalism there has arisen an ever-increasing spirit of rivalry and competition among the great nations of the twentieth century. But, while competition must flourish if the world is to advance, co-operation is of even greater value. Nations are coming to realize it. They are learning that their prosperity and progress come from working together and not by fighting one another. The most advanced expression of this co-operative spirit is found in the two Hague Peace Conferences, of which we have spoken. Their influence should be to strengthen international good-will, on a basis of common sense and humanity, and to uplift the moral and social as well as the industrial welfare of men and women in all lands.

439. The Conservation of Our Natural Resources.— Another matter of great importance to the welfare of our country was a meeting held in the White House in Washington in May, 1908. It was made up of national and State leaders, whom President Roosevelt had called together to consider the conservation of our *Natural resources.* natural resources; that is, the best means of preserving our water, forests, soil, fuel, and minerals.

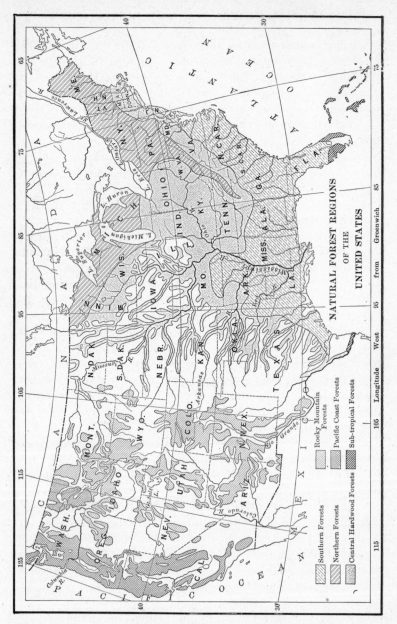

NATURAL FOREST REGIONS
OF THE
UNITED STATES

Rocky Mountain Forests
Pacific Coast Forests
Sub-tropical Forests

Southern Forests
Northern Forests
Central Hardwood Forests

As a people we had been extremely wasteful of these natural sources of wealth, but with a rapidly expanding population the time had come to use them with care. This is especially true in the case of forests, which have a large influence upon the flow of water in rivers and streams. The meeting at the White House did much to strengthen sentiment in favor of preserving our resources. Connected with it is the work of improving our waterways, such as a plan to establish a ship route from Lake Michigan to the Gulf of Mexico.

WILLIAM H. TAFT.

440. President Taft[1] and the Revision of the Tariff (1909). — In the Presidential campaign of 1908, the Republicans were successful in the election of their candidates, William H. Taft as President, and James S. Sherman as Vice-President.

Shortly after his inauguration (March 4, 1909), President Taft called a special session of Congress for the revision of the tariff. There was a sharp difference of opinion as to how this revision should be made, but after several months of heated discussion, Congress passed the Payne-Aldrich tariff bill, which became a law August 5, 1909. This new tariff law, like the "Dingley Tariff" (p. 408), was highly protective. It was therefore

The revision of the tariff.

[1] William Howard Taft, twenty-seventh President of the United States (1909–1913), was born in Cincinnati, Ohio, September 15, 1857. He was graduated from Yale University in 1878, and two years later began the practice of law in his native State. In 1892 he was made Judge of the United States District Court. In 1900 he was appointed president of the United States Philippine Commission, and in 1901 became the first civil governor of the Philippine Islands. He filled this important position with great credit to himself and to his country. He became Secretary of War in President Roosevelt's Cabinet in 1904 and continued in this office until 1908. In the autumn of that year he was elected President of the United States. For this position of responsibility his long experience in the public service seemed especially to have fitted him.

regarded with disfavor by those who believed that there
should be a substantial reduction of duties.

Along with the tariff law, this Congress passed a bill to
create a Tariff Commission, but it was abolished by the
next Congress. It was to investigate the cost of producing foreign manufactured articles, that Congress might
know how high each tariff item must be to protect the
manufacturers here.

441. Postal Savings Banks (1910).—Another law
passed by this Congress established the Postal Savings
Banks. A leading purpose of this law was to develop
habits of thrift among people of small means. It was
thought that those who could save only a little from their
earnings would be encouraged to put their savings into
Postal   these banks; for they are under the control of
banks.   the United States Government and are therefore absolutely safe. Any person of ten years or over can
open an account with a Postal Savings Bank by depositing as
little as one dollar. All deposits pay two per cent. interest.

**442. Arbitration of the Newfoundland Fisheries Dis-
pute (1910).**—For more than a hundred years there had
been much friction in North Atlantic waters as to the
rights of American fishermen there. After many fruitless
efforts to settle the dispute, it was referred by the United
States and Great Britain to The Hague Court of Arbitration, and was adjusted to the satisfaction of both countries.

**443. General Arbitration Treaties of the United States
with Great Britain and France.**—This international dispute concerning fisheries is far from being the only one
settled by The Hague Court. Almost every important
nation in the world has been a party to settlements of this
kind.

Moreover, such progress has been made in this direction that since the First Peace Conference at The Hague
most countries have entered into treaties by which they
agree to settle certain kinds of differences by arbitration.[1]

[1] Our country has signed many such treaties.

Usually, however, questions involving "vital interests, independence, and honor are excepted." President Taft strongly disapproved of such formal exceptions, and nego-

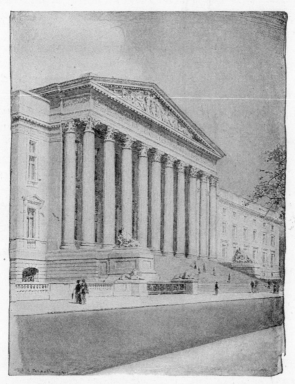

THE NEW DEPARTMENT OF STATE BUILDING.

tiated treaties with England and France without them. But the Senate disagreed with him. It refused to ratify them without important amendments, and would not "delegate to any other body its treaty-making power under the Constitution." As amended, these treaties required further negotiations.

Differences settled by arbitration.

444. A New Treaty with Japan (1911).—To maintain and strengthen our long-standing friendship with Japan, a

new treaty was signed with that country, setting aside the existing treaty—a clause of which declared our right to exclude Japanese laborers.   Their government complained
Japanese exclusion.   that we placed no such clause in our European treaties, and so our new treaty omits it. But there is an understanding between the two countries which allows us to regulate Japanese immigration as before.

445. Arizona and New Mexico Made States (1912).—
In 1912 Arizona and New Mexico were admitted into the Union as States.   Except Alaska and the District of Columbia, all our territory on the mainland has now been

WOODROW WILSON.
*From a photograph, copyright
1912, by Moffett.*

made into States, bringing up the number to forty-eight.   So to-day, **Forty-eight States.** while our national flag contains thirteen stripes to represent the thirteen original colonies, it has forty-eight stars to stand for the States which now make up our great Federal Republic.

446. Woodrow Wilson[1] Elected President (1912).—A question of absorbing interest to all **Issues of 1912 campaign.** the States was the Presidential campaign of 1912.   During the campaign, issues of far-reaching importance were earnestly discussed.

---

[1] Woodrow Wilson, twenty-eighth President of the United States (1913–——), was born at Staunton, Virginia, December 28, 1856. He graduated at Princeton University in 1879, and took the degree of Doctor of Philosophy at Johns Hopkins University in 1886. He practiced law for two years but gave it up in order to devote himself, as teacher and writer, mainly to history, jurisprudence, and politics. After serving as professor of history and political economy at Bryn Mawr and later at Wesleyan University, in 1890 he was appointed professor of jurisprudence and politics at Princeton University. In 1902 he became president of Princeton University, a position in which he remained until 1910, when the people of New Jersey made him their governor. But before the end of his term of office he was elected President of the United States. During that part of his life which he spent as a college professor he wrote a number of books, most of which were in the fields of biography, history, and politics. While president of Princeton University and governor of New Jersey he gave evidence of marked ability as an administrator. All his work was characterized by sincerity of purpose and high standards of public service.

Among these were the tariff, the proper methods of dealing with the business trusts, and the conservation of our natural resources.

On these great national issues, a new political party was formed. Its members called themselves the Progressive Party. It was made up of Republicans and Independents, and some Democrats who held views which they believed to be in conflict with those supported by the Republican and Democratic Parties. The supporters of this party selected as their candidate for President Theodore Roosevelt. The Republicans nominated for a second term President William Howard Taft. Woodrow Wilson, who was the Democratic candidate, was elected.

447. Reforms to Secure Larger Control over Public Affairs for the People.—In this campaign many States made use of primary elections, or primaries, in selecting delegates to the national conventions which were to nominate candidates for the Presidency. It was **Primaries select** believed that in this way the people could **candidates.** have more control in selecting officials to carry out their will. The primaries, as you should know, took the place of caucuses, in which party managers largely, and in many cases entirely, controlled the selection of candidates.

Another reform to help the people to control public affairs is the short ballot, which is used in several States and in many cities having the commission form **The short** of government. Especially in a large city is **ballot.** this reform of great value, because such a city is really a gigantic business corporation, which taxes the people millions of dollars to carry on its various departments—school, park, street, fire, police, and so on.

To succeed in such a great undertaking, the city government should be well organized and well managed. But up to recent years such has not been the case in many of our large cities. The administration has been too complicated and clumsy to get the best work done with the least expense. As a result, there have been much corruption and much waste of money.

To remedy this defect many cities have adopted the experiment of a commission form of government using the short ballot. By this plan, all the legislative and executive functions of the city have been placed in the hands of a small group of men, usually five in number, called a commission, whom the people elect. As the number of officials is small, it is possible to hold each responsible for the kind of service he renders the public. For the same reason also it is easier to find out what sort of candidates are up for election. For the short ballot is quite different from the long ballot, which in some cities contains the names of scores of candidates, of whom the voter knows very little or nothing. The commission form of government is now in use in hundreds of cities in the United States.

Commission form of government.

Aims to fix responsibility.

The same principle has been carried out in the executive departments of State government by making only a few important officials elective and requiring them to appoint their subordinates.

Other plans designed to give the people direct control of their affairs are the initiative and referendum now being tried by a number of States. By means of the initiative, a certain fraction of the voters may propose a statute which the State Legislature must consider. If it refuses to adopt the measure, it must be submitted to the voters of the State to approve or reject at a regular election. By means of the referendum, a certain fraction of the people may demand that any law passed by the State Legislature be submitted to the voters at an election to approve or reject as they see fit.

The initiative and referendum.

Another plan, intended to make it easier for the people to punish an official for wrong-doing or for unsatisfactory public service, is the recall. By means of this plan a certain fraction of voters may demand an election in which the people shall decide whether or not

The recall.

the official in question shall give up his office before the end of the period for which he was elected.

The movement in favor of popular control of public affairs became so wide-spread that in 1913 the Seventeenth Amendment to the Constitution was adopted, requiring that United States senators be elected by the people. Before the adoption of this amendment the United States senators had been elected by the State Legislatures. This method was not wholly satisfactory, for two reasons: (1) because there *People elect senators.* were many cases where improper influences were used with legislators to secure votes for candidates; and (2) because it sometimes happened that a legislature would be deadlocked for weeks and even months before electing a senator. The feeling was wide-spread that too much time was wasted in this way.

448. The Parcel Post (1913).—Another Federal law, which directly affected the people in every part of the land, was the parcel post law. This brought about a marked change in transportation. Before *A marked change in transportation.* the parcel post came into use, parcels and goods that needed to be moved quickly were handled by express companies, while bulky freight was handled by the railroads, as now. But, as the express companies depended upon the railroads for transportation, they served only those whom the railroads served.

By means of the parcel post, the United States mail service can carry on a postal express business reaching any locality that is included in our rural free delivery system, even though it may be far *A cheap means of delivery.* from a railroad station. Moreover, the United States postal express carries packages and other goods within certain limits of size and weights for much less than the express companies used to charge. Merchants and farmers have been quick to adopt this cheap means of delivery, and the work of the parcel post has increased with marvellous rapidity.

449. The Tariff Law and the Income Tax (1913).—
After the enactment of the Payne-Aldrich tariff law of 1909
there followed an increasing demand for more reduction
in duties. In fact, the tariff continued to be perhaps the
leading issue in national politics. Shortly after President
Wilson entered into office, therefore, he called a special session of Congress to consider the tariff question. Following a notable contest, a law was passed (October, 1913)
which made a large reduction in the duties on imported
goods.

This decided revision downward was certain to bring
about a large decrease in customs receipts, and it became
necessary to provide revenue in some other way. A section
was inserted in the tariff revision law, therefore, levying
Income tax to   an income tax. Such a tax had been advo-
raise revenue.   cated for many years and had already been
made constitutional by the adoption of the Sixteenth
Amendment (1913).

The income tax is levied upon incomes of more than
four thousand dollars for any married person living with
              wife or husband, and upon incomes of more
The incomes   than three thousand for all other persons. The
that are taxed. tax upon such incomes is one per cent. An
additional tax is levied upon incomes that exceed twenty
thousand dollars.

450. The Currency and Banking Law (1913).—Another
law having a very important bearing upon the financial
affairs of the people was the currency and banking law
Its threefold   (1913). It provides for the Federal Reserve
object.   System. The object of the law is threefold:
(1) to make the monetary system of the country more
simple and uniform; (2) to provide a plan by which
there shall always be enough money to meet any special
need; and (3) to make it easy for this money to be
obtained in that part of the country where the need is
greatest.

The central body, which has power to control and direct this system, is located at Washington. It is called the Federal Reserve Board. The system includes twelve Federal Reserve Banks,[1] each being a centre of the banking power in its own district. **The Federal Reserve Board.**

All the national banks in any district must become members of the system and purchase stock in its Federal Reserve Bank, each in proportion to its paid-up capital stock and surplus. The State banks also may become members if they apply for membership. Only the banks in the system and the United States Government can deposit money in any Federal Reserve Bank.

By this new currency and banking law all the banks in the Federal Reserve System are joined together to give one another financial aid, just as the forty-eight States of our Federal Union are joined together for government aid.

451. The Panama Tolls (1914).—According to the Hay-Pauncefote treaty between the United States and Great Britain, the shipping of all countries was to pay equal rates for the use of the Panama Canal. Many of our citizens held that "all countries" could legally mean all *other* countries than ours. So Congress passed a law (1913) exempting American coastwise shipping from paying tolls.

Other governments, and likewise many Americans, believed this to be a violation of the treaty legally and, even more, a violation of good faith. President Wilson, in February, 1914, in a special message to Congress, asked for its repeal. After long and able debates in both the House and the Senate, Congress passed a bill for the repeal, but incorporated in it an amendment that it was not to be interpreted as **Panama tolls exemption repealed.**

[1] The banking cities are Boston, New York, Philadelphia, Cleveland, Richmond, Atlanta, Chicago, St. Louis, Minneapolis, Kansas City, Dallas, and San Francisco.

giving up any right of the United States under the Hay-Pauncefote treaty with Great Britain.

452. The United States and the Troubles in Mexico.
—Although the problem of canal tolls was important, it
Trouble with was at times almost overshadowed by a criti-
Mexico. cal situation regarding Mexico. In February,
1913, an uprising in the City of Mexico resulted in the
overthrow and death of Madero, who had been recently
elected by the people as their constitutional President.

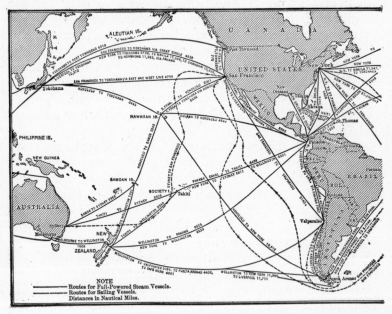

NOTE
——— Routes for Full-Powered Steam Vessels.
——— Routes for Sailing Vessels.
Distances in Nautical Miles.

By the aid of his army, General Huerta became dictator. He soon got control of the centre of the country,
including the capital city. But many of Ma-
Huerta becomes dero's followers, especially in the states of
dictator. Northern Mexico, would not submit to Huerta,
and took up arms in an insurrection that kept growing
in volume and strength. They called themselves Consti-
tutionalists.

President Wilson refused to recognize Huerta on two grounds: (1) he had not been elected by the people in a lawful way; and (2), according to the best evidence obtainable, his hold upon power gave too little promise of stability to justify recognition of him by the United States. Refusal to recognize Huerta.

This refusal led to much bitter feeling toward our government on the part of Huerta and his followers. Meanwhile, the danger to our own people and their interests in

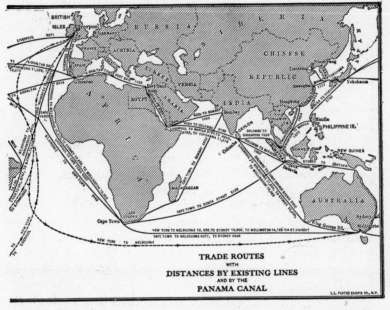

TRADE ROUTES
WITH
DISTANCES BY EXISTING LINES
AND BY THE
PANAMA CANAL

Mexico from the civil war going on there made it prudent to send war-vessels to Mexican waters. On April 10, 1914, a boat-load of sailors from one of our gunboats landed at Tampico to secure gasolene. They were arrested and thrown into prison. Admiral Mayo, commanding the American fleet in the harbor, at once demanded their release. This was granted, and both the Federal general in command at Tampico American sailors imprisoned.

and General Huerta himself expressed regret over the affair.

Admiral Mayo was not satisfied. In accordance with the long-standing custom of nations, he demanded a salute to our flag by the firing of twenty-one Mexican guns.

Vera Cruz captured as reparation.

Huerta refused, and President Wilson sent a fleet of war-vessels to capture Vera Cruz as reparation for the insult to our flag.   On April 21 a force of American marines landed there, and after some fighting and the loss of a small number of men they captured the city and seized the custom-house.

It looked like the beginning of war.   But before there was any more fighting the ministers at Washington from

Mediation.

Argentina, Brazil, and Chile offered to lend their services as mediators. President Wilson promptly accepted the offer.   On May 20 the mediators met at Niagara Falls three American and three Mexican envoys in order to arrange a plan of settlement.

Although the mediators did not succeed in ending the trouble between the United States and Mexico, there was

Latin-American States more friendly toward us.

no war between the two countries.   Moreover, the mere fact that our government was quite willing to accept the offer of mediation from three enlightened and powerful South American states doubtless caused all the Latin-American states to be more friendly toward us as a people. It helped them to understand that we had no thought of making the troubles in Mexico an excuse for getting control, by force, of Mexican territory.

In the autumn of 1915 the United States and the Latin-American powers recognized Carranza as the head of the provisional government of Mexico.

453. The Opening of the Panama Canal (1914).—But an event which is likely to have even greater influence in

The beginning of a new era in our national history.

strengthening friendship and good-will toward us on the part of the twenty Latin-American countries was the opening to commerce of the Panama Canal (August 15, 1914).   There is little doubt that this opening was the beginning of a new era in our national history, and for the following reasons: (1) It supplies a short, quick, and cheap water-route between the ports of the Atlantic and the Gulf seaboard and the ports of the Pacific seaboard. (2) The canal shortens the distance between our Pacific States and Europe as well as between our Atlantic States and Australia, the Philippine Islands, China, and Japan. (3) It is also likely to prove a powerful force for good in our relations with the twelve Latin-American states bordering on the Pacific, for the increase in trade and travel will promote a better understanding and a more friendly feeling.

There is already maintained at Washington an international organization, the Pan-American Union, which aims to develop closer business and commercial relations between the United States and the twenty republics to the south of us, as well *The Pan-American Union.* as to form closer ties of friendship and good-will. It is important that we should work in harmony with our sister republics represented in the Pan-American Union.

454. The United States and the Great War in Europe (1914-1916).—Another event of far-reaching consequence occurred when the great war in Europe suddenly broke out in the midsummer of 1914. This conflict, which involved all the great European powers, put a political strain on the neutral nations who wished to maintain their friendship with *A serious international situation.* all the warring countries. This was especially true of the United States, because the war had a direct influence on our commerce and industry. Not only were the principal markets for our goods and sources of supplies for our factories cut off, but our sea-borne commerce was seriously crippled because most of it was carried on in vessels belonging to the belligerent countries.

But, notwithstanding the violent upsetting of normal trade conditions, in some ways the war has been a source of profit to American business. All the nations at war

needed for their armies, and for their civil population,
Our exports to Europe. vast quantities of munitions, food, clothing,
and other supplies beyond their own capacity
to furnish. For the year ending June 30, 1915, we exported such goods to the value of $857,000,000; in the preceding year the value of all such exports was about $221,000,000. This means that our sales to Europe by reason of the war increased about $636,000,000 during the year. For breadstuffs alone we received about $574,000,000 against only $165,000,000 the year before.

To prevent all supplies from reaching the enemy was of vital importance to both sides. The Allies at the outset completely destroyed the direct ocean commerce of Germany except in the Baltic Sea; while the harm that Germany could inflict on British commerce by submarines and roving cruisers was comparatively small. The Allies then turned their efforts toward cutting down Germany's indirect trade through neutrals. This was a far harder and more delicate task, for it involved the welfare of neutrals and struck heavily at American interests.

Up to the opening of this war food intended for civilians was never considered as contraband and hence could not be lawfully seized at sea when it was on the way to a belligerent port. But changed conditions brought about new methods. Some time after the war began
Each side tries to cut off food supplies from the other. German authorities, including those of cities as well as those of the Imperial Government, assumed control of the distribution of food supplies in Germany. This caused Great Britain to declare, on February 2, 1915, that all food imported into Germany was contraband. Moreover, Germany had placed mines in the North Sea for the defence of her coasts. But these were frequently found far away from the shore, whether through having drifted, as Germany claimed, or "strewn" for offensive purposes, as England claimed. So England established a "war zone" in the North Sea, with only a single lane for neutral vessels. On February

4, 1915, Germany retaliated by declaring a war zone, which included all the waters around Great Britain, and asserted that in this zone she would destroy all enemy vessels. She said it might not be possible to save crews and passengers, and, moreover, that neutral vessels sailing into this zone would be in danger. In return Great Britain announced, on March 3, that she would adopt means to prevent goods of any kind from reaching Germany.

These extensions of contraband and blockade, which were violations of existing international law, led our government to make strong and earnest protests to both sides.

The chief grounds of protest to Great Britain were two: First, that food for a civilian population had never been contraband, and her now making it such Our protest to was remaking international law by her own Great Britain. fiat. Second, that her blockade was not legal. This was partly because it was not universally effective; it did not control, for instance, the Baltic Sea, where the German fleet kept trade open with the Scandinavian countries.

Our protest to Germany demanded a diplomacy of such a delicate nature that many feared a serious break between the two countries. In Germany's submarine Our protest to campaign against England she torpedoed sev- Germany. eral vessels carrying American citizens. The first of these vessels was the Cunard liner *Lusitania*, which was torpedoed without warning off the coast of Ireland, with the loss of many lives, including American citizens. Our government in a note to Germany stated that American citizens had full rights under international law to travel wherever legitimate business called them; that she must make reparation for American lives and property so destroyed; and that in future she must not allow her submarines either to attack American ships or to imperil American citizens travelling on any ships.

Germany declared that our requirements were equiv-

alent to prohibiting submarine warfare altogether, since
Germany's the submarine boats were too vulnerable to
position. resist attack and the wireless system made it
easy to call other vessels to help. She further declared
that she had the right to the only ocean weapon left her
and that the peril of innocent lives was a risk which
neutrals must take or else be in effect allies of the enemies
of Germany. Germany later agreed to make reparation to
the United States; but she at that time refused to admit
that her course was illegal, and the whole question is still
the subject of discussion between the two governments.

TO THE PUPIL

1. Do you think the United States was justified in going to war with Spain at this time? Give reasons for your answer.

2. Why did Dewey go to Manila? Impersonating him, give an account of your experiences.

3. What were the most important results of the war?

4. Explain the policy of the "Open Door." What is meant by the territorial integrity of China?

5. Explain the following: the Hay-Pauncefote treaty, the Isthmian Canal Act, and the treaty with Panama.

6. In what ways is the Pacific Cable of use to the world?

7. What good results would follow if disagreements between nations were settled by peaceful methods?

8. In what ways is co-operation of advantage among individual men and women and also among countries?

9. What is meant by the United States as a world-power?

10. Explain the following: short ballot, commission form of government, the Sixteenth and Seventeenth Amendments to the Constitution, and the income tax.

11. Why are the Latin-American states, south of Mexico, more friendly to us now than they were some years ago? What are the aims of the Pan-American Union?

12. In what ways has the great war in Europe caused trouble between the United States and Great Britain? Between the United States and Germany?

13. Name in order the Presidents of the United States.

CHAPTER XXIV

SOME INDUSTRIAL, ECONOMIC, SOCIAL AND POLITICAL CONDITIONS AND PROBLEMS OF THE PRESENT

REFERENCES: **Scribner's** Popular History of the United States, V.; **Andrews's** Last Quarter Century, II.; **Bogart's** Economic History of the United States; **Wright's** Industrial Evolution of the United States; **Coman's** Industrial History of the United States.

OUTSIDE READINGS: **Boone's** Education in the United States; **Tyler's** History of American Literature; **Richardson's** American Literature; **Stedman's** Poets of America; **Hudson's** History of Journalism in America; various magazine articles.

455. The Natural Advantages of the United States. —As the United States in its vast extent has many varieties of soil and climate, its productions also are varied.

THE ROUND-UP.

Our coasts offer valuable fisheries, and the prairies and the Great Plains furnish excellent pasturage for millions of sheep and cattle. Extensive areas of forest lands supply the best timber, a large region in the South affords suitable land for the growing of cotton, and rich mineral deposits of gold, silver, copper, iron, and coal lie imbedded in the mountain regions. Our coal supply is many times greater than that of all Europe, including England. From all these sources we get abundant raw material[1] with which to supply our factories and still have many things to spare for trade in foreign markets.

456. **The Textile Industry.**—But these natural sources of wealth would be of little value without the power to bring them under control and put them to proper uses. The industrial revolution. This power the American people possess in their inventive genius, their mechanical skill, and their untiring energy. They have, therefore, become leaders in the industrial revolution which began with the

TEXTILE MILL.

invention of steam-driven machinery over a century ago and is still going on. This revolution has brought about such great changes that we may well consider some of its more striking phases.

[1] In the output of iron, copper, coal, wheat, and cotton—the products which with wool are of greatest use in modern industry—our country leads the world. It produces wool also in large quantities.

The textile industry, a leading one in the United States, well illustrates the growth of all. Up to the time of the American Revolution, and even later, the coarser cloths for ordinary use were made by hand in the household and in small shops, while the finer grades were imported from England. It was not until the close of the eighteenth century that the spinning wheel and the hand loom gave place to the spinning machine and the power loom. These new inventions, imported from England, completely changed the making of woolen and cotton cloth.

The spinning machine and the power loom.

The first spinning mill with machinery made after the English models was built by Samuel Slater at Pawtucket, Rhode Island, in 1790. This was the beginning of the factory system in the United States. But the first factory, in the modern sense, that is, a building where all processes from the raw material to the finished product are carried on under one roof, was erected at Waltham in 1814. Since then the extension of cotton manufactures has been steady and rapid. New inventions and processes and increased demand for cotton goods have given the textile industry a wonderful development.[1]

The first modern factory.

Just as the improved machinery in spinning and weaving transferred the making of cloth from the household to the factory, so the invention of the sewing machine (1846) changed the making of men's clothing from a domestic to a factory industry and the manufacture of boots and shoes from a hand-made to a machine-made product. This transfer of industries from the home and shop to the factory greatly lowered the cost of labor and cheapened production. The price of ready-made clothing and shoes was thus brought so low as to come within the reach of even the very poor.

The sewing machine.

457. Iron and Steel.—Another industry which has had a remarkable growth is that of iron and steel. Like the

---

[1] Textiles include clothing and fabrics of every description for household and other uses; textile materials include cotton, wool, flax, silk, and coarser fibres.

making of cloth, it had an early beginning but did not increase much during the colonial period. Common farm
implements, tools, and household utensils were made in
most of the colonies, but the finer grades of cutlery and
edged tools were brought from England.

It was not until the beginning of the last century that
the iron and coal fields of western Pennsylvania began to
be worked, and Pittsburg, now the most important centre of the iron industry, had its first foundry
The use of
anthracite coal.   (1803). During the years that followed, fur-
naces, forges, iron mills, and steel works sprang up in all
quarters. But the impulse which revolutionized the mak-

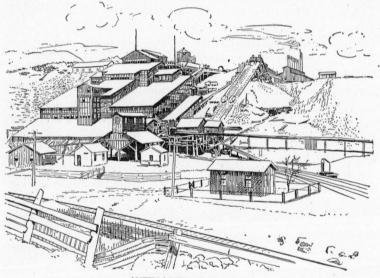

ANTHRACITE COAL MINE.

ing of iron was brought about by the use of anthracite
(hard) coal instead of charcoal in the process of smelting
(1840). It cheapened production and increased the output.

The Bessemer process (1859) wrought a second revolution. This invention, with the use of bituminous (soft)
coal instead of anthracite, gave a wonderful stimulus to the

iron industry. By greatly cheapening the manufacture of steel rails it also played a large part in the rapid extension of the railroad system. For steel rails, being *Steel rails cheapen transportation.* stronger than iron, made possible the use of larger locomotives and heavier trains, and permitted a much higher rate of speed. They are, therefore, the foundation of cheap and rapid transportation, which is a great factor in our industrial life.

Steel is also used extensively in the structure of bridges, of large buildings, and of war-vessels, as well as in the inventions and conveniences of every-day life. Our natural products of iron and coal have been the greatest forces in the development of manufacturing in this country.

458. Railroad Rate Regulation.—The astonishing growth of manufactures and business in this country since the outbreak of the Civil War would have been impossible without the aid of the railroad. After the close *Railroad rates not fair to all shippers.* of that war railroad lines were rapidly extended so as to connect the mining and farming regions with cities and factories. In the course of time most of the important railroads in the country were combined into a few systems, and the lines of each system passed through several States. The great railroad companies owning these systems, in their eagerness to secure business, made certain rates which were not fair to all shippers. Some shippers and places were secretly charged less than the regular freight rates. The business companies who enjoyed the advantage of the lower rates were thus enabled, in some instances, to drive rival companies out of business.

To stop this injustice, Congress passed the interstate commerce act (1887). Its purpose was to regulate trade between the States.[1] This law declares that freight and passenger rates on railroads running from one *The interstate commerce act.* State into another shall be just and reasonable, and shall be uniform, for like service, for all. The Inter-

---

[1] Congress can regulate trade *between* the States. But only the State Legislature can regulate trade carried on entirely *within* any State.

state Commerce Commission (first consisting of five members and later of seven) was appointed to see that the law was carried out.

As the powers of the Interstate Commerce Commission under this law were not large enough, another rate law was passed (1906). It forbids the granting of free passes and
The rate laws of 1906 and of 1910. declares that if any shipper complains of a rate as unjust and unreasonable the Interstate Commerce Commission shall have the power to fix a new rate. Still another law was passed (1910), which created a commerce court to enforce the orders of the Interstate Commerce Commission. It gives the commission power to suspend (for as long as ten months if necessary) a new rate, or any rate, in order to find out by investigation whether or not such rate is just and reasonable.[1]

459. The Federal Trade Commission (1914).—As the Interstate Commerce Commission was given power to oversee and regulate railroads and other transportation interests and the Federal Reserve Board was given large powers in the field of currency and banking, in like manner, for the best business interests of the whole country, a need was felt for another powerful Federal board to regulate and control corporations or trusts holding property in several States.

Accordingly, the Federal Trade Commission bill was passed by Congress (1914). It authorized the appoint-
Threefold powers of the Federal Trade Commission. ment of the Federal Trade Commission with threefold powers as follows: (1) to investigate interstate corporations in order to find out whether they were breaking the laws; (2) to forbid and prevent unfair methods of competition; and (3) to aid the Attorney-General and the United States courts in enforcing the anti-trust laws.

460. Trusts and the Regulation of Trusts.—The railroad, improved machinery, and the opening up of the

---

[1] The rate law of 1910 applies not only to railroads but to telegraph, telephone and cable companies, and also to express companies and sleeping-car companies.

West caused manufacturing to increase with wonderful
rapidity. Business was extended and competition became
intense. As an outcome, rival companies decided that
union was better than strife, and large companies or corporations were organized. A corporation formed by the
union of several companies was called a trust.[1]

GOODS AWAITING EXPORTATION.

The main purposes of the trust were, first, to cheapen
the cost of production, and, second, to lessen and, so far
as possible, to prevent competition. But the people felt
that the prices of trust-made goods, which   The anti-
often included the necessaries of life, were too   trust law.
high. As the trust controlled the market in its given line

[1] Examples of trusts are The Standard Oil Company, The United States Steel
Company, The Sugar Trust, etc. The Standard Oil Company controls the output
of petroleum, in the production and export of which the United States leads the
world. The first oil-well was bored in Pennsylvania in 1859. Since then oil has
been produced in large quantities in Pennsylvania, Ohio, Indiana, Texas, and
in other States.

of goods, it could fix the prices on the raw materials it bought and on the finished goods it sold. Accordingly, the Sherman anti-trust law was passed (1890). This declares, in effect, that all combinations and agreements made for the purpose of controlling the output and sale of goods and of fixing prices are unlawful and are liable to punishment by fine or imprisonment.

461. The Growth of Our Foreign Trade.—Quite apart from attempted regulation of railroads and trusts, the volume of our trade has steadily increased. Our ag-

The United States leads the world in exports.

ricultural and manufactured products have more than kept pace with the needs of our growing population, and the surplus has found a ready market among the nations of the world. The foreign trade of the United States is a fair measure of its economic progress. During our first century as a nation we were largely agricultural and had to depend on foreign markets for many of our manufactured goods. By the close of that century the products of our factories more than equalled in value the products of our farms, and to-day we are the leading manufacturing nation in the world. Moreover, during the period of development, our exports did not pay for our imports. But since 1876 our exports have exceeded our imports, and the United States has advanced to the position of the first exporting nation in the world.[1]

Along with the growth of exports has been an increase of imports, consisting mainly of raw materials used in manufactures, and of luxuries, that is, of those things which

The immense volume of our expanding commerce.

could not be produced at home. The value of our total exports for 1914 was over $2,364,000,000; of our total imports, nearly $1,894,000,000, making an excess of exports of over $470,000,000. This volume of foreign trade is a measure not only of the expanding commerce but of the growing

---

[1] Only three times during that period—in 1888, 1889, and 1893—did our imports exceed our exports.

TRANSPORTATION IN A LARGE CITY, SHOWING ELEVATED ROAD, SURFACE LINE, AND SUBWAY.

wealth of the nation. And when we learn that our domestic commerce is many times as large as our foreign we get a faint idea of the magnitude of the country and of its business operations.

462. Electricity in Modern Life.—As we have seen, steam has come to be of immense service to the world by its use as a motive power in driving machinery. But no less remarkable, perhaps, is the work which electricity has been made to do in many ways The telegraph, the telephone, the marine cable, and wireless telegraphy have already been discussed as useful agents

The many uses of electricity.

in the transmission of thought. About 1880, by the invention of the arc and the incandescent lights, electricity was applied to the lighting of streets and of houses. Soon after, it came into use as a motive power. Trolley-cars, electric automobiles, electric engines, and electric motors for fixed machinery followed.

But two of the most striking uses of electricity are the transmitting of power from falling water to distant cities[1] and the producing of the X-ray, which enables physicians to photograph the bones and to observe the action of the heart and other organs in the living body. By 1900 the uses of electricity had multiplied twentyfold, and yet to-day they are believed to be in their infancy.

463. Inventions as Aids to Human Progress.—From all that has been said about the uses of electricity and steam and the various forms of invention, we see clearly how science has aided man in bringing the forces of nature under his control. Improved machinery as well as improved methods of travel, transportation, and communication have so cheapened the cost of food, clothing, and other things needed in every-day life that the day laborer can now have comforts and conveniences which even the rich did not enjoy fifty years ago.

Moreover, as inventive genius is constantly making new discoveries, we may confidently look forward to changes as wonderful as any that have yet been made. Two of the most recent inventions are the automobile and the flying machine. Before the close of 1910 the automobile had come into extensive use not only as a means of pleasure and recreation, but also for practical purposes in the city and on the farm. In the

The automobile and the flying machine.

---

[1] Important examples of companies engaged in such transmission of power are the Central Colorado Power Company, the power companies of Niagara Falls, and the Southern Power Company. The first transmits power from Shoshone Falls to Denver, a distance of 180 miles; one of the second group, from Niagara Falls to Syracuse, a distance of about 150 miles; and the third to various points, some of which are 150 miles from the place where the power is generated. In all these cases the transmitted power may be used for driving fixed machinery, for propelling trolley-cars, and for lighting purposes.

same year successful experiments with the flying machine, invented by the Wright brothers, led people to believe that the days of aerial navigation might be near at hand.

A CROWDED STREET IN A TENEMENT DISTRICT.
Copyright, 1902, by Underwood & Underwood, New York.

464. City Populations and Municipal Reform. — Our huge industries must be carried on by large bodies of workmen. The result has been an amazing growth of modern cities; and this massing of people in great centres has brought new problems to the front.

When the Constitution went into effect in 1789 only about three per cent. of the people of the United States lived in cities; now not far from forty per cent. are in cities of 4,000 inhabitants and upward. The immense growth of manufactures and commerce has largely caused this change. The massing of large numbers of people in commercial and manufacturing centres furnishes a difficult political problem. Many of the most ignorant foreign-born voters are found in such centres, and, being without intelligent ideas about our government, they can the more readily be induced to sell their votes. As the strength of republican institutions depends upon the morality and intelligence of the people, the practice of buying and selling votes presents a grave danger. But a wide-spread movement in the interests of better city government is making itself felt more and more every year.

465. Education.—All our material advantages would be worth little without a moral and intelligent people to make proper use of them. This the United States understands and has therefore been foremost among the nations **Liberal** of the world in educating its citizens. Every **provision made** State in the Union has its system of public **for public** **schools.** schools, some even providing State universities. As a natural result of such systems the progress of education in the United States has been remarkable.

The nation has also taken much interest in higher education, and the people have reason for pride in the stand-**Interest** ing of their **in higher** universi-**education.** ties. The value of the property owned by colleges and universities in the United States, including grounds, buildings, and productive farms, amounts to hundreds of millions of dollars. Outside the colleges and universities

NEW STEEL TOWER BRIDGE ACROSS THE EAST RIVER, NEW YORK.
Copyright, 1904, by Underwood & Underwood, New York.

there are many professional and scientific schools.

Many special institutions of learning have also been established by gifts and bequests of rich men and women, who have given of their abundance not only for the devel-**Education of** opment of good and strong minds, but also **the weak and** for the training and support of the weak and **helpless.** helpless classes of society, such as the blind, the deaf, the mentally defective. There are in the United States many institutions for those classes that need special help. The nation has made a supreme effort to educate the masses and to improve the condition of the weak and suffering.

In recent years, under the direction of the United States Bureau of Agriculture,[1] much attention has been given to training for life on the farm. There are now more than sixty agricultural colleges established in various parts of the country, **Special training for the farm.** and model farms and experiment stations are to be found in every State in the Union. By means of these opportunities the farmer is learning to make the soil yield much larger returns than was possible before science came to his aid. The advance in scientific farming is one of the most hopeful movements of our time.

Another promising movement is that in favor of vocational and trade schools, that is, schools which give special training for modern industry. The belief is growing that our public schools not only should furnish a general training for life **Training for modern industry.** but also should help to develop that mechanical power and skill and that industrial knowledge which are so much needed in our complex factory system.

466. Woman Suffrage.—Quite as noteworthy is the advance in the higher education of women in the past twenty-five or thirty years. Women now have scholastic advantages formerly limited to men, and have taken their place in many fields of **Advance in the education of women.** activity once exclusively occupied by men. This has come about, however, not only because of a broader general training, but partly on account of the transfer of many household duties to the mill and factory. As we know, many household supplies **Their larger outlook upon life.** which women made by hand in the home a hundred years ago are now made by the use of power machines within factory walls. Women are also doing

---

[1] In 1862 Congress authorized the establishment of the Bureau of Agriculture and also made provisions for the support of agricultural colleges from proceeds of the sales of public lands.

more than they ever did before in the many forms of public service which make for a finer public spirit and a better civic life.

By reason of these and other facts, many believe that women should have the same voting privileges as men. Wyoming was the first State to vote full suffrage to women. There are now eleven States in which women have in all respects equal voting power with men.

467. Newspapers and Periodicals.—The high average of intelligence in the United States has created a great demand for newspapers and magazines. They have be-

RALPH WALDO EMERSON.   JOHN GREENLEAF WHITTIER.

come an immense educational force, giving the people a keener, more intelligent interest in public affairs. But it is well to remember that without the aid of recent inventions the modern daily newspaper would not be possible. The telegraph, the telephone, and the marine cable all aid in gathering the news, while the linotype and the complex printing-press supply the lightning processes of printing. The linotype enables the printer very rapidly to put the news into type by striking the keys of a keyboard as in operat-

The linotype and the complex printing-press.

ing a typewriter. The most advanced printing-press will print, fold, and count 300,000 eight-page papers in an hour, or more than eighty every second.

468. Literature.—For a long time after the settlement of the English colonies the people were too busy with the work of clearing the land and building suitable homes to produce any literature. Washington Irving, born the same

THE LOUISIANA PURCHASE EXPOSITION, ST. LOUIS, 1904. ONE OF THE BRIDGES AND LAGOONS, WITH THE PALACE OF EDUCATION.
Copyright, 1904, by Louisiana Purchase Exposition Co.

year that the Revolution was brought to a close, first attracted public attention by his *Knickerbocker History of New York*. He has rightly been called the "Father of American Literature." J. Fenimore Cooper, his contemporary, was the first American novelist. He wrote the first sea story that attracted the attention of the world, and was author of the famous *Leatherstocking Tales*, describing the life of the American

Irving, Cooper, and Bryant.

Indian.　These stories were written with such freshness and originality that they were eagerly read in many countries.　Our first poet to be recognized in England, William Cullen Bryant, belonged to the same period.　He came into fame by his well-known poem, *Thanatopsis*, written when he was nineteen.

Among the familiar names of later American literature are the following: poets, Henry Wadsworth Longfellow,

THE CAPITOL, WASHINGTON, D. C.

John Greenleaf Whittier, Oliver Wendell Holmes, Edgar

Other familiar names in American literature. Allan Poe, Ralph Waldo Emerson, and James Russell Lowell; essayists, Emerson and Lowell; novelists, Nathaniel Hawthorne, W. D. Howells, Henry James, Harriet Beecher Stowe; historians, George Bancroft, John Lothrop Motley, William H. Prescott, and Francis Parkman.　Much excellent work has been done by living writers, especially in the department of American history, and this work is coming from all parts of the country.

469. Problems of the Hour.—The great educational influences coming from the public schools, from higher institutions of learning, from the newspapers and periodicals, and from the reading and study of good literature are preparing the people rightly to solve the problems of the hour. These problems include the race problem in the South, temperance reform, immigration, the tariff, trust regulation, railroad regulation, conservation of our natural resources, vocational education, the form of government of our cities, the money question, civil service reform, woman suffrage, and the strife between labor and capital. The right solution of these difficult problems demands intelligence, patience, and conscientious effort. We must take time to study them, and we must try to look at them from more than one point of view. If we approach them with a broad and generous spirit, with an earnest desire to find out the truth, we shall be more likely to understand them and to take the proper steps to a satisfactory solution.

470. Relation of the Individual Citizen to the State.—But no matter what problems present themselves for solution, the character of the State is determined by the character of its citizens. We should never forget that a vast territory like ours, with all its wealth, is not necessarily great. The greatness of a country is not measured by what it has in land, productions, trades, and educational institutions, but by what its people are. If they are intelligent and patriotic, ready at all times to do their duty in the interest of the public good, their future is assured.

You, my young reader, owe much to your country for what it has done for you. It has been said America means that America means opportunity. It does. opportunity. It means opportunity to get wealth, power, influence, and honor. It means opportunity to make the most of your powers of body and mind. But, more than all else, it means opportunity to make the institutions of your country better by honest, faithful service, and sincere efforts to know the truth.

Charles Sumner said of our national flag: "The stripes of alternate red and white proclaim the original union of thirteen States to maintain the Declaration of Independ-

Our national flag. ence. Its stars, white on a field of blue, proclaim the union of States constituting our national constellation, which receives a new star with every new State. These two signify union, past and present. The very colors have a language which was officially recognized by our fathers. White is for purity, red for valor, blue for justice."

"I pledge allegiance to my flag and the republic for which it stands, one nation, indivisible, with liberty and justice for all."

TO THE PUPIL

1. Name the natural advantages of the U. S.

2. What is meant by the industrial revolution? Name two inventions that had a large influence on the making of textiles. How did the sewing machine cheapen the cost of clothing?

3. What effect did the use of hard and soft coal have upon the production of iron and steel? How did steel rails cheapen transportation?

4. What was the purpose of the Interstate Commerce Act? What powers were given to the Interstate Commerce Commission by the various rate laws? Why was the Anti-Trust Law passed?

5. Tell what you can of the immense increase of our foreign trade.

6. What is meant by the transmission of power by the use of electricity? Give examples of such transmission.

7. What is meant by municipal reform, and why is it needed?

8. What liberal provision has been made for public schools in this country? What advance has been made in education in recent years?

9. Name four inventions which make the modern daily newspaper possible.

10. What are some of the familiar names in American literature? Name some of the problems of the hour.

11. What is the relation of the individual citizen to the state?

12. Before laying aside the study of this history learn the symbolism, as given by Charles Sumner, of the colors of the " Stars and Stripes," and memorize the " pledge."

CHRONOLOGY

1867. *March* 1, NEBRASKA ADMITTED TO THE UNION.

1868. *July* 28, FOURTEENTH AMENDMENT ADOPTED.

1869. *March* 4, ULYSSES S. GRANT INAUGURATED PRESIDENT.
May 10, FIRST PACIFIC RAILROAD COMPLETED.

1870. *March* 30, FIFTEENTH AMENDMENT RATIFIED.
THE NINTH CENSUS, SHOWING A POPULATION OF 38,558,371.

1871. *January*, ALL STATES AGAIN REPRESENTED IN CONGRESS.

1873. *February*, LAW PASSED DEMONETIZING SILVER.
March 4, ULYSSES S. GRANT INAUGURATED PRESIDENT.
FINANCIAL PANIC.

1876. CENTENNIAL EXPOSITION AT PHILADELPHIA.
FIRST TELEPHONE PATENTED.
August 1, COLORADO ADMITTED TO THE UNION.

1877. *March* 4, RUTHERFORD B. HAYES INAUGURATED PRESIDENT.
July, GREAT RAILROAD STRIKE IN PITTSBURG.

1878. *February*, BLAND-ALLISON SILVER BILL PASSED.
ELECTRIC LIGHT INVENTED.

1879. *January* 1, RESUMPTION OF SPECIE PAYMENTS.

1880. THE TENTH CENSUS, SHOWING A POPULATION OF 50,155,783.

1881. *March* 4, JAMES A. GARFIELD INAUGURATED PRESIDENT.
September 22, CHESTER A. ARTHUR FORMALLY INAUGURATED.

1883. LETTER POSTAGE REDUCED TO TWO CENTS.

1884. *December*, NEW ORLEANS EXPOSITION OPENED.

1885. *March* 4, GROVER CLEVELAND INAUGURATED PRESIDENT.

1887. THE INTERSTATE COMMERCE ACT.

1889. *March* 4, BENJAMIN HARRISON INAUGURATED PRESIDENT.
April 22, OKLAHOMA OPENED TO SETTLERS.
PAN-AMERICAN CONGRESS MET IN WASHINGTON.
November 2, NORTH DAKOTA ADMITTED TO THE UNION.
November 2, SOUTH DAKOTA ADMITTED TO THE UNION.
November 8, MONTANA ADMITTED TO THE UNION.
November 11, WASHINGTON ADMITTED TO THE UNION.

1890. DEPENDENT PENSIONS ACT BECAME A LAW.
July 3, IDAHO ADMITTED TO THE UNION.
July 10, WYOMING ADMITTED TO THE UNION.
MCKINLEY TARIFF BILL BECAME A LAW.
SHERMAN SILVER PURCHASE LAW PASSED.
THE ELEVENTH CENSUS, SHOWING A POPULATION OF 62,622,250.
SHERMAN ANTI-TRUST LAW.

1893. *January* 14, REVOLUTION IN HAWAII.
March 4, GROVER CLEVELAND INAUGURATED PRESIDENT.
May 1, COLUMBIAN WORLD'S FAIR OPENED AT CHICAGO.

1894. *June* 4, PULLMAN BOYCOTT.
  August 27, THE WILSON BILL BECAME A LAW.
1895. *December* 17, PRESIDENT CLEVELAND'S VENEZUELA MESSAGE.
1897. *March* 4, WILLIAM MCKINLEY INAUGURATED PRESIDENT.
  July 24, DINGLEY TARIFF BILL BECAME A LAW.
1898. *April* 25, CONGRESS DECLARES WAR TO EXIST WITH SPAIN.
  May 1, DEWEY'S VICTORY AT MANILA.
  July 1, BATTLE OF SANTIAGO.
  July 3, CERVERA'S FLEET DESTROYED.
1899. *February* 6, TREATY OF PEACE WITH SPAIN RATIFIED.
1900. THE TWELFTH CENSUS, SHOWING A POPULATION OF 75,568,686.
1901. *March* 4, WILLIAM MCKINLEY INAUGURATED PRESIDENT.
  July 1, CIVIL GOVERNMENT ESTABLISHED IN THE PHILIPPINE ISLANDS.
  September 14, THEODORE ROOSEVELT INAUGURATED PRESIDENT.
  HAY–PAUNCEFOTE TREATY SIGNED.
1902. *May* 20, NEW CUBAN GOVERNMENT FORMALLY INAUGURATED.
  THE ISTHMIAN CANAL ACT.
1903. *January* 18, FIRST WIRELESS MESSAGE SENT ACROSS THE ATLANTIC.
  July 4, FIRST MESSAGE SENT BY THE PACIFIC CABLE.
  November 3, THE REVOLUTION IN PANAMA.
  November 18, THE CANAL TREATY WITH PANAMA SIGNED.
1907. THE SECOND PEACE CONFERENCE HELD AT THE HAGUE.
  November 16, OKLAHOMA ADMITTED TO THE UNION.
1908. *May*, MEETING AT WASHINGTON ON THE CONSERVATION OF OUR NATURAL
    RESOURCES.
1909. *March* 4, WILLIAM H. TAFT INAUGURATED PRESIDENT.
  August 5, PAYNE–ALDRICH TARIFF BILL BECOMES A LAW.
1910. THE THIRTEENTH CENSUS, SHOWING A POPULATION OF 91,972,266.
1912. *January* 6, NEW MEXICO ADMITTED TO THE UNION.
  February 14, ARIZONA ADMITTED TO THE UNION.
1913. *February* 25, SIXTEENTH AMENDMENT DECLARED IN FORCE.
  March 4, WOODROW WILSON INAUGURATED PRESIDENT.
  May 31, SEVENTEENTH AMENDMENT DECLARED IN FORCE.
1914. *August* 15, THE OPENING OF THE PANAMA CANAL.

TOPICAL REVIEWS IN AMERICAN HISTORY

(The figures in parentheses refer to pages in the book)

I. DISCOVERERS AND EXPLORERS.
1. European trade with Asia in the fifteenth century (1).
2. Portugal leads in discovering an Eastern route (2).
3. Columbus and his discoveries (3–6).
4. Americus Vespucius and the naming of America (8).
5. Magellan proves America to be a continent (9).
6. Spanish discoverers and explorers (De Leon, Narvaez, De Soto, and Balboa) (13, 14, 18, 19).
7. Voyages and discoveries of the English (Cabot, Drake, Raleigh, and Gosnold) (6, 21, 23, 26).
8. Henry Hudson discovers the Hudson River (63).
9. Cartier discovers the St. Lawrence (87).
10. Champlain explores Lake Champlain (88).
11. Father Marquette and La Salle explore the Mississippi (90).

II. THE SPANISH IN AMERICA.
1. Precious metals the main object of the Spaniards (13).
2. The Spaniards drive the Huguenots out of Florida (15, 16).
3. Advantages of Spain in the New World (16).
4. Reasons for Spanish failure (17).
5. Relations between Spain and England (20, 21).
6. France cedes to Spain all territory between the Mississippi and the Rocky Mountains (102).
7. France regains Louisiana from Spain (219).
8. The purchase of Florida from Spain (239).
9. Spain and the Monroe Doctrine (240).
10. The Spanish-American War (410–417).
11. Spain gives up Cuba and Porto Rico (417, 418).

III. THE FRENCH IN NORTH AMERICA.
1. The Spaniards drive the Huguenots from Florida (15).
2. The work of Champlain (87–89).
3. The French in the Mississippi Valley (89–92).
4. England and France struggle for control in America (93).
5. The last French war and its results (97–103).
6. The French lose control of territory in North America (103).

7. Influence of the French Revolution upon American affairs (207).
8. Citizen Genet defies Washington (208).
9. The " X. Y. Z. Papers " and serious trouble with France (210).
10. France regains Louisiana from Spain and sells it to the United States (219, 220).
11. The attempt of Napoleon III to establish an empire in Mexico (344, 345).

IV. **STRUGGLE FOR CONTROL IN WHAT IS NOW THE UNITED STATES.**
1. Advantages of Spain in the New World (17).
2. Why Spanish colonization failed in North America (17).
3. England's need of America (25).
4. Success of English colonization in America (28–74).
5. The Dutch in New Netherland (63–66).
6. New Netherland becomes New York; why the Dutch failed in colonizing America (67, 68).
7. The work of Champlain (87–89).
8. The French in the Mississippi Valley (89–92).
9. The French lose control of territory in North America (103).
10. The English colonies declare their independence of England (148–150).
11. The Revolution puts an end to English rule in the thirteen English colonies (183).
12. France cedes to Spain all territory between the Mississippi and the Rocky Mountains (102).
13. France regains Louisiana from Spain (219).
14. The purchase of Florida from Spain (239).
15. The attempt of Napoleon III to establish an empire in Mexico (344, 345).

V. **ENGLAND AND THE ENGLISH COLONIES.**
1. Sir Walter Raleigh's attempt to colonize America (23–25).
2. The London and Plymouth Companies (28).
3. Virginia.
   a. John Smith and the settlement of Jamestown (29–31).
   b. Dale's Great Reform (32).
   c. The second great reform (33).
   d. The great need of labor; the labor supply (34).
   e. Tobacco establishes rural life (35).
   f. Berkeley and the people; Bacon's Rebellion (36, 37).
4. Maryland.
   a. Lord Baltimore and the Catholics settle Maryland (37).
   b. Lord Baltimore's proprietary rights (38).
   c. Disputes about boundaries and religion (39).
   d. Prosperity of the people (39).

5. **North and South Carolina.**
    a. Charles II and the grant of land (41).
    b. The form of government (41).
    c. Carolina divided into North and South Carolina (41).
    d. The population (41).
6. **Georgia.**
    a. Why Oglethorpe wished to plant a colony (41).
    b. The settlement of Georgia (41).
    c. Georgia becomes a royal colony (41).
7. **England under the Stuarts** (42).
8. **Massachusetts.**
    a. The Pilgrims migrate to America (44).
    b. Voyage and first winter (45).
    c. The covenant, democracy, and the church (46).
    d. Relations with the Indians (46).
    e. The Puritans and the Massachusetts Bay Colony (47).
    f. The New England township (48).
    g. Church and State (49).
9. **Connecticut.**
    a. Massachusetts gets control of the Connecticut Valley (50).
    b. Massachusetts settles the Connecticut Valley (51).
    c. Thomas Hooker and democracy (51).
    d. The Connecticut constitution (52).
10. **Rhode Island.**
    Religious intolerance in Massachusetts leads to the settlement of Rhode Island (54).
11. **The New England confederacy** (55).
12. **The Quakers in New England** (56).
13. **Trouble with England; loss of the Massachusetts charter** (58).
14. **Andros the Stuart governor in New England** (59).
15. **Industries and trade in New England** (61).
16. **New York.**
    a. Henry Hudson seeks the Northwest Passage (63).
    b. Dutch claims in New Netherland (64).
    c. The patroons (64).
    d. The Dutch win the friendship of the Iroquois Indians and thus secure an extensive territory (65).
    e. New Netherland under Dutch governors (66).
    f. New Netherland becomes New York (67).
    g. New York under English governors (68).
17. **Pennsylvania.**
    a. The Quakers in New England (69).
    b. William Penn and the Quakers settle Pennsylvania (70).
    c. The Quakers live in peace with the Indians (71).
    d. Penn's liberal government (71).
    e. The growth of Pennsylvania (72).

18. **New Jersey.**
    a. The first permanent English settlement (73).
    b. "The Jerseys" and New Jersey (73).
    c. New Jersey becomes a royal province (74).

19. **Delaware.**
    a. The Swedes plant settlements along the Delaware River (74).
    b. The Dutch make New Sweden a part of New Netherland (74).
    c. Delaware becomes a part of Pennsylvania (74).
    d. The people of Delaware allowed a separate assembly (74).

VI. THE INDIANS.

1. Division into families of the Indians east of the Mississippi (75).
2. Character; occupations; wampum; religion (77–79).
3. The clan and the tribe; communal living (80).
4. The Mound Builders (81, 82).
5. Number of Indians; their influence upon the whites (82, 83).
6. Relation of the Pilgrims with the Indians (46).
7. Early Indian wars (84–86).
8. The Iroquois Indians (88, 89).
9. The Quakers and the Indians (71).
10. The conspiracy of Pontiac (103).
11. Burgoyne's Indian allies (158).
12. Tecumseh's conspiracy (228).
13. War with the Creek Indians (235).
14. The Seminole Indians in Florida (239).
15. Grant's Indian peace policy and the reservation system (384–386).

VII. ENGLAND AND THE UNITED STATES.

1. Jay's fruitless treaty with England (208).
2. England claims the right to search American vessels and impress American seamen (225).
3. England and France greatly injure American commerce (226).
4. The War of 1812 (228–238).
5. The Oregon boundary dispute settled by treaty (269–271).
6. The Trent affair (309).
7. England and King Cotton (311).
8. England and the Confederate navy; the "Alabama Claims" settled by arbitration (343).
9. The Bering Sea trouble settled by arbitration (400).
10. The Anglo-Venezuelan difficulty and the Monroe Doctrine (405).
11. The Hay-Pauncefote treaty with England (423).
12. The Panama tolls and the Hay-Pauncefote treaty (443).
13. Great Britain becomes Greater Britain (432).

VIII. STEPS LEADING TO THE CONSTITUTION.
1. The New England Confederation (55).
2. Franklin's Plan of Union (121).
3. The Stamp Act Congress (132).
4. Committees of Correspondence (138).
5. The first meeting of the Continental Congress (145).
6. The second meeting of the Continental Congress (145).
7. The Declaration of Independence (148).
8. The adoption of the Articles of Confederation (188).
9. The Annapolis Convention (190).
10. The Constitutional Convention (190).

IX. THE CONSTITUTION (The topical outline may be found on page 485).

X. WESTWARD GROWTH.
1. Importance of the struggle between the backwoodsmen and the Indians (168–170, 183).
2. Settlement of the Mississippi Valley (213–218).
3. The purchase of Louisiana (220).
4. Lewis and Clark's expedition (221).
5. The use of the steamboat on Western waters (223).
6. The National Road (241).
7. The Erie Canal (245).
8. The railroad and the rapid growth of the West (258, 259).
9. Speculation in Western lands (260).
10. Our claims to Oregon (269).
11. The annexation of Texas (274).
12. The Mexican cession (277).
13. California (279–283).
14. Influence of the West in favor of nationalism (293–294).
15. Influence of the public lands on our national growth (373).
16. Westward expansion (374).
17. The Mormons in Utah (376).
18. The Pacific railroads (378).
19. The arid region and the problem of irrigation (380).
20. Forest reservations (381).
21. Oklahoma made a State (397).
22. Arizona and New Mexico admitted into the Union (438).

XI. TERRITORIAL EXPANSION.
1. The United States at the close of the Revolution (183).
2. The purchase of Louisiana (220).
3. The purchase of Florida (239).
4. The annexation of Texas (274).
5. Settlement of conflicting claims to the Oregon country (269–273).

6. The Mexican cession (277).
7. The Gadsden Purchase (278).
8. The purchase of Alaska (384).
9. Hawaii annexed to the United States (401).
10. The Spanish cessions of 1898 (417).

XII. DEVELOPMENT OF MEANS OF TRANSPORTATION AND COMMUNICATION.
1. Modes of travel and communication in colonial days (117).
2. The flatboat (217).
3. The trail and the pack-horse (217).
4. Steamboat navigation (222, 223).
5. The National Road (241).
6. The Erie Canal (245).
7. The railroad (257, 258).
8. Ocean steamships (264).
9. The telegraph (267).
10. The Atlantic cable (382).
11. The telephone (389).
12. The Panama Canal (423).
13. The Pacific cable (424).
14. Wireless telegraphy (424).
15. Electricity in modern life (459).
16. The automobile; the flying machine (460).

XIII. SOME USEFUL INVENTIONS.
1. The cotton-gin (204).
2. Friction matches (264).
3. The reaping machine (264, 375).
4. The combined reaper and thresher (375).
5. The steam-driven gang-plow (376).
6. The railroad (257).
7. The telegraph (267).
8. The sewing machine, the spinning machine, and the power loom (453).
9. The Bessemer process of making steel (454).
10. The automobile and the flying machine (460).

XIV. SLAVERY.
1. Slavery in the colonies (34, 35, 111, 112).
2. Slavery in the Constitution—the Three-fifths Compromise, the importation of slaves, and fugitive slaves (190, 481, 484; Amendments, Articles XIII, 491; XIV, 492).
3. The cotton-gin and slavery (204).
4. The Missouri Compromise (244).
5. Slavery and the tariff (253).
6. The Abolitionists (271–273).

7. Texas and the Mexican War (274–277).
8. The Wilmot Proviso (278).
9. The Compromise of 1850 (281–283).
10. The Fugitive Slave Law (284).
11. The Underground Railroad (285).
12. The Kansas-Nebraska Bill (287–289).
13. The Dred Scott Decision (294).
14. John Brown's raid (296).
15. Abraham Lincoln and slavery (299).
16. The Emancipation Proclamation (330).
17. The Thirteenth, the Fourteenth, and the Fifteenth Amendments (351, 359, 360).

XV. STATE RIGHTS, NULLIFICATION, AND SECESSION.
1. The Virginia and Kentucky Resolutions (211).
2. Calhoun and nullification (253).
3. Webster and the Union (254).
4. Jackson's feeling toward nullification (255).
5. South Carolina and State rights (255).
6. The State first in the South (300).
7. The Union first in the North (301).
8. State rights, nullification, and secession swept away by the Civil War (352).

XVI. RECONSTRUCTION AND THE NEW SOUTH.
1. President Johnson's plan of restoring the seceded States (357).
2. The freedmen and Southern legislation (358).
3. The Congressional plan of reconstruction (358).
4. The work of reconstruction complete (359).
5. President Hayes withdraws the troops from the South (365).
6. The New South (367).
7. The Atlanta Exposition (369).
8. The freedmen and education (370).

XVII. THE TARIFF.
1. A tariff laid on foreign trade (203).
2. A tariff for revenue with incidental protection (252).
3. A protective tariff (252).
4. South Carolina objects to a high protective tariff (252).
5. New England manufacturers and the protective tariff (254).
6. The tariff question (404, 405).
7. The "Dingley Tariff" (408, 418, 423).
8. The Payne-Aldrich Tariff (435).
9. Tariff revision in 1913 (442).

XVIII. CURRENCY AND BANKING.
1. Jackson and the United States Bank (256, 257).
2. Pet Banks (257).
3. Wild-Cat Banking (260).
4. The Specie Circular (261).
5. The Independent Treasury (263).
6. Greenbacks during the Civil War (391).
7. The Resumption of Specie Payment (390).
8. Silver Legislation (403).
9. Free Silver and the Tariff (407).

XIX. POLITICAL PARTIES.
1. The Federalists and the Anti-Federalists (191, 209).
2. The Democrats-Republicans (209, 211, 213, 230).
3. The Federalist Party and the War of 1812 (230, 236, 237).
4. The Democrats and the National Republican Party (248).
5. William Lloyd Garrison and the Abolitionists (271–273).
6. The Free Soil Party and the Anti-Nebraska Men (278).
7. The Whig Party (290).
8. The Republican Party (290, 299, 358, 360, 389, 404, 407, 425, 435, 439).
9. The Democratic Party (299, 365, 389, 404, 407, 425, 439).

XX. WARS (The topics bearing upon wars may be found in a convenient form in the " Topical Outline of American History," which is included in the book).
1. Indian wars (84, 85, 103, 228).
2. The first three Intercolonial wars (94).
3. The last French war (94–103).
4. The Revolution (126–183).
5. The War of 1812 (229–238).
6. The Mexican War (275–277).
7. The Civil War (305–352).
8. The Spanish-American War (411–417).

XXI. TREATIES.
1. Treaty of peace between France and England in 1763 (103).
2. Treaty of alliance with France in 1778 (164).
3. Treaty of peace with England in 1783 (183).
4. Jay's treaty with England in 1795 (208).
5. Treaty of peace with Tripoli in 1805 (222).
6. Treaty of peace with England in 1814 (238).
7. Oregon boundary dispute settled by treaty in 1846 (271).
8. The treaty of peace with Mexico in 1848 (277).
9. The treaty of peace with Spain in 1899 (417).
10. The Hay-Pauncefote treaty in 1901 (423).

XXII.   THE MONROE DOCTRINE.
1. The principal features of the Monroe Doctrine (240, 241).
2. Maximilian in Mexico (345).
3. The Anglo-Venezuelan difficulty and the Monroe Doctrine (405, 406).
4. The United States and the trouble in Mexico (444).

XXIII.   THE UNITED STATES AND EUROPE SINCE 1860.
1. The Trent affair (309).
2. England resents the capture of Mason and Slidell (309).
3. England and King Cotton; the blockade (311).
4. The battle of Gettysburg and recognition of the independence of the South by England and France (326).
5. The sympathy of English working-men with the South (343).
6. England and the Confederate navy; settlement of the "Alabama Claims" (343).
7. Napoleon III and the Confederate navy (344).
8. Trouble with Italy (398).
9. The Bering Sea trouble settled by arbitration (400).
10. The Anglo-Venezuelan difficulty and the Monroe Doctrine (405).
11. The Spanish-American War (411–417).
12. China and the " Open Door " (420).
13. The Hay-Pauncefote treaty (423).
14. President Roosevelt as peacemaker (425).
15. The Second Peace Conference (427).
16. The United States and the Spanish-American War (417, 429).
17. The United States a world-power (429).
18. The growth of foreign trade (458).

XXIV.   THE PRESIDENTS (For this outline see Appendix D).

XXV.   PRESENT-DAY PROBLEMS.
1. Struggle for popular control of public affairs (439).
2. The tariff (203, 252, 254, 404–405, 407, 408, 418, 423, 425, 435, 439, 442).
3. Conservation of natural resources (433).
4. Railroad rate regulation (455).
5. Trusts and the regulation of trusts (456).
6. Special training for the farm and for modern industry (463).
7. The education of women; woman suffrage (463).
8. Immigration (259, 290, 291, 372–373, 467).
9. Civil service reform (392, 393, 467).
10. Municipal reform (439, 461).
11. The strife between capital and labor (467).

APPENDIX A

THE DECLARATION OF INDEPENDENCE

IN CONGRESS, JULY 4, 1776

THE following preamble and specifications, known as the Declaration of Independence, accompanied the resolution of Richard Henry Lee, which was adopted by Congress on the 2d day of July, 1776. This declaration was agreed to on the 4th, and the transaction is thus recorded in the Journal for that day:

" Agreeably to the order of the day, the Congress resolved itself into a committee of the whole, to take into their further consideration the Declaration ; and, after some time, the president resumed the chair, and Mr. Harrison reported that the committee had agreed to a Declaration, which they desired him to report. The Declaration being read, was agreed to as follows :"

A DECLARATION BY THE REPRESENTATIVES OF THE UNITED STATES OF AMERICA, IN CONGRESS ASSEMBLED.

When, in the course of human events, it becomes necessary for one people to dissolve the political bands which have connected them with another, and to assume, among the powers of the earth, the separate and equal station to which the laws of nature and of nature's God entitle them, a decent respect to the opinions of mankind requires that they should declare the causes which impel them to the separation.

We hold these truths to be self-evident—that all men are created equal; that they are endowed by their Creator with certain inalienable rights ; that among these are life, liberty, and the pursuit of happiness. That, to secure these rights, governments are instituted among men, deriving their just powers from the consent of the governed; that, whenever any form of government becomes destructive of these ends, it is the right of the people to alter or abolish it, and to institute a new government, laying its foundations on such principles, and organizing its powers in such form, as to them shall seem most likely to effect their safety and happiness. Prudence, indeed, will dictate that governments long established should not be changed for light and transient causes ; and, accordingly, all experience hath shown that mankind are more disposed to suffer, while evils are sufferable, than to right themselves by abolishing the forms to which they are accustomed. But when a long train of abuses and usurpations, pursuing invariably the same object, evinces a design to reduce them under absolute despotism, it is their right, it is their duty, to throw off such government, and to provide new guards for their future security. Such has been the patient sufferance of these colonies, and such is now the necessity which constrains them to alter their former systems of government. The history of the present king of Great Britain is a history of repeated injuries and usurpations, all having in direct object the establishment of an absolute tyranny over these States. To prove this, let facts be submitted to a candid world.

1. He has refused his assent to laws the most wholesome and necessary for the public good.

2. He has forbidden his governors to pass laws of immediate and pressing importance, unless suspended in their operations till his assent should be obtained; and, when so suspended, he has utterly neglected to attend to them.

3. He has refused to pass other laws for the accommodation of large districts of people, unless those people would relinquish the right of representation in the Legislature—a right inestimable to them, and formidable to tyrants only.

4. He has called together legislative bodies at places unusual, uncomfortable, and distant from the repository of their public records, for the sole purpose of fatiguing them into compliance with his measures.

5. He has dissolved representative houses repeatedly, for opposing, with manly firmness, his invasions on the rights of the people.

6. He has refused, for a long time after such dissolutions, to cause others to be elected, whereby the legislative powers, incapable of annihilation, have returned to the people at large for their exercise; the State remaining, in the meantime, exposed to all the dangers of invasions from without and convulsions within.

7. He has endeavored to prevent the population of these States; for that purpose obstructing the laws for the naturalization of foreigners; refusing to pass others to encourage their migration hither, and raising the conditions of new appropriations of lands.

8. He has obstructed the administration of justice, by refusing his assent to laws for establishing judiciary powers.

9. He has made judges dependent on his will alone for the tenure on their offices, and the amount and payment of their salaries.

10. He has erected a multitude of new offices, and sent hither swarms of officers, to harass our people and eat out their substance.

11. He has kept among us in times of peace, standing armies, without the consent of our Legislatures.

12. He has affected to render the military independent of, and superior to, the civil power.

13. He has combined with others to subject us to a jurisdiction foreign to our constitutions, and unacknowledged by our laws; giving his assent to their acts of pretended legislation;

14. For quartering large bodies of armed troops among us;

15. For protecting them, by a mock trial, from punishment for any murders which they should commit on the inhabitants of these States;

16. For cutting off our trade with all parts of the world;

17. For imposing taxes on us without our consent;

18. For depriving us, in many cases, of the benefits of a trial by jury;

19. For transporting us beyond seas, to be tried for pretended offenses;

20. For abolishing the free system of English laws in a neighboring province, establishing therein an arbitrary government, and enlarging its boundaries, so as to render it at once an example and fit instrument for introducing the same absolute rule into these colonies;

21. For taking away our charters, abolishing our most valuable laws, and altering, fundamentally, the forms of our governments;

22. For suspending our own Legislatures, and declaring themselves invested with power to legislate for us in all cases whatsoever.

23. He has abdicated government here, by declaring us out of his protection, and waging war against us.

24. He has plundered our seas, ravaged our coasts, burned our towns, and destroyed the lives of our people.

25. He is at this time transporting large armies of foreign mercenaries to complete the works of death, desolation and tyranny, already begun with circumstances of cruelty and perfidy scarcely paralleled in the most barbarous ages, and totally unworthy the head of a civilized nation.

26. He has constrained our fellow-citizens, taken captive on the high seas, to bear arms against their country, to become the executioners of their friends and brethren, or to fall themselves by their hands.

27. He has excited domestic insurrection among us, and has endeavored to bring on the inhabitants of our frontiers the merciless Indian savages, whose known rule of warfare is an undistinguished destruction of all ages, sexes, and conditions.

In every stage of these oppressions we have petitioned for redress in the most humble terms; our repeated petitions have been answered only by repeated injury.

A prince whose character is thus marked by every act which may define a tyrant, is unfit to be the ruler of a free people.

Nor have we been wanting in our attentions to our British brethren. We have warned them, from time to time, of attempts by their legislature to extend an unwarrantable jurisdiction over us. We have reminded them of the circumstances of our emigration and settlement here. We have appealed to their native justice and magnanimity, and we have conjured them by the ties of our common kindred to disavow these usurpations, which would inevitably interrupt our connections and correspondence. They, too, have been deaf to the voice of justice and of consanguinity. We must, therefore, acquiesce in the necessity which denounces our separation, and hold them as we hold the rest of mankind—enemies in war; in peace, friends.

We, therefore, the representatives of the United States of America in general Congress assembled, appealing to the Supreme Judge of the world for the rectitude of our intentions, do, in the name and by the authority of the good people of these colonies, solemnly publish and declare that these united colonies are, and of right ought to be, free and independent States; that they are absolved from all allegiance to the British crown, and that all political connection between them and the state of Great Britain is, and ought to be, totally dissolved, and that, as free and independent States, they have full power to levy war, conclude peace, contract alliances, establish commerce, and do all other acts and things which independent States may of right do. And for the support of this Declaration, with a firm reliance on the protection of Divine Providence, we mutually pledge to each other our lives, our fortunes, and our sacred honor.

The foregoing declaration was, by order of Congress, engrossed, and signed by the following members:

JOHN HANCOCK.

NEW HAMPSHIRE.
JOSIAH BARTLETT,
WILLIAM WHIPPLE,
MATTHEW THORNTON.

MASSACHUSETTS BAY.
SAMUEL ADAMS,
JOHN ADAMS,
ROBERT TREAT PAINE,
ELBRIDGE GERRY.

RHODE ISLAND.
STEPHEN HOPKINS,
WILLIAM ELLERY.

CONNECTICUT.
ROGER SHERMAN,
SAMUEL HUNTINGTON,
WILLIAM WILLIAMS,
OLIVER WOLCOTT.

NEW YORK.
WILLIAM FLOYD,
PHILIP LIVINGSTON,
FRANCIS LEWIS,
LEWIS MORRIS.

NEW JERSEY.
RICHARD STOCKTON,
JOHN WITHERSPOON,
FRANCIS HOPKINSON,
JOHN HART,
ABRAHAM CLARK.

PENNSYLVANIA.
ROBERT MORRIS,
BENJAMIN RUSH,
BENJAMIN FRANKLIN,
JOHN MORTON,
GEORGE CLYMER,
JAMES SMITH,
GEORGE TAYLOR,
JAMES WILSON,
GEORGE ROSS.

DELAWARE.
CÆSAR RODNEY,
GEORGE READ,
THOMAS M'KEAN.

MARYLAND.
SAMUEL CHASE,
WILLIAM PACA,
THOMAS STONE,
CHARLES CARROLL of
Carrollton.

VIRGINIA.
GEORGE WYTHE,
RICHARD HENRY LEE,
THOMAS JEFFERSON,
BENJAMIN HARRISON,
THOMAS NELSON, JUN.,
FRANCIS LIGHTFOOT LEE,
CARTER BRAXTON.

NORTH CAROLINA.
WILLIAM HOOPER,
JOSEPH HEWES,
JOHN PENN.

SOUTH CAROLINA.
EDWARD RUTLEDGE,
THOMAS HEYWARD, JUN.,
THOMAS LYNCH, JUN.,
ARTHUR MIDDLETON.

GEORGIA.
BUTTON GWINNETT,
LYMAN HALL,
GEORGE WALTON.

APPENDIX B

A CHART ON THE CONSTITUTION

Some Steps toward the Constitution........
- New England Confederation (1643).
- Franklin's Plan of Union (1754).
- Stamp Act Congress (1765).
- Committees of Correspondence (1772).
- First Meeting of the Continental Congress (1774).
- Declaration of Independence (1776).
- Adoption of Articles of Confederation (1781).
- Annapolis Convention (1786).
- Constitutional Convention (1787).

Legislative Department............
- House of Representatives.............
  - Manner of election.
  - Term of office.
  - Qualifications.
  - Represents the people.
  - Census.
  - Apportionment.
  - Speaker the Presiding Officer.
- Senate ....
  - Number.
  - Manner of election.
  - Term of office.
  - Represents the States.
  - Qualifications.
  - Sole power to try impeachments.
  - Vice-President the Presiding Officer.

Executive Department............
- President............
  - Term of office.
  - Manner of election.
  - Qualifications.
  - Oath of office.
  - Impeachment.
- Cabinet ....
  - Manner of appointment.
  - Number.
  - Duties.

Judicial Department.
- Judges ....
  - Manner of appointment.
  - Number.
  - Term of office.
- Courts.............
  - Supreme.
  - Circuit.
  - District.

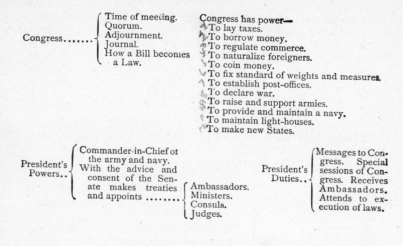

Congress .... {
Time of meeting.
Quorum.
Adjournment.
Journal.
How a Bill becomes a Law.
}

Congress has power—
To lay taxes.
To borrow money.
To regulate commerce.
To naturalize foreigners.
To coin money.
To fix standard of weights and measures.
To establish post-offices.
To declare war.
To raise and support armies.
To provide and maintain a navy.
To maintain light-houses.
To make new States.

President's Powers .. {
Commander-in-Chief of the army and navy.
With the advice and consent of the Senate makes treaties and appoints .... {
Ambassadors.
Ministers.
Consuls.
Judges.
}
}

President's Duties .. {
Messages to Congress. Special sessions of Congress. Receives Ambassadors. Attends to execution of laws.
}

CONSTITUTION OF THE UNITED STATES

WE, the People of the United States, in order to form a more perfect union, establish justice, insure domestic tranquillity, provide for the common defence, promote the general welfare, and secure the blessings of liberty to ourselves and our posterity, do ordain and establish this CONSTITUTION for the United States of America.

ARTICLE I.—Legislative Department.

SECTION I. All legislative powers herein granted shall be vested in a Congress of the United States, which shall consist of a Senate and House of Representatives.

SECTION II. CLAUSE 1. The House of Representatives shall be composed of members chosen every second year by the people of the several States, and the electors in each State shall have the qualifications requisite for electors of the most numerous branch of the State Legislature.

CLAUSE 2. No person shall be a representative who shall not have attained to the age of twenty-five years, and been seven years a citizen of the United States, and who shall not, when elected, be an inhabitant of that State in which he shall be chosen.

CLAUSE 3. Representatives and direct taxes shall be apportioned among the several States which may be included within this Union, according to their respective numbers,[1] which shall be determined by adding to the whole number of free persons, including those bound to service for a term of years, and excluding Indians not taxed, three fifths of all other persons. The actual enumeration shall be made within three years after the first meeting of the Congress of the United States, and within every subsequent term of ten years, in such manner as they shall by law direct. The number of representatives shall not exceed one for every thirty thousand, but each State shall have at least one representative; and until such enumeration shall be made, the State of New Hampshire shall be entitled to choose three; Massachusetts, eight; Rhode Island and Providence Plantations, one; Connecticut, five; New York, six; New Jersey, four; Pennsylvania, eight; Delaware, one; Maryland, six; Virginia, ten; North Carolina, five; South Carolina, five; and Georgia, three.

CLAUSE 4. When vacancies happen in the representation from any State, the executive authority thereof shall issue writs of election to fill such vacancies.

CLAUSE 5. The House of Representatives shall choose their Speaker and other officers; and shall have the sole power of impeachment.

SECTION III.—CLAUSE 1. The Senate of the United States shall be composed of two senators from each State, chosen by the Legislature thereof, for six years; and each senator shall have one vote.

CLAUSE 2. Immediately after they shall be assembled in consequence of the first election, they shall be divided as equally as may be into three classes. The seats of the senators of the first class shall be vacated at the expiration of the second year; of the second class, at the expiration of the fourth year; and of the third class, at the expiration of the sixth year, so that one third may be chosen every second year; and if vacancies happen by resignation, or otherwise, during the recess of the Legislature of any State, the executive thereof may make temporary appointments until the next meeting of the Legislature, which shall then fill such vacancies.

CLAUSE 3. No person shall be a senator who shall not have attained to the age of thirty years, and been nine years a citizen of the United States, and who shall not, when elected, be an inhabitant of that State for which he shall be chosen.

CLAUSE 4. The Vice-President of the United States shall be president of the Senate, but shall have no vote, unless they be equally divided.

CLAUSE 5. The Senate shall choose their other officers, and also a president *pro tempore*, in the absence of the Vice-President, or when he shall exercise the office of President of the United States.

CLAUSE 6. The Senate shall have the sole power to try all impeachments. When sitting for that purpose, they shall be on oath or affirmation. When the President of the United States is tried, the Chief-Justice shall preside; and no person shall be convicted without the concurrence of two thirds of the members present.

CLAUSE 7. Judgment in cases of impeachment shall not extend further than to removal from office, and disqualification to hold and enjoy any office of honor, trust, or profit under the United States; but the party convicted shall nevertheless be

---

[1] Under the census of 1910 one representative is apportioned to every 212,407 people.

liable and subject to indictment, trial, judgment, and punishment, according to law.

SECTION IV.—CLAUSE 1. The times, places, and manner of holding elections for senators and representatives shall be prescribed in each State by the Legislature thereof; but the Congress may at any time, by law, make or alter such regulations, except as to the places of choosing senators.

CLAUSE 2. The Congress shall assemble at least once in every year, and such meeting shall be on the first Monday in December, unless they shall by law appoint a different day.

SECTION V.—CLAUSE 1. Each House shall be the judge of the elections, returns, and qualifications of its own members, and a majority of each shall constitute a quorum to do business; but a smaller number may adjourn from day to day, and may be authorized to compel the attendance of absent members, in such manner, and under such penalties, as each house may provide.

CLAUSE 2. Each House may determine the rules of its proceedings, punish its members for disorderly behavior, and with the concurrence of two thirds, expel a member.

CLAUSE 3. Each House shall keep a journal of its proceedings, and from time to time publish the same, excepting such parts as may in their judgment require secrecy, and the yeas and nays of the members of either House on any question shall, at the desire of one fifth of those present, be entered on the journal.

CLAUSE 4.—Neither house, during the session of Congress, shall, without the consent of the other, adjourn for more than three days, nor to any other place than that in which the two Houses shall be sitting.

SECTION VI.—CLAUSE 1. The senators and representatives shall receive a compensation for their services, to be ascertained by law and paid out of the treasury of the United States. They shall in all cases, except treason, felony, and breach of the peace, be privileged from arrest during their attendance at the session of their respective Houses, and in going to and returning from the same; and for any speech or debate in either House, they shall not be questioned in any other place.

CLAUSE 2. No senator or representative shall, during the time for which he was elected, be appointed to any civil office under the authority of the United States, which shall have been created, or the emoluments whereof shall have been increased, during such time; and no person holding any office under the United States shall be a member of either House during his continuance in office.

SECTION VII.—CLAUSE 1. All bills for raising revenue shall originate in the House of Representatives; but the Senate may propose or concur with amendments, as on other bills.

CLAUSE 2. Every bill which shall have passed the House of Representatives and the Senate, shall, before it become a law, be presented to the President of the United States; if he approve, he shall sign it, but if not, he shall return it, with his objections, to that house in which it shall have originated, who shall enter the objections at large on their journal, and proceed to reconsider it. If after such reconsideration, two thirds of that house shall agree to pass the bill, it shall be sent, together with the objections, to the other house, by which it shall likewise be reconsidered, and if approved by two thirds of that house, it shall become a law. But in all such cases the votes of both houses shall be determined by yeas and nays, and the names of the persons voting for and against the bill shall be entered on the journal of each house respectively. If any bill shall not be returned by the President within ten days (Sundays excepted) after it shall have been presented to him, the same shall be a law, in like manner as if he had signed it, unless the Congress by their adjournment prevent its return, in which case it shall not be a law.

CLAUSE 3. Every order, resolution, or vote to which the concurrence of the Senate and House of Representatives may be necessary (except on a question of adjournment) shall be presented to the President of the United States; and before the same shall take effect, shall be approved by him, or being disapproved by him, shall be repassed by two thirds of the Senate and House of Representatives, according to the rules and limitations prescribed in the case of a bill.

SECTION VIII.—CLAUSE 1. The Congress shall have power to lay and collect taxes, duties, imposts, and excises, to pay the debts and provide for the common defence and general welfare of the United States; but all duties, imposts, and excises shall be uniform throughout the United States;

CLAUSE 2. To borrow money on the credit of the United States;

CLAUSE 3. To regulate commerce with foreign nations, and among the several States, and with the Indian tribes;

CLAUSE 4. To establish an uniform rule of naturalization, and uniform laws on the subject of bankruptcies throughout the United States;

CLAUSE 5. To coin money, regulate the value thereof, and of foreign coin, and fix the standard of weights and measures;

CLAUSE 6. To provide for the punishment of counterfeiting the securities and current coin of the United States;

CLAUSE 7. To establish post-offices and post-roads;

CLAUSE 8. To promote the progress of science and useful arts, by securing, for limited times, to authors and inventors the exclusive right to their respective writings and discoveries;

CLAUSE 9. To constitute tribunals inferior to the Supreme Court;

CLAUSE 10. To define and punish piracies and felonies committed on the high seas, and offences against the law of nations:

CLAUSE 11. To declare war, grant letters of marque and reprisal, and make rules concerning captures on land and water;

CLAUSE 12. To raise and support armies. but no appropriation of money to that use shall be for a longer term than two years:

CLAUSE 13. To provide and maintain a navy;

CLAUSE 14. To make rules for the government and regulation of the land and naval forces;

CLAUSE 15. To provide for calling forth the militia to execute the laws of the Union, suppress insurrections, and repel invasions ;

CLAUSE 16. To provide for organizing, arming, and disciplining the militia, and for governing such part of them as may be employed in the service of the United States, reserving to the States respectively the appointment of the officers, and the authority of training the militia according to the discipline prescribed by Congress :

CLAUSE 17. To exercise exclusive legislation in all cases whatsoever over such district (not exceeding ten miles square) as may, by cession of particular States, and the acceptance of Congress, become the seat of the government of the United States, and to exercise like authority over all places purchased by the consent of the Legislature of the State in which the same shall be, for the erection of forts, magazines, arsenals, dock-yards, and other needful buildings ;—And

CLAUSE 18. To make all laws which shall be necessary and proper for carrying into execution the foregoing powers, and all other powers vested by this Constitution in the government of the United States, or in any department or officer thereof.

SECTION IX.—CLAUSE 1. The migration or importation of such persons as any of the States now existing shall think proper to admit, shall not be prohibited by the Congress prior to the year one thousand eight hundred and eight, but a tax or duty may be imposed on such importation, not exceeding ten dollars for each person.

CLAUSE 2. The privilege of the writ of habeas corpus shall not be suspended, unless when in cases of rebellion or invasion the public safety may require it.

CLAUSE 3. No bill of attainder or *ex post facto* law shall be passed.

CLAUSE 4. No capitation or other direct tax shall be laid, unless in proportion to the census or enumeration hereinbefore directed to be taken.

CLAUSE 5. No tax or duty shall be laid on articles exported from any State.

CLAUSE 6. No preference shall be given by any regulation of commerce or revenue to the ports of one State over those of another ; nor shall vessels bound to, or from, one State, be obliged to enter, clear, or pay duties in another.

CLAUSE 7. No money shall be drawn from the treasury but in consequence of appropriations made by law ; and a regular statement and account of the receipts and expenditures of all public money shall be published from time to time.

CLAUSE 8. No title of nobility shall be granted by the United States : And no person holding any office of profit or trust under them, shall, without the consent of the Congress, accept of any present, emolument, office, or title, of any kind whatever, from any king, prince, or foreign State.

SECTION X.—CLAUSE 1. No State shall enter into any treaty, alliance, or confederation; grant letters of marque and reprisal; coin money ; emit bills of credit ; make any thing but gold and silver coin a tender in payment of debts; pass any bill of attainder, *ex post facto* law, or law impairing the obligation of contracts, or grant any title of nobility.

CLAUSE 2. No State shall, without the consent of the Congress, lay any impost or duties on imports or exports, except what may be absolutely necessary for executing its inspection laws; and the net produce of all duties and impost, laid by any State on imports or exports, shall be for the use of the treasury of the United States; and all such laws shall be subject to the revision and control of the Congress.

CLAUSE 3. No State shall, without the consent of Congress, lay any duty of tonnage, keep troops, or ships of war, in time of peace, enter into any agreement or compact with another State, or with a foreign power, or engage in war, unless actually invaded, or in such imminent danger as will not admit of delay.

ARTICLE II.—Executive Department.

SECTION I.—CLAUSE 1. The executive power shall be vested in a President of the United States of America. He shall hold his office during a term of four years, and, together with the Vice-President, chosen for the same term, be elected as follows:

CLAUSE 2. Each State shall appoint, in such manner as the Legislature thereof may direct, a number of electors, equal to the whole number of senators and representatives to which the State may be entitled in the Congress; but no senator or representative, or person holding an office of trust or profit under the United States, shall be appointed an elector.

CLAUSE 3.[1]

CLAUSE 4. The Congress may determine the time of choosing the electors, and the day on which they shall give their votes; which day shall be the same throughout the United States.

CLAUSE 5. No person except a natural-born citizen, or a citizen of the United States at the time of the adoption of this Constitution, shall be eligible to the office of President; neither shall any person be eligible to that office who shall not have attained to the age of thirty-five years, and been fourteen years resident within the United States.

CLAUSE 6.—In case of the removal of the President from office, or of his death, resignation, or inability to discharge the powers and duties of the said office, the same shall devolve on the Vice-President, and the Congress may by law provide for the case of removal, death, resignation, or inability, both of the President and Vice-President, declaring what officer shall then act as President; and such officer shall act accordingly until the disability be removed, or a President shall be elected.

CLAUSE 7. The President shall, at stated times, receive for his services a compensation which shall neither be increased nor diminished during the period for which he shall have been elected, and he shall not receive within that period any other emolument from the United States, or any of them.

CLAUSE 8. Before he enter on the execution of his office, he shall take the fol-

[1] This clause is no longer in force. Amendment XII. has superseded it.

lowing oath or affirmation :—" I do solemnly swear (or affirm) that I will faithfully execute the office of President of the United States, and will, to the best of my ability, preserve, protect, and defend the Constitution of the United States."

SECTION II.—CLAUSE I. The President shall be commander-in-chief of the army and navy of the United States, and of the militia of the several States, when called into the actual service of the United States ; he may require the opinion, in writing, of the principal officer in each of the executive departments, upon any subject relating to the duties of their respective offices ; and he shall have power to grant reprieves and pardons for offences against the United States, except in cases of impeachment.

CLAUSE 2. He shall have power, by and with the advice and consent of the Senate, to make treaties, provided two thirds of the senators present concur ; and he shall nominate, and by and with the advice and consent of the Senate shall appoint, ambassadors, other public ministers and consuls, judges of the Supreme Court, and all other officers of the United States, whose appointments are not herein otherwise provided for, and which shall be established by law ; but the Congress may by law vest the appointment of such inferior officers, as they think proper, in the President alone, in the courts of law, or in the heads of department.

CLAUSE 3. The President shall have power to fill up all vacancies that may happen during the recess of the Senate, by granting commissions which shall expire at the end of their next session.

SECTION III.—He shall from time to time give to the Congress information of the state of the Union, and recommend to their consideration such measures as he shall judge necessary and expedient ; he may, on extraordinary occasions, convene both Houses, or either of them, and in case of disagreement between them with respect to the time of adjournment, he may adjourn them to such time as he shall think proper ; he shall receive ambassadors and other public ministers ; he shall take care that the laws be faithfully executed, and shall commission all the officers of the United States.

SECTION IV.—The President, Vice-President, and all civil officers of the United States, shall be removed from office on impeachment for, and conviction of, treason, bribery, or other high crimes and misdemeanors.

ARTICLE III.—Judicial Department.

SECTION I.—The judicial power of the United States shall be vested in one Supreme Court, and in such inferior courts as the Congress may from time to time ordain and establish. The judges, both of the Supreme and inferior courts, shall hold their offices during good behavior, and shall, at stated times, receive for their services a compensation which shall not be diminished during their continuance in office.

SECTION II.—CLAUSE I.[1] The judicial power shall extend to all cases, in law and equity, arising under this Constitution, the laws of the United States, and treaties made, or which shall be made, under their authority;—to all cases affecting ambassadors, other public ministers, and consuls;—to all cases of admiralty and maritime jurisdiction;—to controversies to which the United States shall be a party;—to controversies between two or more States;—between a State and citizens of another State;—between citizens of different States;—between citizens of the same State claiming lands under grants of different States, and between a State or the citizens thereof, and foreign states, citizens, or subjects.

CLAUSE 2. In all cases affecting ambassadors, other public ministers and consuls, and those in which a State shall be party, the Supreme Court shall have original jurisdiction. In all the other cases before mentioned, the Supreme Court shall have appellate jurisdiction, both as to law and fact, with such exceptions and under such regulations as the Congress shall make.

CLAUSE 3. The trial of all crimes, except in cases of impeachment, shall be by jury, and such trial shall be held in the State where the said crimes shall have been committed; but when not committed within any State, the trial shall be at such place or places as the Congress may by law have directed.

SECTION III.—CLAUSE I. Treason against the United States shall consist only in levying war against them, or in adhering to their enemies, giving them aid and comfort. No person shall be convicted of treason, unless on the testimony of two witnesses to the same overt act, or on confession in open court.

CLAUSE 2. The Congress shall have power to declare the punishment of treason; but no attainder of treason shall work corruption of blood, or forfeiture, except during the life of the person attainted.

ARTICLE IV.—General Provisions.

SECTION I.—Full faith and credit shall be given in each State to the public acts, records, and judicial proceedings of every other State; and the Congress may by general laws prescribe the manner in which such acts, records, and proceedings shall be proved, and the effect thereof.

SECTION II.—CLAUSE I. The citizens of each State shall be entitled to all privileges and immunities of citizens in the several States.

CLAUSE 2. A person charged in any State with treason, felony, or other crime, who shall flee from justice, and be found in another State, shall, on demand of the executive authority of the State from which he fled, be delivered up, to be removed to the State having jurisdiction of the crime.

CLAUSE 3. No person held to service or labor in one State, under the laws thereof, escaping into another, shall in consequence of any law or regulation therein, be discharged from such service or labor, but shall be delivered up on claim of the party to whom such service or labor may be due.

This clause has been modified by Amendment XI.

SECTION III.—CLAUSE 1. New States may be admitted by the Congress into this Union ; but no new State shall be formed or erected within the jurisdiction of any other State ; nor any State be formed by the junction of two or more States, or parts of States, without the consent of the Legislatures of the States concerned as well as of the Congress.

CLAUSE 2. The Congress shall have power to dispose of and make all needful rules and regulations respecting the territory or other property belonging to the United States ; and nothing in this Constitution shall be so construed as to prejudice any claims of the United States, or of any particular State.

SECTION IV.—The United States shall guarantee to every State in this Union a republican form of Government, and shall protect each of them against invasion, and on application of the Legislature, or of the executive (when the Legislature can not be convened), against domestic violence.

ARTICLE V.—Power of Amendment.

The Congress, whenever two thirds of both houses shall deem it necessary, shall propose amendments to this Constitution, or, on the application of the Legislatures of two thirds of the several States, shall call a convention, for proposing amendments, which, in either case, shall be valid to all intents and purposes, as part of this Constitution, when ratified by the Legislatures of three fourths of the several States, or by conventions in three fourths thereof, as the one or the other mode of ratification may be proposed by the Congress ; provided that no amendment which may be made prior to the year one thousand eight hundred and eight shall in any manner affect the first and fourth clauses in the ninth section of the first article ; and that no State, without its consent, shall be deprived of its equal suffrage in the Senate.

ARTICLE VI.—Miscellaneous Provisions.

CLAUSE 1. All debts contracted, and engagements entered into, before the adoption of this Constitution, shall be as valid against the United States under this Constitution, as under the Confederation.

CLAUSE 2. This Constitution, and the laws of the United States which shall be made in pursuance thereof ; and all treaties made, or which shall be made, under the authority of the United States, shall be the supreme law of the land · and the judges in every State shall be bound thereby, any thing in the Constitution or laws of any State to the contrary notwithstanding.

CLAUSE 3. The senators and representatives before mentioned, and the members of the several State Legislatures, and all executive and judicial officers, both of the United States and of the several States, shall be bound by oath or affirmation to support this Constitution ; but no religious test shall ever be required as a qualification to any office or public trust under the United States.

ARTICLE VII.—Ratification of the Constitution.

The ratification of the conventions of nine States shall be sufficient for the establishment of this Constitution between the States so ratifying the same.

> Done in convention, by the unanimous consent of the States present, the seventeenth day of September, in the year of our Lord one thousand seven hundred and eighty-seven, and of the independence of the United States of America the twelfth.

In witness whereof we have hereunto subscribed our names.

GEORGE WASHINGTON,
President, and Deputy from Virginia.

CONSENT OF THE STATES PRESENT.[1]

NEW HAMPSHIRE.
JOHN LANGDON,
NICHOLAS GILMAN.

MASSACHUSETTS.
NATHANIEL GORHAM,
RUFUS KING.

CONNECTICUT.
WILLIAM SAMUEL JOHNSON,
ROGER SHERMAN.

NEW YORK.
ALEXANDER HAMILTON.

NEW JERSEY.
WILLIAM LIVINGSTON,
DAVID BREARLEY,
WILLIAM PATERSON,
JONATHAN DAYTON.

PENNSYLVANIA.
BENJAMIN FRANKLIN,
THOMAS MIFFLIN,
ROBERT MORRIS,
GEORGE CLYMER,
THOMAS FITZSIMONS,
JARED INGERSOL,
JAMES WILSON,
GOUVERNEUR MORRIS.

DELAWARE.
GEORGE READ,
GUNNING BEDFORD, JR.,
JOHN DICKINSON,
RICHARD BASSETT,
JACOB BROOM.

MARYLAND.
JAMES MCHENRY,
DANIEL OF ST. THOMAS JENIFER,
DANIEL CARROLL.

VIRGINIA.
JOHN BLAIR,
JAMES MADISON, JR.

NORTH CAROLINA.
WILLIAM BLOUNT,
RICHARD DOBBS SPAIGHT,
HUGH WILLIAMSON.

SOUTH CAROLINA.
JOHN RUTLEDGE,
CHARLES C. PINCKNEY,
CHARLES PINCKNEY,
PIERCE BUTLER.

GEORGIA.
WILLIAM FEW,
ABRAHAM BALDWIN.

Attest: WILLIAM JACKSON, *Secretary.*

[1] Rhode Island was not represented in the Federal Convention.

AMENDMENTS[1]

To the Constitution of the United States, Ratified according to the Provisions of the Fifth Article of the Foregoing Constitution.

ARTICLE I.—Congress shall make no law respecting an establishment of religion, or prohibiting the free exercise thereof; or abridging the freedom of speech, or of the press; or the right of the people peaceably to assemble, and to petition the government for redress of grievances.

ARTICLE II.—A well-regulated militia being necessary to the security of a free State, the right of the people to keep and bear arms shall not be infringed.

ARTICLE III.—No soldier shall, in time of peace, be quartered in any house, without the consent of the owner, nor in time of war, but in a manner to be prescribed by law.

ARTICLE IV.—The right of the people to be secure in their persons, houses, papers, and effects, against unreasonable searches and seizures, shall not be violated, and no warrants shall issue, but upon probable cause, supported by oath or affirmation, and particularly describing the place to be searched, and the persons or things to be seized.

ARTICLE V.—No person shall be held to answer for a capital or otherwise infamous crime, unless on a presentment or indictment of a grand jury, except in cases arising in the land or naval forces, or in the militia, when in actual service in time of war and public danger; nor shall any person be subject for the same offence to be twice put in jeopardy of life or limb; nor shall be compelled in any criminal case to be a witness against himself, nor to be deprived of life, liberty, or property, without due process of law; nor shall private property be taken for public use without just compensation.

ARTICLE VI.—In all criminal prosecutions, the accused shall enjoy the right to a speedy and public trial, by an impartial jury of the State and district wherein the crime shall have been committed, which district shall have been previously ascertained by law, and to be informed of the nature and cause of the accusation; to be confronted with the witnesses against him; to have compulsory process for obtaining witnesses in his favor, and to have the assistance of counsel for his defence.

ARTICLE VII.—In suits at common law, where the value in controversy shall exceed twenty dollars, the right of trial by jury shall be preserved, and no fact tried by a jury shall be otherwise re-examined in any court of the United States, than according to the rules of common law.

ARTICLE VIII.—Excessive bail shall not be required, nor excessive fines imposed, nor cruel and unusual punishments inflicted.

[1] Amendments I. to X. were declared in force December 15, 1791.

ARTICLE IX.—The enumeration in the Constitution of certain rights, shall not be construed to deny or disparage others retained by the people.

ARTICLE X.—The powers not delegated to the United States by the Constitution, nor prohibited by it to the States, are reserved to the States respectively, or to the people.

ARTICLE XI.[1]—The judicial power of the United States shall not be construed to extend to any suit in law or equity, commenced or prosecuted against one of the United States by citizens of another State, or by citizens or subjects of any foreign state.

ARTICLE XII.[2]—The electors shall meet in their respective States, and vote by ballot for President and Vice-President, one of whom, at least, shall not be an inhabitant of the same State with themselves; they shall name in their ballots the person voted for as President, and indistinct ballots the person voted for as Vice-President; and they shall make distinct lists of all persons voted for as President, and of all persons voted for as Vice-President, and of the number of votes for each, which lists they shall sign and certify, and transmit sealed to the seat of the government of the United States, directed to the president of the Senate;—the president of the Senate shall, in the presence of the Senate and House of Representatives, open all the certificates, and the votes shall then be counted;—the person having the greatest number of votes for President, shall be the President, if such number be a majority of the whole number of electors appointed; and if no person have such majority, then from the persons having the highest numbers not exceeding three on the list of those voted for as President, the House of Representatives shall choose immediately, by ballot, the President. But in choosing the President, the votes shall be taken by States, the representation from each State having one vote; a quorum for this purpose shall consist of a member or members from two thirds of the States, and a majority of all the States shall be necessary to a choice. And if the House of Representatives shall not choose a President whenever the right of choice shall devolve upon them, before the fourth day of March next following, then the Vice-President shall act as President, as in the case of the death or other constitutional disability of the President. The person having the greatest number of votes as Vice-President, shall be the Vice-President, if such number be a majority of the whole number of electors appointed; and if no person have a majority, then from the two highest numbers on the list, the Senate shall choose the Vice-President; a quorum for the purpose shall consist of two thirds of the whole number of senators, and a majority of the whole number shall be necessary to a choice. But no person constitutionally ineligible to the office of President shall be eligible to that of Vice-President of the United States.

ARTICLE XIII.[3]—SECTION 1. Neither slavery nor involuntary servitude, except as a punishment for crime, whereof the person shall have been duly convicted, shall exist within the United States, or any place subject to their jurisdiction.

[1] Declared in force January 8, 1798. [2] Declared in force September 25, 1804.
[3] Declared in force December 18, 1865.

Section 2. Congress shall have power to enforce this article by appropriate legislation.

ARTICLE XIV.[1]—Section 1. All persons born or naturalized in the United States, and subject to the jurisdiction thereof, are citizens of the United States and of the State wherein they reside. No State shall make or enforce any law which shall abridge the privileges or immunities of citizens of the United States; nor shall any State deprive any person of life, liberty, or property, without due process of law, nor deny to any person within its jurisdiction the equal protection of the laws.

Section 2. Representatives shall be appointed among the several States according to their respective numbers, counting the whole number of persons in each State excluding Indians not taxed. But when the right to vote at any election for the choice of electors for President and Vice-President of the United States, representatives in Congress, the executive or judicial officers of a State, or the members of the Legislature thereof, is denied to any of the male inhabitants of such State, being twenty-one years of age and citizens of the United States, or in any way abridged except for participation in rebellion or other crime, the basis of representation therein shall be reduced in the proportion which the number of such male citizens shall bear to the whole number of male citizens twenty-one years of age in such State.

Section 3. No person shall be a senator or representative in Congress, or elector of President or Vice-President, or hold any office, civil or military, under the United States, or under any State, who having previously taken an oath as a member of Congress, or as an officer of the United States, or as a member of any State Legislature, or as an executive or judicial officer of any State, to support the Constitution of the United States, shall have engaged in insurrection or rebellion against the same, or given aid or comfort to the enemies thereof. But Congress may, by a vote of two thirds of each house, remove such disability.

Section 4. The validity of the public debt of the United States, authorized by law, including debts incurred for payment of pension and bounties for services in suppressing insurrection or rebellion, shall not be questioned. But neither the United States nor any State shall assume or pay any debt or obligation incurred in aid of insurrection or rebellion against the United States, or any claim for the loss or emancipation of any slave; but all such debts, obligations, and claims shall be held illegal and void.

Section 5. The Congress shall have power to enforce, by appropriate legislation, the provisions of this article.

ARTICLE XV.[2]—Section 1. The rights of citizens of the United States to vote shall not be denied or abridged by the United States, or by any State, on account of race, color, or previous condition of servitude.

Section 2. The Congress shall have power to enforce this article by appropriate legislation.

---

[1] Declared in force July 28, 1898.   [2] Declared in force March 30, 1870

ARTICLE XVI.[1]—The Congress shall have power to lay and collect taxes on incomes from whatever source derived, without apportionment among the several States, and without regard to any census or enumeration.

ARTICLE XVII.[2]— SECTION 1. The Senate of the United States shall be composed of two Senators from each State, elected by the people thereof, for six years; and each Senator shall have one vote. The electors in each State shall have the qualifications requisite for electors of the most numerous branch of the State legislature.

SECTION 2. When vacancies happen in the representation of any State in the Senate, the executive authority of such State shall issue writs of election to fill such vacancies: Provided that the legislature of any State may empower the executive thereof to make temporary appointments until the people fill the vacancies by election as the legislature may direct.

SECTION 3. This amendment shall not be so construed as to affect the election or term of any Senator chosen before it becomes valid as part of the Constitution.

[1] Declared in force February 25, 1913.   [2] Declared in force May 31, 1913.

TO THE PUPIL

1. What colonies united to form the New England Confederation, and what were its purposes and results? What was Franklin's plan of Union, and why was it not adopted? What did the Stamp Act Congress do? What was the leading object of the Committees of Correspondence?

2. Under what circumstances was the first meeting of the Continental Congress held? What led the colonies to adopt the Declaration of Independence?

3. When did the States adopt the Articles of Confederation? Explain the weakness of the central governing power, Congress, under the Articles of Confederation. Tell what you can about the Annapolis Convention; the Constitutional Convention.

4. Under the Constitution, what are the three departments of our government? Which of them makes the laws? Which sees that they are carried out? Which interprets them and tries cases arising under them?

5. Of what does the legislative department consist? How are members of the House of Representatives elected? For how long? What are their qualifications?

6. How many people does each member of the House represent? What is the unit of representation? How can you find the number of representatives in any State? How many in your own? Why?

7. What do the Senators represent? How are they elected and for what term of office? What are their qualifications?

8. What exclusive functions has the House? the Senate?

9. What are the qualifications of the President? How is he elected? For what term of office is he elected? What is meant by the impeachment of the President?

10. What is the President's Cabinet? How many members had Washington's Cabinet? How many in the Cabinet now? What are the duties of the Cabinet officers?

11. Name the three kinds of national courts. How many judges are there in the Supreme Court? How are they appointed and what is their term of office? Why should we have national courts?

12. Explain the three courses which a bill must take in order to become a law. Name the powers of Congress enumerated in the chart.

13. What military power has the President? How are treaties and important appointments made? What duties of the President are named in the chart?

APPENDIX C

TABLE[1] OF STATES AND TERRITORIES

No.	Name.	Date of Admission.	Area in Square Miles.	Representatives in Congress, 1914	Electoral Votes,[2] 1912
1	Delaware[3]	1787	2,050	1	3
2	Pennsylvania...............	1787	45,215	36	38
3	New Jersey................	1787	7,815	12	14
4	Georgia....................	1788	59,475	12	14
5	Connecticut...............	1788	4,990	5	7
6	Massachusetts.............	1788	8,315	16	18
7	Maryland..................	1788	12,210	6	8
8	South Carolina............	1788	30,570	7	9
9	New Hampshire...........	1788	9,305	2	4
10	Virginia...................	1788	42,450	10	12
11	New York.................	1788	49,170	43	45
12	North Carolina............	1789	52,250	10	12
13	Rhode Island..............	1790	1,250	3	5
14	Vermont...................	1791	9,565	2	4
15	Kentucky..................	1792	40,400	11	13
16	Tennessee.................	1796	42,050	10	12
17	Ohio......................	1802	41,060	22	24
18	Louisiana.................	1812	48,720	8	10
19	Indiana...................	1816	36,350	13	15
20	Mississippi................	1817	46,810	8	10
21	Illinois...................	1818	56,650	27	29
22	Alabama...................	1819	52,250	10	12
23	Maine.....................	1820	33,040	4	6
24	Missouri..................	1821	69,415	16	18
25	Arkansas..................	1836	53,850	7	9
26	Michigan..................	1837	58,915	13	15
27	Florida...................	1845	58,680	4	6
28	Texas.....................	1845	265,780	18	20

[1] The population, the capital, and the largest city of each State may be found on the map between pages 420 and 421.

[2] In 1912 the total number of representatives in Congress was 435. Add to this number 96 for the number of senators in the Senate, and the result is 531 Electoral votes.

[3] The dates opposite the first thirteen—the "Original Thirteen"—indicate the year when the States ratified the Constitution.

No.	Name.	Date of Admission.	Area in Square Miles.	Representatives in Congress, 1914	Electoral Votes,[1] 1912
29	Iowa......................	1846	56,025	11	13
30	Wisconsin..................	1848	56,040	11	13
31	California.................	1850	158,360	11	13
32	Minnesota.................	1858	83,365	10	12
33	Oregon....................	1859	96,030	3	5
34	Kansas....................	1861	82,080	8	10
35	West Virginia..............	1863	24,780	6	8
36	Nevada....................	1864	110,700	1	3
37	Nebraska..................	1867	77,510	6	8
38	Colorado..................	1876	103,925	4	6
39	North Dakota..............	1889	70,795	3	5
40	South Dakota..............	1889	77,650	3	5
41	Montana..................	1889	146,080	2	4
42	Washington................	1899	69,180	5	7
43	Idaho.....................	1890	84,800	2	4
44	Wyoming..................	1890	97,890	1	3
45	Utah......................	1896	84,970	2	4
46	Oklahoma.................	1907	70,430	8	10
47	New Mexico...............	1912	122,580	1	3
48	Arizona...................	1912	113,020	1	3
	Alaska....................	....	577,390	..	..
	District of Columbia........	....	70	..	..
	Hawaii....................	....	6,740	..	..

[1] See note 2 on opposite page.

APPENDIX D

PRESIDENTS OF THE UNITED STATES

President.	State.	By Whom Elected.	Term of Office.
George Washington	Virginia	Whole people.	Two terms; 1789-1797.
John Adams	Massachusetts	Federalists.	One term; 1797-1801.
Thomas Jefferson	Virginia	Dem.-Rep.	Two terms; 1801-1809.
James Madison	Virginia	Dem.-Rep.	Two terms; 1809-1817.
James Monroe	Virginia	Dem.-Rep.	Two terms; 1817-1825.
John Quincy Adams	Massachusetts	Rep	One term; 1825-1829.
Andrew Jackson	Tennessee	Dem	Two terms; 1829-1837.
Martin Van Buren	New York	Dem	One term; 1837-1841.
William Henry Harrison	Ohio	Whigs	One month; 1841.
John Tyler	Virginia	Whigs	3 yrs. 11 mos.; 1841-1845.
James Knox Polk	Tennessee	Dem	One term; 1845-1849.
Zachary Taylor	Louisiana	Whigs	1 yr. 4 mos.; 1849, 1850.
Millard Fillmore	New York	Whigs	2 yrs. 8 mos.; 1850-1853.
Franklin Pierce	New Hampshire.	Dem	One term; 1853-1857.
James Buchanan	Pennsylvania	Dem	One term; 1857-1861.
Abraham Lincoln	Illinois	Rep	One term and 6 wks.; 1861-1865.
Andrew Johnson	Tennessee	Rep	3 yrs. 10 mos.; 1865-1869.
Ulysses Simpson Grant	Illinois	Rep	Two terms; 1869-1877.
Rutherford Burchard Hayes.	Ohio	Rep	One term; 1877-1881.
James Abraham Garfield	Ohio	Rep	6 mos. 15 days; 1881.
Chester Alan Arthur	New York	Rep	3 yrs. 5 mos., 15 days; 1881-1885.
Grover Cleveland	New York	Dem	One term; 1885-1889.
Benjamin Harrison	Indiana	Rep	One term; 1889-1893.
Grover Cleveland	New York	Dem	One term; 1893-1897.
William McKinley	Ohio	Rep	One term and 6⅛ mos.; 1897-1901.
Theodore Roosevelt	New York	Rep	3 yrs. 5⅔ mos. and one term; 1901-1909.
William Howard Taft	Ohio	Rep	One term; 1909-1913.
Woodrow Wilson	New Jersey	Dem	Serving.

INDEX

ABOLITIONISTS, 271–273
Acadians, removal of, 99
Adams, John, 149; presidency of, 209–212; sketch and portrait, 209
Adams, J. Q., sketch, 245; portrait, 246; presidency of, 245–248; defends the right of petition, 273
Adams, Samuel, 138–140; 143, 149; portrait, 149
Africa, 2, 432
Agricultural colleges, 463
Agriculture, in Colonial times, 34, 35, 39–41, 106, 111, 113; in the South, 253, 367; in the West, 375–377, 380, 381; experiment stations in, 463; model farms in, 463
Aguinaldo's rebellion, 420
Alabama Claims, 344
Alabama, Confederate cruiser, 344
Alabama, secedes, 302
Alaska, purchase of, 384
Albany (Fort Orange), 64
Albany Plan of Union, 121, 122. *See also* Franklin's Plan of Union
Algeria, 222
Algonquin Indians, 76, 89, 94
Alien and Sedition Laws, 211

Alleghany Mountains, 94, 168, 169
Alleghany River, 96
Allen, Ethan, 145
Allies, 448
Alsace and Lorraine, 431
America, naming of, 8; found to be a continent, 9
Americus Vespucius, 8, 9
Amsterdam, New, 64
Amusement, in Colonial times, 110, 112, 113, 116
Anæsthetics, discovered, 268
Anderson, Major, 305, 306
André (än'drä), John, 178, 179
Andros, Sir Edmund, 59–61, 68
Antietam, battle of, 324
Anti-Federalist Party, 191, 209
Appomattox Court House, Lee surrenders at, 347
Arbitration, 400, 401, 406, 407; court of, 428, 436
Arbitration treaties, general, 436; of United States with Great Britain and France, 436
Arc light, 460
Arid region, 380, 381
Arizona, 438

KEY TO PRONUNCIATION.*

a as in fat.	ē as in mete.	ō as in note.	ū as in mute.
ā " " fate.	ë " " her.	ö " " move.	ü German ü, French u.
ä " " far.	i " " pin.	ô " " nor.	oi as in oil.
ā̂ " " fare.	ī " " pine.	u " " tub.	ou " " pound.
e " " met.	o " " not.		

A double dot under any vowel indicates the short *u*-sound, as in but.

* According to Century Dictionary.

Arkansas, 354
Armada, Spanish, 21
Armistead (är'mis-ted), General, 328
Army, Continental, 145, 147
Arnold, Benedict, 145, 157, 159, 163; his treason, 177–179
Arthur, Chester A., sketch, 392, 393; portrait, 392
Articles of Confederation, 185–188
Ashburton Treaty, 354
Asia, European trade with, 1
Astoria, 269
Atlanta Exposition, 369
Atlantic Cable, 382, 383
Atlantic Fleet, 427
Atlantic Ocean, feared by sailors, 3
Australia, 432
Australian Ballot System, 400
Austro-Hungary, 431
Automobile, 460

Bacon's Rebellion, 37
Bahama Islands, Columbus at, 6
Balboa discovers the Pacific, 18
Baltimore attacked by the British, 234
Baltimore, Lord, 37, 38
Bancroft, George, 466
Bank, United States, 256, 257
Bank notes, 260, 261, 262
Barbary States, war with, 222
Barclay, Captain, defeated by Perry on Lake Erie, 233
Beauregard (bō're-gärd), General, 305
Bell, A. G., 389
Bennington, battle of, 158, 159
Benton, Thomas H., 255
Bering Sea trouble, 400, 401
Berkeley, Sir William, 36, 37
Bessemer process, 454, 455
Blacklists, 395
Bladensburg, 234
Blaine, James G., 398, 400
Blanco, Governor-General, 411
Bland Silver Bill, 403
Blockade, during War of 1812, 231, 232; during Civil War, 311–314; block-
ade of Cuban coast, 414; blockade of Vera Cruz, 446; of Great War, 448, 449
Bon Homme Richard (bo-nom'rē-shär'), 173
Boone, Daniel, 169
Border ruffians, 289
"Boston Massacre," 138
Boston, settled, 48; evacuated by the British, 148
Boundaries of the United States in 1783, 183; Northwest, 269–271; Southwest, 277
Bowling Green, 315
Boycott, 395
Braddock, General, his defeat, 98
Bradford, Governor, 46
Bragg, General, 334
Brandywine, battle of the, 162
Breckenridge, John C., 299
Brewster, Elder, 46
Brooklyn Bridge, 394
Brooks, Preston S., assaults Charles Sumner, 289, 290
Brown, General, 233
Brown, John, at Harper's Ferry, 296
Bryan, William J., 407, 418
Bryant, William Cullen, 466
Buchanan (bu-kan'an), James, sketch, 294; portrait, 294; presidency of, 294–304
Buell, General, 316
Buena Vista, battle of, 354
Buffalo, 245, 419
Bull Run, first battle of, 307, 308; second battle of, 323
Bunker Hill, battle of, 146, 147
Burgoyne (ber-goin'), General, his invasion, 157–164; his surrender, 163
Burnside, General, 324
Burr, Aaron, 213; his conspiracy, 223, 224
Butler, General, 317, 331

Cabinet, the President's, 200, 395
Cable, Atlantic, 382, 383; Pacific, 424, 425

Cabot, John, seeks the Northwest Passage, 6, 8

Cabot, Sebastian, explores the coast of North America, 8

Cahokia, 169

Calhoun, John C., and nullification, 253, 254; portrait, 253

California seeks admission to the Union, 281; admitted to the Union, 354

Cambridge, 51

Camden, battle of, 175

Canada, 87, 88, 102, 145, 432, 433

Canal, Isthmian, 423; Erie, 245, 246

Canary Islands, Columbus at, 4

Canonicus, 47, 55

Cape Cod, 46

Cape of Good Hope, 2

Cape Verde Islands, Cervera's fleet at, 413

Carolina, North and South, 41

Carpet-bag rule, 360, 361

Carranza, 446

Carteret, 73,

Cartier (kär-tyā'), 87

Carver, John, 46

Catholics, 37, 39

Cavaliers, 36, 112

Cedar Creek, battle of, 339

Centennial Exhibition, 388, 389

Central America, 398

Cervera, Admiral, 413, 414, 417

Chambersburg, 339

Champlain (sham-plān'), 87–89, 123

Champlain, Lake, 88, 97, 123, 151, 157, 234

Chancellorsville, battle of, 325

Charles I., 42, 43–47, 48

Charles II., 42, 43, 58, 59, 70

Charleston, 305

Charlestown, 48, 147

Charter Oak, 60

Charter, 28, 38, 45, 54, 60, 64, 70

Chattanooga, battle of, 335, 336

Cherokee Indians, 75, 385

Chesapeake, *Leopard* fires upon, 225, 226

Chicago, 260

Chickamauga, battle of, 333, 334

Chickasaw Indians, 75, 385

Chili, trouble with, 398

China and the "open door," 420

Chinese immigration, 377, 378

Chippewa (chip'e-wä), battle of, 233, 353

Choctaw Indians, 385

Christian Commission, 350

Church of England, 44

Cities, growth of, 461; government of, 461; commission form of government, 439; populations, 461

Civil rights, of the freedmen, 358

Civil service reform, 392, 393

Civil War, principal steps toward, 301, 302; principal events of, 305–348; results of, 351, 352

Clark, George Rogers, in the Northwest, 169, 170, 183

Clay, Henry, 244, 256

Clermont, 223

Cleveland, Grover, sketch, 393; portrait, 393; 402, 404

Clinton, DeWitt, and Erie Canal, 245

Clinton, General, 163, 166, 175, 176, 178, 182

Coal, 452; use of anthracite, 454

Cold Harbor, battle of, 337

Coligny (ko-lēn'yē), 15, 122

Colleges, 462

Colonies, life in the, at the close of the French and Indian Wars, 105–117; groups of, 105, 118, 119

Colorado, 381

Colored troops in the Civil War, 332

Colombia, Republic of, 423

Columbia River, 269, 270

Columbia University, 114

Columbian Exposition, 402

Columbus, Christopher, his plans, 3; portrait, 3; his difficulties, 4; first voyage of, 4; trials on his first voyage, 5; discovers America, 6; other voyages, 6; last days, 6

Commerce, American, 186, 458, 459

Commission form of government, 439, 440

Committees of Correspondence, 138

Common storehouse, in Virginia, 29, 32

Compass, mariner's, 2

Compromise, Missouri, 244; with South Carolina, 256; of 1850, 283, 284

Concentration, 411

Concord, battle of, 142–145

Confederate States of America, organization of, 302

Confederation, Articles of, 185–188

Congress, Continental, first meeting of, 141; second meeting of, 145; has little power, 167, 168, 185–187

Congress, Acts of, Alien and Sedition Laws, 211; Embargo, 227; National Road, 241, 242; Missouri Compromise, 244; Tariff of 1816, 252; Tariff of 1828, 253; Compromise of 1850, 283, 284; Kansas-Nebraska Bill, 287, 288; Reconstruction, 358, 359; Tenure of Office, 360; Homestead Bill, 374; Civil Service Reform, 393; Presidential Succession, 394, 395; Pension Bill, 397; Bland Silver Bill, 403; Sherman Act, 403; McKinley Bill, 404; Wilson Bill, 405; Dingley Bill, 408; Isthmian Canal Act, 423; Payne-Aldrich Tariff Bill, 435; Postal Savings Banks, 436; Parcel Post, 441; Currency and Banking Law, 442; Tariff of 1913; Income Tax, 442; Interstate Commerce, 455; Federal Trade Commission, 456; Sherman Anti-trust Law, 458

Connecticut, early history of, 50–54; and the Northwest Territory, 188

Conscription, North, 332; South, 333

Conservation of Natural Resources, 433

Constitution captures the *Guerrière*, 231

Constitution of the United States, events leading to, 189; ratified, 190; slavery compromises in, 190; strict and liberal construction of, 200

Constitutional Convention, 190

Continental currency, 168

Conway Cabal, 165, 166

Cooper, James Fenimore, 465

Co-operation among nations, 433

Cornwallis, General, 154, 176, 179–183

Coronado, 122

Cortez conquers Mexico, 18

Cotton export, 311, 367–369

Cotton-gin, invention of, 204, 205

Court of Arbitration, 428

Cowpens, battle of, 179, 180

Creek Indians, 385

Creek Indians, war with, 235

Crève-Cœur (krev-kër'), 91

Crimes and punishments, 109, 115

Cromwell, Oliver, 43

Crown Point, Fort, 101; Americans capture, 145; Burgoyne captures, 157

Cuba, island of, 6, 286, 410

Cuba, Republic of, 421–423

Cuban Reciprocity Act, 423

Cubans rise against Spain, 410

Cumberland destroyed by the *Merrimac*, 313

Cumberland River, 315

Cunard Steamship Line, 264

Cushing, Lieutenant, 328

DAKOTA, NORTH, 375

Dakota, South, 375

Dale, Sir Thomas, 32

Darien, Isthmus of, 18

Daughters of Liberty, 131

Davenport, John, 52

Davis, Jefferson, sketch, 302; portrait, 302; elected President of the Confederacy, 303; flight and capture of, 348

Dawes Act, 386

Dawes, William, 143

Declaration of Independence, 148–150

"Decrees," 226

De Kalb (de kalb), John, 165

Delaware, early history of, 74

Delaware, Lord, 32

Democratic Party, 209, 248, 299, 404, 407, 418
Democratic-Republican Party, 209, 211, 230
Deposits, removal of, 257
De Soto (sō'tō), lands in Florida, 14; discovers the Mississippi, 15; portrait, 16
Detroit, 232
Dewey, Admiral George, 412, 413
Diaz, 2
Dingley Tariff, 408
Dinwiddie, Governor, 96
Discoveries, by Portugal, 2, 8; by the Spaniards, 4–6, 13–15, 18, 19; by the English, 8; by the Dutch, 63; by the French, 87–91
Discovery, aids to, 1
District of Columbia, slavery in, 283
Dorchester Heights, 148
Dorr rebellion in Rhode Island, 354
Douglas, Stephen A., 288, 299
Dover (N. H.), 62
Draft riots, 332
Drake, Sir Francis, 22, 26
Dred Scott decision, 294, 295
Dutch, in New Netherland, 63–68; reasons for their failure, 68
Dutch West India Company, 64

Eads, Captain, and the Mississippi jetties, 366
Early, General, his raid in the Shenandoah, 338
Eaton, Theophilus, 52
Education, 109, 111, 112, 114, 462, 463
El Caney, 416
Electoral Commission, 389, 390
Electoral Count Bill, 390
Electricity, 459
Elizabeth, Queen, 20, 23, 27
Emancipation Proclamation, 330, 331
Embargo, 227
Emerson, Ralph Waldo, 466
Endicott, John, 47
England, her need of America, 25; and

the American Revolution, 126–183; impresses American seamen, 225; injures American commerce, 226; and the Civil War, 309–311 and 343–345; and Venezuela, 405–407; friendship of, 407; a colonizing nation, 431, 432
Era of good feeling, 247
Ericsson, John, and the Monitor, 313
Ericsson, Leif, 11
Erie Canal, 245
Erie, Lake, battle of, 232, 233
Eutaw Springs, battle of, 192
Expansion, territorial: backwoodsmen in the Revolution, 169–171; purchase of Louisiana, 220; purchase of Florida, 239; annexation of Texas, 274; Mexican Cession and Gadsden Purchase, 277, 278; purchase of Alaska, 384; Hawaii annexed, 401; Spanish cessions in 1899, 417
Exploration, Portuguese, 2; Spanish, 4–6, 9, 13–15, 18, 19; English, 8, 23, 26, 27, 30; Dutch, 63; French, 87–92; Lewis and Clark, 221, 222
Exports, 447, 448, 458, 459
Express companies, 441

Factory System, 453
Fair Oaks (Seven Pines), battle of, 322
Faneuil Hall, 129
Far East, 420
Farragut, Admiral David G., at New Orleans, 317; sketch, 342; at Mobile Bay, 342
Federal Reserve Banks, 443
Federal Reserve Board, 443, 456
Federal Reserve System, 442
Federal Trade Commission, 456
Federalist Party, 191, 198, 209, 211, 230, 237, 238
Fifteenth Amendment, 360
Filibustering Expeditions, 286
Filipinos, rebellion of, 420
Fillmore, Millard, sketch, 281; portrait, 283
Fisheries, in colonial days, 61, 106;

Newfoundland fisheries dispute ar-
bitrated, 436

Five Forks, battle of, 346

Five Nations (see Six Nations), 76

Flag, American, 164, 468

Flatboat, 216

Florida, purchase of, 239; admitted to
the Union, 354

Flying machine, 460

Foote, Commodore, 315

Foreign trade, growth of, 458

Forest reservations, 381

Fort Dearborn, 260

Fort Donelson, 315

Fort Du Quesne (dü-kān'), 97, 98, 100

Fort Edward, 158

Fort Henry, 315

Fort le Bœuf, 96

Fort Lee, 152, 153

Fort McHenry, 234

Fort Moultrie (mōl'tri), 150

Fort Necessity, 97

Fort Niagara, 98

Fort Orange (Albany), 64

Fort Stanwix, 159

Fort Sumter, 305, 306

Fort Ticonderoga, 101, 129, 145, 157

Fort Washington, 96

Fort William Henry, 124

Fortress Monroe, 321

Fourteenth Amendment, 360

France, her struggle with England for
control of America, 93–103; American
treaty with, 164; aids the Americans
with her fleets, 172, 181; at war with
England, 206; regains Louisiana, 219;
injures American commerce, 226

Franco-Prussian War, 431

Franklin, Benjamin, 98; his plan of
union, 121; sketch, 121; and the
Declaration of Independence, 150;
portrait, 162; in France, 164

Franklin Plan of Union, 121, 122

Fredericksburg, battle of, 324

Freedmen, and Southern legislation,
358; and education, 370, 371

French forts, 95

French Revolution, 207

French War, Last, 94–103; causes of,
94; principal events of, 96–102;
treaty of peace, 102; other results of,
103

Fugitive Slave Law, 284

Fulton, Robert, 223

Fur trade, 64–66, 91, 113, 114

GADSDEN PURCHASE, 278

Gage, General, 140, 142, 143

Gang-plow, 376

Garfield, James A., portrait, 390; sketch,
392

Garrison, William Lloyd, 271, 272

Gates, General, 163, 175

Genet (zhe-nā), Citizen, defies Washington, 208

George III., 135–140, 183

Georgia, early history, 41; secedes, 302

Georgian Bay, 90

Germantown, battle of, 192

Germany, United, 431, 432

Gettysburg, battle of, 325–329

Gilbert, Sir Humphrey, 23

Gold, discovery of, in California, 279,
280

Gorges, Sir Ferdinando, 62

Gosnold, Bartholomew, 26

Gourges (görg), Dominique de, in Florida, 16

Government, colonial, 118–121

Grant, Ulysses S., at Fort Donelson,
315; at Shiloh, 315, 316; at Vicksburg, 329, 330; at Chattanooga, 334,
335; sketch, 335; portrait, 337; in
campaigns about Richmond, 337–348;
captures Lee's army, 347, 348; President, 362; his Indian policy, 384, 385

Great Meadows, 97

Great War in Europe, 447–450

Greater America, 429

Greater England, 432

Greater France, 432

Greater Germany, 432

Greater Russia, 432
Greeley, Horace, 348
Greenbacks, 390–392
Greene, General, 179–181
Greenland, 11
Grenville, Lord, 129
Griffin, 90
Griffin's Wharf, 140
Guam, 417
Guantanamo, 415
Guerrière (gär-ryär), captured, 231
Guilford Court House, battle of, 180
Gulf of Mexico, 17
Gunpowder, 1
Guthrie, 397

HAGUE, THE, 427, 428, 436
"Hail Columbia," 210
Hale, Nathan, 152
Half Moon, 63
Halifax, 148
Hamilton, Alexander, favors a strong union, 200; financial policy of, 202; portrait, 202; killed by Burr, 223
Hamilton, Colonel, 169, 170
Hampton Roads, 312–314
Hancock, John, 143, 145, 150
Harper's Ferry, 296
Harrison, Benjamin, 396; sketch, 402; portrait, 402; elected President, 404
Harrison, William Henry, 228; sketch, 267; portrait, 268
Hartford, 51, 54, 60
Hartford, at Mobile Bay, 343
Hartford Convention, 236, 237
Harvard College, 109
Havana, 411
Hawaii (hä-wī'ē), revolution in, 401, 402
Hawthorne, Nathaniel, 466
Hay, Secretary, 421
Hay-Pauncefote treaty, 423
Hayes, Rutherford B., sketch, 365; withdraws troops from the South, 365; portrait, 366; election of, 389, 390
Hayne, Robert Y., 254
Hayti, 6

Hennepin, 123
Henry, Patrick, 131, 141, 191
Henry VII., 8
Hessians, 149, 155
Higher education, 462
Hobson, Lieutenant, 415
Holland at war with England, 167
Holmes, Oliver Wendell, 466
Holy Alliance, 240
Homestead Bill, 374
Hood, General, 341
Hooker, Joseph, 325, 335
Hooker, Thomas, 51–52
Horseshoe Bend, 235
House of Representatives, elects Jefferson as President, 213; impeaches Andrew Johnson, 360; in the Constitution, 486–491
Howe, General, 146, 152, 160–163, 166
Howells, W. D., 466
Hudson, Henry, discovers the Hudson River, 63
Hudson Bay Company, 270
Hudson River, 63, 64, 67, 150, 157
Huerta, General, 444–446
Huguenots (hū'ge-nots), in France, 15; their settlements, 16; Spanish destroy settlements of, 16
Hull, Captain Isaac, 231
Hull, General William, 232
Hutchinson, Anne, 55

IBERVILLE (ē-ber-vēl'), 123
Idaho, 375
Illinois, 353
Immigration, foreign, table of, 259; 290, 291, 372, 373
Impeachment, President Johnson's, 360
Imports, 252, 253, 458
Impressment of American seamen, 208, 225
Income tax, 442
Indentured servants, 34
Independence Hall, 150
Independence of the United States, 183
Independent Treasury, 262

Indian Territory, 390, 391

Indiana, 353

Indians, division of, 75; character of, 76; occupations of, 77; their canoes and snow-shoes, 77; wampum, 78; religion, 79; clan and tribe, 80; communal living, 80; number of, 82; influence of, upon the whites, 83; early wars with, 84–86; aid Burgoyne, 158; use of, by the English, 168; reservation system, 386

Incandescent light, 460

Industrial revolution, 452

Initiative, 440

Intercolonial Wars, 94–103

Internal improvements, 246, 247, 261

Interstate Commerce Act, 455

Interstate Commerce Commission, 456

Inventions: gunpowder, mariner's compass, printing-press, 1, 2; cotton-gin, 204; steamboat, 222; reaping machine, 264; friction matches, 264; telegraph, 267; wireless, 424; cable, 382, 424; steam plow, 376; telephone, 389; sewing machine, 453; spinning machine, power loom, 453; Bessemer process of making steel, 454; X-ray, 460; automobile and flying machine, 460

Iowa, 354

Iron, 453–455

"Ironsides, Old," 231

Iroquois (ir-ō-kwoi') Indians (see Five Nations and Six Nations), 64, 65; and Champlain, 88; enemies of French, 89; and fur trade, 93; and St. Leger, 159

Irrigation, 380, 381

Irving, Washington, 465

Isthmian Canal Act, 423

Italy, trouble with, 398

Italy, United, 430

Jackson, Andrew, at battle of New Orleans, 235, 236; in Florida, 239, 240; presidency of, 250–262; sketch, 250; portrait, 251

Jackson, C. T., 268

Jackson, Thomas J. ("Stonewall"), in the Shenandoah, 322; sketch, 325; and portrait, 327

James I., 30, 42–44

James II., 42, 43, 59

James, Henry, 466

Jamestown, settlement of, 29

Japan, treaty with, 285; new treaty with, 437

Japanese immigration, 438

Jay, his treaty with England, 208

Jefferson, Thomas, 132; writes Declaration of Independence, 150; opposes a strong union, 200; presidency of, 213–227; sketch, 213; portrait, 216

Jesuit missionaries, 90

Johnson, Andrew, presidency of, 356–363; sketch and portrait, 357; his plan of reconstruction, 357, 358; impeached, 360

Johnston, Albert Sidney, 315

Johnston, Joseph E., 307, 322, 329, 337, 340, 348

Joliet (zho-lyā'), 90

Jones, John Paul, 164, 173, 174

Kalb, John, 165

Kansas, struggle for, 287–289; admitted to the Union, 354

Kansas-Nebraska Bill, 287, 288

Kaskaskia, 169

Kearsarge, sinks the Alabama, 344

Kenesaw Mountain, battle of, 341

Kentucky, Resolutions presented by, 211; life in, 216

Key, Francis Scott, 234

King George's War, 94

King Philip's War, 85, 86

King William's War, 94

King's Mountain, battle of, 176

Knickerbocker History of New York, 465

Knights of Labor, 395

Knox, Henry, 200

Kosciusko (kos-i-us'kō), 165

Ku-Klux Klan, 361, 362

LABOR, in Virginia, 34, 35; in the North and South, 292, 293; railroad strikes, 387, 388; Knights of Labor, 395

La Fayette (lä-fā-yet'), portrait, 160; sketch, 162; in Virginia, 181

La Salle (lä-säl'), explores the Mississippi, 90; his aims and work, 91, 92

Lake Erie, Perry's victory on, 232, 233

Lands: railroad and Western, 258; speculation in Western, 260, 261; public lands and Western expansion, 373-375; arid region and irrigation, 380; forest reservations, 381

Las Guasimas, 415

Latin-American states, 446

Lawrence, Perry's flagship, 232, 233

Leatherstocking Tales, 465

Lee, Charles, 153, 154, 160, 165, 166

Lee, Richard Henry, 149

Lee, Robert E., sketch, 322; in Peninsular campaign, 322; portrait, 324; at Antietam, 324; at Fredericksburg, 324; at Chancellorsville, 325; at Gettysburg, 325-329; in campaigns of 1864 and 1865, 337-347; his surrender, 347

Leisler (līs'lér), Jacob, leads an uprising against Andros, 69

Lewis and Clark's Expedition, 221, 222

Lexington, battle of, 142-145

Liberator, William Lloyd Garrison's, 271, 272

Lincoln, Abraham, sketch, 299, 300; portrait, 300; presidency of, 305-348; assassinated, 348

Lincoln, General, 175

"Line of Demarcation," 6

Linotype, 464

Literature, 465, 466

London Company, 28, 29

Long Island, battle of, 151, 152

Longfellow, Henry W., 466

Lookout Mountain, battle of, 335

Louis XIV., 91

Louisburg, 94

Louisiana, 353

Louisiana Purchase, 220, 221

Louisiana Purchase Exposition, 425

Lovejoy, Elijah P., 273

Lowell, James Russell, 466

Loyalists, 134, 151

Lumber trade, 61

Lundy's Lane, battle of, 233

Lusitania, 449

MCCLELLAN, GEORGE B., in the Peninsular campaign, 319-323; at Antietam, 324

McCormick's reaping-machine, 264, 375

McCrea, Jane, 158

McDonough (mak-don'ō), Thomas, on Lake Champlain, 234

McDowell, General, 307, 321

McKinley, William, author of McKinley Bill, 404; portrait, 404; sketch, 408; conduct of Spanish War, 411; assassination of, 418

Madero, 444

Madison, James, portrait, 228; sketch, 228; presidency of, 228-238

Magellan (ma-jel'an), wonderful voyage of, 9

Mails, 198

Maine, 244

Maine, 411

Malolos, 420

Malvern Hill, battle of, 322

Manassas (ma̤-nas'as), battle of (*see* Bull Run)

Manhattan Island, 64

Manila, 412, 413, 420

Manufactures, in New England, 61, 227; in the North, 252; in the South, 253, 367, 368

Marion, Francis, 176

Marquette (mär-ket'), Father, 90

Marshall, Chief Justice, 212

Maryland, early history of, 37-40; and the Northwest Territory, 188

Mason, John, 84

Mason and Dixon's Line, 39

Mason and Slidell seized on the *Trent*, 309

Massachusetts Bay Company, 47, 48

Massachusetts, early history of, 44–59

Massasoit (mas-a-soit'), 47

Maximilian, Archduke, in Mexico, 345

Mayflower, Pilgrim vessel, 45

Mayo, Admiral, 445, 446

Meade, George G., portrait, 329; at Gettysburg, 325–329

Mediation, 446

Menendez in Florida, 16

Merrimac, Confederate ironclad, 311–314

Merrimac River, 47

Merrimac, United States collier, 415

Merritt, General, 413

Mexican War, 274–277

Mexico, Cortez conquers, 18; secures independence, 240; troubles with Texas, 274; at war with United States, 275–277; Maximilian in, 345; troubles in, 444–446

Michigan, 354

Middle Colonies, 113–116; mixed population of, 113; occupations of people in, 113; education in, 114; crimes and punishments in, 115; life and manners of the Dutch in, 115

Miles, General, 420

Mills Bill, 404

Mimms, Fort, massacre at, 235

Mining, 279, 280, 452

Minnesota, 354

Minutemen, 143

Missionary Ridge, battle of, 336

Mission stations, 90

Mississippi, 353

Mississippi River, discovered by De Soto, 15; explored by French, 89–92; flatboats on, 217; navigation, 220; in War of 1812, 235; importance of, in Civil War, 314–318; jetties, 366

Mississippi Valley, French in, 89–92; settlement of, 213–222

Missouri, 244

Missouri Compromise, 244, 245

Mobile Bay, battle of, 342, 343

Mohawk River, 89, 157

Money, during Revolution, 167, 168; Shays's Rebellion, 187; Jackson and United States bank, 256; wild-cat banking, 260; in Civil War, 390, 391; resumption of specie payment, 390; silver legislation, 403

Monitor, Union ironclad, 311–314

Monmouth, battle of, 166

Monroe Doctrine, 240, 241, 405, 406

Monroe, James, presidency of, 239–245; sketch, 240; portrait, 241

Montana, 375

Montcalm, General, 99, 102

Montgomery, 145

Monticello, 213

Montreal, 145

Moore's Creek Bridge, battle of, 192

Morgan, Daniel, at battle of Cowpens, 179, 180

Mormons, 376, 377

Morris, Robert, 156

Morristown, 156, 160

Morse, Samuel F. B., and the telegraph, 267, 268

Morton, W. T. G., 268

Motley, John Lothrop, 466

Mound Builders, 81, 82

Mount Vernon, home of Washington, 196

Municipal reform, 461

Murfreesboro, battle of, 324

Napoleon I., 218–220, 229

Napoleon III., and the Confederate navy, 344; and Mexico, 345

Narragansett Indians, 47, 55

Narvaez (när-vä-äth') explores Florida, 19

Nashville, battle of, 355

National Republican Party, 248

National road, 241, 242

Natural resources, 433, 435

Navigation Laws, 36, 59, 126

Navy, United States, in the Revolution, 172; in War of 1812, 230; our new, 399, 400

Nebraska, 288

Negroes, in Union army, 332; freedmen in reconstruction days, 358–363; progress, 370, 371. *See also* Slavery

Negro suffrage, 360

Nevada, 355

New England, industries and trade of, 61; occupations of the people in, 106; religion and church worship in, 106; education in, 109; crimes and punishments in, 109; life and manners in, 109, 110; and protection, 254

New England Confederacy, 55, 56

Newfoundland, fisheries dispute, arbitration of, 436

New France, the founding of, 87–92; in the Intercolonial Wars, 93–102; given up to England, 102. *See also* Canada

New Hampshire, early history of, 62

New Haven colony, 52

New Jersey, early history of, 73

New Mexico, 438

New Netherland, early history of, 64–68; becomes New York, 68

New Orleans, battle of, 235, 236; capture of, 316, 317; Cotton Centennial, 368, 369

New Sweden, 74

New York, under English governors, 68, 69; and the Northwest Territory, 188

New York City, 246

New Zealand, 432

Newspapers, 117, 263, 464

Niagara Falls, 446

Nina, ship of Columbus, 4

Non-Importation agreements, 133, 139

Non-Intercourse Act, 227

Norfolk Navy Yard, 311

North, economic conditions in, 293; advantages of, 303

North America, mainland discovered, 8; claimed by England, 8

North Carolina, early history of, 41; secedes, 306

North Dakota, 375

North German Confederation, 431

North Sea, 448

Northern point of view, 301

Northmen, 11

Northwest Boundary, 269

Northwest Passage, 8

Northwest Territory, conflicting claims to, 188

Nova Scotia, 8, 11, 99

Nullification, 211, 253–256

Ocean Steamships, 264

Oglethorpe (ō'gl-thôrp), James, 41

Ohio Company, 96

Ohio River, Fort Du Quesne on, 97; flatboats on, 217; value to Westerners, 216, 217; part of boundary lines, 242

Oklahoma (ok-lạ-hō'mä), territory opened to settlement, 396

Old North Church, 143

Old South Church, 130, 139

Olney, Richard, 407

"Open Door," 420

"Orders in Council," 226

Ordinance of 1787, 188, 189

Oregon, 354

Oregon, 414

Oregon Country, 269–271

Ostend (os-tend') Manifesto, 286, 287

Oswego, 159

Otis, James, 128

Pacific Cable, 424

Pacific Ocean, discovery of, 18

Pacific railroads, 378–380

Pack-horse, 217

Paine, Thos., writes *Common Sense*, 149

Pakenham (pak'en-ạm), Sir Edward, 236

Palo Alto (pä'lō äl'to), battle of, 354

Palos, 4

Panama Canal, 423, 443, 446, 447

Panama, Isthmus of, 18

Panama, revolution, 423; treaty, 424

Panama tolls, 443

Pan-American Congress, 397

Pan-American Exposition, 419

Pan-American Union, 447

Panic, financial, of '37, 262; of '57, 294; of '73, 386, 387; of '93, 403

Paper money, 168, 187, 390, 391

Parcel post, 441

Parkman, Francis, 466

Parliament, English, 126, 127, 134, 135, 136, 139, 186; Acts of, 186; Sugar Act, 127, 136; Stamp Act, 128-133, 149; Townshend Acts, 136-138; Boston Port Bill, 140, 149, 164; Massachusetts Act, 140

Parties, Federalist, 191, 247; Anti-Federalist, 191; Republican, 209, 299; Democratic-Republican, 209; Democratic, 209, 299; National Republican, 247, 248; Whig, 290; Free Soil, 290; Progressive, 439

Partisan warfare in the South, 176

Patroons in New Netherland, 64, 65

Payne-Aldrich Bill, 435, 436

Peabody, George, 370

Peace Conference, first, 427, 428; second, 427

Peace movement, 427-429

Peking, 421

Pemberton, General, 329, 330

Penn, William, proprietor of Pennsylvania, 70-72; portrait, 70

Pennsylvania, early history of, 70-72

Pennsylvania, University of, 115

Pensacola, 240

Pension Bill, 397

Pepperell, Colonel, 94

Pequot Indians, 84

Periodicals, 464

Perry, Commodore, in Japan, 285, 286

Perry, Oliver H., his victory on Lake Erie, 232, 233

Personal Liberty Bills, 284, 285

"Pet banks," 257

Petersburg, explosion of mine at, 338

Petition, right of, 273

Philadelphia, 71

Philippine Islands, 417, 420

Pickett, General, 328, 329

Pierce, Franklin, portrait, 286; sketch, 286; presidency of, 287-294

Pilgrims, go to Holland, 44; aims and character of, 45; voyage to America, 45; settle at Plymouth, 46; covenant and democracy, 46; relations with the Indians, 46, 47

Pinckney, Charles C., 210

Pinta, ship of Columbus, 4

Pitt, William, 100, 133

Pittsburg Landing, battle of, 315, 316

Pizarro (pi-zä'rō), conquers Peru, 19

Plains of Abraham, 102

Plantation system in early colonial days, 35, 39; in later times, 253, 292

Plymouth colony, 46, 56

Plymouth Company, 28

Pocahontas, 31

Poe, Edgar Allan, 466

Polk, James K., sketch and portrait, 275; presidency of, 275-281

Ponce de Leon (pōn'tha dā lā-ōn'), discovers Florida, 13, 14

Pontiac, his conspiracy, 103

Pope, General, 323

Population, in 1790, 195; table of, 372

Port Bill, Boston, 140

Port Hudson, surrender of, 330

Porto Rico, 417, 418

Portugal leads in discovering an eastern route, 2

Postal savings banks, 436

Postal service, 117, 198

Potomac, Army of, 319

Power loom, 453

Powhatan (pow-ha-tan'), 31

Prescott, Colonel, 146

Prescott, William H., 466

Presidency, change in form of election, 213; the joint high commission, 389, 390; Presidential Succession Act, 394, 395; in the Constitution, 491, 492

Primaries, 439
Princeton, battle of, 156
Princeton College, 115
Printing-press, 464
Prisoners, difficulties about exchange of, in Civil War, 332
Privateering, in Revolution, 172; in War of 1812, 232
Problems of the hour, 467
Progressive Party, 439
Proprietary colonies, 38, 41, 62, 70, 118–120
Protective Tariff, 203, 252–254, 404, 405, 407, 408, 418, 423, 425, 435, 439
Providence, R. I., 55
Provincial Congress, 142
Prussia, 430, 431
Public debt, 260, 261
Public land, 259, 260, 373–375
Public schools, 263, 462
Pullman boycott, 405
Puritans, 47–59; obtain a charter, 47; settlements, 48; government, 49; religious intolerance, 54–58; persecute the Quakers, 56, 57; have trouble with England, 58, 59
Putnam, Israel, 103, 146

Quakers, 56, 57, 69, 70
Quebec, capture of, by Wolfe, 101, 102
Queen Anne's War, 94

Railroads, 257, 258, 367, 378–380
Railroad rate regulation, 455, 456
Raleigh, Sir Walter, portrait, 21; sketch, 22; colonies, 22–25
Rapidan River, 337
Recall, 440
Reconstruction, Johnson's plan of, 357, 358; congressional plan of, 358, 359; work of, complete, 359; difficulties and results of, 363
Referendum, 440
Religion, motive for colonization, 37, 44; Puritan intolerance, 49, 54, 55–57. See also Catholics

Religious intolerance among the Massachusetts Puritans, 54–59
Representative assemblies, 33, 38, 39, 49, 50, 118–120, 131, 134
Republican Party, 290, 299, 404, 407, 418
Reservations, Indian, 386
Resumption of specie payments, 390–392
Revere, Paul, 143
Review of the army at Washington, 355
Revolution, American, causes of, 126–141; principal events of, 142–183; results of, 183
Rhode Island, settled, 54, 55; religious toleration in, 55
Rice, cultivation of, 41
Richmond, Va., Confederate capital, 302; evacuated by Lee, 346
Right of search claimed by England, 225
Rio Grande River, 275
Rivers, twofold use of, 217
Roanoke Island, 23–25
Rochambeau, 182
Rolfe, John, marries Pocahontas, 31
Roosevelt, Theodore, portrait, 417; sketch, 419; 424, 425, 426, 439
Rosecrans (rōze-cranz), General, 333, 334
Ross, General, 234
"Rotten boroughs," 134
Rough Riders, 415
Roxbury, settled, 48
Royal colonies, 41, 62, 74, 119
Russia, 432

Sacramento River, 279
St. Augustine, 16
St. Lawrence River, 87
St. Leger (sănt lej'er), in western New York, 159
St. Mary's, settlement at, 38
Salem witchcraft, 108
Sampson, Admiral, 415, 418
San Francisco, 280
San Juan Hill, 416
San Salvador, 6

Sanitary Commission, 350
Santa Maria, ship of Columbus, 4
Santiago, battle of, 416
Savannah, Sherman captures, 341
Savannah, 264
Say-and-Sele, Lord, 52
Saybrook, 54
"Scalawags," 361
Schley, Commodore, 411, 414
Schuyler, General, 158, 163
Schuylkill River, 165
Scott, General, 233
Scrooby, England, 44
Seal fisheries, 400, 401
Secession, of South Carolina, 300; doctrine of, 301; of the remaining Cotton States, 302; of Virginia, North Carolina, Tennessee, and Arkansas, 306
Seminole Indians, 239, 240, 385
Semmes (semz), Captain, 344
Senators, United States, elected by the people, 441
Separatists in England, 44
Serapis, 173
Seven Days' battles, 322
Seven Pines, battle of. *See* Fair Oaks
Seven Weeks' War, 431
Seven Years' War, 94
Seventeenth Amendment, 441
Sewing machine, 453
Shafter, General, 416
Shays's Rebellion, 187, 188
Shenandoah Valley, Jackson in, 322; Early in, 338; Sheridan in, 339
Sheridan, Philip H., in the Shenandoah, 339; portrait, 339; at Cedar Creek, 339; sketch, 339; at Five Forks, 346
Sherman Act, 403, 458
Sherman, James S., 435
Sherman, Roger, 150
Sherman, William T., sketch, 340; portrait, 341; captures Atlanta, 341; his "March to the Sea," 341; captures Johnston's army, 348
Shiloh, battle of, 315, 316

Shipbuilding, in the colonies, 61, 106
Short ballot, 439, 440
Silver, Spanish search for, 19; silver legislation, 403
Six Nations. *See* Five Nations and Iroquois Indians
Sixteenth Amendment, 442
Slater, John F., 370
Slater, Samuel, 453
Slavery, in Virginia, 34, 35; cotton-gin and, 204, 205; in the North and the South, 243; and the Civil War, 301
Slidell, seized on the *Trent*, 309
Smith, Captain John, his services to the Virginia colonists, 30; sketch, 31; portrait, 31; returns to England, 31
Smith, Joseph, 377
Smuggling, 127, 128
Solid South, 365
Sons of Liberty, 131
South, economic conditions in, 292, 293; advantages of, 303; seizes national property, 304; condition at the close of the Civil War, 356; the new, 365–371; troops withdrawn from, 365
South America, discovered and explored, 8–10, 18, 19; colonies in revolt from Spain, 240; and the United States, 397, 446, 447
South Carolina, 41; objects to Protection, 252, 253; and State Rights, 255, 256; secedes, 300
South Dakota, 375
South Sea. *See* Pacific Ocean
Southern Colonies, 111–113; occupations of the people of, 111; education in, 111; life and manners in, 112
Southern point of view, 300
Spain claims Florida, 16; advantages of, in the New World, 16, 17; reasons for failure, 17; relations with England, 20, 21; rise of Cubans against, 410
Spaniards, precious metals main object of, 13; and the Indians, 15; destroy Huguenot settlements, 16
Spanish-American War, 410–417

Specie Circular, 261
Specie payments, 390, 391
Speedwell, 45
"Spheres of Influence," 431
Spinning machine, 453
Spoils system, 251
Spottsylvania Court House, battle of, 337
Stage coaches, 117, 197
Stamp Act, 128–131; Stamp Act Congress, 132; repeal of, 133
Standard Oil Company, 457
Standish, Myles, portrait, 48
Stanton, Secretary, 349
Star of the West, 305
Star-Spangled Banner, 234
Stark, John, 159
State Rights, 254–256, 300, 301
Statue of Liberty, 396
Steamboat, Fulton's first, 222; launched on the Ohio River, 223
Steel, 453–455
Stephens, Alexander H., sketch, 303
Steuben, Baron, 165
"Stonewall" Jackson. *See* Jackson, Thomas J.
Stowe, Harriet Beecher, 285
Straits of Magellan, 9
Strikes, railroad, 387, 388, 405
Stuyvesant (stī've-sant), Governor, 68
Submarine, 449, 450
Suffrage, for negroes, 359–361
Suffrage, for women, 463, 464
Sugar and Molasses Act, 127
Sugar Trust, 457
Sullivan, General, 152
Sumner, Charles, assault on, 289, 290
Supreme Court, 200, 295, 492, 493
Surplus, 404
Sutter, Captain, 279
Swedes, settlement made by, 74

Taft, William H., sketch of, 435; portrait of, 435; and revision of the tariff, 435; and arbitration, 436, 437
Tampico, 445

Tariff, 203, 252–256, 404, 405, 407, 408, 418, 423, 425, 439, 442
Tariff Commission, 436
Tarleton, 179
Taxation, 39, 43, 130; without representation in America, 134; without representation in England, 134
Taylor, Zachary, 276; portrait, 280; sketch, 281
Tea, tax on, 139, 140
Tecumseh (te-kums'e), 228
Telegraph, 267, 268, 379, 424
Telephone, 389
Temperance movement, 264, 265
Tennessee, life in, 216
Tennessee, Confederate ironclad, 342
Tennessee River, 315
Tenure of Office Act, 360
Territories, slavery in, 287, 288, 295, 299
Texas, annexation of, 274; admitted to the Union, 354
Textile industry, 452, 453
Thames River, battle of, 233
Thanatopsis, 466
Thanksgiving Day, 110
Thirteenth Amendment, 358, 360
Thomas, General, 333, 336
Tilden, Samuel J., 389
Tippecanoe, battle of, 228
Tobacco, 33–35, 40
Tories. *See* Loyalists
Township, New England, 48, 49
Trade, Colonial, 126–128
Trade Schools, 463
Travel, modes of, 117, 197, 215, 217, 223, 241, 242, 257
Treaty at close of Last French War, 102; at close of Revolution, 183; Jay's, 208; at close of War of 1812, 238; with Mexico, 277; Hay-Pauncefote, 423; with Japan, 437, 438
Trent Affair, 309
Trenton, battle of, 154, 155
Trolley-cars, 460
Trusts, 456–458
Tuscaroras (tus-ka-rö'räs), 76

Tyler, John, sketch, 267, 268; portrait, 269

"UNCLE TOM'S CABIN," 285
Underground Railroad, 285
Union, steps toward: New England Confederation, 55, 56; Franklin's Plan of Union, 121, 122; Stamp Act Congress, 132; Committees of Correspondence, 138; first meeting of the Continental Congress, 141; second meeting of the Continental Congress, 145; Declaration of Independence, 148-150; Articles of Confederation, 185-189; Constitutional Convention, 189, 190; results of Civil War, 351, 352; results of Spanish-American War, 417
United States, a world-power, 429, 430
United States, natural advantages of, 451, 452
United States Bank, 256, 257
United States Bureau of Agriculture, 463
United States Steel Company, 457
Universities, 462
University of Pennsylvania, 115
Utah, 375

VALLEY FORGE, suffering at, 164, 165
Van Buren, Martin, sketch and portrait, 262; presidency of, 262, 263
Venezuela (ven-e-zwē-lä') and England, 405-407
Vera Cruz (ve'rä kröz), 354, 446
Vermont, 352
Verrazano (ver'rät-sä'nō), 87
Vespucius, Americus, 8
Vicksburg, capture of, 329, 330
Victor Emmanuel, 430
Vincennes, 169
Vinland, Northmen visit, 11
Virginia, early history of, 29-37; and the Northwest Territory, 188
Virginia and Kentucky Resolutions, 211

Vocational schools, 463
Vulture, 178

WABASH RIVER, 89
Wallace, Lew, 338
Waltham, 453
Wampanoag Indians, 47
Wampum, 78
War of 1812, causes of, 229, 230; principal events of, 231-236; results of, 238
Wars: Indian, 84-86; Intercolonial, 94; Last French, 94-103; Pontiac's, 103; Revolution, 126-183; Barbary States, 222; Tecumseh's conspiracy, 228; of 1812, 229-238; Creek, 235; Mexican, 275-277; Civil, 301-352; Spanish-American, 410-417
War zone, 448, 449
Warren, Joseph, 143, 146, 147
Washington, D. C., made the national capital, 203; captured by the British, 234
Washington Elm, 144
Washington, George, his journey to the French forts, 96; at Great Meadows, 97; with Braddock, 99; takes command of the American army, 147; in the Revolution, 147-183; presidency of, 194-209; sketch, 195; inaugurated, 195; formality of, 198-200; his cabinet, 200
Washington, Lawrence, 96
Webster, Daniel, and the Union, 254; portrait, 255
Wells, Horace, 268
West, rapid growth of, 259; influence of, in favor of nationalism, 293; expansion of, 374-376
West Point, 177, 178
West Virginia admitted to the Union, 307
Western lands, speculation in, 260
Western migration, 213-224
Wethersfield settled, 51
Weyler, General, 411
Whig Party, 290
Whiskey Rebellion, 203, 204

White Plains, battle of, 192

Whitney, Eli, invents cotton-gin, 204, 205

Whittier, John Greenleaf, 466

Wild-cat banking, 260

Wilderness, battles of, 337

Wilkes, Captain, 309

Williams, Roger, 54, 55

Williamsburg, 131

Williamsburg, battle of, 321

Wilmot, David, 278

Wilmot Proviso, 278

Wilson Bill, 405

Wilson, Woodrow, sketch, 438; portrait, 438; and the troubles in Mexico, 445

Windsor settled, 51

Winthrop, John, 51

Wireless telegraphy, 424

Wisconsin, 354

Witchcraft, Salem, 108

Wolfe, General, captures Quebec, 101, 102

Woman suffrage, 463, 464

World-powers of Europe, 430

World's Columbian Exposition, 402

Wright Brothers, 461

Writs of Assistance, 128

Wyoming, 464

X-Ray, 460

X. Y. Z. Papers, 209, 210

Yale College, 109

Yorktown, McClellan at, 321

Young, Brigham, 377